Tigers at White City
Glasgow Speedway 1928 to 1968

Jim Henry

London League Publications Ltd

Tigers at White City
Glasgow Speedway 1928 to 1968
© Jim Henry
Forewords © Jim McMillan and Bert Harkins

The moral right of Jim Henry to be identified as the author has been asserted.

Front & back cover design @ Stephen McCarthy.

All photographs are from the John Somerville Collection unless otherwise credited to the photographer or provider of the photo. No copyright has been intentionally breached; please contact London League Publications Ltd if you believe there has been a breach of copyright.

Front cover photos: Tommy Miller in action; Back cover: Jim McMillan ready for action in 1967 and a poster from the sport's early days at White City.

This book is copyright under the Berne Convention. All rights are reserved. It is sold subject to the condition that it shall not, by way of trade or otherwise, be lent, resold, hired out or otherwise circulated without the publisher's prior consent in any form of binding or cover other than that in which it is published and without a similar condition being imposed on the subsequent purchaser.

A CIP catalogue record for this book is available from the British Library.

Published in February 2023 by London League Publications Ltd, PO Box 65784, London NW2 9NS

ISBN: 978-1-909885-31-8

Cover design by Stephen McCarthy Graphic Design
46, Clarence Road, London N15 5BB.

Editing and layout by Peter Lush

Second printing February 2024

Printed and bound by CPI Group (UK) Ltd, Croydon, CR0 4YY

Foreword: A Glasgow speedway legend

My experience of Glasgow White City does not stretch back over half of the era covered by Jim's book.

I started watching speedway in 1953. I recall going to White City with my grandfather and still remember watching Tommy Miller who was the top Tiger and a particular favourite of mine.

A really enjoyable part of watching the action was the spectacle of racing under the lights with the rest of the stadium in darkness. The riders of the day in their polished black leathers and mounted on sparkling chromed framed bikes were a particular attraction.

I was soon hooked. However, it was not until after 1964 when the speedway returned to White City, and my brother Bill was a Tiger, that I resolved to give it a go. I started out on the shale at Cowdenbeath in the winter of 1965 and 1966 and rode at White City as Tiger until the stadium was closed at the end of 1968 and subsequently demolished to make way for the M8. I now look back fondly on my career on the shale. It is great to be still involved in the sport, albeit from the outside of the fence.

While much of the book covers eras before I started watching, and then riding, it sets out lots of interesting facts on the history of my first team. It tells how my team became the Tigers and why the colours are red and white. It also gives an insight into to how they performed in the past, their highs and lows, and how the star riders I heard older fans talking about had ridden. Often mentioned names were Will Lowther, Joe Crowther, Gruff Garland, Buck Ryan, and Bat Byrnes who were before my time. I remember seeing others the fans talked about like Australians Junior Bainbridge and 'Last Bend Bob' or 'Cowboy', Bob Sharp.

I enjoyed watching the 1964 and 1965 Tigers and then joining them on the track, initially as a junior partner, before progressing to be the top Tiger in 1968. It was a big ask to replace Charlie Monk but it was a challenge which I am happy say I was able to rise to.

I remember my uncles Doug and Willie Templeton who both feature in the book. Doug started out on the grass and raced for the Tigers in 1953 and 1954. Willie, who also raced on the grass, started on the shale in 1954 just a meeting or so before the Tigers closed down. In the 1960s I fondly remember Uncle Willie as a team mate and mentor as I learned my speedway skills at White City and other tracks around the country. My brother Bill, also a Tiger in the 1960s era, helped me progress as a speedway rider.

I was also interested in details of the Tigers career of Ken McKinlay who I saw from the stands. Ken was still very much a star in my early days. Stylish and immaculately turned out, Ken was a hard, but fair, opponent. I got to know Ken when he was the Rider–Manager of my first tour to Australia in 1968. He took me under his wing, mentoring me on the often big Australian circuits.

One-time Tiger Gordon McGregor was also riding in my early days and, by the time I raced against him in the mid to late 1960s, he still had a fair turn of speed. I also recognised many names of visiting riders who I saw at White City or raced against in the post war the era.

The book paints a picture of a long-gone period, it gives a factual record of the meetings showing Tigers exploits home and away, plus it gives details of riders' careers with the Tigers. John Somerville's excellent photographs put faces to many of the names which is a definite bonus.

I hope you will enjoy reading about my Tigers 'ancestors' and family as much as I have.

Jim McMillan
Rugby, November 2022

Foreword: A Young Tiger's Tale

'Glasgow White City', a magical name to a young Glaswegian boy who fell in love with the sport at that iconic stadium on Paisley Road West.

I grew up in Govan Fire Station, my Dad was a Glasgow Fireman (or Firefighter as they say these days) and we lived in the Fire Station, a stone's throw from White City and on a Wednesday night, you could hear the sound of the unsilenced JAP speedway machines echoing all the way down from the stadium.

My dad used to take me there every week and if he was on nightshift one of the other Firemen would take me there to sample the thrills and spills of Speedway and the lovely aroma of a Speedway rider's After Shave, Castrol 'R'.

Ian Hoskins was the Tigers' promoter and my favourite riders were the Australian Ron 'Junior' Bainbridge and the young Ken McKinlay. Tommy Miller was the top Tiger at that time, but with his low handlebars and armchair style, he made it look so easy by gating and winning almost every race so I preferred the riders who had to battle from the back. Riders like Kiwi Peter Dykes and Australians "Cowboy" Bob Sharp and Arthur Malm were not heat leaders but they were still big favourites with the Tigers fans.

Ian Hoskins was forever a showman and always had an interval attraction to entertain the crowd, everything from an Egyptian 'Yogi' lying on a bed of nails, to someone jumping off a high tower onto a bucket of water, Mr. Hoskins knew how to keep the fans entertained.

He even gave the riders various nicknames, 'Tartanic' Alf MacIntosh was "The Tartan Terror", Ken McKinlay was "Hurri Ken" and "Atomic" Tommy Miller and there was even a novice who served on the whaling boats and was known as "Whaler" Joe Ferguson.

I was the super keen Tigers fan and even had my 18 inches Hercules bicycle painted in the Tigers colours of red and white. On many a Thursday morning I would go to school and be quite hoarse from all the cheering I had done the night before! So, as a young fan, my ambition was to be a Speedway rider when I grew up and to ride for the Glasgow Tigers.

Most of my school classmates were football fans and wanted to play for Rangers or Celtic, but my ambitions lay in the sport of speedway and that ambition never wavered.

By the time I left school, Speedway in UK was going through a difficult period and there were no tracks left in Scotland, White City had closed its doors and their riders transferred to other teams down south. I rode Cycle Speedway for the Mansewood Lions in the Glasgow Cycle Speedway League and we wore the genuine Wembley Lions race jackets which had been donated to us by that famous London club. Little did I know that many years later, I would race Speedway as captain of the REAL Wembley Lions, a fantastic coincidence. Eventually I did some motorcycle road racing for a season just as Ian Hoskins was reopening Old Meadowbank in Edinburgh to bring speedway back north of the border.

I bought a very old JAP speedway bike from fellow Glaswegian, Jimmy Tannock and set about trying to become a speedway rider. It wasn't easy as there were a couple of dozen other young novices trying to get onto the track at the same time. Eventually, after a few seasons of trying, I managed to squeeze in at reserve for the Monarchs just as Ian Hoskins and Trevor Redmond were reopening White City and putting the Tigers back on the track.

As much as I would have liked to have signed for Glasgow, I was now making progress with Edinburgh and as they had given me my first opportunity in the sport, I thought I had better stay with the Monarchs, not that Glasgow ever asked me to sign for them so there was no other choice! I did, however, wear that famous Glasgow Tigers race jacket once when I guested for the Tigers in a league match.

As I progressed with Edinburgh, my visits to White City were always the highlight of my season. The track was over 400 yards long with tight corners and it was like riding down the M1 motorway then suddenly having a hairpin corner appear. It was a difficult track to ride but I really enjoyed it there and especially riding against home track specialists, Jimmy McMillan and Charlie Monk, they really had the track 'dialled in' and it took a gigantic effort to try to beat them.

And so, the mighty White City stadium fell victim to the march of time as the new motorway cut through that hallowed ground. Glasgow Tigers continued to race at Hampden Park, Coatbridge, Shawfield and now Ashfield, but, to this one-time schoolboy Tigers fan, nothing will compare to being at White City on a Wednesday night with the grandstands in darkness, only the track lit by floodlights, and the roar of the bikes as they raced into the first corner ... and, as I said before, White City was pure magic."

Bert Harkins
Hemel Hempstead, November 2022

Jim McMillan and Bert Harkins riding for Scotland at Reading in June 1977 in the World Team Cup.

Introduction

Glasgow is a city that is hard to sum up in a few short paragraphs. It was founded in the sixth century as a monastic settlement around the Cathedral. It has grown and expanded manifold and is now the major city in Scotland. It has taken in what were at one time separate settlements. The location on the River Clyde gave it access to the seas and trading opportunities, many of which are now considered unsavoury. The new world brought much wealth to the city. Tobacco, sugar and cotton were massive sources of income.

It had the coal deposits underneath large areas of the extended settlement and other industrial minerals, including ironstones, and stone for building in its hinterland in the Clyde Valley and surrounding areas as source of raw materials to take advantage of the Industrial Revolution.

These raw materials were used in what were once thriving sectors such as shipbuilding, and railway engine manufacturing. 'Clyde Built' was synonymous with quality. It has been a centre of learning for many centuries and training professionals, engineers, medics, and business leaders to name a few occupations.

The anticipated promise drew ever more folk into the area from the length and breadth of the west coast and islands of Scotland and from further afield. Equally, it was often the embarkation point got those seeking a new life in the USA.

While there were what would be described as posh areas, the city also had massive housing areas for engineers and artisans and many notorious slum areas. These often housed newcomers to the city and those down on their luck. Rehabilitation and regeneration schemes have largely addressed the problems of yesteryear.

Today, Glasgow is still the leading settlement in Scotland, at the hub of vast hinterland within relatively short travel times. Most of the shipyards, steel industries, tobacco trades and fabric manufacturing mills have gone. However, it is a tenacious city and modern Glasgow has overcome these losses and has a wide range of activities which help it retain its major city status.

White City Stadium

The stadium, known as the White City Sports Stadium, was built in the winter of 1927 and 1928. It opened for greyhound racing on 7 April 1928. The speedway track, presumably built as a 440-yard running track, did not feature speedway until a couple of months later. The stadium had stands on the southern edge alongside Paisley Road West and uncovered standing spectator accommodation in the rest of the stadium. The stadium could accommodate between 20,000 and 25,000 spectators.

The speedway track was used for midget car racing in 1937, and was also used for stock car racing in the early 1960s. There was also show jumping on the centre green.

Given the by now somewhat run-down stadium was on the route of the M8 motorway, proposed in 1967, the speedway promoters pulled out at the end of 1968. However, the track continued to operate as a greyhound stadium until April 1972, 44 years after it opened for business.

Having written a book on the pre-war days in Glasgow, this book originally started life as a project to cover the 1940s and 1950s with the rise and fall of the sport at White City.

It was Peter Lush who suggested that the book should be re-focussed and cover the whole era of speedway at White City. This meant a late, unplanned, dive into the 1964 to 1968 to add to rest of it. I have found it a rewarding exercise and have been helped in the endeavour by Doug Nicholson's web site covering this era.

A further refocus saw the first part of the book focus on team racing. We have reformatted and abridged some of the pre-war material, but the remainder is new. It can never dot absolutely every 'I' nor cross ever 'T', but I like to think it fully covers the history of speedway at White City Stadium in the period from 1928 to 1968.

I have tried to present the story in a neutral manner. As an Edinburgh fan since 1961, this could have been difficult. However, I spent 25 years as Clerk of the Course at Powderhall, Shawfield and Armadale with the Monarchs and time at Linlithgow. I remained neutral when 'on duty'. The rules require office holders to be impartial and I think I shook a few visiting team managers when they asked, for example, what gates were 'you' taking I would reply "Edinburgh are taking…"

I am aware that there may be bits of history not covered, but I tried to concentrate on the speedway action without going into detail on the promoters and other information.

Jim Henry
December 2022

Acknowledgements

Many, many people have helped bring this book to fruition. I am especially indebted to Peter Lush and Dave Farrar of London League Publications Ltd who had the faith in me to take on board publishing this book. Peter went over my text in very meticulous manner, knocking it into shape.

I owe a big thanks to my long-suffering wife Anne who often saw me vanish upstairs to the computer. This did, often, allow her to enjoy peace and quiet to watch curling, football, and tennis when the various big events were being screened. Whilst I was compiling the base information, I was fortunate to be able to call up the help of fellow researchers who were gathering information about the venues of interest to them.

I hope the following is a reasonably comprehensive list of those who helped fill in the gaps that could not be gleaned from newspapers or the speedway press of the day. Norrie Isbister, Willie Durward and George McKenzie gave some great insights to the pre-war era while Jack Monteith and Jimmy Tannock gave me some interesting insights into the Tigers era of the 1945 to 1956 era.

I would like to thank Jim McMillan for doing the foreword for me. Jim watched the Tigers in 1953 and 1954, catching the tail end of the post-War era. Jim became a Tiger himself in 1966 rising to star status in 1968. He has solid links with two of the eras the book covers.

The Scottish track information came from magazines and other material from collections held by Mike Hunter, Ian Moultray, Derek Carruthers, John Somerville, John Houston, Dennis Darling, Norrie Tait, Raymond Jarvie, Andy Reid, Robin Goodall, Keith Gilbert, Bluey Scott, Norrie Isbister, Tom Blackwood, and Peter Colvin. Latterly information came from web site files complied by Steve Wilkes and Gary Done. Kenny Taylor is also thanked for information re his father's role in 1967.

Doug (Nicky) Nicholson is thanked for allowing me to draw upon his views on the Tigers meetings 1964 to 1968 on his website and a large number of small bits which have helped me paint a bigger and wider picture of the White City's last days. Sadly Raymond, Norrie Isbister, Tom, Peter and Steve are not with us to read the finished article.

South of the border I was helped by John Jarvis (Bristol); Colin Parker, Stuart Stait-Aris and Chris Durno (Coventry), Nigel Nicklin and Roger Beaman, (Birmingham /Cradley Heath); Tony Lethbridge (Exeter); Mike Craven (Fleetwood); Barry Stephenson (Halifax); Roger Thorpe (Ipswich); Alan Jones and Tim Grant (Leicester); Norman Briggs and Graham Gleave (Liverpool); Barry Wallace, Phil Hood and Joe Wake (Newcastle); Bryan Tungate, Mike Kemp, and Mike Gardner (Norwich), Glyn Shailes and Jim Gregory (Oxford); Colin Rugg (Plymouth); Gordon Day and Richard Hine (Poole); John Sampford (Rayleigh); Vic Butcher (Southampton); Terry Campbell (Stoke); Rob Bamford (Swindon); Alan Bates (Walthamstow); Mark Sawbridge (Wolverhampton) and Keith Farman (Yarmouth).

The foregoing lists makes tough reading for me as many of those who helped me are no longer with us.

Others who have helped me a lot are Andy Reid and Duncan Luke, who helped with programme scans and other items. Nigel Bird, Les Hawkins, Arnie Gibbons also chipped in, together with collectors who helped but wish to remain anonymous. Colin Jewes helped with regional competition data.

If I have omitted anyone from the list then I apologise unreservedly.

Matt Jackson has kindly provided his profiles of the riders who raced for the Tigers in both post-War eras. Matt worked with Hugh Vass who laid the foundations for much of the immediate post war ea. Much of the rider information has been set aside to concentrate on the riders' time with Tigers. Matt also read over the text files spotting my typos, challenging some statements and advising me on inaccuracies on the personal facts about many riders. Another pair of eyes help accuracy of the text.

Keith Corns has helped with scans of programmes and has dug me out of a hole or three. His forensic skills are amazing and his dogged determination to get the answer to some of my "daft laddie" questions demonstrates his inexhaustible patience and good nature.

I would also like to thank staff in The National Library of Scotland and The Mitchell Library in Glasgow for digging out and returning newspapers time after time.

Newspaper sources include: *The Scotsman; The Edinburgh Evening News; The Edinburgh Evening Dispatch; The (Glasgow) Herald; The Daily Record; The Bulletin and Scots Pictorial; Glasgow Evening Times; Glasgow Evening News; The Glasgow Citizen; The Motherwell Times; The Wishaw Press.*

Magazine Sources include: *The Speedway News; The Speedway Star; Speedway Star and News; The Speedway Gazette; The Speedway World; Broadsider and The Stenners Annuals.*

I have drawn odd snippets from a number of books but the two main sources have been: *Glasgow Tigers - Into the 80s - 25th Anniversary Handbook with Statistics* by Ian Steel and published by David Thompson and Ian Steel. *The Complete History of the British League* by Peter Oakes. Others include *The Speedway Hoskins* by Ian Hoskins; *The First Book of Scottish Speedway; Speedway* in Scotland by Jim Henry and Ian Moultray; *Glasgow Speedways – The Pre-War Years* by Jim Henry.

Most photographs have been supplied by John Somerville from his superb and ever-growing speedway photograph archive. Other photographs were supplied by Ian Moultray from the Friends of Edinburgh Speedway and the Norrie Isbister photograph archive which he curates. Bill Hamilton added photographs from his own collection. Some photos used in my original book are re-used in this one include some from newspapers of the day and were fully acknowledged in the original book.

If the book includes any in the ownership of others not acknowledged I apologise for not giving them due credit. I make no claims on the copyright of any of the photographs. I also thank Dave Wardrope for removing the two large drawing pins from my original photograph of the Christmas card photo taken at Ian Paterson's collection.

Jim Henry
December 2022

Thank you

London League Publications Ltd would like to thank Steve McCarthy for designing the cover, the staff at Ashford Colour Press Ltd and CPI Antony Rowe for printing the book; John Somerville for supplying the photos, and Jim Henry for all his work on the book.

Peter Lush and Dave Farrar

Contents

1. 1928 and 1929: Early days — 1
2. 1930: League speedway — 9
3. 1931: Half a season — 27
4. 1939: Relaunch with Johnnie Hoskins — 37
5. 1940: A short wartime season — 47
6. 1945: Speedway relaunches — 51
7. 1946: League speedway returns — 55
8. 1947: National League racing — 69
9. 1948: Improving — 83
10. 1949: Powerful at home, weak away — 99
11. 1950: So close — 113
12. 1951: "Somewhat disappointing" — 131
13. 1952: Scottish Cup winners — 147
14. 1953: "Terrific and terrible" — 165
15. 1954 and 1956: Short seasons — 183
16. 1964: Speedway returns to Glasgow — 187
17. 1965: The British League — 199
18. 1966: Scottish Cup triumph — 213
19. 1967: Charlie Monk's last season — 225
20. 1968: Final season at White City — 237
21. Glasgow riders 1946 to 1954 — 251
22. Glasgow riders 1964 to 1968 — 276
Appendix: Statistics and records — 290

Matt Jackson wrote and researched chapters 21 and 22. More information about the early meetings at Glasgow can be found in *Glasgow Speedway 1928 to 1940*, available on Amazon Kindle.

About the author

A fan of Edinburgh Monarchs since 1961, Jim Henry became interested in speedway history in the 1980s. With Graham Fraser he founded *The Speedway Researcher* magazine and this spawned the website which carries, thanks to many helpful contributors, a large and ever-growing record of speedway meetings in the UK since 1928. Jim compiled information for Scottish venues and has written the history of *Glasgow's Speedways 1928 to 1940,* originally published as *Glasgow's Speedways – The Pre-War Years,* and *Where Eagles Dared – Speedway in Motherwell* on his own and, with Ian Moultray, written *A History of Marine Gardens Speedway* and *Speedway in Scotland*. He moved on from track raking at  Powderhall, Edinburgh to become Clerk of the Course at Powderhall, Shawfield, Armadale and Linlithgow between 1989 and 2014. Jim is well acquainted with Glasgow having spent four years as a student at the University of Strathclyde, starting about when White City closed in 1968. A retired town planner, Jim has been chair of his local Community Council, is a volunteer at the National Mining Museum Scotland taking a special interest in Mining Memorials in Scotland and was Secretary to the WSRA Members in Scotland Committee. Jim is marred to Anne and they have two sons and four grandchildren.

White City Stadium in 1938.

1. 1928 and 1929: Early days

White City Stadium was built in early 1928, specifically as a greyhound racing and sports stadium. It was built on an undeveloped triangular site bounded by Paisley Road West to the south, Helen Street to the west and a railway line to the north. This strongly influenced the track shape with long straights and fairly tight bends. It was a 440-yard-long track that required a bit of skill to ride.

1928

It opened to the public on Easter Saturday, 7 April 1928, and speedway was introduced to the stadium on 29 June, by the Glasgow Nelson club, when a single meeting was staged.

June

It was suggested the poorly advertised meeting on 29 June would be the first of a regular series of meetings run by the Glasgow Nelson Motor Cycle Dirt-Track Club. The crowd turn out is not known but it was mentioned as being quite poor.

The 350cc event was won by Jimmie Pinkerton who won the eight-lap event in a time, which must have been clocked by the newspaper reporter, at four minutes and one second. There was no official timekeeper for this event. Jimmie went on to win the unlimited capacity event. His clean sweep was prevented by an engine failure in the first heat of the 600cc event. Allan Campbell collected the £3 winner's prize money.

Race times suggest that the track was in a difficult condition or that it was, with the long straights and tight bends a bit hard to master.

The riders who took part, Jimmie Pinkerton, Jimmy Valente, Bill Dickie and Allan Campbell had, by now, gained experience of Celtic Park, and were well capable of keeping up with their peers.

The prize money was quite poor compared with that on offer at Celtic Park and probably did little to attract big names which may have just helped draw a crowd.

August

On Saturday 11 August a motorcycle gymkhana was staged at White City by a local motorcycle club. Jimmie Pinkerton took the opportunity to demonstrate the art of broadsiding to those attending the event.

1929

The birth of speedway in Glasgow had seen four new tracks in action, but none lasted. White City, which was one of the four, lasted a single meeting in June of 1928. Some people had reservations about the rebirth but their fears proved unfounded. The White City promotion staged 50 meetings and lost a further three to rain.

The crowd levels fluctuated. The holiday periods and wet nights reduced the numbers but, given good weather and no other 'one-off' counter attractions, the Glasgow public demonstrated a demand for speedway. Once, when Sprouts Elder was the star visitor, fans were locked out of the full stadium. The weather was a major issue. There were some meetings staged when the track had been soaked by rain earlier in the day and some in falling rain. One was abandoned halfway through and three never started. At least one meeting was carried to a conclusion when the track conditions made it farcical.

The Glasgow public's loyalties were reflected in the crowd for the meeting for 3 August being well down. They chose to go to Ibrox Stadium, home of Glasgow Rangers FC, to watch the annual sports event rather than speedway.

The regular Glasgow Handicap and Scratch Race events were presented on Tuesday evenings and Saturday afternoons most weeks from 20 April until almost the end of September. The attraction of racing under lights saw a change to Friday evenings, although this may have been due to a fall in supporter numbers and a desire by the stadium owners to run greyhound meetings on Saturday nights. As it was, after one Friday night event, the Edinburgh based promoters cut back to one night a week until the end of the season.

During the May Holiday weekend, the promotion ran three meetings in four days with the extra event on Monday afternoon. Nice weather failed to draw the anticipated crowd.

The meetings were staged with imported riders and locals. Up to 35 riders could appear, but not all had a chance to race. Five riders per handicap race heat involved up to 30 riders. A further five could be in the junior event.

The visitors usually had lower handicap start advantages than the locals, but visitors won a fair share of events. Top visitor was the brilliant Australian Billy Galloway. He collected all the trophies twice over and had a four meeting unbeaten spell. Sprouts Elder was reasonably successful. He cleaned up three meetings including the White City Championships in August. Other visiting 'clean up' riders were Arthur 'Buster' Frogley, Drew McQueen, Reg Heller and Billy Lamont.

From the locals, Norrie Isbister cleaned up twice and Jimmie Pinkerton did the double once. They were veterans of 1928, but the big find of 1929 was Andy Nicholl. Blantyre lad Nicholl began with a big handicap advantage reflecting his novice status. By the end of September his handicap was down to one second, reflecting his new star rating. Other locals had their share of handicap wins, demonstrating the value of a big start and track experience.

Tiny Blantyre has made a big contribution to Scottish speedway over the years and it had its own two speedways at the Greyhound Stadium and Craighead Park.

Scots and English riders

The record of riders who rode at White City is not complete. However, at least 65 Scottish riders appeared at White City in 1929. There was a large turnover of Scots in the junior ranks. However, in the handicap events and scratch races the number of Scottish riders who were regulars was much lower.

Norrie Isbister and Drew McQueen in action at White City in May 1929.

Programme from the first full season at White City.

There was not a great interchange with Edinburgh-based riders. The regulars included Norrie Isbister, Jimmie Pinkerton, George Pinkerton, Andy Nicholl, Andy Marr and Willie Durward.

At least 55 English riders visited White City regularly. Most rode two or three meetings in a row. Whether they came up and stayed for the week is not known. Some fitted in meetings at Marine Gardens, giving a couple of Saturday meetings but most rode only in Glasgow. While they did not win many championships, the English riders did reasonably well.

One English rider was female competitor Eva Askquith. According to reports she rode well and was invited back, but was thwarted on her trip north by fog. Originally only programmed for a match race with Norrie Isbister, which she lost, Eva took part in the handicap and scratch events. Her heat win in the latter with a fast time drew praise from the press.

Wales only had early visitor Aubrey 'Taffy' Williams and adopted Scot Billy Llewellyn. Williams was a sand-tracker turned dirt-track rider. Blacksmith Llewellyn was from Blantyre and was a regular at White City. Gordon Spalding, described as a native Scot by the press and by George McKenzie as having a strong Welsh accent, also rode in Glasgow in 1929.

Australians and Americans

The Antipodes were represented by 19 Australians and no Kiwis. The most successful was Billy Galloway. The Australians did not win many honours and only a clean-up by Billy Lamont and Gold Armlet win by Syd Parsons appear in the winners list.

Despite this, they were popular visitors and were often given a big build up on the basis of their exploits at home. Big stars Frank Arthur and Vic Huxley were unlucky at White City.

Two Americans appeared at White City. One was Ray Tauser, who thrilled the crowd with his riding, but never collected a trophy. The other was Mr Speedway himself, Lloyd 'Sprouts' Elder. He rode in eight meetings and always boosted the crowd. Bike problems let him down on occasions, but when they ran well, he usually 'cleaned up'.

The track

The quarter-mile track at White City had very long straights and tight bends which required skill to ride. However, the early track surface was not good. It was only after a hard-hitting article by a local journalist that the track was modified in shape, slightly shortened and the bumps, or to use the press word 'humplocks', removed. Times improved throughout the season. The best at the season's end were more than 10 seconds below those at the opener.

The season was, if anything, a bit intense. It was not helped by the weather which deterred all but the diehard fans. However, it was a success in a city which had apparently turned its back on the sport in its inaugural year. The mix of locals and visiting stars was successful and the big favourite was Billy Galloway. Norrie Isbister and Jimmie Pinkerton were in close competition for favourite home star status.

This season saw the introduction of team races, a taster for the Northern League in 1930. Glasgow's first team event was at White City Manchester on 1 May. Glasgow lost 23–4. The team was Norrie Isbister, Andy Marr, Chris Hughes and Allan Campbell. Six more meetings including team racing were held towards the end of the season.

League activity passed Scotland by because the most northerly track in the English Dirt-track League was Newcastle Brough Park. Team activity was started late in the season with three team events. They were raced over four heats with four points awarded for a win, two for a second and one for third. These matches operated on the basis of fixed pairings.

Left: American star Sprouts Elder when he won the Glasgow Handicap event and scratch race on 27 April 1929.
Right: Billy Galloway with the Open Trophy Race that he won at Glasgow in 1929.

With Newcastle Brough Park, operating as a member of the Northern Dirt-track League, the Gosforth venture also entered into team events. Glasgow could have been the first team opponents for this Newcastle side on 28 August. The results for the match do not indicate the fourth member of the Glasgow side, but in a press advert Jack Reilly was listed in the eight riders and all other seven featured in the meeting. It is possible that George Pinkerton could have been involved as he featured in the side that raced the home leg at Glasgow.

From reports the match was not particularly full of incident. Jim Holder fell in heat 2. Heat four was the most interesting as it was re-run twice. In the first attempt Andy Marr fell and the race was brought to a halt. In the second attempt it was Arnie Cattell who came to grief resulting in the race being halted. In the re-run of the re-run, Glasgow secured their first and only heat win. Scoring used the four points for a win, two for second and one for third place.

Newcastle went on to draw 14–14 with Wembley, beat Edinburgh and a Belle Vue side. Gosforth staged a couple of Inter-County events in 1929 and a Tyneside versus Scotland fixture. Scottish riders were popular visitors to Newcastle and a Scotland side with Holder, Isbister, Allan Campbell and one unknown rider, thought to be Jack Reilly, raced and lost to a Tyneside team on 4 September.

'Speedway', in the *Citizen* reported on the 10 September meeting: "An excellent programme was again witnessed at White City last night, and the innovation of a series of matches with Gosforth (Newcastle) riders raised so much excitement that more of this type of event will be seen. In the first match George Pinkerton slammed into a good lead at the start, but a spot of unintended sliding nearly put him down. However, with Norrie Isbister out, George was forced to turn it all on to finish in front of the two visitors. A splendid encounter.' Norrie had been well away but his tyre burst, ending his race.

"Jim Holder rode number two under the effects of a previous crash and unluckily managed to spill again.' Jim actually remounted after his fall and completed the race. 'Arthur Moser had been last on the first bend, but when he realised the position rode pretty desperately to emulate Pinkerton's feat of leading home the visitors. A splendid effort by Cattell of Gosforth now put the Sassenachs in the lead for the first time. For a time, it looked as if Thompson was going to increase that lead by getting second place, but a magnificent effort by Isbister saw the Glasgow boy squeeze into second place. With Jim Holder suffering from the effects of his weak shoulder, Arthur Moser was left to ride alone against the brothers Sanderson in the last event. and with the score 11 points to 10 in favour of Gosforth the plot was that Arthur had to win to make a draw of the series ... and win he did – with one of his most brilliant rides in 93.0 seconds" The final result was Glasgow 14 Gosforth 14.

The gradual transition into team racing continued. On 17 September, the second-half was unusual because the riders were split into two teams and points allocated by finishing order. Despite there being two home men and two visitors in each heat, it was still an individual event. The home riders did not do well. Galloway was their only heat winner and George Pinkerton chased Elder in their heat. The *Citizen* said: "George Pinkerton made Sprouts keep his finger away from the 'button'. The Final was a chapter of spills with the three stars all coming to earth. Elder was quickest to get up and get going again and claimed second place." The 28–14 score can be accounted for if the winner is awarded four points and second place two points, with no other scorers.

The following week, the team match was reported: 'The series of races with Gosforth, Newcastle Speedway provided some thrilling work, particularly when, despite a vicious slide, Jimmie Pinkerton ran through a fast field to score for White City in match one. Nicholl, with Cattell at his exhaust, clocked 90.3 seconds to win match two. George Pinkerton was sadly troubled with plugs hereabouts – indeed he oiled no less than four in quick succession. Jimmie Pinkerton and Andy Nicholl also annexed matches three and four respectively to give White City a win over Gosforth by 19 points to 9.' So, Glasgow had their only win in a team match in 1929.

The individual meetings continued, but on 8 October, history was made with the first meeting between teams representing Glasgow and Edinburgh. The crowd was considered by the *Daily Record* to be poor, although Billy Galloway said it was good. They saw the Glasgow team in the third team match at White City. This was the first full scale meeting between the two rival cities, and after four heats the result was 17–10 in Edinburgh's favour.

McQueen raced to a very quick win in the opening heat, and with team mate Bill Barclay in third place behind Glasgow's Arthur Mann. Edinburgh opened up a 5–2 advantage thanks to the scoring system of four points for a win, with second and third place collecting two and one points respectively. McKenzie took the second race with Pinkerton following him home in second. Jimmie Valente fell on the last turn and pushed home as the second Edinburgh rider, Andy Milne, had spilled earlier in the race.

Galloway said in the *Daily Record* that Milne had tried to get between the Glasgow riders and the fence on one bend, when the space available was only enough for a rabbit. Milne tried the same on the next bend and collected the fence, a trip to the ambulance tent and treatment for cuts and concussion. The race produced a 4–3 for Edinburgh. This crash ruled Milne out of the return at Marine Gardens.

Heat four was raced next for some reason, and was won by Glasgow's Arthur Mann. He was in the side because Andy Nicholl was injured. Gordon Spalding, replacing Andy Milne, grabbed second as the only other scoring finisher, George McKenzie fell and retired, unlike Isbister who fell, remounted, fell again and pushed "manfully, if leisurely, up to the post, and then collapsed over his mangle[bike]".' Unfortunately for him, the steward had seen Isbister receive outside assistance after one of his falls and excluded him.

The final heat saw McQueen complete his maximum and Edinburgh take maximum points from the heat. Bill Barclay took his chance to grab second spot when Jimmie Pinkerton 'collected an earful of cinders' (fell). Valente took third spot. Edinburgh carried off the superb Distillers White Horse Trophy, with a 10–8 win. Glasgow should not have risked of including Jimmie Valente. His experience at White City was limited. He was race rusty coming back late in the season. This, along with not including Galloway, was an error on Glasgow's part.

The last meeting of the season at Marine Gardens on 12 October saw Edinburgh beat Glasgow 16–12 over four heats, with scoring on the 4–2–1–0 system. George McKenzie's two heat wins turned the match round after Glasgow took a 5–2 opening heat lead. This meeting was Valente's Edinburgh swan song. He had come out of retirement for Glasgow and raced at White City on the Tuesday before. Pinkerton skippered Glasgow; Drew McQueen captained Edinburgh.

McQueen was due to race in a triangular event with two Australians, but withdrew due to an injured hand. The injury was sustained in the first heat of the match. Had Drew stayed aboard the score would probably have been greater than 16–12. Equally, had Glasgow used their star man, Billy Galloway in the team, the result might have gone in favour of White City.

Edinburgh retained the White Horse Distillers Ltd. Trophy which they had won in Glasgow and kept it until the middle of 1930. Individual meetings continued for a couple of weeks. The first full season at White City finished on 22 October. A remarkable 53 meetings had been staged at White City. The season's star was runner-up in each of the main events at the last meeting. 1929 was Billy Galloway's year, and would have been an even bigger year for him had he not left for a while and also avoided injury.

Documents from the 1930 season at White City

WHITE CITY SPEEDWAY
IBROX GLASGOW

Competitor's Pass

FOR

Date... 13 MAY 1930

Admit to Competitors' Enclosure

ROBERT W. SINCLAIR
Speedway Manager.

WHITE CITY SPEEDWAY
IBROX GLASGOW

Mechanic's Pass

FOR

Date... 27 MAY 1930

Admit to Competitors' Enclosure

ROBERT W. SINCLAIR
Speedway Manager.

---

52 GREAT KING STREET,

EDINBURGH, 6 JUN 1930 19

DEAR SIR,

The Glasgow Dirt Track Racing Club

I have to inform you that you have been selected to ride at the Race Meeting to be held on 10 JUN 1930 at 4.45 p.m.

All Competitors must be at the Track with their Machines ready for racing before 4.15 p.m., and report to the Official in charge of the Pits not later than 4.20 p.m.

Competitor's and Mechanic's Passes enclosed herewith.

Your Racing Number for this Meeting is ....

Yours faithfully,

ROBERT W. SINCLAIR,
Speedway Manager.

2. 1930: League speedway

Glasgow reopened in mid-April 1930 with proposals to run twice a week. The Friday meetings lasted until early May, when the meetings were reduced to Tuesdays only. The loss of Saturday meetings staged in 1929 may have been due to crowd numbers or pressure from the greyhound meetings, but Friday nights were not popular. The introduction of speedway in the East End at Carntyne probably had no effect on the White City crowds. The meetings at White City were a mixture of team meetings and individual meetings.

The Glasgow promotion ventured into league speedway in the Northern League. The league added some variety to the individual meetings as staged in 1929. It was planned for 13 teams to contest this league. Unfortunately, it was never completed and Belle Vue won with the highest points total. This was well deserved because they won every away fixture except against Leicester Super, where they claimed a draw. The league used six-heat matches with three points for a win, two for second and one for third. Tracks were represented by four-man teams, plus a reserve. Normally each team member took three rides, but occasionally a rider had four rides. Meeting formats were not fixed and this was left to the home promotion to determine.

The Glasgow fans welcomed back Billy Galloway as their League team captain. Fellow Australian Colin Stewart was signed to back him up. The rest of the side would come from local talent. Andy Nicholl was included in the squad along with Arthur Mann. Arthur Moser was the reserve. Only once did this line-up ride together. Injury, illness or outside interests saw to that.

Stewart missed the first home meeting due to 'flu, Moser broke a collarbone, Nicholl could not get time off work to travel to Leicester, and then broke a collarbone in the pre-match parade at Belle Vue. Billy Galloway broke bones in a crash at Edinburgh.

The press often demanded that the younger lads be given a chance. When they did get to ride, they did not score more than the established riders. It is a pity that the Glasgow promotion did not try to bring in a proven star or two, in addition to Col Stewart, to give the league side a biting edge and send the fans of team racing home happy more often.

Scotland provided 40 riders for the 1930 season. Jimmie Pinkerton, who many years later was awarded an OBE, transferred to the short-lived Glasgow Carntyne venue, where he broke his arm in the opening meeting. Jimmie returned for very briefly in mid-season before retiring. His brother George appears to have also dropped out around the same time.

Bill Dickie moved to White City without much success. Willie Durward continued to improve without winning any events. Andy Marr maintained his interest and Sandy Smith was one of the few juniors, like Alfie Williams and Sam Aitkenhead, to gain senior status. The local riders were popular and the supporters club had asked for a Glasgow based riders only event. The management obliged and on 22 July no visitors were on the bill.

There were 55 English riders who raced at White City in 1930. Most were one meeting visitors with their league team, but a few stars did make it up for the big events. Blantyre's Billy Llewellyn was the only Welshman at White City. Billy improved during the year and was a member of the league team on a few occasions.

Two of the Australians were Galloway and Stewart, while a few appeared with visiting teams. Jack Chapman was the only Australian to win an event. With Galloway out for much of the middle of the season it was Stewart who became the star man. While he shone in team events, he only won one individual event. Four Australians were attached to White City for a short period in the early season as they tried to sell sidecar speedway to the Scottish public. It never really caught on.

Belle Vue had the first Danish riders on their books. Kai Anderson and Walter Ryle both rode once at White City but did not warrant scratch rider status. Belle Vue also had the first Norwegian, a rider called Paul Sande.

The sole American visitor was ever popular Sprouts Elder. As before bike problems restricted his returns, but he could still draw a crowd to Glasgow. It was still a feather in any rider's cap to beat Sprouts.

The move from the Douglas bike to the Rudge was in progress and the Glasgow riders were involved. By the end of the season most top riders had moved to the single cylinder four-valve machine and the track reduced in depth to suit this equipment.

The writing was on the wall for speedway in Glasgow as crowd numbers fell over the year. The lack of success for the league team representing a very sports orientated City did not help. Being devoid of out-and-out stars, capable of winning most of their races, probably didn't help either. 1930 was a season of highs and a lot of lows.

April

The *Daily Record* said about the 15 April meeting: "Last night again heard the White City Stadium resound with the roar of dirt-track machines. A gigantic card on which 35 'A Grade' riders figured was submitted, the handicaps ranging up to four seconds, the maximum allowance this year."

Billy Galloway was chasing the Rudge dealers for a new machine, while Col Stewart had one. Unfortunately for him at over 4,000 revs it developed a miss-fire. He borrowed a bike from Rev Cox. This was not good as it must have had a slightly buckled wheel, causing it to wobble about.

Galloway used a Douglas belonging to Arthur Mann. He must have been alarmed to see Galloway in a very unusual prang. The *Glasgow Evening News* said: "Everyone present will long remember Billy's amazing perception when a riderless machine was thrown against his own. He grabbed hold of the handlebars with his left hand and steered both for about 30 yards before coming to a halt."

Belle Vue's Frank Varey won the Handicap event from Glasgow's Andy Nicholl. In the scratch event for the Scottish Silver Gauntlet, Nicholl showed his gentlemanly nature. After a few false starts the heat with Varey and Nicholl got underway. Varey, thinking it was yet another false start when he saw a wrongly displayed red flag, halted. All the others sped off and, when Andy was told about this, he called for a re-run. This was accepted and Varey won. What the other riders in the race thought is not recorded. Galloway was not happy. Varey was a non-finisher in the Gauntlet Final but, after beating Col Stewart in the Match Race contest heat, beat Squib Burton in the Final.

After many thrills the four finalists lined up to try to win the Scottish Silver Gauntlet. 'It looked odds on Varey scoring a hat-trick, but he retired at the end of the first lap with engine trouble. Campbell came a cropper soon after, as did Mann in the third lap. Burton finished alone.

Galloway advised his *Daily Record* readers that he thought the Rex Acme used by Burton was the first to be seen in Glasgow. Clearly he had forgotten Norrie Isbister's bike on which he had started 1929. He also outlined that: "I got bored touring round admiring the scenery and stayed out of the scratch race. Col borrowed another bike and after putting up a good show came down in a slide on the pits corner. That allowed Ernie Willis who had been off but restarted to get into second place. Moral - Its always worth trying."

The crowd turned up at White City on 19 April expecting to see Jack Parker and his brother Norman in action but were out of luck. Train troubles prevented their trip and, following their telegram to Glasgow, a telegram to Marine Gardens produced two able replacements in George McKenzie and Len Stewart.

The *Daily Record* said: "George McKenzie proved an able substitute for he took premier place in the three chief items, Andy Nicholl, the local lad being runner-up on each occasion."

Billy Galloway was also a non-starter as he had 'flu. So the fans missed Galloway taking on the Parkers. The *Bulletin and Scots Pictorial* commented: "Much disappointment was felt among the 10,000 spectators when it was made known that Billy Galloway was suffering from influenza and would be unable to take part in the proceedings."

McKenzie, however, was an able replacement and kept the crowd on their toes. He had a great race with Andy Nicholl in their match race.

The other telling remark from the *Herald* was about the crowd: "The second meeting of the season at White City, Glasgow showed a big drop in attendance, only 10,000 people being present." The Parkers should have drawn more. Maybe it did, but then maybe word got around about their non-arrival and Galloway's absence before customers paid at the turnstiles.

Glasgow started their home Northern League fixtures on 22 April against Leicester Super. Glasgow won 23–13 and Galloway scored a nine-point maximum. Stewart was unwell and did not ride.

The match started with heat 2 first. It was quite exciting; Bert Spencer raced into a lead only to be bored out and passed by winner Andy Nicholl. Heat 1 followed and 'Speedway' wrote in the *Evening Citizen:* "It was one long gasp. Galloway took the lead and Stevens went clean berserk in his efforts to chip Billy from the white line. Even the mechanics watched the grim tussle (absolutely unprecedented) and I myself became so excited that I had to ascertain Billy's winning time from the pits marshal."

Heat 3 was a 5–1 to Glasgow. In heat four there was more excitement. 'Stevens rode very desperately in the fourth tussle that a purler was always a possibility and on the second lap it came. Mann ripped into the lead but by yielding a few inches in the last bend he allowed Spencer through to win in 92.4 seconds. Galloway and Mann made siccar (sure) in the fifth round. Billy, of course, streaked away on his own, but we had a really tense half minute with Mann and Wilkinson. It was anybody's berth with only the finishing straight to go but a violent broadside fetched the Leicester boy's chain off and finished him. Even at this hopeless stage the visitors sportingly played up and Stevens had the rewards of his previous strenuous efforts by a splendid win in the last event in 89.3 seconds.' Andy Nicholl was excluded from this race after he left the track.

Harold Stevens ended the evening in hospital, after a crash in heat four of the Glasgow Handicap event. The *Citizen* captured the moment: "Stevens' broadsiding in his previous races had thrilled the crowd and he was attempting the same tactics in his handicap heat in an endeavour to overhaul the leader. In the second lap he came down in a slide at the east corner, being flung several yards along the track." He was hit by a following rider.

The attendance was considered to be poor on 25 April, but the fans saw some good racing. The *Glasgow Herald* noted: "Shining new machines were a feature at White City Speedway, Glasgow last night and among others Billy Galloway brought out his new Rudge.

The machine behaved splendidly in heat and semi-final (of the Handicap). Billy was the star, his new bike doing the business, but let it go in the Handicap Final when his bike packed in."

Galloway was also in the scratch race final. The *Glasgow Herald* outlined: "The Final with the inclusion of both Scottish Captains – Drew McQueen, Marine Gardens and Billy Galloway, White City – promised thrills and it did, but only for a short time. Galloway skidded on the first bend of the first lap and retired while McQueen did likewise on the second bend. With Billy out of contention it was Andy Nicholl who gained the benefit to complete his double. Andy only had Arthur Moser running along with him at the end. Drew McQueen re-mounted to trail in in third place rather than retiring from the event."

An odd tail-piece was contained in the *Govan Press*. It advised that the Silver Gauntlet Final was almost ready to start when the manager realized the trophy was not in the stadium cupboard. After a panic and longer than usual track preparation, the trophy was returned from a motorcycle showroom window where it was on display.

26 April was very wet at Leicester and the riders were quite daring to give it a go. The meeting lasted for three of six scheduled heats before it was called off. Billy Galloway said in the *Daily Record* that he had seen rain in Glasgow, but this surpassed the downpours in Scotland. Bike problems occurred due to the wet weather. Freddie Hore had an engine failure in heat two, but managed to restart the bike and grabbed second place. George Pinkerton raced in his only league match with a last in heat three. The abandonment and expunging of the record means that his name is not in the league record books. However, the team photograph records George's lone outing.

Billy Galloway said in the *Daily Record*: "They scared up a set of bagpipes and someone to work them and played us round the track. We, the Glasgow team, in a Ford lorry. That was the first time I'd ever lapped in one."

Leicester was a one-third of a mile track hence each heat was raced over three laps only. A mile and a third race was probably out of the question. The *Daily Record* said: "Although there were few spills there were many thrills at last night's dirt-track meeting."

Danish riders from Belle Vue, Walter Ryle and Kai Anderson visited White City on 29 April, but it was Eric Langton who was the talk of the terraces. Billy Galloway felt that the Danish riders were at home on the White City circuit and despite their scratch handicap ratings, they failed to show up as star riders.

The *Daily Record* was impressed by Langton and said: "We had the vanguard of the Belle Vue team with us last night and, quietly, between ourselves, that motor of Eric Langton's must be fed on nitro glycerine.

The Silver Sash did not appear to provide so many thrills. The Final was a two race event. Up front Langton and Galloway contested first place, whilst at the rear Andy Nicholl and Jack White fought it out for third place. Nicholl claimed the superior place on the line by a half-wheel margin. This event took three attempts to get started and after the starter 'sent the field away…it was soon obvious that, barring a spill, Langton would get the chequered flag, which he did in 87.5 seconds.

The match race between Langton and Galloway showed us two really quick motors handled by master tacticians. One would have expected the Manchester boy to yield the white line to Galloway on his first visit to the track, but, by reason of his violent acceleration, Eric annexed the inside and ran round as if it had been a rail. Both riders gave almost perfect examples of speedway speed and style and Langton's effort, in particular, was the best of the whole evening."

May

The programme for 2 May had a couple of unusual items. First, there was a demonstration by Australian sidecar speedway racers Allan Bruce and Keith Horton. It was one of many at venues up and down the country, but never caught on.

Second, there was a relay race between a team from Glasgow and one from Belle Vue. The format was a series of three two-lap races and the team with the best aggregate time was the winner. Belle Vue's time was 140.8. According to the *Daily Record*: 'There was not a dull moment at last night's dirt track meeting at the White City, Ibrox. Perhaps the most exciting event was the demonstration for the first time in Great Britain of motor sidecar racing by Alan Bruce and Keith Horton from Down Under'.

On the solos, the *Record* said: "Although the Manchester riders failed to show anything out of the ordinary in the handicap event, they fully made up for this in the scratch race for the Scottish Silver Gauntlet. No fewer than three of their quartet, Dunn, Harrison and Wilcock, lined-up for the Final along with Bill Naismith who came down on the first bend. The race, however, was a thriller, for it was only on the line that Dunn, a lad of 17 years, got home from Harrison."

'Velox' of the *News* gave an interesting insight into the relay: "The *bête noir* of previous relay races has been the too great influence of the start. The chances of four men should be jeopardized by a bad start by one of them was farcical and inept - and by making them each ride two laps instead of one thus gave the slow beginner a chance to recover ground lost at the start.

"As the first two riders representing Glasgow and Manchester complete the first lap, the second men from each team will move their machines on the inside of the track leaving the outside line clear for the finish of the first race. Immediately the front wheel of the leading man crosses the line his colleague will be pushed off, the other having to await the arrival of his leader. Thus there are only four change overs in the eight laps.' Provisions were made for falls and for engine failures by way of time penalties.

An idea to revive this event in 1996 was 'knocked on the head' by the sport's insurance company, but later Barry Briggs staged a relay race at a meeting he promoted. Clearly it could be dangerous if not carefully planned, but the relays must have been interesting to watch.

Glasgow faced the Belle Vue Northern League team on 6 May in their second home league match. Glasgow were ahead only once, but ran the Manchester team closer than Edinburgh had done. 'Speedway' in the *Citizen* felt that had Glasgow raced Belle Vue later in the season the result might have been different.

'Speedway' reported: In heat 1 Frank Varey opened the Belle Vue onslaught, then "Andy Nicoll, inspired and determined, took the lead in match two. He left no daylight between himself and the white line; nor could Harrison run outside the Blantyre boy. The Manchester rider crocheted a pattern all over the track in an effort to get past but Nicoll stuck to it."

"Arthur Franklyn got away best in the third tussle, but Galloway and Nicoll both wriggled to the front in the first lap. Billy thereupon piled it all on and got away with it (he confessed afterwards that his throttle jammed full open) what time Nicoll and Franklyn tore into each other for second place."

Stewart diced with Harrison in heat four as Varey took the lead: "Despite brilliant riding, tremendous two-wheel slides of 30 yards or more, and real track craft, a motor that seemed hopelessly under-geared sent all Colin's fine work up in smoke on the straights and he had to rest contented with third place."

"The fifth race saw two visitors, Franklyn and Harrison, tearing it up nicely with Galloway waiting his chances. Two vacant patches of white line allowed Billy through and although the visitors filled both hands with throttle and courage, our man stuck to the inside border and passed the post in 86.9. A feature of the heat was the grim riding of Bill Naismith who ploughed into each bend at a speed that even Sprouts could not hold – but inevitably [he] collected (fell off). Stout boy Bill."

Bill Naismith was Glasgow's reserve and replaced Arthur Mann, who had not scored in his two rides.

The sixth race did not go as expected. "Most people had the last race settled in the third lap with Varey No.1 and Haigh runner-up. An unlucky over-slide sent Haigh overboard, however, within sight of the post and Stewart seconded Varey's 89.6 seconds."

Varey fell in the Glasgow Handicap final. Belle Vue's Bob Harrison won it. Franklyn won the Scottish Silver Sash to complete a Belle Vue whitewash.

The *Glasgow Herald* said that the meeting on 9 May would be the last regular Friday night event at White City Speedway. Despite ideal weather it only drew 11,000 fans.

Drew McQueen enjoyed the scenery of the Scottish Lowlands and Highlands, as he took part in the Scottish Six-Day Trial. While he did not make it to Preston for the Northern League match the night before, he did take a break to turn out for the Glasgow fans. He had to go back to Perth for the sixth and final day of the event. Maybe it was because of lack of attention, but his speedway mount did not perform to standard, and his winnings were well down. His bike failed in the Handicap Final.

Eric Langton also had machine troubles. This caused his defeat in the Handicap semi-final, and the Scottish Gold Armlet final. Had his bike been on song, he probably would have 'cleaned up'. Edinburgh's Australian, Syd Parsons, rode according to the *Herald*, but does not appear in any of the results available. Syd's performance was poor for him.

The *Daily Record* said the [Armlet Final] "... looked a certainty for [Langton] but, 50 yards in front after the first lap his machine gave out. This left Bill Naismith, Andy Nicholl and George Pinkerton to fight it out to the finish and that trio passed the winning line in that order."

Sidecars were on the bill. Alan Bruce and Keith Horton gave a wheel-to-wheel display with the former just easing over the line ahead by a few inches. They then tried to set a new one lap record. Bruce was the faster, but his 22.7 seconds was a bit slower than the solos.

On the junior front, Sam Aitkenhead appeared in the results for the first time. He went on to be a popular performer at White City.

Glasgow visited Marine Gardens on 10 May for a four heat challenge match for the Inter-City Cup. They ran the home team close before losing 12–10. Edinburgh had won the cup at White City in 1929. The rules allowed three challenges a season, which took place at the holder's track.

After a prang in his first team race and a paid win behind Len Stewart, George McKenzie 'cleaned up' the meeting. His Gold Sash win was on a machine which covered the final two laps with a buckled rear wheel and flat tyre. Edinburgh were lucky that the bike troubles which plagued the Macs in the match waited until the second-half to affect Stewart and Parsons, otherwise Edinburgh may have failed to score.

The *Edinburgh Evening News* noted: "Among the gossip notes in the official programme it was stated that Drew McQueen was wondering if his machine worries would ever end. He would have cause for more wonder after Saturday night. Machine worries concerned most of the riders but again McQueen had far more than his share of them. He did not earn a single point in the match. Due largely to the same cause, however, neither did Galloway, the Glasgow team captain, give any assistance to his side. In two of the races only two riders managed to complete the course. The best performance was by Len Stewart, who took first place in his two races. Parsons had one first and, with a defective engine, he merely crawled in for third place in his other race. McQueen had looked like winning the same race when his chain came off."

Billy Galloway had a crash with George McKenzie in the second Gold Sash semi-final. This resulted in a broken collar bone and lengthy spell on the sidelines. His injury hit Glasgow's league campaign as they did not have the fire power to replace him. It is likely that this injury contributed to his decision to retire at the end of the season.

Glasgow had their third league meeting at home on 13 May. After Belle Vue they faced the equally daunting Manchester White City, who turned up two men short. Missing were the Jervis brothers, Arthur and Hubert, often known as Hugh.

The three riders who did turn up, Frank Charles, Wally Hull and Buzz Hibberd, managed to win the match 19–16 to take the league points.

'Speedway' of the *Citizen* reported: "It was a mixed grill which we were served at White City last night; keen racing, a record equalled, another one broken, a few lurid crashes that turned out not to be serious after all and defeat of the local team by these very fast riders from Manchester.

"Bill Naismith made us gulp in the first match when he collided with the safety fence and somersaulted half-a-dozen yards. His injuries were latterly diagnosed as a dislocated shoulder and bruised knees." Walter Hull won heat two easily: "The real thrills in this event was the desperate endeavours of Colin Stewart to charm more speed out of his motor to keep Buzz Hibberd out, but the efforts of both were in vain for Mann followed Hull home."

Heats three and four did not provide any thrills, but heat five did: "Arthur Mann, by sheer good handling, put White City (Glasgow) in the lead in the fifth match though not without every inch being contested by Buzz Hibberd. Arthur was furiously behind until the last bend and by trimming the grass as Buzz wiped the fence, the home boy got his wheel in front and kept it there."

The last heat saw Frank Charles and Wally Hull facing Andy Nicholl and Col Stewart. The Manchester pair raced away to a 5-1 and victory in the match. They scored 8+1 and 9 points respectively. Buzz Hibberd chipped in with two. This was an unusual meeting. In the Handicap event heats, "It was really remarkable to see Charles, Hull and Hibberd in that order sewing up their respective seams through bucking, twisting and baulking opposition and their excellent finishing was much appreciated."

It was another wet night in Rochdale on 17 May. This was Rochdale's opening league meeting and it is not well reported. The reporter was not helped by Glasgow's failure to use numbered race-jackets, so their names were not announced. Despite this, Rochdale Observer reported on six incident packed heats: "There was many causes contributing to the defeat of Glasgow. First, they were not such good riders as the Rochdale team, and secondly, their machines caused them a lot of trouble. On the whole, the league match was not of an exceptionally exciting character; the fact that the Glasgow team did not wear distinguishing numbers made matters worse. It appears that Glasgow arrived without team numbers and asked to be supplied by the Rochdale directors. There were none to be had, so the Glasgow men rode without, and whenever they were placed at the final of the team heats, the names of the Glasgow men were not announced. According to the speedway regulations each team is responsible for providing their own numbers... the contest started in a lively manner, only two of the four riders finishing the course. Sticpewich and Jack Atkinson were the Rochdale men and at the first bend the former fell, his right leg trailing dangerously. Arthur Mann to avoid Sticpewich went wide to the fence and fell. Meanwhile, Atkinson was going at fine speed on his new Rudge and registered first points with the best time of the meeting - 84.72 seconds. In the second heat Rochdale were unfortunate. Breaks machine failed in the second lap and Austin Humphries, with a good lead, was pulled up on the last bend, his back tyre twisting off. Sticpewich and Ingham had things their own way in the next heat, neither of the Glasgow men finishing the four laps. In the remaining heats of the match, Sticpewich recorded two firsts, Breaks a first and a second place and Atkinson a third position. The most notable incidents in these three heats was the improved riding of Breaks and Austin Humphries' plucky continuation, notwithstanding a flat back tyre. Although his wheel was wobbling dangerously, he fought for third position and almost managed it."

In the next three heats Rochdale took 12 points to Glasgow's six and won 20–13.

Glasgow had their bike troubles as ever. In the pre-match parade Billy Llewellyn's bike holed a crankcase and he may not have ridden in the match unless he borrowed a bike. Andy Nicholl's number one bike had a broken throttle cable and his second bike had a puncture.

'Speedway' reported on the 20 May meeting which had the usual format of two main events, the Glasgow Handicap and the Scottish Gold Torch.

Heat two of the Handicap saw a close finish as Col Stewart and Eric Langton chased after Peter Coia. At the end of the race Langton just passed Cola, but Stewart was not so fortunate. "In heat five Billy Llewellyn just about blew his two seconds start over Frank Charles. 'If Billy had not had a 'grandfather of a lurch' in the first lap he would have had an even better time."

The best was the last race, the Handicap final. It was "a triumph for Langton. In a rasping finish he was at the head of a 20 feet long procession comprising Stevens, Mann and Nicholl and the crowd let loose the breath they had been holding for 90.5 seconds and asked for more."

"They got it [in the Scottish Silver Torch]. Inspired probably by the Manchester method all riders put their machines into 30 foot slides for the bends and nobody moved a square inch of enamel in the process. Charles and Langton in particular gave really wonderful examples of what motorcycles should not be able to do – but did."

The management were pleased with the 20,000 crowd. They considered that the reduction to one meeting per week was the main reason for the increased numbers.

Not everyone was happy. 'Velox' of the *Glasgow Evening News* berated the Glasgow riders for not riding fast enough and keeping to the white line: "Billy Lamont laughs at the jibe that he goes mad on the track. It is only his style – he flies at everything. I believe he opens the taps full and does his best to keep the bike on the track. Sprouts Elder is not quite so ruthless. He flies up the straights and in the bends intuitively shuts off for barely a second." 'Velox' was beginning to think that some local riders had lost sight of the fact that there is no formula for success, and should open their eyes and taps.

Glasgow had an unfortunate start to a league match when Nicholl collided with one of his team-mates on the parade lap, before the match on 24 May. He broke his collarbone and reserve Billy Llewellyn replaced him. Belle Vue's virtually three-man side tore Glasgow apart.

Heat one was a 5-1 to Belle Vue. Arthur Franklyn and Len Myerscough beat Arthur Moser and Billy Llewellyn. Frank Varey won the next from Stewart with no other finishers. Another second place for Stewart in heat three when he followed home Arthur Franklyn with Billy Llewellyn third.

Belle Vue won heat four. Frank Varey got his second win and Glasgow provided Arthur Moser in second place with Mann third. Stewart beat Len Myerscough with no other finishers.

There was a last heat decider. A 5–0 to Glasgow could have given them victory. With Varey and Franklyn in the last heat, an away win was unlikely. True to form, Varey won it; the final score was 21–13.

27 May was a black day for dirt-track racing in Glasgow. The fans had watched a home 18–17 defeat at the hands of Warrington, with a last-heat decider when Col Stewart fell. Nothing prepared them for the coming events.

In the second-half, the popular, single, 26-year-old Londoner Eddie Reynolds fell on the second bend of the second lap while leading the Handicap opening heat. He was hit by Arthur Moser who could not get his bike laid down to avoid him. Eddie's injuries were, unfortunately, fatal. He was Glasgow's first speedway fatality and Scotland's second. War hero Walter Brown from Musselburgh had been killed at Marine Gardens a little over a year before, in a very similar accident.

Arthur was flung into the air by the impact and turned two somersaults before landing 10 yards up the straight from the point of the crash. The meeting continued to heat four of the Handicap event, but was then abandoned after the rider's death was announced. Eddie, a tailor by trade, lived in Glasgow. His loss was sorely felt by the crowd and his fellow riders.

The *Govan Press* captured the moment: "When the awful news was given over the loud speakers the crowd were horrified and thunderstruck and no one was surprised when the management decided to abandon the meeting." A few weeks later, the inquiry into the fatal accident was satisfied that this was just a racing accident and the formal verdict, which does not apportion blame, recorded.

The events surrounding Eddie's injuries over-shadowed the track record established by Col Stewart in the second heat of that ill-fated Handicap event.

'Velox' of the *News* said of the league match: "Once again the White City league team have had to admit defeat. This time it was the lads from Warrington Speedway that took away the points from the Ibrox last night. They can count themselves a little lucky, however, for although they lined up for the last match a point to the good it looked as if the local pair engaged here – Colin Stewart and Arthur Mann – would have come first and second. Although Arthur managed to secure first place, Col, in trying to manoeuvre past his colleagues came a cropper, thus letting the visitors ride into second and third place to win the series by a single point."

June

The *Glasgow Herald* commented that there were riders from six tracks present on 3 June. The results only feature five: White City, Glasgow; White City, Manchester; Belle Vue, Manchester; Coventry; and Liverpool. Carntyne could have been the sixth, but Broncho Bianchi was listed as unattached following the demise of the other Glasgow venue a few weeks before.

Racing was reported as being exciting and "There were a series of spills, the most serious of these occurring in the second semi-final of the Glasgow Handicap event. Frank Varey and Tommy Price [not the Wembley rider] crashed badly when the former tried to cut in at the bend. Varey had to be carried off on a stretcher suffering from an injured shoulder and was later removed to the infirmary. Tommy Price sustained a severe cut to the forehead."

Racing rules of the day demanded that a rider had to be a certain distance clear of their fellow riders before trying to cut in to the white line. Frank was a robust racer and cut things a little too fine. The *Govan Press* was critical: "Varey's riding was very lucid and when he ran into Tommy Price... at the Ibrox bend and 'I was expecting that' was on most people's lips. Daring riding is one thing and recklessness is another. No one wishes a repetition of last week's tragedy, and if Varey ever again serves up a display like he did on Tuesday night, he will drop right out of favour with the fans at White City. Price suffered a nasty gash at the side of his right eye – a narrow escape. Varey was slightly injured about the shoulder and was able to leave Glasgow on Wednesday night."

Coventry's Tom Farndon was a star visitor, and his status was recognised when he was asked to replace Frank in the match race with Stewart. Farndon won as Stewart fell on the last lap.

The Northern edition of *Auto* had a short report on the 4 June meeting at Sheffield. It said the obvious, that the visitors were well-beaten. Jack 'Broncho' Dixon and Jack Chapman had a private duel in the opener and the race was won in a track record time for four laps rolling start. Dixon completed his maximum of nine points for the home team. Jack Chapman was also unbeaten by a visiting rider. Glasgow's best effort was a couple of second places by Llewellyn and Isbister in a 26–10 defeat.

The Sheffield 'Blades' visited Glasgow on 10 June. As well as the league match, 18–17 to Glasgow, the crowd saw Jack Parker's skills. Apparently, he entertained the crowd by 'running rings' round track manager Mr Sinclair. It is assumed he did this on his bike.

On the more serious business of racing, Parker set a new one lap track record at 20.6 seconds and a new four lap flying start record. He beat Col Stewart in a match race. 'Speedway' said: "Both bored into it like smoke with Colin leading until he came off after two laps. Jack passed, but waited until Colin was level – they both tore off again. Once more Colin sat down but although Jack won he insisted on a re-run, and got it – and the spectators loudly applauded his sportsmanship."

Parker rode in the Handicap Final, winning through in heat two. He suffered from his scratch status in the Final. 'Norrie Isbister got in front in the Final of the Handicap, and despite furious pursuit, was never headed. Parker was settling nicely when White executed such a lurid slide that Jack pulled up. He resumed in the rear of Chapman and white and when Chapman sat down on the pit bend he followed White past.' Parker had to settle for third. He set a new track record in his Scottish Silver Gauntlet heat, but fell in the Final.

Chapman excelled in the league match with a nine points maximum. Glasgow had no stars to match the Australian, but won the match by an odd-point with a solid display from all their riders.

Glasgow's reserve, Jack White, rode in the last heat of the match, because Arthur Mann's bike refused to start. In at the deep end in a last heat decider Jack did well to finish second.

Glasgow raced Rochdale for Northern League points at White City on 17 June. Despite having five heat winners they lost 19–17. Rochdale were never behind after a second heat 5–1 from Frank Atkinson and Buster Breaks put them ahead. Rochdale were handicapped by the non-appearance of Bill Sticpewich, promoting a 'Jack' Wilson into the team in his place. 'Jack' was probably Geoff Wilson who rode for Rochdale at Gosforth the following night.

The opening heat went to Col Stewart who beat Austin Humphries. Humphries had a faster bike and Stewart's track craft carried him to victory. The upshot of the battles between Stewart and Humphries was that a special match race later on in the meeting.

Jimmie Pinkerton came back from injury sustained at the Carntyne opener in mid-May. However, his attempts in the team were frustrated by a badly sprained wrist. Glasgow were not well off for star riders, with Galloway and Nicholl still out. Pinkerton was not the answer and maybe they should have signed a couple of stars, as was suggested by their manager, Sinclair, after Nicholl was injured.

Rochdale's 'Buster' Breaks's real Christian name was John. He was, at one time, a publican in Bristol and returned to Rochdale for the 1970 re-opening meeting at Milnrow Road. Bill Sticpewich was an Australian who had a brother called Charlie, but sometimes raced as Paddy. Bill moved to Leeds when Rochdale closed in mid-1930.

'Speedway' was amazed by George Cumming's antics on 24 June: "Scotty Cumming slid, wobbled and streaked in his heat of the Handicap, but he stuck grimly to the rear of Stewart and Coia until a particularly scarlet slide let him down."

On the bill was Sprouts Elder, who was on a new bike, a Rudge. 'Speedway' thought that it changed his approach: "He has changed over to a Rudge this year and there isn't quite the spectacular man-eating look about his riding, but he comes out of the bend at the same terrifying pace – and few there be that can catch him."

Elder had bike trouble in the Handicap event: "He oiled a plug in the semi-final, however. Our man Colin took 92.4 to make the Final his own." Stewart came from the back. 'Speedway' said: "Mann and Campbell seemed to have a sitting lead in this race when Colin breezed in from nowhere to third in the second lap and then sneaked sweetly past."

Stewart faced Elder in a match race and the American won by five millimetres – *'Speedway's'* distance. The event was worthy of a re-match and "In a re-run, Colin took the lead and though he inspected fences he never lost hold of the precarious couple of yards and Sprouts had an excellent view of his rear tyre when the chequered flag was waved in 86.5 seconds."

Harry Whitfield started a happy weekend on 27 June. By the end of the weekend, Harry was £200 richer. He won £100 at White City and a similar prize at Marine Gardens the next evening.

The *Glasgow Evening Times* was underwhelmed by the whole meeting. The report noted: "Heat number one fizzled out in the run round (to the start) as Harry Butler's machine decided to have nothing further to do with the business.' (Other reports had Drew McQueen in heat 1) 'The next heat (heat 2) was proceeded with, and run to an end in spite of being virtually finished in the first lap. Colin Watson had the race won too easily for thrills."

Heat three saw Arnie Cattell replace Tiger Sanderson: "After Scot Michie had retired Arnie did his best to challenge Syd Parsons, but failed. We were still waiting for our first thrill. And it came in heat four. Colin Stewart, the Glasgow hope, got off rather badly, and Alby Taylor was a couple of yards to the good right away. That assured a good race, Stewart set off in pursuit, gained the lead and won by barely 3 yards. Much better.

"But heat five made us sigh. Down came Hatch, Stan Catlett gave up and Arthur Mann toured in alone. In the next heat one saw some freakish riding by Jimmie Pinkerton. He took the corners in a series of leaps and how he kept the saddle for three corners as he did is something of a mystery. He came down on the fourth and Austin Humphries got the flag without a cheer.

"Then heat 7. Sprouts Elder was there. We stood on tiptoe but not for long. Atkinson and White were his rivals. White skidded and fell and Atkinson gave up. Elder led by over a lap when his Rudge spluttered to a standstill. White remounted and won. A championship event heat won in 119.9!

"We were ready for anything then. The next heat was an ordinary affair. The riders kept to their saddles; the machines behaved too; but Len Stewart's win was easy. Heat nine saw Cliff Watson fall out. Harry Whitfield, the 'dark horse', took 87.1 to complete the heat for a soft win.'

The semi-finals started with Colin Watson beating Tom Farndon after Syd Parsons fell. In the Final: "It was a perfect start. A wild swerve spoiled Colin Stewart's chances - Whitfield and Watson were separated by less than five yards. Stewart shut his teeth to make it and crashed heavily. Poor Colin, the hardest of luck. But the pair of Wembley men made a great race of it. Inch by inch Whitfield made ground and in the second lost it and a blinding last minute effort just gave him victory, a really gallant Champion and a most enjoyable finale to a very disappointing meeting."

White City Championship contestant Scott Michie was a Scotsman. Hailing from Dumfries, he had started out as Laurence Michie at Marine Gardens in 1928, before seeking his fortune at Rochdale in 1929.

July

The Glasgow crowd, was tired of the Edinburgh monopoly of the White Horse Distillers Ltd. Trophy. Edinburgh should have defended it at Marine Gardens as in the trophy rules. The trophy, one of two donated by White Horse Distillers Ltd., was a magnificent bit of silverware.

The *Glasgow Evening News's* 'Velox' said about the meeting on 1 July: "If a little slow in getting started, the races were fast and keen once under way and I heard the meeting compared favourably with the Championship."

'Speedway' reported: "At long last the White Horse Trophy has come to Glasgow and in the main we have Colin Stewart to thank for it. He won all his matches in good time and though the rest of the team were hardly as fast as the Edinburgh boys, the White City registered a dogged and determined win.

"At the start of the last match (heat) the issue was still in doubt with the score of 16 to 14 in favour of Glasgow. Realising this, Colin Stewart wound it well up and took the first bend and the lead. His namesake Len was just as determined and along with Drew McQueen darned patterns all over the track in furious effort to displace Colin."

The *Govan Press*, told its readers that Johnnie Walker was "the only Govan rider on the White City staff and is a partner in the well-known local motorcycle agent Walker Bros of Paisley Road West."

The day after 3 July, the *Lancashire Daily Post* headlined: "Racing Cancelled Owing To Heavy Rain", but just because the league match against Glasgow was off, that did not mean there was no activity: "The Speedway match arranged to take place at Farringdon Park last night was cancelled on account of the weather. A certain amount of water had lodged at one of the bends and the track was generally in a heavy state.

A few thousand people gathered at the track and a good proportion of the riders expressed their willingness to race, however, Mr Meagher the managing director and the ACU Steward thought that the track would cut up badly, become unsafe and that good performances would be impossible. The crowd that had gathered therefore had a free view of some riders, including 'Tipple and Topple', the trick riders, doing a few practice runs round the track."

The Glasgow Supporters Club were a little parochial. They wanted a meeting confined to local riders. They could be seen as xenophobic because many visiting teams arrived at White City and won. This evening was no exception. Newcastle Gosforth won 20–16 on 8 July. Arthur Mann was a passenger in the league match; his engine would not perform. His sole point was gained on a borrowed bike.

'Cinder Sifter' in the *Glasgow Evening Times* rarely spared anyone's sensibilities: "The air around Ibrox way last night was full of sighs of disappointment which came from loyal White City Speedway supporters and others. The reason – another and deserved defeat for the home team. To speak the truth the league match was devoid of thrills, except for the solitary duels between Colin Stewart and Gordon Byers of Gosforth. Gosforth aggregated 20 points, largely due to the steadiness of Byers and his team-mate Alec Hill."

'Cinder Sifter' added: "Now White City frequenters are realizing and have realized for weeks now that Colin Stewart has to win every race that he takes part in for the home team to gain a respectable score of points. Week after week the same thing has happened, and no response to Stewart's daring is forthcoming from his team-mates. Indeed, the Glasgow White City team might be called 'Stewart's team'. It is evident that the remaining trio are completely failing to justify their selection, yet they are never displaced from the chosen four." The writer then lambasted the promotion for not replacing riders who were out of form, suggested alternatives and was fairly critical.

'Speedway' largely ignored the meeting, and reported on the other events. These often held more local interest or were the best races: "All the fun was reserved for the handicap events, which Bill Walker neatly initiated by wriggling his Python into first place. We saw something of the old Moser in the first heat; flat out, sliding desperately, throwing pieces of track about, and then calmly winning. Then, most people had to look for Hugh Adamson's number to make sure it was really him, he and Johnnie Walker had a real poem of a scrap in heat 2." The handicap event provided thrills: "One of the finest races we have seen this season was the second semi-final. Aitkenhead, Isbister, Byers and Campbell flattened into everything with Aitkenhead leading for four hurricane laps. A clothes rope could have been flung round all four riders at any one time and although the latter won a single misfire would have put him last."

The match at the one third of a mile lap Melton Road circuit in Leicester on 12 July was not seen as a classic by the *Leicester Mercury*. It was described as "a surprisingly tame affair."

The reporter bemoaned the lack of dirt on the track and thus the Douglas machines had nothing to hold them up in the turns. The Rudge-mounted men could hold the line on the slicker track.' The blame lay with Jock Hallas, speedway manager, who was, according to the reporter, "tremendously keen on having the European track record lowered at Melton Road Speedway, but I consider he is letting the thrills slip by for the sake of the speed craze. I like to see broadsiding, so do the crowds, but you will never get it on a track bare of cinders." Average speeds of 47 miles per hour were recorded by Hal Herbert and Arthur Sherlock, but Jack Chapman nearly made Hallas's night with a run 0.4 seconds off the mark.

The results from the *Leicester Mercury* do not agree with another Leicester paper for the Glasgow riders' scores. The *Mercury* gave third place to Arthur Mann in heat two, and had Les Stewart riding for Glasgow when it was Col. Without Galloway's fire power, on a genuine Australian size track, Glasgow were very weak.

On 19 July, 'Speedway' commented: "Despite torrential rain a really excellent turnout watched the show at White City." They were not rewarded by a home win; Liverpool won the Northern League match 26–10.

'Cinder Sifter' noted: "... the track [was] exceedingly heavy, especially at the west end, where there were pools of water. Perhaps from the home supporters' point of view, it would have been better had the meeting been abandoned before Glasgow lost so many points to such a superior skilful Liverpool team."

He added: "a ray of hope penetrated the gloom in Andy Nicholl, who signalled his long-awaited return to the Ibrox cinders by steady, if not daring riding. Andy of course, will require time to regain his old nerve, and if Billy Galloway can turn out soon there will be sound hopes for Glasgow not doing so badly in future engagements."

Norrie Isbister drew some applause, 'Speedway' said: "A return to something like his old form for Norrie Isbister kept our hands out of our pockets." In the handicap second heat he had one of the best scraps of the evening, when he clung desperately to the few inches of rain that separated him and Wotton. Eventually Isbister passed in 96.7.

Most spectators remained until the end of the handicap. Aitkenhead and Isbister were up against "a pair of Tigers" in the visitors, Blain and Boulton in the Final. "Sam skilled off everyone to win."

According to the *Herald's* report on 22 July: "The Fair Holiday (traditional Glasgow Holiday period, usually the last two weeks in July) and inclement weather conditions were responsible for a poor attendance at last night's meeting at White City Speedway, Glasgow, which was confined to local riders. The going was heavy and times consequently were slow, but there was no lack of thrills."

Star of the Handicap was "Young Sam Aitkenhead" who was "recently of the junior ranks and who will shortly feature in the White City league team, who showed that he retained his winning spirit for he carried off the handicap race for the third time in succession."

The *News* also said that Aitkenhead "has certainly made himself a popular fellow on the Ibrox cinders by his daredevil style and pluck, for Sam is a sticker all the time, and has earned his place in the local team in which he will be included next week."

Another youngster who was going well was Johnnie Short. He had a crack at the one lap track record. Given the state of the track and his relative inexperience, his time of 22.3 was not bad, even though it was two seconds off the record.

The main event of the evening was the Gold Armlet. The winner would keep the prize. Glasgow's Australian favourite, Col Stewart, carried off the trophy. Ever innovative, the White City promotion showed their fans car racing. The demonstration was brought to a halt when one of the machines broke a spring.

Glasgow's visit to Liverpool on 23 July saw Liverpool equal their score at White City with an easy win. Only Stewart came remotely close to the chequered flag. He had a lead in heat four but lost to Larry Boulton. In heat two, all four riders fell off their machines, thankfully without serious injury. Some re-mounted to complete the course.

The first rain-off of 1930 in Glasgow on 29 July deprived the Glasgow fans of seeing Edinburgh attempt to win back the White Horse Distillers Ltd. Trophy. Edinburgh's last 1930 meeting had been staged the previous Saturday; the future appeared to promise a series of monthly meetings to end the season.

Details of the teams were not fully advertised. The Edinburgh side was due to include McQueen, McKenzie, Len Stewart and McGregor. The meeting was also expected to feature the return of Billy Galloway.

Above: Col Stewart.
Left: Jimmie Pinkerton.
Both riders made an important contribution to the early years of speedway at White City.

Edinburgh were due to return for the re-staging on 5 August, but the closure of Marine Gardens caused the change to a challenge between the 'Reds' and 'Blues' at White City. The match included Drew McQueen, Bill Barclay and Bob McGregor for the 'Reds'.

Billy Galloway had a poor return after injury. The *News* said: "Billy Galloway, who was making his first appearance since his accident gave flashes of his old skill, but he is far from himself yet." The Blues' other trio were on maximums, either full or paid. Sam Aitkenhead had a successful home team debut. This line-up had some new blood, but was not a real test.

While the prizes went south on 12 August, the local riders put up a fight. The *Herald* said: "Isbister was the one who seemed capable of bringing the best out of Frank Charles." The main guests were Sprouts Elder, Frank Varey and Frank Charles. All of them were fliers, and even with a bike going well, Sprouts was hard put to beat the White City, Manchester man.

Yet again Sprouts' equipment was not right. He failed to stay the pace in the Handicap heats. He started at the back and passed two of his rivals before bike failure allowed Arthur Moser to win.

In the Final, 'Speedway' said: "They renewed the discussion in the Final and again it seemed as if Norrie was impassable, but from the tangle of riders who were flagged-off simultaneously Frank Charles emerged winner in 89.9 seconds with Isbister second."

Reported in the Warrington local paper, The match between Warrington and Glasgow on 15 August saw: "In the first two heats decided, Glasgow came first but Warrington competitors followed with second and third places, which placed both teams on equal terms at the end of the second round. Hornby and Hatch registered the maximum number of points in the third heat, whilst in the following race the Glasgow riders were disqualified by the ACU Steward for riding on the green verge - this gave Warrington a lead that was almost impossible to overcome. In the remaining two heats Warrington scored seven points against the visitors five. The last two events were most exciting, Stewart and Isbister cutting inside cleverly after racing behind Hornby and Hatch.' Glasgow lost 23–12. The next night, Glasgow scored one more point in going down at Liverpool.

But for sterling work by the local fire brigade on 19 August, this meeting would have been rained-off. The races were a lottery and at the end of five heats of the match with Preston, only the visitors' Joe Abbott had a bike that was still functional. Treating the event as the farce which the league had become, Glasgow allowed Preston to field Joe in the last heat to keep the crowd happy. Joe's win was academic as Glasgow were so far ahead that the last heat scarcely mattered.

Abbott's 10 points were all but two points short of his team's total and probably a record for a rider in this league.

Glasgow took wet weather with them to Preston on 21 August. *Auto* described the track as 'a quagmire.' It continued: "These uncomfortable conditions linked with strangeness proved too big an obstacle for the plucky Glasgow league team, who gallantly fought out a one-sided battle for points."

'Good Sport at White City' was the heading of the *Glasgow Herald* report of the clash between London (Wembley) and Glasgow on 26 August.

The *Evening Times* headline was 'Wembley Wizards too good for Glasgow'. The paper's report said: "The best of the three races was made in the third race. Colin Stewart jumped into the lead immediately and Greenwood just was thwarted. Strange indeed to see Arthur Atkinson filling last place of the four riders. Isbister's somewhat alarming experience, falling in the second heat of the match, necessitated Arthur Moser being substituted in the fourth event. Buster Frogley was well off his mark, and though he elected to ride wide his speed was too much for Billy Galloway and his team-mate Evans, who just managed to finish third, in front of Moser. Colin Stewart had his work cut out to ward off Norman Evans in his second last match, the Londoner trying his best to close with and beat the Glasgow idol. Last of all came an awesome moment when Galloway went down in front of George Greenwood whose somersault from his machine was perhaps wild but nevertheless effective. Buster Frogley was thus left a hundred-to-one chance of completing his double which he did by beating Andy Nicholl."

The *Times* also considered that "An abundance of spills marred the preliminaries of the Glasgow Handicap and even in the first semi-final, an event one would have expected to be a tit-bit of the evening with Atkinson, Frogley and Sam Aitkenhead in opposition, a clash occurred which put Aitkenhead and Frogley out of the running for the premier honour."

The visitors impressed the *Herald's* writer: "All the visitors rode magnificently and were worthy of their victory. Had Glasgow had fewer fallers, they might just have given the men from North-West London a bit of a fright."

September

The *Herald* said the crowd was down on normal levels on 2 September due to the counter attraction of football at nearby Ibrox Stadium, the home of Glasgow Rangers.

However, despite the missing crowd, "the sport was interesting, promising form being shown by the local riders, five of whom contested the first semi-final (of the Handicap). Even in the second semi-final there were four home men with Percy Dunn the only outside representative."

Was this a trial for Dunn? The Belle Vue based Northumbrian joined Glasgow in 1931 as part of their ill-fated Northern League team.

The Silver Gauntlet provided thrills for the fans. The battle between Billy Galloway and Gordon Byers in heat one was 'notable'. The Final was 'a splendid race, Ivor Creek and Galloway riding neck-and-neck for three laps', before Galloway pulled away to win.

Off track interest centred on Billy Galloway. 'Velox' said 'It was a happy occasion for little Billy Galloway. All season he has been pursuing another kind of 'Miss', now he has won her and gleefully told me of his engagement last night.' Galloway's pleasure helped his track performances 'and the happy event coincided with the return of fortune's smile. Never did Billy ride better than in pulling off the big double.'

Not to be outdone, Col Stewart was pleasing his public. He tailed Clem Cort in his heat for almost all four laps before nipping past to win. He fell in the semi-final.

The *Times* reported this meeting on 9 September: "As anticipated the attendance at the White City Speedway, Glasgow last night was most gratifying, while the sport itself reached a high standard that was only to be expected from such a meeting. The 10,000 spectators present were completely satisfied.

"It was a fitting tribute that Glasgow fans should have the good fortune of witnessing Sprouts Elder and Harry Whitfield, two great riders, whose appearance no doubt added enthusiasm to the proceedings."

The *Glasgow Herald* reported favourably on the meeting on 16 September: "Glasgow's dirt-track racing season has almost finished, but the interest in the sport still maintains as shown by the attendance of 12,000 spectators." The *Times* observed: "As one of the last treats of the year's dirt-track racing...we had as visitors Jack Parker, the renowned English rider; Gordon Byers of Newcastle and that provider of thrills, Joe Abbott, the Preston captain."

The Glasgow Championship was a draw and the riders scored two points for a win and one for second. The format, was three riders in each heat. Nine riders contested the event. Joe Abbott, Jack Parker and Col Stewart each scored seven points. The *Times* reported: "The Glasgow riders were rather ordinary in comparison, but Colin Stewart and Norrie Isbister kept up the interest, the former riding up to form to annex seven 7 points and Isbister, providing the thrills at the expense of the points gained five."

A report said of the first semi-final: "The Abbott-Parker duel provided many thrills, first one then the other gaining the ascendancy, until Parker essayed a spectacular skid to get the verdict."

The second semi-final saw: "Col Stewart had a relatively easy task as neither Isbister or Galloway rode up to form."

The Final featured three riders. The winners of the semi-finals and the fastest second: "The Final provided another Abbott-Parker duel in which Abbott, because of his less spectacular riding, proved superior."

This was Colin Stewart's last meeting at Glasgow. In 1931 he returned, but as a Wembley rider. He made a farewell speech and "was accorded a wonderful ovation by the spectators."

The last meeting was meant to be 19 September, with the Supporters Trophy event between the Blantyre-based riders and the Glasgow men. Rain and flooding caused a postponement. The meeting was to benefit the St. Andrew's Ambulance Association and the infirmaries. Twenty two riders were expected to take part.

The last meeting of 1930 was on 23 September and drew a poor attendance of 300. The charities would have seen little benefit from the event. The members of the winning Blantyre-based riders team received a small trophy for their 10–8 victory.

It seems that this was the first leg of a two leg event. An advert for an event at Motherwell's Paragon Speedway featured Blantyre versus Glasgow. Whether this was staged is not known.

The *Times* reported: "There was nothing to enthuse over at last night's meeting at White City Speedway, Glasgow. The wretched weather conditions completely spoiled the evening's proceedings and there was an unsatisfactory attendance. There would be no more than 300 spectators and the meeting was intended to benefit our hospitals and other deserving institutions."

So ended the 1930 season on a wet and dismal note. It was also the last meeting for the rider who had for two seasons lit up White City, Billy Galloway.

3. 1931: Half a season

Tuesdays became the regular speedway night in Glasgow in 1931. Apart from a couple of events at Marine Gardens, Glasgow were the sole Scottish Speedway flag carriers.

The promoters entered a team in the League and Cup competitions, but when there was no team racing, went back to individual events. One even went back to a match race format with two or three riders in each heat. The press believed that the 1931 fans wanted team racing and lamented that as Glasgow was so far away from most tracks, sending a team was not a practicable proposition.

The teams grew in size from four riders to six with one reserve. The team matches were extended from six heats to nine, and each pair raced every pair from the opponents.

Glasgow entered the much reduced Northern League, which started with Belle Vue, Leeds, Leicester (Super), Preston, Sheffield and Glasgow. The teams were to meet four times a season. In addition to the league, the National Trophy was extended to take in the Northern League clubs and some non-league outfits including York and Wombwell. A Northern Trophy was also instituted.

Glasgow faced all its opponents once home and once away. They faced Belle Vue for a second time at White City and Leeds twice at Fullerton Park. The only home wins were against Leicester Super and Preston. Away from home, Glasgow were walloped regularly.

In the National Trophy, Preston won at White City, then trounced the Glasgow team at Farringdon Park. Glasgow had originally been drawn against Warrington, but their closure gave them a bye into the next round. The Northern Cup match at Leeds saw another defeat for Glasgow. The track closed before the second leg was run.

For the 1931 season Glasgow had to replace Billy Galloway who had retired, and Col Stewart who had joined Wembley. In their place came the top Scots from 1928 to 1930, Drew McQueen and George McKenzie. Another recruit was Percy Dunn from Belle Vue. The rest were riders who had raced in the 1930 team. With hindsight the team lacked out-and-out heat-leaders, a mistake given the strengthening undertaken by many of the other teams.

The number of Scots riding at White City fell to just 16. They included pioneers Norrie Isbister, Drew McQueen and George McKenzie. Andy Nicholl and Alfie Williams continued to ride. Many had, however, retired from the sport, never to return. Scottish riders won about half the individual trophies.

Thirty-nine English riders rode at White City. Most successful was Eric Langton with four event wins. He was closely followed by Frank Charles on two and Joe Abbott, Gordon Byers, Frank Varey and Dusty Haigh each won once.

Billy Llewellyn was the only Welsh rider. Only six Australians rode at White City, a far cry from the pioneer days when there were five times that number. Gustav, or Bill as he was known, became one of very few Germans to race in Scotland. He came on one of Preston's visits and scored a couple of points.

The track was still prone to flooding when the weather was really wet. Two meetings were lost to the weather. Wembley never returned, but Leeds did.

The wind down of speedway, partly due to the economic recession in the industrial areas, caught up with Glasgow. The track lasted for half-a-season when their team was poor at home and dismal away. The closure signalled the end of a short era and track activity at White City did not return until 1939.

Most Glasgow riders retired from the sport. Norrie Isbister and Andy Nicholl had short spells at Belle Vue and Drew McQueen ended the season at Leeds. McQueen rode at West Ham in 1932. When the sport revived in the late 1930s only Drew McQueen, Norrie Isbister and the little known Tom Shearer returned.

April

The new season opened with a two event meeting on 7 April. George McKenzie, Drew McQueen and Percy Dunn faced some of the 1930 Glasgow team. Star guests were Ginger (Harold Riley) Lees and Frank Charles. Billy Galloway had retired and watched the action from the stands, taking notes for his weekly reports in the *Daily Record*.

McKenzie did not progress from the heats of either event. He was the first Glasgow rider to endure 'Glasgow Luck', which was a season-long battle with chains. McQueen reached the semi-finals, but did not progress to the finals. Dunn was out of luck too – his motors refused to perform. Not a great start for the newcomers.

The only bright spot was Andy Nicholl, who used his speed at the start to grab the white line and follow it to win the Glasgow Handicap Final. A walk-over against Dunn gave him a place in the Match Race Final but he could not catch the visiting stars.

Fellow Glasgow favourite Norrie Isbister was similarly afflicted in the opening heat. Peter Coia followed Frank Charles home in the heat and semi-final of the Scratch Race, but an engine failure in the Final relegated him to last place.

'Speedway' of the *Citizen* observed: 'The match races fizzled rather badly, the only worthwhile scrap being between McQueen and Charles. The visitor was heartily cheered for his sportsmanship in pulling up when McQueen bought one on the east bend in the first lap. In the re-run McQueen's Douglas was not quick enough for Charles' Rudge and the latter took the flag.'

Glasgow opened their 1931 Northern League campaign on 14 April against tough opposition in Belle Vue and lost by 10-points. Glasgow were without Andy Nicholl who had 'flu and he was replaced by Arthur Moser, who was promoted from reserve.

Top man for Glasgow was Alfie Williams. He was, described by the *Daily Record* as the "outstanding performer." The reporter said: "He was using special 'dope', – he was the only Scot who did – and right well did his bike respond. He was the man of the moment in our side, for he had a couple of firsts in the league match and was also first past the post in his scratch heat. Once he gained the lead there was no catching him and he fully earned the vociferous cheering that greeted his victories."

McQueen, according to Billy Galloway had problems as "somebody or something put the Indian sign on Drew McQueen and he kept breaking chains and sliding on his pants in the most un-Drew like fashion. Those slices of ill-fortune accounted for a good lot of the margin of ten-points." But there was something else. Galloway talked about the team-riding tactics used by Belle Vue and suggested that this was sadly lacking from Glasgow. He noted that in heat one "Indian Allen stuck to the line and Frank Varey whizzed round about half way out. They weren't scrapping with each other; they did not care who won and who was second so long as both first and second wore a Belle Vue shirt. In team racing you must use your head for more than wearing a crash helmet."

Glasgow's luck was out in heat one when Drew had chain trouble. George McKenzie broke a chain in heat two and Norrie Isbister had his broken after he had been hit by Arthur Franklyn. Galloway wrote: "Norrie Isbister did a most alarming acrobatic stunt in the eighth heat of team racing. He and Varey were pulling neck-and-neck stuff when Norrie got into a wobble, did a marvellous somersault and landed heavily on the back of his neck. It looked rather serious from the stand but after taking a count of nine Norrie managed to stagger to the pits."

Chain trouble was a common problem and required the introduction of Renold chains which solved the problem of a build of dirt and subsequent breakages.

According to the *Daily Record* it was not an accidental fall: "Varey over slid and to save him Norrie Isbister pulled his bike round. The front wheel locked and the front forks bent. This of course was the finish of Norrie's Rudge, but he competed in the scratch event." Varey stayed on the machine and with Jim 'Indian' Allen claimed another Belle Vue 5–1."

Frank Varey had more than mechanics with him on this visit to Glasgow: "Frank turned up with a new member of his retinue on Tuesday. This was a page boy, gorgeous in a red uniform with gold buttons. We all stood around and watched respectfully. It is understood that he was the Belle Vue mascot."

Sam Aitkenhead was a surprise winner of the Scratch event. He kept going when all others, Arthur Moser apart, were falling off."

Without a league match, the meeting reverted to the old format on 21 April. The star visitor was Frank Charles of Leeds. The *Daily Record* said: "Norrie Isbister delighted his supporters by carrying off the Handicap Final. George McKenzie and he had a tremendous tussle and only Norrie's early lead carried him over the line first. The runner-up must have had the fastest time of the meeting in the last lap of this race." Billy Galloway commented: "The two Franks, Varey and Charles put up the best argument of the season so far in the first heat of the match race when a blanket would have covered them for four laps. George McKenzie was also among those scheduled to take part, but engine trouble pulled him out early in the piece."

Galloway noted that Fred Wilkinson was trying a Norton machine. He considered "it is an admirable tool in its way but quite unsuited for the Glasgow track. Leicester Super is a third of a mile round which gives a bike like the Norton a chance to get wound up, but you can't get any winding up done on the Glasgow track with its narrow bends. The result was that Wilkinson went round epileptically jumping from cinder-to-cinder."

Drew McQueen was a notable absentee from this meeting. It was suggested by Galloway that he was thinking of retiring. McQueen had personal problems due to the failure of his Edinburgh-based company and had to devote his immediate attention to that.

Andy Nicholl was back, 'but he was still suffering from the effects of the 'flu. He reached the Final of the Handicap, but finished last.' He had raced Frank Varey in the first heat of the scratch race, but he wasn't fit enough to take on Varey. He did make the semi-final but scratched.

In the scratch event first semi-final, 'Varey, Charles and Watson were the starters. Cliff put his hand up for a false start, but they sent the others off without him. Varey fell, and Cliff, deciding to make the best of a bad job, set off in a frantic hurry which ended in his sitting down on his left ear. So Charles finished as he pleased. Varey was washed and halfway into his clothes when they decided to re-run this race, so they pulled him out of his civilized garments, put him back into his leathers. Then he broke a chain in the first lap and Charles won again!'

A cold wet night at Preston on 23 April was not warmed up by the speedway racing. Glasgow were not expected to put up a very good show according to the *Speedway News* reporter, and the home riders gave the crowd the treats and won the match 35–18.

To be fair to the Glasgow side, the state of the slippery track did not help their cause. The home riders were more at ease on the surface. Ham Burrill recorded his first league race win and Gustav (Bill) Kellner proved an astute signing. Burrill's tally of three would probably have been more, had he not broken a chain prior to the start of heat eight. Eric Airey stepped in and also suffered a chain break, after the race had started.

Drew McQueen's return to the Glasgow side on 28 April was obviously in some doubt, as the programme did not feature him in the line-up. His return demoted Arthur Moser to reserve and Sam Aitkenhead rode just in the second-half. The match against Preston went to a last-heat decider, which, for once, went Glasgow's way. They won 28–25.

McQueen's return maybe brought some luck to Glasgow. The opposition had some bad luck, including engine trouble for Joe Abbott.

According to the *Daily Record:* "Glasgow registered their first win in the Speedway league ... interest was kept up till the last race which produced a bit of a sensation. Larry Boulton of Preston had finished first and a draw in the match proclaimed when the Scottish Auto Cycle Union judge gave out Arthur Moser, Glasgow had won the heat, Boulton being disqualified for boring out Moser in the straight." Boring out meant forcing wide by pushing the rider from their preferred riding line. Moser was riding as a replacement for McQueen, who had failed to get his bike started. He borrowed a bike from Norrie Isbister which was a runner, but failed to beat the clock which had given him three minutes to reach the starting line.

Glasgow's win looked safe as Nicholl took the lead for the all-important three-points, closely followed by Moser. Unfortunately, Nicholl broke a chain, leaving Moser in the lead. As mentioned above, Moser was overtaken by Boulton, who ran him close on the exit to a bend. Moser did not consider that Boulton had used unfair tactics in his passing move, but the SACU Steward saw things differently.

Billy Galloway said that the Steward "could see better than Arthur, and there is something in that. What happened was that Boulton was coming out of the scoring board bend when he went into a fierce two-wheeled skid out towards Arthur who had to shut off." This was the first exclusion of a Preston rider. The Preston captain, Joe Abbott, also was penalised by the Steward for his riding in the Scratch Race Final.

May

Billy Galloway's column in the *Daily Record* was pessimistic: "I was sorry to see this week's attendance at the White City meeting – the poorest of the season and sorrier still to have to admit that the racing was uninspiring. A dry track may have been the cause of the poor racing; it was certainly responsible for a lot of the falls.

"Only Joe Abbott of Preston gave us something we could really be enthusiastic about, helped at times by Gordon Byers of Leeds who spread a few fireworks about the track."

He was impressed that there were no false starts on 5 May, well, none the starter saw. He commented: "... thought I spotted two that were not so clean cut as they might have been, but the starter was satisfied and his word goes. The good starts may have been due to the fact that before the racing began each of the boys got a circular intimating that anyone responsible for false starts would be fined. Dirt-track riders are out to make money, not throw it away by inattention to the regulations, so I can imagine the lads were determined to be careful."

It was a couple of years before speedway sorted out the problems with false starts by using a starting gate. Even that did not stop false starts, but helped reduce them.

Left: Drew McQueen Right: George McKenzie. McQueen joined Glasgow in 1931. McKenzie was the Glasgow captain.

On the meeting, Galloway said: "In the scratch and handicap races, the semi-finals and finals provided the best racing of the meeting, but at that, in most every case, it lasted for a couple of laps or so. Generally, after the competitors had got round twice or three times they became strung out and it was a case of follow-my-leader to the winning flag. This was what happened in most of the races on the programme and no one wants processions."

He continued: "I don't want to be too critical, but after Tuesday I am almost compelled to say that team racing is perhaps the only thing that remains to hold the interest of the onlooker. All the best racing we have had this year has been given us in the team matches, but it is useless I know to hope we can have them at every meeting. We are too far away from the majority of tracks for that I'm afraid."

After his departure from the handicap event in the heats, Joe Abbott was in great form. He was unbeaten in the scratch event and a best of three match races with George McKenzie.

'Speedway' of the *Citizen* noted changes to the stadium on 12 May. The White City track was re-shaped before this meeting. The inner-edge of the bends was changed to a smooth semi-circle from the pointed ends of the past.

He also noted that it was good team-riding that won the day, rather than individual brilliance by the Glasgow riders. He said: "There were no outstanding performers among our boys, but all pulled their weight." Leicester, on the other hand, had a star: "The star rider was A.W. Jervis, the captain of the Leicester Super team. Faster on the straight and trickier on the bends, Jervis was never troubled in any of his league contests and he carried off the maximum number of points."

Billy Galloway, in the *Daily Record,* singled out Percy Dunn of Glasgow for praise in this 31–23 home win: "Percy hit his best form he's been in all season and gained eight-points for White City. He gathered his first three in the second heat which was a thriller and a half, first one then another of the riders taking the fresh air and leaving the dust to the rest until the final lap, after everyone had had his share, Percy Dunn snapped it up for keeps and shot home, closely followed by Herbert and Williams."

'Speedway' said in heat three "McQueen was easily the star ... everyone but Drew was well away, but in a magnificent effort he needled past the leaders in one lap and was never headed. Nicholl added another two-points."

George McKenzie broke a chain in the fourth race when he was second, following on Herbert. He tried to push home for third place but was pipped at the post. After he had hit the fence and shorn off his foot rest, Jack Wood had the crowd watching him. He demonstrated his good sense of balance and completed the race, hanging on to third place.

Leicester Super might have done better had Tommy Price and Cliff Watson appeared for them. Price was injured and Watson's car broke down at Lancaster. Leicester promoted reserves Jack Wood and George Hazzard, who was a Belle Vue rider, into the team, but they only contributed three-points, less than Price and Watson were likely to score.

Star visitor for the meeting on 19 May was Belle Vue's Eric Langton. The *Daily Record* said he "was in irresistible form at White City Speedway, Ibrox. The manner in which he handled his machine thrilled the 5,000 spectators and the verdict of most people present was that he gave the finest display of riding seen at the White City this season.

"He carried off the flying start scratch event in the splendid time of 84.9 seconds and went on to gain more glory by lifting the standing start event. In this event he came within two seconds of the ground record, a wonderful performance on a strange track."

Billy Galloway added the details of the meeting in the *Daily Record:* "Eric Langton, Max Grosskreutz (known to the troops, I regret to say as 'Crossguts') and Col Stewart were the visiting attractions."

Max Grosskreutz had to borrow leathers from local lad Bill Walker. Max had been stopped by the police on his way north, who advised him his kit back had fallen out the car some 20 miles back.

Galloway was not impressed by the latest Glasgow experiment: "The other event of the evening was an innovation in the shape of a scratch race from a standing start. Why the standing start I don't know, unless the idea was that a standing start from scratch would give the lesser lights a better chance in the all-important early stages than a flying start. Anyway, it did not work out that way for the best riders nearly always have the best machines. In the standing start they picked away perhaps a shade sooner than those of the other men with the result that the standing start from scratch really operated to the latter's disadvantage. Personally, I think the handicap with the standing start a better scheme." Obviously, the riders were pushed off at the same time with the engines dead and it was not a proto clutch start.

An impressive 20,000 fans turned up to Belle Vue's Hyde Road on 23 May to watch their Northern League team rip into a Glasgow side that won just one heat. The *Speedway News* correspondent was a bit scathing, saying that while a big home win keeps the team fans happy, "a monotonous succession of hollow victories must defeat its own subject. There can be little doubt that the majority of the 20,000 present at Belle Vue last Saturday would have been better pleased had the opposition been able to make some sort of fight."

Drew McQueen managed to beat Arthur Franklyn in heat three, after Franklyn had eased into a lead early on in the race. Franklyn apart, the Belle Vue riders won as they pleased; races between the home men provided thrills for the fans.

Billy Galloway commented: "The Belle Vue meeting was a poor show. I am told the track was under water in spots and very slippery nearly all over. Alfie Williams was shaken after a bad fall." The final score was 40–24 to Belle Vue.

Glasgow rode in their first knock-out cup style National Trophy competition on 26 May. Defeat in this the home leg, 52–43, ended their hopes of progressing to the next round.

The *Daily Record* considered the damage was done in the last part of the match: "Three-quarters of the struggle had gone and only two-points separated the rivals (in Preston's favour), but misfortune dogged the footsteps of the home boys in the last quarter and Preston finished up with a well-deserved lead of nine-points ... Strange to say, Arthur Moser, usually a reserve man in the home side, carried off most points for the White City, gaining 11 points out of a possible 12."

Billy Galloway noticed that Les Wotton's mechanic had long blond hair and was in fact his wife. For a long time, the ban on women riders applied to pits staff as well.

By way of a slight distraction, Glasgow fans were invited to vote for four out of McQueen, McKenzie, Isbister, Nicholl, Williams, Moser, Mann, Aitkenhead and Llewellyn. The top four were to have places in the Glasgow Championship which, for the winner, was a passport into the World Championship.

The proposed National Trophy match at Preston on 28 May fell victim to threatened rain. The track, however, was actually in good condition.

June

The *Daily Record* said on the day of the meeting, 2 June: "We'll be hearing the roar of Wembley Lions tonight at the White City, Ibrox. The speedway management are to be congratulated on bringing such a renowned team up to Scotland for Glasgow's Civic Week. The Wembley team, thwarted by the weather, was Colin Watson, Norman Evans, Harry Whitfield, Colin Stewart, Jack Ormston and Wally Kilmister. The meeting was rained off.

The National Trophy return match on 4 June was always going to be an uphill struggle. The 70–26 score gave Preston a massive 122–69 aggregate victory.

Joe Abbott completed the tie undefeated. For Glasgow Percy Dunn and Norrie Isbister were best. Isbister would have scored more, but for machine trouble when he blew a tyre when leading Eric Airey. He and Percy Dunn were the only Glasgow riders to win heats late on in the match.

On 9 June popular visitor Frank Charles and his Leeds team were hit by the weather and the Northern League meeting was rained off. The *Speedway News* report on the meeting on 13 June bemoaned that Leicester Super were poor away from home, yet on the one-third of a mile Melton Road circuit reigned supreme. The track was ridden flat out.

Billy Galloway said that the Glasgow boys were under-geared for the fast-riding track. He added: "The score at Leicester was 'the Vauxhall's horsepower' on Tuesday night. In other words, it was 15-39, with the heavy end going to Leicester Super. I'm told that the dust was so thick that some of the boys never saw much of the racing, which was a change from recent conditions at White City ... on the bends it was almost impossible for the riders to see what they were doing..."

Glasgow were without Percy Dunn on 16 June against Leeds due to an injury at Leicester Super and Billy Llewellyn took his place; Arthur Mann coming in as reserve. Arthur Moser was recovering from another broken collar bone, sustained in a practice at White City.

The *Daily Record* said: "Frank Charles was the outstanding performer on the track, his fast riding and cornering being one of the main features of the meeting. His total of nine-points was almost equalled by one of his team-mates, Roy Barrowclough, who lifted eight-points for the winners. Andy Nicholl was Glasgow's most successful rider, his steadiness on the cinders being the only bright thing in an otherwise poor display by the home team."

Billy Galloway commented on George McKenzie, that he was "disappointing once again. He has a new and super-hot JAP engine which eats up plugs at a rate a crocodile would eat up kippers. An appetite like that leads to bother." Maybe a little unfair, at least McKenzie was trying to get the best equipment. Leeds won the league match 31–23. Galloway said that "The racing generally only reached the fairly good standard. Leeds took the lead right away through Frank Charles, with Norrie Isbister and Sam Marsland scrapping for second place. Norrie got there by a wheel."

The second-half had an unusual incident when, in the second semi-final Billy Llewellyn's bike nearly caught fire. Marsland's bike did, however, catch fire after he had fallen. Drew McQueen fell in the Final.

Glasgow had another heavy away defeat on 18 June, this time at Sheffield. The *Speedway News* considered: "The score in no way exaggerated their [Sheffield's] superiority, for the simple truth is that Glasgow had no rider in the same class as Dusty Haigh." The piper who led the Glasgow team out on parade failed to stir the riders into action, on a wet night.

The writing was on the wall for Glasgow after two heats, and, had Broncho Dixon's motor been on song, the score might have been worse for the visitors. However, had Norrie Isbister's motor been faithful for the whole meeting, he might have added to his top score of 5, including a race win. Drew McQueen was almost a heat winner in heat five. After passing Eric Blain and leading for three laps by sticking to the white line, he could not hold Blain who passed him on the outside. He settled for second place. The final result, a 35–19 defeat, was Glasgow's best away performance in 1931.

In the event on 23 June, five riders contested the White City Championship, with the winner of one tie going to the Final. Andy Nicholl, who had a bye to the second round, faced the winner of the other first round contest. It was an odd arrangement.

McQueen emerged victorious, having disposed of Norrie Isbister in the first round and Andy Nicholl in the Final. According to the *Daily Record*, Drew won "the title of track Champion and he will now compete in the preliminary rounds of the World Championship series." Falls played an important part in McQueen's victory as Isbister fell in the first race, and while he rode in the second race, was out of sorts.

The best score by a Glasgow rider away from home in the league was achieved by McQueen at Fullarton Park on 27 June, when he raced to eight points. It would have been a maximum had he not burst a tyre when leading Roy Barrowclough. As it was, he hung on for the last lap for second place. Leeds won 39–14, despite McQueen's efforts.

Glasgow's cause was not helped by a heat two fall from Andy Nicholl and bike troubles for Sam Aitkenhead, which saw him being lapped, depriving the visitors of a gift third place.

There should have been a double-header, with Glasgow facing Leeds in both League and Northern Cup action on 30 June, but the Yorkshiremen withdrew. In their place, the promoters advanced Belle Vue's second visit. "Easily the finest dirt-track meeting of the season was the unanimous verdict of the about 7,000 spectators" said the *Daily Record*. "Thrill after thrill was experienced and I was genuinely sorry for one or two of the more ardent supporters who must have shouted themselves hoarse. The league match against Belle Vue was the cause of all the excitement and not until the second last match did the Champions of the North gain a commanding lead over our boys. Drew McQueen, our re-appointed captain, was the darling of the Glasgow side. The manner in which he lifted all his races would have made even the most pessimistic of our fans clap his hands with joy – nothing could go wrong. His engines responded to every touch and not even the famous Eric Langton, who proved himself to be in irresistible form at the Test match last Saturday, could stop Drew's winning ways." Belle Vue won 30–24.

Billy Galloway was impressed by the race between McQueen and Langton, and also by heat five which featured a hectic battle between Andy Nicholl and Walter Hull. The latter named pair 'sharing the fresh air alternately. Andy got the last gasp and the flag.' In the next, an apparent dead-heat was awarded to Len Woods when half-a-point to both him and George McKenzie was considered more appropriate.

The real issues happened before the last heat: 'In the match there was another unfortunate incident. These things seem to go in groups. The visitors were comfortably in the lead by now and it seems it is their habit to drop one of the team and give the reserve rider a chance so that the public may see how he performs. It also gives him a chance to earn a few pennies and strikes me as a rather sporting act. In this case Oliver Langton stood down in favour of reserve Wilf Mulliner, but officials refused to let Mulliner ride under the circumstances. Belle Vue gnashed their teeth a bit, but there was nothing doing so Frank (Varey) refused to let Oliver ride. Eric Langton was therefore Belle Vue's sole representative.' Langton won this despite having a flat tyre.

July

The Glasgow promotion finally brought in a new signing on 7 July in an attempt to freshen-up the side. Down to reserve went George McKenzie, displaced by the new rider who was a Belle Vue asset and had been a reserve or second-string at Leicester Super, George Hazzard. It was too little too late. Hazzard took his three rides and fell in each. The other George took one ride, replacing Percy Dunn, and scored a point.

The *Daily Record* said: "Glasgow Speedway made a heroic effort to avert defeat last night against Sheffield ... all seemed lost after the finish of the sixth race, but a brilliant recovery in the seventh and eighth matches brought them only a point from their rivals' total.

"The task was too great for our last pair, however, Hazzard, our new rider falling off and Andy Nicholl only managing second place." As it was, Glasgow lost 28–25.

The writer was impressed with the track Champion: "Drew McQueen again won most of our points, his riding being splendid, although not being so reliable as in the last meeting or two. He and Norrie Isbister took part in the finest piece of team racing seen at the White City this year. It was in the race when the Glasgow team pulled up their socks.

"If one had watched closely, one would have seen a little conflab between Drew and Norrie take place before the race and then McQueen shift his position from the inside of the track to third place. At the start Drew took the lead and held it for three laps, while Norrie kept back Broncho Dixon; then the leader slackened off and let Norrie take the front in the last bend, while the hindered Dixon was roaring behind them. The scheme worked, both our men ending up with the two premier places although unfortunately for the Sheffield rider, he had a spill in a wonderful effort to haul in the winners. Dixon was cheered to the echo when he completed the race by pushing his machine home."

Galloway was not too critical of George Hazzard's performance, suggesting that "it would hardly be fair to bring forth the block and axe after his first performance. I believe he is only on trial meantime, so he will probably turn up the wick a bit when he gets at home on our cinders. The said cinders incidentally were by no means in good shape for the meeting due to the afternoon's thunderstorm."

Thus ended the 1931 season. A proposed double-header with Leeds was planned for 14 July, but the management cancelled it, announcing that no further meetings would take place. There was a possibility that the Belle Vue management were about to move in, but this never materialised. Glasgow White City would be without speedway until 1939.

In what may be the first ever double-header for team racing, Leeds faced Glasgow twice in the one meeting on 11 July. The first fixture was the first leg of the Northern Cup, which Glasgow lost 35–18, and the second was the Northern League match, which Glasgow lost 31–17. Glasgow had closed after the meeting the previous Tuesday and the side did well under the circumstances.

The first meeting started with a cracker of a heat. The *Speedway News* reported: "The rival captains both lived up to their reputations in the opening heat, when they indulged in the best race of the night. McQueen was leading at the last bend, but Charles did not ease up for a moment, and was rewarded by the narrowest possible win." Leeds were unlucky, or Glasgow lucky as Roy Barrowclough had an engine failure, which spoiled his possible maximum and Gordon Byers fell twice.

Drew McQueen dropped out of the World Championship chase when he lost 2–0 to Roy Barrowclough in match races. Barrowclough took the lead in the opener and Drew chased him for three laps, before his bike packed in. In the second Drew led for a while by hugging the white line, but Roy rode round him to take the victory.

Without the injured Gordon Byers, Leeds promoted Harry Watson into the side for the league match, while Glasgow did likewise with Percy Dunn replacing Arthur Moser.

Frank Charles only won once. The Leeds top-dog was Roy Barrowclough with a nine-point maximum. Drew McQueen was top Glasgow man on five, his tally reduced by an engine failure in his last heat. The league meeting opener again featured McQueen and Charles and again was a cracker.

Heat seven was declared void. All one report says is that Charles was knocked off his bike. Others say that Norrie Isbister crashed with Charles, and as both were unable to continue, the heat was declared void.

Leeds, like Glasgow were on shaky ground financially. George McKenzie recalled that after the meeting they were paid in change from the gate money.

George told the author that the riders had travelled some way north in a convoy of cars. They stopped and set up a camp fire to brew up some tea and the share out took place round the camp fire. Maybe somewhat embellished there will be more than a grain of truth in the story as George's memory was pin sharp to the end.

This was the end of George's speedway career, but he did ride grass track events after 1931 and retained his skills as a mechanic. The author recalls George instructing one of the famous Men in Black, a group of enthusiasts including Jim Gregory, Terry Stone, and John Stallworthy, on how to repair a malfunctioning Douglas. Further, the author recalls Ian Paterson's story about the problems he was having setting the timing on a pioneer days JAP using the factory timing disc when George dropped in. After Ian explained his problem George quoted alternative timings to a very sceptical Ian who, nonetheless, jotted down the numbers. Ian gave up on the JAP but returned to it a while later. Ian decided to use George's numbers and was amazed that they allowed the engine to be timed perfectly.

4. 1939: Relaunch with Johnnie Hoskins

Success in 1938 at Edinburgh's Marine Gardens prompted Johnnie Hoskins to take up the promotional reigns at White City and revive the sport in Glasgow in 1939. Both Edinburgh and Glasgow hoped to ride in the National League Second Division, but these hopes were dashed due to opposition by Hackney Wick and Bristol. These two clubs objected to the Scottish sides, saying that their riders were not full-time and would find it difficult to reach far-flung northern venues.

A crumb of comfort was held out in a late season competition. This was the Auto Cycle Union Northern Cup, which was staged on a league basis. Both Scottish clubs along with Belle Vue Seconds, Newcastle and Sheffield were to race home and away, but the outbreak of the Second World War unfortunately prevented completion.

The Glasgow Lions simply does not sound right. The more familiar name of 'Tigers' was not adopted until 1946. In Edinburgh, their team was called the 'Thistles'. It lacks the familiar ring of the Monarchs.

Glasgow, who had used red and blue in the earlier period, did adopt the familiar red and white colours in 1939. The insignia was a rampant lion with its head turned forward on a red background. The team manager was an Australian, Jack Clementson, who had started the season as a rider at White City.

The emphasis in speedway was, by now, on team racing. Prior to the ACU Cup events, a side called Glasgow raced team fixtures against both First Division and Second Division sides. They raced a similar type of team representing Edinburgh and faced two representative sides: the Colonies – Australia, New Zealand and Canada – and an Australia team. This covered 11 of the 17 meetings. A Scotland versus England match can be more accurately described as Scottish-based riders of Division Two status against their English counterparts.

In the ACU Northern Cup, Glasgow raced three times at home, beating Edinburgh and losing to Sheffield and Newcastle. Belle Vue were due the week after the closure due to the breakout of the War.

Away from home, Glasgow lost at Edinburgh and Newcastle. The top scorer in a relatively settled side was Will Lowther, who was with Middlesbrough until they closed. Belle Vue loanee Harold Jackson and Bob Wells also scored well. The latter was from Hertfordshire and had also been at Middlesbrough. He rode for Wembley after the war.

For most of the challenge matches, the Glasgow side was never the same two weeks running. Gruff Garland was an ever-present, and Harold Jackson appeared eight times. Elwood Stillwell and Joe Crowther each rode five times, but most of the Glasgow side, 14 riders out of 27, made single appearances.

The Glasgow Track Championship was the highlight of the season. The Milne boys, Jack and Cordy, sons of a man from Lossiemouth in Moray, were involved. With fellow Americans Wilbur Lamoreaux and Benny Kaufman, the Stars and Stripes dominated the meeting. A top scorers final featured the four and Jack Milne became Track Champion.

Sir Harry Lauder presented the trophy to the winner and made sure the crowd knew of Jack's Scottish ancestry. His presence was a strong influence on the Milnes' attendance, as Mr Milne (Senior) was keen to meet the world famous entertainer. Sir Harry must have liked speedway as he visited Marine Gardens too. It was his local track, only a lap's length or so from his birthplace in Portobello.

The riders

Scots were in a minority. The native Scots who had raced in the pioneer era had almost all retired. Dick Dennie had one ACU Cup outing and Bill Nisbet managed a non-league outing. Leo Lungo, Dave Lamb and Chuck Pinkerton were all restricted to second-half outings. Norrie Isbister appeared as a reserve in the Championship, before a track injury ruled him out of the sport, as a rider, for good. Both Lungo and Isbister were on Edinburgh's books.

Twenty-five English riders rode at White City in 1939, in both home and visiting sides. Most did well and rode to form. Doubtless the Glasgow Lions fans would have preferred them to stay, but they usually returned to star for their own team.

Australia and Canada provided riders for the Glasgow fans to support. The Australians included Gruff (Cecil) Garland – who did well – and Jack Hancock, Curly (Noel) Thompson and the Jamieson Brothers who were less successful. Elwood Stillwell and Fred Belliveau were the Canadians. From Denmark in 1939, Jens Fisker Henning 'Morian' Hansen made a couple of visits.

Glasgow had a young lady, Millie Laidlaw, who wanted to try speedway. Despite her pleas, helped by some press coverage, she was not allowed to fulfil her ambition. In those days, the ACU rules did not allow 'female persons' into the pits, let alone ride a bike.

Speedway came back, buoyed by a Glasgow economy financed by rearmament work and was a reasonable crowd-puller again. The lack of a regular team until the start of the ACU Cup was compensated for by stars riding for the Glasgow Lions. Unfortunately, they did not produce any home-grown stars, but saw the emergence of Durham butcher Joe Crowther and his sidekick Will Lowther.

Fans managed to see the World Champions from 1936 and 1937, Van Praag and Milne, riding, and 1938 Champion Bluey Wilkinson visited as Sheffield's team manager.

The ACU Cup side did not do well, but beat Edinburgh, when the pundits were predicting defeat.

The outbreak of War came at a time when speedway was about to re-establish itself in Glasgow and the short season in 1940 showed its popularity.

May

"Fifteen thousand people at White City Stadium on Saturday night 6 May were thrilled by the speedway racing" was how the *Daily Record's* 'Speed Ace' started his report on the first meeting in Glasgow since May 1932. He outlined: "Glasgow lost the Inter-City match to Newcastle's team of experts. Colin Watson, captain of Glasgow gave a magnificent display. Although he is 42 years of age and served three years in the Great War, he rode with the daring of a youngster. The Lions lost their first home meeting 31–23.

"The most thrilling of events of the evening was the Final of the Clydesdale Scratch Race. Phil Bishop, Maurice Stobart, Billy Lamont and George Pepper raced neck-and-neck for the first lap; then Bishop and Lamont shot forward. Lamont went over the grass and was disqualified. Maurice Stobart came on with a rush and almost pipped Bishop on the line."

The *Sunday Mail* reported: "There were few spills, but plenty of thrills at the White City Stadium last night when the speedway season opened with a visit from Newcastle's team. Fifteen thousand saw Glasgow lose, but not ingloriously. They put up a grand fight and considering the Newcastle team are in the running for their league Championship, their win by a margin of eight-points was no sensation."

Left: Harold Jackson. Right: Leo Lungo. Both riders are wearing the Glasgow Lions race-jackets.

This report was making favourable comments about the young Scottish rider Bill Nisbet, suggesting that it would not be long before he would be appearing in the Marine Gardens team. Sadly, Bill never really fulfilled this early promise in the 'Thistles' race-jacket.

After the meeting, the *Mail's* 'Crash Helmet' spoke to the promoter, Johnnie Hoskins, who said: "Although Glasgow lost the Inter-City race, I think you'll agree that the boys put up a good show. However, I am negotiating for the signing of a world famous rider to strengthen the team. I can't disclose his name at the moment, but if I clinch the deal it will create a minor sensation."

The sensational signing was West Ham's Harold 'Tiger' Stevenson. The *Daily Record* said: "Tiger Stevenson, who has come to ride at White City Stadium, Glasgow, on 13 May delighted the 20,000 crowd on Saturday night by his prowess on the speedway, and he received a cheer all to himself after the first race.

"In the third heat of the Gold Helmet race Stevenson and team-mate Curly Thompson collided. Thompson sustained a fractured foot and had to be removed to the Victoria Infirmary. Tiger escaped with minor injuries. It was a close run affair in the Glasgow - Middlesbrough match, the English team getting the verdict by 27 points to 25 points."

'Cinder Sifter' said in the *Times*: "The Glasgow team (known as the Lions) lacks just that extra bit of pep to make them a combination that will rival the best in the country, and it is with that in view that Johnnie Hoskins hopes to introduce Andy Menzies, an Australian from the Wembley club."

The meeting at White City on 20 May was followed by a fireworks display. It was planned before the Glasgow team achieved its first home win in 1939. Johnnie Hoskins was still making changes. Out to Edinburgh went Jack Hancock and back to Australia went the brothers Jamieson, who had failed to meet his standards. Gruff Garland was the only one of six from the previous week kept and was handed the captaincy.

The *Daily Record* thought that Hoskins would "go about his work this week in a little happier frame of mind. His team won on Saturday and the crowd of 18,000 did not forget to cheer when the Glasgow boys had their first victory of the season. Glasgow defeated Sheffield, which is managed by Bluey Wilkinson, World Champion speedway rider, by 30 points to 24. Bill Longley put up a fine display for Glasgow, getting the maximum nine points. His chief worry was in the eighth heat when Ernie Evans tried to get past the post first. Longley seemed to get an extra kick out of his motor and crossed over the line barely a wheel length ahead of Evans. Gruff Garland, Glasgow's new captain, ran into more than a spot of bother. In the first race he punctured and plunged out of control into the safety fence, but fortunately he was unhurt. He got the job of faking up his bike again and in the seventh heat led all the way to best Stan Williams, one of Sheffield's best riders."

The *Glasgow Evening Times* mentioned newcomer Jock Hamilton "who was given the opportunity of showing his prowess by taking the place of Frank Woodroofe [and] made such a good impression that Johnnie Hoskins signed him up for the Glasgow team immediately he finished second in his first heat of the Inter-City race." Jock had raced south of the Border and with the Scottish diminutive of Jock, was worth a try in a side lacking much home-grown talent. For whatever reason, he never appeared in the Glasgow side again.

For their meeting report of 27 May, the *Daily Record* advised that the weather "was ideal for the spectators, but not for the riders." It added: "the boys found it difficult to keep on their machines. No fewer than ten riders were unseated, but none was seriously injured.

"In the third heat of the Glasgow v Colonies races, the two veterans of speedway racing Colin Watson and Charlie Spinks collided. Both were unhurt and Spinks managed to carry on for third place. A more serious crash occurred in the fifth heat when Harold Jackson came down the second time round. All eyes were on Tiger Stevenson who was close behind, but with a clever thrust of his machine he steered clear. The crowd sighed with relief, but not for long. Tiger, in his quest for supremacy, gained on George Pepper too quickly, his front wheel collided with Pepper's machine. Down he went in a cloud of dust and was carried from the track suffering from concussion."

Eric Chitty sang a couple of songs to the crowd at the interval. The *Sunday Mail* started its report: "Eric Chitty, the crooning speedway rider, certainly had something to sing about last night. A record crowd of 20,000 saw him win the Scottish Silver Torch in brilliant style, and in addition lead the Colonies team to victory against Glasgow."

Singing speedway riders are rare, but Len Silver, Howdy Byford, Malcolm Brown and John McNeill are four others. In 1928 a song called *My Speedway Hero* was supposed to have been the first of its kind, and is supposed to have been sung by Sprouts Elder. It had impromptu revival at the 1998 High Beech celebrations and sounded nothing special.

June

The side representing Glasgow is probably the best way to describe the team on 3 June. It was bolstered by three stars from Wembley for a challenge match against First Division Southampton. The Wembley riders scored 27 points out of 34 scored by Glasgow. All three were unbeaten. Malcolm Craven collected the track record in heat six.

Another newcomer to the Glasgow ranks was Elwood Stillwell who was, despite a Canadian tag, possibly born in the USA. A painter by trade, Elwood had rode at the Toronto Exhibition track in 1932 and came to the UK in 1938 to ride for Newcastle.

The *Citizen* reported: "Real thrills were provided in the Search for Talent races. These events have become a popular feature with White City enthusiasts and, with the steady improvement in racing as the riders become more accustomed to the track, the events are proving more keen. Leo Lungo won the Final of the series, with Joe Crowther second and Dick Dennie third."

The *Daily Record* correspondent for 10 June was Glasgow captain Gruff Garland. His team won 32–21. Gruff, or Cecil to his parents, felt he had arrived "when I did that lap of honour at the White City on Saturday night after having won the Scottish Silver Gauntlet. I felt like a million dollars, not because I had won the principal event on the programme, but because I had the satisfaction of knowing that I had now justified my position as captain of the Glasgow team."

Gruff said that he had welcomed the encouragement from the Glasgow crowd, but realised that his bike was not up to it. The machine was seven-years old. He had invested in a new engine which had helped ride faster.

Garland went on: "With a new outfit I went out there on Saturday and did something and I can promise you I'm going to do a lot more before I'm finished. If Glasgow is not at the top of the tree in speedway racing before very long, it won't be my fault.

"We certainly slipped it across Newcastle, but chief credit for that victory goes to Cliff Parkinson. Cliff was in great form." Cliff Parkinson scored a maximum and set a new lap record of 20.6 seconds.

Gruff praised Joe Crowther: "he is a good boy and should be encouraged. He won the search for talent with ease." The *Citizen* noted: "A new departure from the usual programme was made...by the introduction of two match races, one for the four highest point scorers (in the match) and an International event in which Australia, Canada, Denmark and England were represented. The top scorers race saw Stobart join three Glasgow riders and finish in third place in the re-run. Elwood Stillwell fell in the first running and was excluded.

"In the International Race Stillwell and Hansen crashed at the first bend of the first lap. The accident looked serious at first, but both riders were able to go off for attention unassisted." Cliff Parkinson beat Billy Lamont in the re-run.

Frank Woodroffe, whose correct name was Woodroofe, took part in the meeting on 17 June as a member of an Australian side, captained by Charlie Spinks who scored a maximum and the *Daily Record* said "was the outstanding performer."

The report added: "A notable feature was the splendid riding of young Joe Crowther. Included in the Glasgow team for the first time, this lad cornered like a veteran and became the favourite of the 15,000 crowd.

"Glasgow were unfortunate in their battle royal with Australia, the team from Down Under winning by six-points. The third heat was a thriller. Harold Jackson leapt to the front as the gates flew up and second time round was still in the lead. Woodroofe was striving desperately to get level with the Glasgow rider and with one lap to go flashed into the lead. Jackson, however, went after the Aussie crack like a flash. On the second last bend he drew level and thundered into the straight a length ahead to win by two lengths."

According to the *Sunday Mail:* 'Glasgow struck a packet of trouble, captain Garland went down in the first, Curly Thompson's bike conked in the second and Andy Menzies was injured in the fifth. Three Aussies in the Glasgow side who maybe just could not feel anything, but traitorous riding against an Australian side.' The Australians won 30–24.

The *Glasgow Evening Times* considered: "Great things were expected of Isbister in the special challenge race with Curly Thompson. Unfortunately, Norrie fell at the last bend of the first lap. He rose to the occasion, however, by getting on his bike again and tore round the track in spectacular fashion.' The *Citizen* scribe observed that 'Norrie Isbister, who was riding on this track when the sport was last in Glasgow, still gives the crowd plenty of thrills.'

Edinburgh defeated Glasgow at Marine Gardens on 20 June by 10 points, 32–22 in this Inter-City Challenge. Only Glasgow's captain, Gruff Garland, kept the flag flying for the visitors. However, Joe Crowther, promoted from the novice class, did well, scoring two-points in the match, and reached the Scottish Silver Helmet Final. Laurie Packer and Jack Gordon were both unbeaten in the match and Oliver Hart won his last two races after a machine failure in his first. Oliver took the other major honours, winning the Captains Match Race from Gruff Garland, and then in a Top Scorers Match Race came second. In the Scottish Silver Gauntlet, Hart made a good start and held on to win his first trophy of the season.

The *Daily Record* was thrilled by Cliff Parkinson who "put up one of the best performances of his career on Saturday [24 June]. He snapped into it at the start, in fact (he) was only one fifth of a second off the track record in his first race, and was the only rider with full points in the Glasgow v New Cross event. Cliff certainly did his part in helping Glasgow to a 12-point victory. He won every race in which he rode and rounded off a good night's work with the Scottish Gold Helmet in his keeping."

The *Scottish Daily Mail* concentrated on Joe Crowther saying he "crashed when riding in the sixth race. He appeared hurt, but got up to re-mount his machine to earn a cheer though finishing last." The Glasgow crowd certainly loved a trier.

July

Readers of the *Sunday Mail* were told: "The Glasgow Wembley duel was close. Score was even till the fifth when Rol Stobart's machine failed and gave Wembley an advantage of two-points. However, in the eighth heat he made amends, getting second position with Harold Jackson gaining the premier award. In this heat Cliff Parkinson's machine went dead and Gilbert Craven also had to give up." This was description of 1 July was one of the more cryptic reports of a meeting. The *Citizen* said: "Glasgow's victory was brought about by sheer determination. They only got one first place out of nine heats, but to level matters up they were getting seconds and thirds." Glasgow won 28–25 against their London namesakes.

The *Daily Record* commented: "With one more First Division scalp on their belt Glasgow will enter the Second Division of the National Speedway League with confidence. We were all delighted when the White City boys slipped it across New Cross. However, as if to show that the win was no fluke, captain Gruff Garland and his merry men went out on Saturday and gave Wembley a licking. Johnnie Hoskins is still determined to make a few changes in the team. He wants at least two other star men to wear Glasgow's colours."

All the match reports for 8 July were sympathetic towards Edinburgh, advising readers that the team from the capital were dogged with bad luck throughout the night. Glasgow defeated their eastern rivals 34–18 and won 56–50 on aggregate. It was an unfortunate night for Edinburgh. Every Edinburgh rider crashed at some juncture of the meeting. George Greenwood, the Edinburgh captain came a cropper on more than one occasion. He had a really nasty smash in the Captains' Match Race, featuring himself and Gruff Garland, but escaped with a severe shaking and a shoulder injury.

In heat one of the Inter-City match, both Garland and Greenwood had machine trouble, leaving Mick Mitchell and Harold Jackson to fight it out. Jackson won and was in scintillating form all evening. He scored a maximum in the match, and then won two special races in the second-half, but was involved in a collision in heat three of the Scottish Silver Torch with Gilbert Craven, and spoiled his chances of 'clearing the boards.'

The meeting on 15 July moved the *Citizen* to say: "They were certainly in a big hurry, the American aces of the dirt-track who competed in the Glasgow Championship. Dominated — not competed – is the word, for there were few, even in such a star-studded list as Saturday's, who could live with them as they hurtled round that Ibrox track in real US style.

"Here are the representatives of the Stars and Stripes who sent the track record dropping like a thermometer in a refrigerator – Jack Milne, New Cross; brother Cordy Milne, Southampton; Wilbur Lamoreaux, Wimbledon and Benny Kaufman, also Southampton. And whenever Johnnie Hoskins brings them back to White City don't forget to get out and see them. They gave Glasgow its best speedway night ever. The track record of 85.4 seconds, set up a couple of weeks ago by Andy Menzies was bettered eight times in twenty one races."

The trophy was presented by Sir Harry Lauder, who sung for the crowd. Promoter Hoskins was, doubtless, pleased with his guest who was a big draw in his own right. Tragic news probably broke at this meeting. Frank Charles, a great performer at Glasgow, had been killed in a gliding accident in the afternoon.

Glasgow entered into the ACU Northern Cup competition with a match against Sheffield on 22 July and were beaten by a narrow two-point margin, 43–41. According to 'Speed Ace' of the *Daily Record:* "It certainly was a close contest, the score being level on no fewer than four occasions.

"The last heat was the decider. Glasgow needed five-points for a win and four-points to draw. The crowd roared its approval when Fred Belliveau and Harold Jackson leapt to the front. It looked as if Glasgow were going to get these precious five-points, but Jackson and the Sheffield riders, Ossie Powell and Paddy Mills came down in the second bend. The race had to be re-run and that was Glasgow's downfall. Jackson and Belliveau went away again with Mills close on their heels. Round they roared and the positions were unaltered till the finishing straight, when Mills, with a terrific burst of speed, passed and beat the Glasgow lads by a length." In the re-run Powell fell at the first bend.

The *Citizen* covered the second last race as well as the last one: "When the penultimate heat came along, Sheffield led 37–35 after 12 heats, in which the balance had swung from one side to the other. And this is how heat thirteen went. Doug McLachlan came down in lap three. In the last circuit, Gilbert Craven crashed at the last bend. Broncho Dixon went on to win from Joe Crowther.

"White overalled mechanics dragged Craven's bike from the track. The Glasgow manager Johnnie Hoskins dashed down to the track to tell the dazed rider that he could still wheel the machine home for third place and one-point. Craven set off pushing the bike for the finishing line. McLachlan just ahead, also pushing his machine towards the official with the chequered flag. He got there first and Craven pushed his bike on to the grass. But when he was told McLachlan had only completed his third lap, he upped again and just managed to get over the line before dropping prone, exhausted by the effort."

The last two heats seem a comedy of errors. McLachlan should have been excluded for being lapped if he had only completed three laps by pushing. Craven should have been excluded for leaving the track. In the last heat one report says that Jackson was the primary reason for the race being stopped, as he fell first and Mills ploughed into his bike.

Edinburgh avenged their White City defeat by beating Glasgow 56–27 at Marine Gardens on 25 July in the ACU Northern Cup. George Greenwood got well away in the first heat to put Edinburgh one up. In the next heat Oliver Hart clocked the fastest time of the meeting, one minute 20.8 seconds. The next nine heats all went to Edinburgh, before Gruff Garland, the Glasgow captain, won the twelfth for Glasgow's first success. The last two heats also went to the home side.

In the sixth heat, Laurie Packer and Joe Crowther, who were fighting for second place, both came down and Will Lowther, who was last, also fell but re-mounted to finish half-a-lap behind Jack Chapman.

In the ninth, Harold Jackson and Gruff Garland snatched the lead at the first corner, but after the first lap Jack Chapman and Laurie Packer moved past Garland, and then on the third lap Chapman got past Jackson for an Edinburgh 4–2.

George Greenwood and Oliver Hart both registered 12-point maximums and Jack Chapman was also unbeaten by a Glasgow rider. Glasgow's Gilbert Craven won the reserves race, and Oliver Hart won the Scottish Silver Torch from George Greenwood and Jack Hyland.

Lowther's heat spill occurred while taking avoiding action, which ended with him crashing into the fence at speed after failing to find a clear way past the fallers. Will, like the other two, was uninjured, and he managed to re-mount to collect second place. The crowd cheered Will on, impressed by his grit and determination.

Will, along with Crowther and Garland, became a valuable performer for Glasgow Tigers in the immediate post-war era. He later moved to Newcastle in a swap for one of the Hodgson brothers (Jack), before ending his career at Motherwell. Gruff Garland, also an immediate post-war Tiger, turned out for Bradford and the Ashfield Giants before retiring to Australia. Crowther left Glasgow in 1950, joined Motherwell and then retired to manage Leicester.

Glasgow took revenge on Edinburgh, 45–36, at White City on 29 July, their first win in the Northern Cup. However, the score does not convey a true indication of the terrific tussle the teams had. Only in the last two heats Glasgow forged ahead to make certain of victory.

A heat one crash took Bill Birtwell out of the meeting, suffering from concussion. This reduced Edinburgh's chances. Heat three was gifted to Glasgow when the two Edinburgh riders suffered from 'over eagerness at the gate', which 'resulted in some queer happenings … Laurie Packer and Jack Chapman gave their machines too much throttle as the tapes flew up. Their bikes went up in the air and they fell backwards on the track.' Packer was unlucky in that the bike landed on him but, fortunately, he was unhurt.

The *Daily Record* commented: "The 'Hampden Roar' in miniature was heard at the White City on Saturday night when the SACU officials disqualified Bob Wells for cutting-in. It was a roar of protest for it seemed evident to most of us that Wells was not the culprit. I (Speed Ace) thought that disqualification was hardly called for, but in any case it was Jack Hyland who committed the offence, not Wells. After the meeting I had a word with Wells who was indignant about the whole affair. Said Bob: 'There can be no doubt that it was a wrong decision. Even Hyland admits that.'"

What 'Speed Ace' did not say was that there was a three-man pile-up on the Paisley bend, so the race had to be stopped and someone disqualified. The *Citizen* said: "The cup competition certainly has whipped up enthusiasm.'

At the end of heat 12 Glasgow led by only three-points, but the brilliant riding of Fred Belliveau and Joe Crowther, and then in the next heat Harold Jackson, the one-time newsagent, and Dick Geary gave them a nine-point victory."

The outstanding rider was Edinburgh's George Greenwood, who scored a maximum in the match, and won the Scottish Silver Torch.

The second half saw Chuck Pinkerton hit the fallen Norrie Isbister who sustained career ending injuries. It was a sad ending to Norrie's career which went back to the first ever meeting in Glasgow on 9 April 1928 at Glasgow Nelson. Despite this, to the end, Norrie never lost his love of the sport.

August

The Glasgow team were programmed to meet West Ham Hawks, the Hammers second team, at Custom House on 1 August, in a second-half challenge match. Unfortunately, the track was waterlogged and the fixture rained-off. The home management had engaged a piper to lead the visitors out, but he was not needed.

West Ham visited Glasgow four days later. The *Glasgow Herald* said: "West Ham, one of London's many speedway racing teams, beat Glasgow by a single point ... on Saturday. Several members of the London team have had considerable experience of the Glasgow track and it was presumably a factor that helped them gain the verdict."

The *Sunday Mail* reported: "In the first race Gruff Garland was thrown off his machine at the starting point. His machine careered along the track and it was only with difficulty that Buck Whitby avoided crashing into it." There were no cut out mechanisms to stop the machines.

In another brief report, the *Daily Record* observed: "Glasgow found it impossible to hold captain Tiger Stevenson of West Ham. He collected full points in the Inter-City match and would have won the Scottish Gold Helmet into the bargain, but for a piece of bad luck. In the Helmet Final, Stevenson roared to the front and kept a good lead all the way. He was winning in a canter as he entered the finishing straight, then his bike conked out and that put him out of the running."

The *Record* went added: "Captain Gruff Garland let the Glasgow team down badly. We lost by one point – 42 points to 41 – but that should never have happened. Our skipper only collected three-points." True, Gruff had taken a couple of falls, but it was a bit unfair to lay the blame solely at his door.

The *Citizen* commented: "Glasgow and West Ham gave a 15,000 crowd some of the best speedway racing at a White City meeting since the game returned to the town three months ago. Bob Lovell's win for West Ham in heat four was the most exciting piece of work of the evening. Lying last, he overhauled team-mate George Enright and then Elwood Stillwell. He chased Gruff Garland to the last bend, hung on the white line while the Glasgow skipper went wide, and won by a wheel."

The *Speedway News* reported the ACU Northern Cup fixture at Brough Park on 7 August. The headline was: "Glasgow Outclassed", which was reflected in the result, a 58–22 home win. Newcastle were without Billy Lamont and Rol Stobart and the damage might have been worse if they had been at full strength.

It was incorrect to call the meeting on 12 August Scotland versus England. First, there was only one Scot in the Scotland side, and, secondly, George Pepper, riding for England side, was Canadian. The *Glasgow Herald* got it right: "A team comprising members of the

Marine Gardens and White City tracks defeated a Second Division English side." The portrayal of the meeting was not accurate. The sides could have been called Scottish-based riders and English-based riders. The *Herald* went on: "Scotland took the lead right from the start, and considering the keen struggle between the riders it was remarkable that only one of them fell, O(liver) Hart, Edinburgh, being the only one requiring treatment."

The *Sunday Mail*'s interest was in the second-half: "The Gauntlet heat which Crowther won was the most thrilling of the evening. Oliver Hart got out smartly as the tapes flew up, but on the first corner Crowther was on his tail. There was a terrific roar from the crowd when Joe got in front, but it wasn't long before Hart was leading the way. However, Joe won through on the last bend, and pipped Hart by inches. Another youngster giving a good account of himself was Leo Lungo. Lungo, who acted as one of Scotland's reserves, rode magnificently in one of the heats and was only yards behind England's captain at the finish."

It was a wet night in Glasgow on 19 August. The *Herald's* headline was: "Promising Meeting Spoiled By Rain". The report said: "Heavy rain and a track which in places represented a miniature lake, spoiled what promised to be an attractive Northern Cup match. Newcastle, however, weathered the conditions better than the Glasgow team and gained an overwhelming victory of 53 points to 39.

"Racing was held up after the tenth heat owing to one of the electrical wires breaking, and when the lights were turned on again the rain that had fallen during the interval almost swamped the track. The conditions thereafter played havoc with the machines and in the races that followed there was frequent troubles with motors. The times too were considerably high and even in the All-Star Match Race it took Will Lowther 117 seconds to complete the four laps – 33 seconds more than usual." The crowd was 15,000, despite the wet weather.

The *Daily Record* gave the winners on 26 August a great write up: "The Edinburgh Speedway proved on Saturday that they had two class riders in George Greenwood, their captain, and Oliver Hart. The White City, Glasgow ran off their Best Pairs and the Edinburgh lads walked away with it, collecting 19 points, just one short of the maximum.

"The Newcastle pair, George Pepper and Kid Curtis, were second with 16 points and incidentally George won every race in which he competed and bagged the Silver Helmet into the bargain. Gruff Garland, the captain of Glasgow, is coming back into the limelight. He had three firsts and a third, and with Joe Crowther's help, managed to knock up 15 points which was good enough for third place."

Despite the advert on the front cover of the programme indicating the Belle Vue second team would visit the following week, this pairs event was the last pre-war meeting at White City. Speedway in Britain more or less shut down over night. A few tracks, including White City, did stage meetings in 1940, but most did not reopen until after the hostilities were over.

5. 1940: A short wartime season

Many writers have suggested that the use of petrol hastened the closure of all tracks except Belle Vue during the Second World War. This may have been a contributory factor, but of greater concern to the authorities was the potential loss of life should the enemy decide to bomb a sports crowd. Floodlights were not acceptable as they would have been an easy target for enemy action.

Unlike the First World War, sport – with some restrictions – was encouraged by the government and local authorities, as they realised that it would provide some relaxation and entertainment for the civilian and military populations. In the winter, association football and both rugby codes were active; cricket was played in the summer. In speedway, a small number of tracks organised meetings in 1940. Belle Vue was the only track to stage regular meetings throughout the War.

Glasgow's 1940 season ran for six meetings before wartime restrictions, including rider availability, closed it down. White City did not reopen for speedway until hostilities were over in 1945.

The Lions raced five team meetings using riders who were still available. Three defeats, by Belle Vue, Harringay and The South were compensated for by wins over West Ham and Harringay. Meeting formats varied. A league style 14 heat opener was followed by a test match-style event with 18 heats against West Ham. Harringay and The South each rode in 12 heat matches and the last encounter with Harringay had 15 heats.

Glasgow raced one match against Belle Vue. The programme for this meeting suggested that there were hopes to stage league speedway, but this never happened.

Gruff Garland was again an ever-present, along with Will Lowther. He was criticised in the press for his poor machine preparation for some meetings. The war effort hauled off Harold Jackson and George Pepper after four and five events respectively.

Glasgow signed Edinburgh's George Greenwood. He was injured in his third and last outing. Leo Lungo also joined the Lions and was an ever-present.

Overall, the short season appears to have been popular with Glasgow's speedway supporters, although, maybe, unpopular with the powers that be who were concerned about public safety.

May

The *Daily Record* reported that on 8 May there were "thrills and spills once more at the White City Speedway last night." Meanwhile, 'Cinder Sifter' in the *Times* reported: "A crowd equally as good as that which has attended any previous meeting, and a thrilling night's sport during which the record time of 82.0 seconds was repeated by Frank Varey, gave speedway racing another great send off for the opening meeting."

The *Daily Record* added: "Glasgow had the worst of luck in the opening match of the season against Manchester. The last heat was the decider with the score previously standing at 39-points for Glasgow and Manchester 38.'

'Harold Jackson went flashing ahead from the starting gate and was six lengths in front at the end of the first lap. He gradually increased his lead and looked like winning for Glasgow when his bike stalled in the last lap. Tommy Bateman, Manchester, cut in front before Jackson's bike came to life again. In his effort to catch up, Jackson came a cropper. Bateman going on for first place. Jack Gordon, Manchester, was second with Will Lowther third, Manchester winning by three-points."

George Pepper was outstanding for Glasgow with 12 points and Frank Varey, the Belle Vue skipper, was also in good form, scoring 11 points.

On 15 May, the *Daily Record* reported that "Bill Longley of West Ham was the star at the White City Speedway, Glasgow, last night, although his team was beaten by 59 points to 48. Bill won every race in which he competed. His last heat was a smasher. Getting off to a bad start, he was well behind at the first lap but by clever, daring riding he managed to catch the field and nip through on the last bend to win by a bike length. Gruff Garland and Harold Jackson make an excellent combination. Their team work for Glasgow was a pleasure to watch. George Pepper was also in grand shape for Glasgow and the surprise of the evening, Leo Lungo, a local rider, was shoved into the last heat and came through on top, beating none other than Eric Chitty, one of West Ham's crack riders. Jack Gordon came down in the second last heat and sustained a dislocated shoulder."

The problems of war-time are clearly shown by comparing the team sheets with the results. The advertised West Ham line-up was Arthur Atkinson (injured), Keith Harvey (did not ride), Eric Chitty, Dick Geary (did not ride), Bill Longley, Kid Curtis, Wilf Jay (did not ride) and Ron Clarke. George Saunders and Jack White rode for West Ham, who had six riders compared to Glasgow's eight. Glasgow's side saw Jack Gordon replace Maurice Stobart and Leo Lungo filled-in for Jack Hyland.

The *Daily Record* reported about the meeting on 22 May: "At the White City Speedway last night, Harringay had a run-away victory over Glasgow, getting the verdict with a margin of 14 points. Glasgow put up a hard fight, but against such a crack First Division team they hadn't a chance.

"Jack Parker, the Harringay captain, gave a grand show and collected the maximum points. He was pipped, however, in the Silver Helmet heat by Glasgow's best rider of the evening, Bill Longley. Gruff Garland, the Glasgow skipper, had a lot of trouble with his machines."

The Royal Racing Cheetahs appeared at this meeting. Pitted against greyhounds, they demonstrated their turn of speed at White City. Well, that was the idea, but 'Skids Stewart' of the *News* was not impressed: "They might be the fastest animal in the world, but they certainly did not prove it last night. If I cut out the cigarettes for a week and got my wind back, I believe I could give the Cheetah a run for its money over 100 yards."

'Skids' also reported the speedway: "Although Glasgow were beaten by Harringay they were not disgraced. To come within striking distance of Harringay is its self an achievement. The maximum crowd figure was reached last night. They closed the gates shortly after the start. I'll bet Johnnie Hoskins is congratulating himself on fixing up Bill Longley. Bill did quite a tidy spot of points collecting and in addition won the Scottish Silver Helmet, inflicting on Jack Parker his only defeat of the evening. Most thrilling event of the night was the second heat of the match race. Bill Pitcher and Alec Statham got off to a grand start. After two laps they were still in the lead, with George Pepper in third. It looked all over bar the shouting. Pepper put on a terrific effort entering the last lap and the crowd shouted themselves hoarse when he nipped through to win top honours." Harringay won 43–29.

At home, Belle Vue intended to welcome back Joe Abbott into their ranks to face Glasgow on 25 May. The programme said that "fans should not expect too much from him. Long working hours and repercussions from old injuries have found their mark in past months. Give him a hand and then watch for fireworks." Bill Kitchen took Joe's place.

The programme also featured Ernie Price a brother of the northern Tommy Price (not the Wembley rider). On the Glasgow side, Kid Curtis was absent and his place was taken by Scottish-Australian Ron Johnson.

The programme hinted that this was a league match and that Glasgow and Belle Vue were in a league, which was an amalgamation of tracks still running despite the wartime restrictions. The 'league' did not materialise.

The *Daily Record* reported on the meeting on 29 May: "In a tight affair at the White City Speedway last night, 29 May, Glasgow were beaten by an English select by a narrow margin of four-points. George Greenwood, riding for the first time in Glasgow colours, had a nasty spill and fractured his elbow."

'Skids Stewart' in the *News* noted: "Greenwood was injured in the eighth heat", then added: "George Greenwood is as tough as they make them! When he was carried off with his right arm badly smashed up, he waved the other arm to the crowd as much as to say 'Don't worry about me, I'll be OK."

'Skids' considered: "We certainly had a packet of trouble at the White City last night. We lost the match against the South by four-points." He continued: "Bill Longley's bike was not behaving itself and Will Lowther could not strike his form ... Another member of the Glasgow team who deserves a big hand is George Pepper. George and Eric Chitty came down in a nasty bump in the first bend of the Scottish Silver Torch final. The judges said 're-run it', so the bold Mr Pepper received some medical attention, jumped on his bike and romped home the winner. Eric Chitty preferred to sit that one out and the race was run with three riders."

It was announced that the Stockport-based former newsagent Harold Jackson, had been called up by the Army and would not ride at Glasgow again. Also, George Pepper was called up by the Air Force.

Harold returned from the War and went on to become a leading light at Belle Vue in an administrative capacity, while George Pepper was killed on active service.

June

The prize for the winner of this event on 5 June was the Scottish Silver Torch and it was carried off by Canadian Eric Chitty. The *Daily Record* said: "Although Jack Parker had the highest number of points in the Glasgow Championship at the White City Speedway last night, he was pipped for the award in the Final by Eric Chitty. The four highest point scorers rode in the Final and Chitty, with a daring piece of riding, managed to collar the Championship. Bill Longley was right in form last night and Gruff Garland put up a good performance. Norman Parker was well up the list considering he was riding a borrowed machine. George Pepper won his first heat, but after that his bike gave him a lot of trouble."

It was a revenge meeting for Glasgow on 12 June. The *Daily Record* noted: "Glasgow had a run-away victory ... last night beating Harringay by 12 points. Bill Longley of Glasgow was undoubtedly the star performer, winning every race in which he competed, the All-Star Match Race into the bargain. Eric Chitty made the cinders fly and was second highest scorer for Glasgow. The Harringay captain, Jack Parker, and Bill Pitcher were the outstanding riders for the visiting team'"

So ended the short 1940 season. The meeting planned for the following week never took place due to further restrictions on crowd numbers.

Will Lowther rode for Glasgow before and after the Second World War, as well as in 1940. Note the thigh bar projecting out from the bike above Will's right leg. A rider using a bike with a thigh bar was prone to breaking his leg if he fell or crashed his machine.

6. 1945: Speedway relaunches

Victory in the European theatre of the Second World War allowed some return to normality. Part of that was reopening speedway tracks. Glasgow White City was one of the first back in action in 1945. Belle Vue had run throughout the War and started on 31 March. Bristol followed suit with a meeting on 2 April and the same day Newcastle reopened for a full season.

The pre-war Glasgow sides relied heavily on riders from other teams and, in essence the 1945 meetings adopted a similar approach. The men from pre-war days were gradually being released from wartime duties, although their performances depended on whether their equipment that would last the pace.

Promoter Johnnie Hoskins ran White City, Newcastle's Brough Park and the new track at Bradford's Odsal Stadium which opened on 23 June. The latter hosted the first post-war side labelled Glasgow. This team bore little similarity to the Glasgow side that faced London in the first fixture at White City on Wednesday 15 August 1945. The only regular in the Glasgow team was Canadian Eric Chitty. The team changed from week to week.

Glasgow had four fixtures and the supporters also saw a Best Pairs and an international between Scotland and England.

Ron Johnson and Bill Kitchen captained teams that faced each other twice. The season closed on 17 October with individual competitions – the Scottish Senior and Junior Championships. No matter the makeshift nature of the meetings, the Glasgow public lapped it up and 22,000 packed the stadium for the last meeting.

August

Glasgow's first meeting was on Saturday 11 August 1945 at Bradford. The home side won 46–37. The Glasgow team included two 1939 Lions, Joe Crowther and Will Lowther. Malcolm Craven top scored with 9+1. Next best was Tommy Allott on eight, who had visited the Odsal track a few times. The other Glasgow riders were Bert Spencer, Wilf Jay, Norman Hargreaves and Ron Mason.

White City opened on Wednesday 15 August, promoted by Johnnie Hoskins. He was keen to bring new blood into the sport and invited anyone who was interested. He said: "I'm expecting a good response from lads who were dispatch riders in the services and I'm sure, in a sporting city like Glasgow, we'll find these gentlemen."

The Daily Record covered the meeting: "It was too damp at the White City Glasgow last night for the riders to raise much of a dust on but speedway racing, revived in the city after five years, aroused great enthusiasm in a crowd of over 10,000. 'Wednesday night is speedway night again' was on the programme and if last night's thrills are common this is a sport which is going to get a real grip on Glasgow." The report concluded: "Glasgow was riding against London but all the riders were guest stars."

"Riding was very good considering the conditions" Hoskins said. *The Record* added that: "Glasgow had new favourite sport stars. Lt. Com. Geoff Godwin for instance. Eric Chitty, too, perhaps Number One favourite and Glasgow's captain was in good form. So was Ron Clarke who seems to glide out of nowhere at the right time, Tiger Hart and Bill Kitchen London's captain." Glasgow won 61–47. Oliver Hart top scored with an 18-point maximum. The first home Glasgow team featured captain Eric Chitty, Will Lowther, Oliver Hart, Joe Crowther, Geoff Godwin, Ron Johnson and Alec Grant at reserve.

The first post-war international was staged on Wednesday 22 August. The home team had two native Scots – Ron Johnson and the barber from Bellshill, Leo Lungo. They were supported by an assortment of riders from other nations while England fielded a fully representative side. Johnson and Lungo scored six points between them; most of Scotland's points were scored by Chitty, Clarke and Bill Longley. Kitchen was best English rider and was well supported by Malcolm Craven. The match went to the wire and a last heat 3–3 made sure Scotland won by one point.

Two cobbled together sides named Glasgow and Newcastle produced a close fixture on Wednesday 29 August watched by a 15,000 crowd. A couple of good heat results could have turned it Newcastle's way, but Glasgow won 56–51.

Chitty was the top Glasgow man on 16, but had better support from Johnson and Crowther. He was twice beaten by Newcastle's top scorer on 17, Alex Statham. Ron Johnson scored a five-ride maximum while Joe Crowther had only one win in his 12 points.

September

Bike troubles let down Glasgow on Wednesday 5 September. Johnson, Chitty, Ken Tidbury and Spinks all had bike failures. However, North London also had bike stoppages. The quickly recruited Glasgow side faced a similar North London team. The visitors had only seven men, but held the home side until near the end. There was no last heat decider. A last heat 5–0 for the visitors made the score, 42–39, which flattered them.

North London's Bill Kitchen looked set for a maximum, but Oliver Hart had other ideas. Oliver halted the march of the Lancashire hero who in 1946 became a Wembley Lion.

Hoskins's tracks kept it in the family with Glasgow visiting Newcastle on Monday 10 September. Will Lowther and Bill Kitchen both representing the Diamonds. The Tynesiders won 49–35. Johnson was top scorer for Glasgow on eight, but the rest failed to score well. The bikes ran properly for Glasgow; the problem was riders falling with Johnson, Craven, Spinks and Crowther all losing points this way.

The first post war best pairs event attracted 18,000 fans to White City on Wednesday 12 September. They watched Kitchen and Lowther combine to win with 21. Ron Johnson was second top scorer with 14 but partner, Australian Charlie Spinks, collected only three, so they finished second. Chitty was the only rider with a maximum 15, but his partner, Geoff Godwin, failed to score. Chitty's solo efforts were enough to give them third place.

The crowd dipped a little to 16,000 on Wednesday 19 September but this was acceptable in those still austere days. After the War, people were desperate for entertainment, as was shown the following season. Yet again, Chitty led Glasgow to a victory. The 46–37 margin against 'The Rest' was reasonably convincing. The track was in poor condition, but it didn't deter Johnson who broke his record of 86.4 seconds by 1.1 seconds. In heat seven he was overanxious and was disqualified for touching the tapes. Johnson and Bill Kitchen both clocked 21 seconds for a flying start lap record. In the challenge event Johnson won, not easily, with Kitchen on his tail. The *Record's* Bill Manson said about the match on 26 September that Kitchen, whose challenge that he could recruit a team and beat Glasgow led by Ron Johnson, wasn't an empty one. Bill's side stopped Ron's overwhelming run of successes at White City, winning 50–34.

Left: Ron Johnson who captained the Glasgow Tigers in 1945. Above right: White City programme for the Scottish Championship on 17 October 1945.

The White City Stadium in the foreground of this panoramic picture.

Heat twelve was a thriller, Charlie Spinks skidded badly on the second bend, collided with the safety fence and careered off the track across the grass park. He was lost in the darkness in midfield. Then the bike flew into view minus the rider – to crash through the barrier at the other side. However, fans' screams turned to cheers – Charlie sauntered off the park uninjured.

Johnson made amends by winning his Glasgow Victory Cup heat easily. The Final wasn't so easy but Johnson, with his daredevil cornering, left Chitty behind to win. It was his sixth cup of the season.

The final race of the evening was a treat; Johnson faced Kitchen. Johnson jumped into the lead, but Kitchen left him at the bend. Then Johnson drew him in again. The lead changed hands race long and on the last bend it looked like Kitchen would win, but Johnson grabbed some extra horsepower from somewhere to win by a wheel.

October

Speedway was still holding the public interest. The visiting team billed The Midlands attracted 21,000 to White City on Wednesday 3 October. Despite this support, Glasgow only had the twin spearhead of maximum men Chitty and Oliver Hart on form. The rest, including Frank Varey, were not at the races. Next best for Glasgow was Bill Longley with 3+2.

The Midlands, who won 46–37, had Malcolm Craven on 10 with Phil 'Tiger' Hart and Ron Clarke on nine each. The rest of The Midlands riders gave the top three solid backing.

The end of the short season was drawing close. After the thumping for Glasgow the week before, it was prudent of the promoters to stage a match on Wednesday 10 October without any territorial links.

The rematch between the two sides captained by big rivals Johnson and Kitchen was close run affair which produced a draw. Johnson's team built a 10-point lead, then saw it whittled away. His side was expected to win, but without non-show Alex Statham, they were a man down and toiling.

The intense rivalry of the two captains was not carried into the second half when Kitchen loaned Johnson a bike for the second half final which he used to win the race.

The meeting on Wednesday 17 October goes down in Scottish Speedway history as one of the most unusual. Watched by 22,000 it brought down the curtain on 1945.

There were two Scottish Championships, a senior event, won by Ron Johnson, and a junior event, won by Norman Evans. In the senior event, two riders failed to turn up. Their rides distributed among riders for the Junior Championship, so the Senior event had six reserves. The junior event also started two riders short and their rides were allocated among the competitors.

The missing riders were not the main problem. The big concern was the whereabouts of the truck coming north with the methanol for the meeting. The vehicle broke down en-route. Another lorry sent to collect the fuel also broke down. So the meeting continued until the riders ran out of fuel at the end of the Junior Championship, heat seven. By this time the three considered to be the main contenders, Evans, Lowther, and Gordon, had completed their four rides. With nobody else in contention Evans was awarded the Junior Championship. Another odd point is that the meeting programme was reprinted in the 1960s. It can be identified as the reprint because it lacks a printer's name.

Fortunately, this was in reality an open meeting – the 'championships' had no official standing in the sport.

7. 1946: League speedway returns

Speedway re-established a league structure for the 1946 season. The War was now over, and although many men were still in the Armed Forces, there was a huge demand for entertainment. Glasgow rode in the Northern League – in practice a second tier under the National League. The other five teams were Middlesbrough, Sheffield, Norwich, Birmingham and Newcastle. Each team raced the others twice at home and twice away for a programme of 20 league fixtures. Every track in the sport was well supported – it was the start of a golden age for speedway which lasted until the early 1950s.

Ian Hoskins recalls in his book *History of the Speedway Hoskins:* "The mainstay of the new Tigers were two Geordies ... Will Lowther, the captain, and Joe Crowther ... Will was an introvert who had a gammy left leg which he used to stick out before him in the corners like a crutch. Crowther was an extrovert who would have a go from anywhere and he quickly became the darling of the crowds."

April

This was an all-ticket return for the Tigers new season on 10 April. The stand cost three shillings and sixpence (3/6 or 17.5 pence) while the ground cost one shilling and nine pence (1/9 or 8.75 pence).

The fans saw Wembley's Bill Kitchen on fine form. He lowered Ron Johnson's track record by 2.9 seconds to 82.4 seconds while winning The Glasgow Cup. The former track record holder was carried off after a heat six fall. Johnson rode wide on the second bend, hit the fence, and bounced back into Kitchen's path. Kitchen won the rerun from Jeff Lloyd.

He won the trophy with 14 points, one more than Bradford's Ron Clarke. Glasgow fans were pleased with the efforts of their riders, Wal Morton, Will Lowther, Joe Crowther and Maurice Stobbart.

The following week, 17 April, in brilliant weather, 17,000 Glasgow fans watched a best pairs event. It was won by Bill Longley and Will Lowther who team rode their way to victory. Lowther scored eight and followed Longley home in their five outings for 21 points. They just beat West Ham's Eric Chitty and Newcastle's Jeff Lloyd who scored 20. Bill Kitchen rode with Glasgow's Bill Baird and missed out on a rostrum place. Kitchen was unbeaten but did not score a maximum – he dead-heated with Wal Morton and totalled 14.5 points.

On 22 April 1946 the Glasgow Tigers made their post-war debut. Their name was chosen by Ian Hoskins in preference to the Glasgow Dynamos. He was not allowed to use the 'Lions' name from 1939. The red and white stripes came from Sunderland FC which Hoskins supported. The Tigers won their first fixture, a challenge match at Newcastle's Brough Park, 43–40. The team was skippered by Wal Morton who scored six points, and included Londoner Eddie Lack five, Cumbrian Maurice Stobbart 6+1, pre-war Glasgow Lions Joe Crowther 11, Will Lowther 12, Stan Beardsall 1 and Ken Tidbury 2+1 and Terry Tight 0, at reserve. Tight replaced Dennis Gray. Eddie Lack was the Tigers' hero with a last heat win to clinch victory.

The Tigers, described as 'the babes of the Northern League' were seen as a force to be reckoned with after their display against Sheffield on 24 April. Splendid team work was the basis of Glasgow's victory, but they had to defend their 61–47 lead in the second leg of this National Trophy first preliminary round tie.

Sheffield were a courageous team but were puzzled by the tight White City bends. Notable events including Ken Tidbury's point in heat six when he pushed his bike to the line. He collapsed after his efforts. Eddie Lack fell in heat five in spectacular fashion. He was leading when he performed a 'flying trapeze' act – his bike hurtled across the centre green.

Heat 17 finished early because the marshal miscounted. After three laps Stobbart was declared the winner. However, the error was spotted. In the rerun he was only second. Lowther top scored for the Tigers on 16, while Morton scored 14+2. Bill Baird made his Glasgow debut in this meeting.

The following evening, at Owlerton Stadium, Sheffield won 61–47 and levelled the aggregate score, forcing a replay. It looked as though Sheffield would not make it. However, they reeled in Glasgow and levelled the scores after a last heat decider.

With unbeaten Tommy Allott taking the win, his partner Tommy Bateman had to make the decisive score. He managed to get third place behind Lowther. His attention was on fighting off the other Glasgow rider, Crowther. For Glasgow, Lowther top scored with 14 and Joe Crowther added 11. Morton chipped in with 9+1.

May

Despite winning at Newcastle two weeks before, the Tigers lost 44–40 to the Diamonds at White City in a thrill packed meeting watched by 18,000 on May Day. Engine troubles and spills were the Tigers' main problems. They had a chance to finish level in the last heat, but Leo Lungo took the lead and stayed there to score the vital three points.

The Tigers' Gruff Garland, the wee Australian leg trailer who was a Lion in 1939, had arrived from Australia. He had the fans on their toes with excitement. His unorthodox cornering looked dangerous, but brought him dividends. Lowther and Crowther both raced to maximums but apart from Garland with seven points, had little support.
Lungo, who regularly raced in Glasgow and Edinburgh before the War without being a star, top scored for Newcastle with 9+1.

At Newcastle on 6 May the Tigers had some different riders from the Wednesday before, ran the Diamonds close in a Northern League fixture, losing 44–40. Jeff Lloyd, the rising Newcastle star, was unbeaten. One of Tigers' 'terrible twins', Will Lowther, top scored with 11 points with support from Wal Morton on nine and Crowther with eight. Had Garland been present the Tigers may have won. Charlie Oates was not riding, and Glasgow used Butch (John) Williams. He was a West Ham mechanic and pre-war West Ham Hawks rider, but only rode twice, failing to score and then falling. Twice the Tigers only had one rider in a heat.

Glasgow made the best of the replayed National Trophy tie first leg on 8 May. The 19,000 crowd was right behind their team. The visitors had machine troubles. However, the Glasgow second strings were weak. Tidbury and Baird failed to score and six of their rides were taken by reserves. Would Glasgow be able to defend their 62–45 lead at Owlerton? Glasgow's other six riders were more solid and Morton returned to form with 13+1. Garland, now officially a Glasgow rider, did well with 10 points. Lowther and Crowther both scored 10+2. The latter lost points trying to protect Eddie Lack's lead in heat six when he miscalculated Bateman's speed and lost the lead. For Sheffield, Tommy Allott scored a six-ride paid maximum.

This hard-fought tie went to the last heat at Owlerton the next evening. The score at the end of heat 17 was 58–44 to Sheffield. The home side needed a 5–1 or better to win the tie. Allott and Williams went to the tapes for Sheffield. For Glasgow, the two riders selected by Ian Hoskins were Wal Morton and Gruff Garland. Despite doing well from the gate, the Glasgow men met with misfortune. Garland fell after being pushed wide by Williams and did not remount to finish. Morton either suffered an engine failure or fell when he was too close to the fence, gifting Sheffield a tie winning 5–0. Sheffield got a bye into the first round proper of the National Trophy, where they were well beaten by National League Bradford.

The Tigers threw away their chance of a first Northern League home victory on 15 May. The Birmingham Brummies grabbed a last heat win. Lowther registered a maximum and Crowther only dropped points in one race. Glasgow started badly with a 5–1 reverse, they did take the lead by heat three but could not sustain this, going behind in heat six. The Brummies, were consistent, taking second and third places. They had enough points for a draw going into the last heat, but held Glasgow to a 4–2 to win 42–40. Had Stobbart been awarded the point in heat five when he fell victim of Phil Hart who was excluded and had either Morton or Lack completed heat seven, they would have scored a 4–2 and taken a league point from the fixture. Stobbart bravely rode his other races nursing a knee injury which required stiches. Tidbury and Stan Beardsall, the Glasgow reserves, failed to score and, at the end of the meeting, were told they had been dropped.

Wednesday 22 May was a red – and white – letter day for Tigers because they won their first league match. It was not plain sailing. Morton suffered engine failures in his four starts in the match and his second half outing. The Tigers re-introduced Baird and Oates at reserve and they chipped in 3 and 2+1 in a 44–38 victory. Lowther recorded another full maximum while Stobbart had a paid maximum 9+3. Norwich fought hard and the scores were level at heat 10, but the Tigers then won three of the last four heats for victory.

Lowther was praised for his efforts. He won the Miss Edna Stewart Trophy from Garland who had stalked him for three laps before Lowther pulled away. Miss Stewart, who laid out £50 in sponsorship, later married Junior Bainbridge. Mr Hoskins (Senior), ever the showman, donned a fur coat to congratulated Lowther with a bundle of flowers.

The Tigers were on a roll as they went to the high-speed Norwich track and took an unexpected 43–41 win. The inspiration for this result on 25 May was Norwich based Morton, who showed the locals the way round with a full maximum. He was well supported, particularly by Lowther with 10 points. Crowther and Lack were the Tigers' last heat heroes when they grabbed a match winning 5–1. The Tigers didn't win many on the road so it was a result to be savoured. Still experimenting with the reserve berths, the Tigers gave an outing to John Lockley. He failed to score. He had ridden in 1945 and briefly at Preston in the 1930s.

Some journalists considered Glasgow were emerging as a force to be reckoned with after their 58–26 win over Sheffield on 29 May. The *Speedway News'* did not agree, believing that Sheffield were a shadow of their former selves without Tommy Allott, normally worth double figures at White City. The visitors' Stan Williams was unlucky at the start of heat five. Impeded by a track staff member at the gate, he closed the throttle and stalled his bike. He missed out on this race but won his last two riders. Like Norwich the week before, Sheffield had two obscure names at reserve. Norman Clark, Sheffield team manager, rode to ensure they had seven riders. They also borrowed Glasgow second half rider Bert Shearer, who scored a point by finishing ahead of Clark. Lowther returned another full maximum while Garland and Crowther both scored 9+1. It was Glasgow's best win of the season, later equalled against Birmingham.

June

The Tigers travelled to Birmingham on 1 June and lost 46–37 in a league fixture. They held the home side to 3–3 results in 10 of the 14 races and won a single heat 4–2 on the 440-

yard athletics track shared with Birchfield Harriers. The Tigers had seven of the 14 race winners. Lowther scored a full maximum and Morton scored 10 points, but the Tigers' tail was a bit too long. This was not unusual in the years to come.

The secondary knock-out trophy in 1946 for the Tigers was the Northern Trophy. They faced Newcastle in the opening tie with the first leg at Brough Park on Monday 3 June. Glasgow may have won but for Crowther's crash in heat 10. The incident looked 'quite grim', but he bounced back to race again on a borrowed bike. His had ended up wrapped round a fence post and was quite seriously damaged. The Tigers were two points down before the last heat, but Morton and Lack took a vital 4–2 over Sid Littlewood to take the draw.

The Tigers had borrowed Newcastle based Ted Adler for the reserve berth and his two points were valuable. He finished both his rides in a scoring position. He took a point in the reserves only heat twelve after Oates had an engine failure. He then replaced Crowther and scored a point because his partner had an engine failure. Lowther was beaten by home star Jeff Lloyd twice but still managed to record a respectable 13 while Morton and Garland scored 11 and 7+1 respectively.

The season's big individual competition was the British Riders' Championship, which temporarily replaced the World Championship. Glasgow held the first of two qualifying rounds to be staged at White City on 5 June. Another wet night in Glasgow saw the track likened to a duck pond. However, it produced splendid racing and the honours went to Sheffield's Tommy Allott with an unbeaten 15.

Top Tiger was Wal Morton on 11, one point ahead of Lowther. Crowther scored 9.5. He had an uncomfortable ride in heat nine when his fuel cap fell off. He was covered in methanol for most of the race. He dead heated with Reg Lambourne. Allowing methanol to evaporate off the skin is a chilling experience.

He had been bothered by engine troubles and the bike that soaked him was Eddie Lack's. Crowther's bike expired just before the heat and he narrowly missed a time exclusion as he accepted the borrowed machine.

The next heat was a thriller involving Phil Hart and Morton. At the flag it was Hart, the Englishman who had started racing in Australia, ahead.

Two Birmingham riders in the meeting, Roy Dook and Stan Dell, were posted missing at Sheffield the following evening. Their bike trailer had lost a wheel on a remote stretch of road and repairs took ages before they could continue. They arrived in Birmingham on Friday 7 June to explain themselves.

Two composite sides, Newcastle & Middlesbrough and Sheffield & Glasgow entertained Norwich fans on 8 June when the Stars were away. Stan Williams was programmed for Sheffield & Glasgow but didn't ride. Tommy Bateman took his rides from heat seven onwards and Ernie Silver was drafted in to take Bateman's heat 13 ride. Why Bateman raced in heat four is not clear, because he should have replaced Williams. Maybe the fans were not concerned in this Special Victory Night event. The Tigers riders, Morton, Crowther, Lowther and Garland scored the most for their team which won 50–33.

In the Northern Trophy, despite holding the advantage of the draw at Newcastle from the first leg, the Tigers' passage to the next round was uncertain until near the end of the return leg on 12 June. It was described as one of the best meetings at Glasgow even though there was a run of drawn races between heats five and 14.

The fans were excited that Glasgow progressed to next round. Their 50–46 victory was sealed by Garland and Lack. In the last heat, the Tigers duo faced Norman Evans and Syd Littlewood and it looked tough. However, Garland managed a last bend burst to win while

Lack, completing a 2+1 return, secured third place. Lowther scored 13+1 while Crowther scored 12. Jeff Lloyd rode masterfully and was brightest Diamond as he scored 14 points from five rides. He also won the second half final – the first visiting rider do this in 1946.

The Diamonds' Terry Tight was awarded a trophy for being the first Newcastle novice to win an away heat.

In true Johnnie Hoskins fashion, the public were entertained by the speedway and other attractions. This evening the half-time interval attraction was a ladies' hockey match between Babcock and Wilcock Ladies and India of Inchinnan Ladies.

Returning to Northern League action, Stan Williams was top man at Sheffield on Thursday 13 June. Stan, a one-time Sheffield programme salesman, opened his account with a second behind Jack Bibby in a 5–1. Tommy Allott defeated the top visitors, Lowther with 10 points and Crowther, who scored eight. He did not get the better of Morton who scored nine. Glasgow gave a reserve berth to Bert Shearer, but he failed to score in a 45–39 defeat.

The secondary league style competition in 1946 was the Auto Cycle Union Cup (ACU Cup). The Tigers faced Birmingham in the opening match in Glasgow on 19 June. It was a night of fast racing. The match should have been run over 16 heats, but only featured 14 by mistake. The 47–36 home win was allowed to stand.

This was the visitors' first defeat in Scotland and reports blamed defeat on missing riders Doug Wells and Bob Lovell. Birmingham had further trouble when Glasgow's Baird, who replaced Shearer, crashed in heat four. His rider-less machine collided with Brummies' Laurie Packer and Percy Brine. This put Brine out of the meeting, aggravating a back injury sustained earlier that week. Not even a 5–0, gifted them by Lowther and Lack, could save Birmingham.

Wal Morton was the top Tiger with 11 points, while Garland scored 9+1. Lowther, who had an engine failure won his other outings.

A special charity meeting on Thursday 20 June at Norwich drew a crowd of 9,000. The Stars faced a combined Newcastle and Glasgow team. The combined team with Morton and Garland should have given Norwich a better contest. The result underlined their growing strength with Norwich winning 51–33.

Brough Park track specialist Lowther, who crashed breaking his collar bone at Sheffield on 20 June, and skipper Morton, laid up on doctor's orders, missed Glasgow's visit to Newcastle on 24 June for an ACU Cup fixture. Lowther made up some of his lost earnings by writing for the *Scottish Sunday Express*. His absence reduced the Tigers' chances of winning. However, 36 points by a weakened team was a good return, but 11 short of Newcastle's 47. This was another 16 heat ACU Cup match which was raced over 14 heats by mistake.

Littlewood and Stobbart had a coming together in heat nine which ended with the Newcastle rider falling, much to the home fans' annoyance. The Tigers were encouraged by Scottish music played by a girls pipe band.

The Tigers had a new rider at reserve, former commando, Sergeant Major Wallie Thompson. He scored one point and had ridden for Newcastle earlier in the season. The best Tiger was Crowther with 11 points, while Stobbart notched 10.

On 26 June, the Tigers were weakened by the absence of Lowther and Morton, but were splendid in defeat. They kept things close with a much stronger Norwich side for a while, but the visitors dominated the last three races with a 4–2 and two 5–1s to win 46–37.

The track was in great condition and Crowther's opening heat win was near the track record. He went on to complete his maximum. Norwich's strength was their second strings where the Tigers had passengers in Baird and debutant, Jack Tye, in the body of the team and John

Lockley at reserve. Tye was racing for the first time in six years. He had two engine failures at the starting gate and a fall.

Around this time, Billie Bates was attending the early morning practice sessions riding an aged Scott machine.

July

Still without their two heat leaders on 3 July against Middlesbrough in a home Northern League fixture, Glasgow's troubles were compounded by an injury to Crowther in heat seven. It put him out of the match, robbing the Tigers of what little major fire power they had. The outcome was Glasgow's biggest league defeat so far, 50–34.

Glasgow had fighters in Lack and Stobbart. Without a full side it was an uphill struggle against a Middlesbrough team who went on to win the League. Garland was the top Tiger on nine points, with one heat win. Stobbart rose to the occasion in heats two and 11 when he defeated top class visitors Wilf Plant and Fred 'Kid' Curtis. These were two of Glasgow's race wins but only returned 3–3 results. Maurice ran a last and fell between his two wins. Tigers had another debutant, Percy Brine, but he only scored one point and did not ride again. The visitors' Frank Hodgson won every race he entered, four in the match and the second half.

Norwich's veteran Australian, Bert Spencer, proved he was one of the best riders in the League in the British Riders' Championship round at White City on 10 July. He won all his races, but did not have things all his own way. Crowther challenged him in heat 10.

Glasgow fans were pleased with Crowther's 12 points, confirming he had recovered from his shaking the week before. He was level with Stan Williams and a point behind Frank Hodgson. The 18,000 crowd had their money's worth. The other Tigers did reasonably well, Garland scored eight points and Stobbart seven.

A new Johnnie Hoskins idea was the Paisley Sealed Handicap Trophy. It gave the riders a handicap bonus score to add to the points they scored on the track. He tried it out at White City on 17 July and brought in some National League stars to bolster the field. Belle Vue's Jack Parker, and Odsal's Ron Clarke, Fred 'Friar' Tuck and Bill Longley had no handicap points. Parker finished with a 15-point maximum. This was equalled by Newcastle's Jeff Lloyd who scored 13 plus 2 handicap points. Parker won the run-off.

It had been the intention that any decider should be on a handicap basis. However, the promoters had not told anyone and the pair went from the gate together. The race was over three laps and credit to Parker who won despite a deflating tyre. The original idea was to withhold the handicaps until the end of the meeting, but it was decided to reveal them at the interval.

The local press was not too complimentary saying "Parker's riding lacks spectacle but he is extremely fast on the corners and that is what really matters." He was presented with the Trophy by Nan McNamara, Paisley Carnival Queen and British Women's Ice Skating Record Holder.

It was back to league racing at White City on 24 July. Once again, Glasgow were beaten but not outclassed. Glasgow had an early lead before Sheffield's superior strength came through and the visitors won 47–37. Tommy Allott won all his races in the meeting.

Stobbart impressed *Cinder Sifter* in the *Times,* who noted that his improved performance was a welcome surprise and he showed more confidence than usual. He did well to score nine points, equalling Garland and one behind Crowther.

Glasgow nearly threw away points in heat eight when both Shearer and Thomson fell. However, Thomson remounted to take a point. The Sheffield riders did not realise that he had remounted and were cruising round when Dick Geary noticed him. Both visitors had to sprint to score full points.

Pundits thought the Bellahouston Cup in the second half of the meeting produced the best racing. Garland won heat one in a fast time of 87.1 secs. Allott, Crowther and Tommy Bateman also qualified for this final, which Allott won.

The clash of the Hoskins teams resulted in a 46–38 win for Newcastle on Monday 29 July at Brough Park. Morton eased himself back into action from reserve, scoring 6+2. Lowther, normally a Tyneside specialist, returned scoring nine points.

Lowther was back to his old form for the return against the Diamonds at White City two days later. The fans were shown how good the Tigers could be. With a full-strength team they trounced Newcastle 52–32. Lowther just missed a maximum, Morton scored 10 and both Garland and Crowther scored 9+1.

Fast riding Newcastle captain Jeff Lloyd was outstanding with a maximum, but he could not rally his team enough to do better.

A 21,000 crowd saw the most thrilling racing so far this season. Though Glasgow took a commanding 12-point lead in the first five heats, the visitors never flagged. They drew the next five races, but then three wins put Tigers in an unassailable position.

Again, the second half Govan Trophy impressed. Stobbart gave Lowther one of his hardest tests this season. After a thrilling four laps Stobbart qualified for the Final with Ron Clarke, who beat Lowther in a special match race, Morton, and Jeff Lloyd. The final line-up looked good, but after the first lap, it fizzled out leaving Clarke an easy winner.

The record crowd meant the riders being awarded 30 shillings (£1.50) per point.

August

Birmingham were considered to be 'off colour' on Saturday 3 August and Glasgow were at full strength for their visit to Perry Barr. The Tigers' team-riding was far superior to Birmingham's and their steadiness in all circumstances displayed just that quality the home riders lacked. All the Tigers scored consistently with Crowther on nine points, and Lack on eight their leading lights. The former won three races in fine style and in his remaining heat fell while battling for first position with Phil Hart. Crowther remounted and the crowd gave him a special cheer when he made up half a lap and almost succeeded in taking a point. Lack, vastly improved since his last visit to the midlands, rode with rare dash and spirit. In heat five Hart tried his hardest to nurse Bob Lovell into first place, but was forced to abandon the attempt when Lack pressured them on the last lap. The Birmingham captain went ahead, but Lack surprised him by getting inside on the last bend to record an excellent win.

Reports indicate that the Birmingham riders were getting into trouble on the first bend, then trying too hard to catch the leader rather than team riding. The home heat leaders were also guilty of hogging the better inside gates, which would have been better occupied by the second strings. The result was that Glasgow had a rare win at Perry Barr, 45–39.

Glasgow seemed to have done enough in a Northern Trophy semi-final first leg match on 7 August at White City.

Norwich's skipper, Bert Spencer, had a fall in his first ride and then an engine failure. Without a motor, he did not ride again. The races he did finish he won in style.

Maurice Stobart (top) and Wal Morton (bottom) were both important riders for the Tigers in 1946.

Left: Edna Stewart, who presented trophies for second half events at White City in 1946. She went on to marry Glasgow legend Junior Bainbridge at Dumfries in 1948.
Right: Will Lowther was a loyal rider for the Tigers (and Lions) before and after the War.

Glasgow Tigers programme against Birmingham in 1946.

The match featured an uncommon dead-heat 5–1 for Glasgow. The referee could not split the Crowther–Lowther duo in heat three. Crowther had an unusual unbeaten score of 14.5 points. Lowther scored 11.5 while Lack scored 10+2 from five rides. The Tigers won 54–42, so had a 12-point lead for the second leg at The Firs.

Oliver Hart rode in the second half winning the August Trophy and an extra race featured Crowther, Jay and Lack.

Sheffield Tigers climbed to the top of the Northern League on Thursday 8 August thanks to a 48–36 win over Glasgow. Sheffield fans were horrified to see Tommy Allott take a long sliding fall during a duel with Glasgow skipper Wal Morton. They were even more horrified to see him lie still as the other riders raced on for two laps. However, the cold sponge did the trick. Allott walked from the track and won his other three outings. Bateman had to stand up on his footrest to win one of his races when his saddle fell off. For Glasgow Stobbart top scored with 9+2; Wal Morton scored nine including two heat wins.

A wet track at The Firs gave a home advantage. Watched by 13,000 fans, their riders won the Northern Trophy second leg 59–36 on Saturday 10 August to win the tie on aggregate 101–90. They moved into the lead overall in heat 12 and never looked back.

Glasgow did not give up without a fight. For a time, the Tigers managed to peg back Norwich. Wal Morton lived in Norwich and liked to show his neighbours he could handle a speedway machine. He was the best Tiger on 13 points. Joe Crowther scored 8+1 and Stobbart 7+2. Will Lowther had a poor night, scoring only two points.

Despite a couple of zeros from their reserves, Glasgow saw good returns from Crowther, Lowther and Morton in their 51–42 ACU Cup win over Sheffield at White City on 14 August. Yet again Allott was the visitors' top rider but, while he scored well, he lacked support. Glasgow had 13 of the 16 race winners, but only picked up three second places and six thirds. Lowther and Crowther both scored 13+1, losing only to Allott while Morton scored 10. Stobbart scored 4 in the races he finished. His total was reduced because of two falls and an engine failure. Lack was rested to allow his injured hand time to heal.

The public address system broke down. Race times were displayed to the crowd chalked on a blackboard carried round on the tractor. The track lights were dim and it was thought that they would soon fail as well. Despite all this, the press pundits noted that Glasgow were always an attraction.

The second leg at Owlerton was on the next night. Glasgow were nine points ahead and they were very anxious to repeat this performance at Sheffield. Despite Glasgow pulling back to four behind from an earlier 12-point deficit, the home riders rallied to win the match and the tie. Glasgow were unfortunate in finding Tommy Allott, Sheffield's favourite in the British Riders' Championship, on top of his form. He recorded a maximum in their 55–41 win.

The fans and reporters enjoyed the spectacle, the latter noting it was a grand meeting, good, clean riding and every heat a race. For Glasgow Lowther, with 9+1, and Morton and Crowther, both on nine, led the visitors' challenge. Brian Wilson, a Belle Vue asset who rode for several teams in his career, was at reserve for Glasgow, scoring one point.

The Tigers had another setback at White City when champions-elect Middlesbrough Bears won 47–37 on 21 August. The Bears provided the stiffest opposition of the season. None of the home riders had an answer to the rampaging Bears, only winning five races between them. Reserves Wallie Thomson and newcomer Joe Arlet managed a single point between them. In the second half Odsal's Oliver Hart won his match races against team mate Ron Clarke 2–1. Visiting captain Frank Hodgson won the Knights of Speed Trophy in the fastest time of the night.

The next evening, Middlesbrough won decisively, 54–30 against Glasgow at Cleveland Park. The Tigers' cause was not helped by Stobbart twice failing to finish. Lowther's opening race fall and last race engine failure reduced his score to five. Yet again the reserves had a miserable night, scoring just one point, compared to the Bears' duo of Len Tupling and Ed 'Crusty' Pye.

The best Tiger was Wal Morton on nine points with Crowther on eight. Only three heats had four finishers – the Glasgow riders had six engine failures compared to just two for the Bears. A Bears junior team whitewashed a Tigers team with Bob Murray, G McLellan, Niven McCreadie and Billy Bates on the wrong end of four 5–1 defeats.

Six days later, for the second consecutive week Middlesbrough won at White City. The ACU Cup points went south. The Bears won 54–42. Slow times were recorded because the track was described as 'something resembling a miniature duck pond.' Wet tracks don't often provide good racing and this proved no exception. However, the conditions obviously suited the Bears. Despite a fightback, from 14 points down at heat 13, Glasgow could do nothing against a superior team. Numerous skids and nasty falls occurred. Crowther managed a respectable 12 points and Stobbart scored 10.

September

The Glasgow fans were treated to an international meeting on 4 September. It attracted the biggest crowd of the season, 25,000, who saw an exciting meeting. The Britain side were beaten 58–50, but not disgraced, by an Overseas Select.

The British team included Crowther, Lowther and Morton in their line up and Garland rode for the Overseas side. Only good form from Lowther provided any home advantage. Britain's best were Belle Vue star Jack Parker and Newcastle's Jeff Lloyd who both scored 12.

Canadian Eric Chitty of West Ham, a 'resident' in Glasgow in 1945, topped the Overseas chart with 17 while Australian Bill Longley scored 16.

It was back to Northern League action on 11 September. A 20,000 crowd saw the Tigers give their best show of the season, a runaway 58–26 win over Birmingham. Lowther and Morton scored maximums and had solid support. Stobbart collected 8+2 while Crowther scored eight.

The most exciting race was a Clydesdale Cup heat featuring Lowther, Garland, Hart and Dell. Dell won on the line and went to win the final.

Even without captain Frank Hodgson, who was racing at Wembley in the British Championship Final, Middlesbrough were more than a match for Tigers on Thursday 12 September. The Bears' second strings overcame a determined Glasgow side 54–41 in this ACU Cup match.

Crowther top scored for Glasgow with 13, but lacked sufficient support to upset the Bears. Morton scored 9+1 and Stobbart took 7+1 from four completed races before his engine failed in his last outing. Lowther and Morton were both excluded for tapes offences while Stobbart and Garland both had engine failures in the same heat.

The meeting at White City on 18 September was a fixture filler. A Best Pairs event, on a heavy track, turned out an exciting finale. The meeting format did not bring all the pairs together during the regulation 20 heats and, as it transpired, the top two pairs who both gathered 23 points from five outings did meet.

The tie between Sheffield's Tommy Allott and Stan Williams from Sheffield and Middlesbrough's Frank Hodgson and Kid Curtis required an extra race to decide the winners.

Unfortunately, the race ended up level on points and the trophy winners were decided by a match race. After a thrilling four laps Hodgson won by inches from Williams. Tigers had three pairs, Lowther and Lack on 15 points, Crowther and Garland nine and Baird and Stobbart seven.

The Tigers visited Cleveland Park and again the Middlesbrough second strings, Gordon, Jack Hodgson and Godwin were praised for their efforts. Glasgow lost this Northern League fixture 52–30 on 19 September. The Tigers best were Lowther and Crowther, both with eight points. The reserves, Thomson and Peter Lloyd both failed to score.

Newcastle, even without Jeff Lloyd, injured the week before, were a stern test for the Tigers in an ACU Cup match at White City on 25 September, the home team winning 51–45.

Outstanding performer was Lowther with 14, but most applause went to Angus (William) McGuire, a 27-year-old former Army dispatch rider from Hamilton. McGuire, riding on a speedway bike for the first time in a meeting, did so spectacularly.

Crowther was not his usual self and lost the second half match race to Bradford's Ernie Price. He was a late replacement for Jeff Lloyd who had been due to meet Crowther for the Northern Match Race Championship. Only two races were necessary – Price won both. He also won the Sauchiehall Trophy.

Glasgow were no match for the Stars at Norwich on Saturday 28 September, losing in the ACU Cup 64–32. A couple of 5–1s early in the proceedings put the home side comfortably ahead and they romped home easy winners.

Only on rare occasions was a home man out of a points placing. While no Norwich rider collected a maximum, they were solid throughout. Morton showed his liking for The Firs circuit despite a fall and scored 11. Only Lowther, with eight, gave any real support. Crowther had a poor night with 2+1.

The fixture at Brough Park, on Monday 30 September was billed as friendly, not a Challenge match. Newcastle borrowed Bradford's Bill Longley to replace Jeff Lloyd and beat Glasgow 50–34. Syd Littlewood was on course for a maximum but fell in his last outing.

Lowther, who scored eight, was subdued and the best Tiger was Morton on nine. Crowther was the only other Tigers heat winner. The racing was described as being keen and the last heat provided the best action.

October

The local press headlined the match with Norwich on 2 October with "Wooden Spoon For Tigers" and described them receiving the 'wooden spoon' from the visitors. It was the last home Northern League match of the season and Norwich's 44–40 win was deserved. Glasgow won only three of the 14 heats while six were drawn.

The Tigers' faithful looked at the prospects of a draw before the last heat as Lowther and Morton could collect first and second places to give them five points. Lowther won to complete his full maximum, but Morton fell gifting the race points and the match to Norwich. He ended the match with eight points, the same as Crowther.

Sheffield's Tommy Allott, was a guest visitor. He won his special match race against Bert Spencer, Morton and Norman Evans of Newcastle and carried off the Visitors Cup beating Jay, Mills and Spencer.

The Glasgow Supporters' Cup saw Morton and Lowther came to grief in the final leaving Crowther and Stobbart to finish in that order.

The Tigers visited Norwich on Saturday 5 October in their last Northern League fixture. It was another expected home win for the Stars. This time the result was 51–32 in the Stars' favour. The Tigers managed only three race winners and only one heat win, but did enough to ensure that the Stars only had one unbeaten man, Ted Bravery with a paid maximum.

Crowther bounced back and received the plaudits for a 51–38 'friendly' win over First Division Bradford (Odsal) on 9 October. The third placed Division One team included captain Alex Statham, Ernie Price and Ron Clarke.

Crowther started off racing as a champion in the third heat using an engine that had been prepared by track mechanic Dick Stewart. After occupying third place he worked his way through against stiff opposition to collect his first win. He followed with a second, a first and a third.

Glasgow's success, however, lay in the inclusion of guest stars including Bill Kitchen, Wembley's captain and West Ham's Eric Chitty. Kitchen opened the meeting by attempting a new record for the four laps, but failed by 0.2 seconds to beat his own previous time of 82.8 seconds. He won the remaining honour, the Wooden Spoon Trophy by beating Chitty and Clarke.

The Tigers completed their ACU Cup matches with a 62–34 defeat at Birmingham on Saturday 12 October. Glasgow, with their traveling support giving voice to their *Rippety Roaring Tiger* song, faced a Birmingham team boosted by the return of Phil Hart and Stan Dell. They both made match winning scores.

Only Crowther threatened the home team's top guns. Even then he only won one race as he collected 10 points. Lowther and Stobbart were Tigers' only other race winners scoring 8+1 and five respectively. Wal Morton had a poor night after starting with an engine failure. Such was Brummies superiority they had 14 of the heat winners and took heat advantages in 10 heats.

Even although it was a 'friendly' fixture, the visiting Wembley Lions, the National League Champions, meant business on 16 October. It seemed that Wembley intended to rub the Tigers into the home dirt. They arrived at White City the day before "in high glee" and immediately "started to tell anyone willing to listen of their intentions".

The Wembley bandwagon was well equipped to ensure any breakdown could be addressed from a number of spare bikes or by using a full-scale mobile workshop. The team had five mechanics and their manager, Alex Jackson.

The Glasgow team was boosted by guests Eric Langton of Belle Vue and Wimbledon's Oliver Hart, but the duo did not shine as brightly as expected. As a consequence, Wembley won. Eric scored 6+1 and Oliver scored six. Hart had a solo run in the rerun of heat 11. The other three starters were all excluded. Crowther was the home team's top scorer on 7+1, Lowther got seven and Garland 5+2.

George Wilks, the often unsung hero of the Lions, was their star with a full maximum in their 43–38 win. Bob Wells, with a paid maximum, and Bill Kitchen were stars. Kitchen might have joined George Wilks, but for a last ride engine failure. Bill Gilbert and Alf Bottoms did little and reserves Charlie May and Bronco Wilson took a couple of extra rides apiece.

Bill Kitchen had better fortune in the second half winning the Farewell Trophy to bring Tigers' first season to a close.

The season closed for a Tigers side that had its highs and lows home and away but the net result was they never enjoyed a consistent enough spell to take any silverware. In the league, winning only four home meetings out of 10 saw them finish bottom of the table. However, there was potential for the future.

One rider Ian Hoskins tried to sign was an American called Clayton Glover, who he met in a carpark in Carlisle on his way to a meeting in England. However, the next week, he got a phone call from the Glasgow police. It turned out that Glover was a deserter from the American Army and would be arrested if he turned up at White City. He did not turn up and Hoskins made his excuses to the crowd.

Peter Morrish in his book *British Speedway Leagues 1946 – 1964* said that "No less than six home defeats put paid to Glasgow White City but strange to relate, Will Lowther, Joe Crowther, Wal Morton, Gruff Garland and Maurice Stobart all topped a hundred points. With Eddie Lack making a bright start many of the defeats were by a fairly narrow margin for the teams in the Northern League were reasonably well balanced."

8. 1947: National League racing

Reflecting the growth of the sport, the Northern League became the National League Second Division. However, apart from Bristol, all the teams White City would face were in the midlands or the north of England. The teams also competed in the British Speedway Cup. The new Third Division had teams from the south of England and the midlands. White City continued as the only Scottish team in the sport.

Glasgow's line up included Eddie Lack who bought a new Mosley framed JAP for the season, but he crashed out after one meeting. Bruce Venier, a Canadian who raced for Newcastle before the War lasted two meetings. He did not finish a race in 12 starts and promptly retired. Maurice Stobbart had retired. Veteran Wal Morton was expected to return, but did not. Glasgow retained Will Lowther, Joe Crowther and Gruff Garland. Scots Bill Baird, Bert Shearer, Angus McGuire and Billie Bates started in the line-up, but moved on as the Australian and New Zealand riders arrived. Baird had a spell at Bradford (Odsal) when they were having rider problems mid-season.

The initial cover for Eddie Lack was Wembley's Harold Sharpe. Maurice Stobbart came back to help out for one meeting. The first new Australians to arrive were Junior Bainbridge and Buck (Keith) Ryan. They joined the Tigers by the end of April. They had paid for their passage to England, and Ian Hoskins recalled: "They were high on optimism and low on experience. They came complete with Aussie bikes that had handlebars like the horns of a steer and thick, heavy rear tyres." Hoskins said that Bainbridge was "small in stature with a quick temper and an engaging smile." Ryan was more cautious on the track, having broken his neck in an accident in Australia.

Bill Murray had one outing, Fred Rogers a few and Ron Howes, a promised loanee from West Ham, never materialised. The next Australian was Bat (Bernard) Byrnes who came in early in May while Wigan born New Zealander Harold Fairhurst arrived towards the end of May. In early June Tigers added Norman Lindsay after he found top league activity at Harringay a bit too challenging.

April

A threatened riders strike was resolved and the new season opened in Glasgow on 9 April with a challenge match. Tigers used a race jacket with two vertical white stripes on a red background. The work on the track looked like it could cause problems at lunchtime, but the crew, directed by Johnnie Hoskins, completed it in time.

The fixture attracted 17,000 fans to watch Lowther and Garland, both score full maximums against Oliver Hart's Select. Hart's team had some riders from the new Wigan outfit who had been put in the Second Division probably for geographical reasons. Glasgow had Bruce Venier in the side, but he fell twice and was excluded for breaking the tapes once. Despite this, the Tigers won 43–39. Eddie Lack, recently demobbed from the RAF, scored a very promising 10. Venier, McGuire and Bates failed to score.

For Oliver's team, Jack Gordon was supported by Harry Welch but the rest, Oliver included, were poor. Bill Kitchen appeared in the second half, winning the match race against Gruff, Lowther and Hart, and the second half trophy.

The Tigers' heat leaders rode well at White City on 16 April, but the rest struggled and they lost 44–38 to Norwich Stars in the league. Bruce Venier fell in all his four outings and his second bad meeting saw him retire from the sport. Unlucky Lack crashed out in his opening ride and missed the rest of the campaign. He was in hospital until the end of May.

Lowther scored his second maximum of the season and Garland had his second double figure return with 10. Crowther returned to action with 7+4.

To fill the gaps, team manager Ian Hoskins was waiting for Australians Willie Waddell, who rode as 'Bonnie' Waddell. His full name was Rex King Waddell, but he did not come to Glasgow. Keith 'Buck' Ryan did join the Tigers. Glasgow had seven juniors: Bob Murray, Johnny Gordon, Niven McCreadie, Joe Arlet, Malcolm Riddell, George Wylie and G McLellan, but they could not provide the immediate boost needed.

Norwich were one of the better teams in the league, but already it seemed that Glasgow would struggle to climb up the league.

The team's injury problems were compounded on 23 April when Garland fell in his first outing and damaged his foot. A burst blood vessel ruled out further action and from then on, they struggled to contain Sheffield.

Missing Lack, the Glasgow called up Maurice Stobbart. He scored 5+1. Glasgow had Harold Sharpe, on loan from Wembley, at reserve and he scored 3+1. Lowther put up the greatest amount of resistance with nine points while Crowther scored 8+1.

Sheffield lost the services of Jack Bibby in the same heat as Garland. His severe shaking ruled him out of the meeting. They could afford to carry a passenger as White City specialist Tommy Allott scored a maximum. The visitors won easily, 52–31.

Lowther, with 10 points, and to a lesser extent, Crowther with eight, put up a fight against the home men at Owlerton the next night. However, the visitors, missing three established riders, were no match for the home side and lost 58–26. For the third time in a row, two Glasgow riders, McGuire and Jack Lloyd, (probably Peter Lloyd from Middlesbrough) failed to score. However, some reports have Bill Murray rather than Lloyd in the team.

Another defeat on the road for the Tigers happened on Saturday 26 April. Birmingham were a strong team at Perry Barr, and weakened visitors like Glasgow resulted in a 60–24 home win. Glasgow did not have a heat winner and drew only three heats.

Lowther was best Tiger on six points and Crowther only managed 5+1. Glasgow gave Fred Rogers, a future Norwich star, an outing but his one point probably failed to impress. Ian Hoskins probably regretted this in the future.

A narrow 43–41 win over newcomers Wigan at White City on 30 April, gave the Tigers their first league win of the season. This was due in part to their new signings: Ron 'Junior' Bainbridge and Keith 'Buck' Ryan. They gave the Glasgow fans new hope and served the team well. Buck, born at Mittagong in New South Wales, started out in 1939 and practiced during the war with Vic and Ray Duggan on the Mud Flats. He came to Britain on the advice of Charlie Spinks.

Crowther led the Tigers with a maximum, supported by Lowther with nine points, and Bill Baird on 8+1. Bill was a last heat hero, narrowly defeating the Warriors' Reg Lambourne for the odd, but vital point as he followed home Bert Shearer for a match winning 5–1.

May

Reports indicated that Ian Hoskins was trying out local grass track racers, including Arthur Fox, George Ingham, Sandy McQueen and Ron Hyman to bring on some Scottish talent. None of them, apart from Hyman, appear to have tried out speedway again.

In the match, the Tigers saw off league newcomers Bristol on 7 May. Lowther was again the star with a maximum, but he had sound support from the other riders. The next best were Crowther on 7+1 with Baird and Ryan on seven.

The Bulldogs, who had staged open meetings in 1946, started well, leading up to heat five, but in heat six an exclusion for Billy Hole allowed the Tigers to level with a 5–1 from Bainbridge and Bates. From then on, the Tigers eased in front and when Bates followed home Ryan in heat 12, the Tigers had the match won. Tigers closed by losing a 5–1 to Bristol's top two, Jack Mountford and Mike Beddoe. The final score was 48–36 to the Tigers.

Brave Australian leg trailer Garland came back prematurely on 14 May against Birmingham, riding with his injured foot in plaster (or 'wearing a stookie' in Scotland). He failed to score in two outings. His cause wasn't helped when he was excluded for crashing with Ernie Appleby in heat six. This time he hurt his other foot. Despite this handicap, the Tigers gave the Brummies a run for their money before losing 44–40. The lead had changed hands a few times and the visitors nosed ahead in heat 11 and stayed ahead to the end.

Heat 14 was raced to a conclusion before the Steward decided on a rerun without Laurie Packer who had, he decided, broken the tapes at the start of the race. Lowther missed the start in the first race, but made no mistakes in the rerun. Ian Hoskins was leaping up and down and throwing his hat into the air as the original race continued. At its conclusion he headed for the Steward's box and made his case in an animated manner, securing the rerun. Lowther scored another maximum, while Crowther added nine points. The fans watched bicycle polo in the interval, with Bonawe facing Royal Albert.

Around this time, it was announced that Carntyne would be used as a training track. However, there is no evidence that this actually happened.

Three Tigers were trying hard and scoring reasonably well, but the remainder, despite putting as much effort into their riding, did not give their team much of a boost. On 16 May, at Bristol, the Tigers had three men, Bainbridge, Baird and Bates on a duck. Lowther was the top Tiger with nine points, while Shearer, who dead heated with Mike Beddoe in heat 13, scored 7.5 and Crowther added seven. The Knowle track in Bristol was becoming a fortress for the Bulldogs. No Bristol rider managed double figures, but their strength in depth saw a 57.5–26.5 home win. Each Bulldog collected at least one bonus point.

Despite the big difference in the scores, the Tigers gave their hosts Norwich a tough time and provided fans with good racing. It was the team's third meeting in four days. Far from fit Garland returned on 17 May, replacing Bates. He only scored four points in this 58–25 league defeat. Bainbridge had another poor meeting and failed to score in two outings. Crowther was top scorer with seven points while Lowther managed six.

Jack Freeman, Norwich's reserve, made a hole in the stout wooden safety fence in one race but survived to complete his programmed rides. Roy Duke and Geoff Revett dead-heated and scored 4.5+1.5 each.

Glasgow had a new rider at reserve against Middlesbrough on 21 May, former Harringay rider, Australian Bernard 'Bat' Byrnes. He did well, scoring seven points. He replaced Baird in the Tigers line up. However, Lowther, who scored 13, apart, the Tigers had a poor night in this British Speedway Cup fixture at White City. Garland continued his comeback with eight.

The Bears were without Kid Curtis, who returned home to be with his sick child who thankfully made a full recovery. The 58–38 result suggests that the Bears were not weakened by his absence. The visitors moved into the lead in heat two and never looked back.

Glasgow pioneer and White City track official Norrie Isbister came back for a demonstration ride to show fans what he could do on a dirt track Douglas, but the expected appearance of Ian Hoskins' South American 'find' Jack Downs did not happen. He never got going at practice the morning before. However, a big find made an unspectacular debut. Gordon McGregor rode in the second half and came last. He spent many weeks in the second half before progressing to a place in the team.

Bill Baird surprisingly moved to First Division Bradford from early July until mid-August, when his progress was halted by a serious hand injury.

The Tigers travelled to Middlesbrough the next night, but returned pointless from a British Speedway Cup meeting, losing 62–33. Lowther lost to Frank Hodgson in his first race, but won his next four rides to gather 14 points. He also set the fastest time of the night. Next best was Garland with six points and Crowther, who completed only two rides, on five. The Bears had four riders on double figures, and the other four, Ossie Osborne apart, scored solidly. Lowther got no real support with four Tigers on two points and one failed to score. The new Australians were still trying to find their feet.

Crowther was injured in a fall and was expected to be out of action for at least three months. Thankfully this was an overestimate.

The Glasgow May Monday meeting on 26 May was a best pairs meeting. It went to the wire because two pairs tied at the end of the 20 heats. Ron Johnson, and Billie Bates collected 19 points, with Johnson scoring a maximum 15. They were matched by a Tigers pair. Bainbridge with a respectable eight and fellow Australian Garland on 11, gave them 19 points which earned them a run-off for the trophy.

Johnson won, but Bates fell leaving both pairs tied 3–3. It was decided that the outcome would be settled by a run off with the Johnson facing Garland. Johnson was a star at New Cross, and he took the flag to give the native Scots the trophy. The difference between the Glasgow and New Cross tracks was substantial. The Old Kent Road track was known as 'The Frying Pan' and was 262 yards long, while White City was 430 yards.

Wembley's Bill Kitchen scored 14, but unfortunately for him, his partner Harold Sharpe only scored four and the Wembley duo finished joint third. The Tigers had two other pairs, Lowther and Ryan on 17 taking fourth and Byrnes and Fairhurst, making his debut, on 12

Glasgow had no answer to the might of Sheffield who were ahead from heat two in a British Speedway Cup match at White City on 28 May. Seven heats were drawn but the visitors won the rest bar two to take the match 54–42. Lowther was in great form with 14 points, but the rest did not follow his lead. Glasgow's efforts were not helped by Crowther's absence due to the injury sustained at Middlesbrough. Next best for Tigers were Byrnes and Garland, both on six.

The second half reserves event featured the tall Wigan born Kiwi Harold Fairhurst and he finished last in his only outing.

Sheffield expected Glasgow to be a pushover after their win the night before, but events on 29 May did not turn out that way. The visitors rode well without ever really causing the home team problems. Sheffield won 56–40 in the British Speedway Cup. Sheffield had three good scorers and another three scored soundly. Glasgow included debutante Harold Fairhurst at second reserve and he scored 3+1 from three outings. He replaced Scottish rider Bert Shearer. Lowther was the only visitor to score double figures with 13, but a long weak tail trailed after him.

The following evening, the Tigers travelled to Bristol, this time for a British Speedway Cup fixture. The Knowle's small track had many Tigers all at sea. Bristol won 59–37 with relative ease. There was another first-class display from Lowther, with 11+1. Fairhurst took extra rides, replacing opening race faller Ryan. He gave Lowther sound backing with 7+3, while Garland scored six. Yet again, the Tigers had a long tail while Bulldogs were strong throughout. Glasgow went behind from heat two, and apart from a glimmer of resistance in heat four, they could not catch up.

The fixture compilers were not kind to Glasgow. The team had been to Sheffield and Bristol before their fourth match in as many days at Birmingham. They did not fare any better in Birmingham on Saturday 31 May. The strong Birmingham team did not ride as well as expected, but repeated the previous night's score, 59–37. This was despite them trying out new team pairings at Perry Barr. The home fans, used to big home wins, had expected more.

The highlight for Tigers was Bill Baird's heat 11 burst from the back. He came through to win as the leader of a very close race. His seven points was one of the more memorable efforts for the man from Forth in Lanarkshire. However, it was almost a Tigers one-man band as Lowther impressed with some fine riding and a 15-point maximum.

The Brummies gave former Wimbledon rider Ken Brett his debut and he passed muster. His new team mates all scored solidly with no standouts. Maybe not a memorable win for Birmingham, but another away match for the Tigers to forget.

June

After a Sunday off, the Glasgow tour continued at Newcastle on the Monday night. The score of 63–45 to the Diamonds did not reflect the quality of the racing on 2 June. Lowther showed his love of Brough Park with an immaculate 18 point maximum. Unfortunately, as was often the case, he failed to find the support necessary produce a result. The next best Tiger was Byrnes on seven points. Despite his experience Garland, on five, was not piling up the points and clearly Glasgow still missed Crowther's fire power. The new overseas riders were still finding their feet and not giving Ian Hoskins the boost for the team he wanted. The Diamonds built up a good lead as the night progressed in this National Trophy first leg tie

Back home on 4 June, at the end of an eight-day tour which gave them two nights off, Tigers started with a points mountain to climb to reach the next round of the National Trophy. Unfortunately, after giving their best shot, they won 60–46 on the night and were eliminated narrowly on aggregate 109–105. They struggled until heat 14 when a 5–1 from Baird and Fairhurst set them on the victory trail.

Yet another Australian, Norman Lindsay, joined the team, taking their Australia and New Zealand contingent to six, over the decreed limit. Norman had ridden in the UK before the War, and made a sound debut with an impressive 11+2. The other Australians were still, Garland apart, having problems with White City. Only Garland scored a respectable nine points. Byrnes scored three and Ryan 3+1. Lindsay, with Byrnes plus £250 had become Tigers while 1946 skipper Wal Morton became a Harringay asset. Glasgow would receive another £500 if Morton averaged six points a match, a target he failed to achieve.

Lowther dropped a point to Norman Evans, earmarked for Glasgow in 1946 before ending at Newcastle, who had a poor night due to engine problems. It was the efforts of Wilf Jay that kept Diamonds in the cup.

Ken Le Breton, riding for Newcastle, but destined to set Glasgow alight in 1949, made his White City debut. He scored 6+1 from five rides, but better was to come from him.

Middlesbrough's Frank Hodgson dominated the Glasgow round of the British Riders' Championship with a maximum 15 on 11 June. He and the runner up, Norwich's Bert Spencer on 14, proved too good for Tigers' Lowther who was third with 13. Wigan's Dick Geary was fourth with 12. Will's efforts at Glasgow and in the other rounds carried him through to the next round. The other Tigers in the line-up were Garland, Byrnes and Lindsay with eight, five and two points respectively. Lindsay replaced Tamworth's Vic Pitcher, who despite manager Hoskins' pleas to the Speedway Control Board, did not bank qualifying points.

Another trip to Newcastle on Monday 16 June saw a creditable Tigers' performance. They just missed out, losing 43–41 in a league match. The Tigers were four points down going into heat 14 and needed a 5–1 for a draw, but Baird could not pass Doug McLachlan to join Lowther, who completed another Brough Park maximum. Glasgow held a lead early on, but Norman Evans and Grant combined for their second 5–1 in heat 10 to put the Diamonds on track for victory.

After scoring two points in his first outing, Lindsay had to pull out after three rides due to a recurrence of malaria. Garland with 6+1 and Byrnes on six were the next best Tigers.

The shoots of revival continued to sprout. Lowther, on a new bike, scored a maximum on 18 June and his efforts inspired the team to give the Tigers a 45–38 League victory. The teams had an equal number of race winners, but the six bonus points to two in Glasgow's favour reflected the Tigers' team riding. Newcastle kept the scores close until the end, but not enough to win.

The Tigers' fans showed their appreciation of Lowther's efforts by presenting him with a wallet of notes. He had opened the match by winning heat one, a race that saw Ryan and Alec Grant crash into each other. Facing only one opponent, Norman Evans, Will had his work cut out to beat the experienced Diamond.

The Tigers all scored well with none except Lowther really shining. Garland scored nine and Byrnes scored 7+1. Ryan fell in his opener, then managed only one point from his three other rides. Neither side recorded a 5–1 heat win; eight races were drawn. Also unusual was a second half handicap event.

Lancashire side Wigan Warriors visited Scotland for the first time on 25 June on British Speedway Cup business. They had the Tigers' fans worried for much of the match. The Warriors were 40–38 up after heat 13, but this stunned the Tigers into action and two 5–1s won the match by the end of heat 15. The last heat 4–2 was a bonus for the Tigers' fans.

Despite regularly missing the starts, Lowther scored a 15-point maximum. He stood head and shoulders above his team mates. Wigan's top rider, Dick Geary, gave Lowther his toughest test. They met in the opening and closing heats with Lowther winning both. Byrnes was next best Tiger with 9+1 while the others chipped in enough for a 52–45 win and the Cup points on offer.

Yet again, Ian Hoskins tried out a second half handicap event. Lowther came from the back to win before continuing to clean-up of the meeting by winning his heat and the final of the Star-Spangled Scratch Race.

A trip to Cleveland Park in Middlesbrough was always a daunting prospect for any team in this era. It was no surprise on 26 June that the relatively inexperienced riders representing Glasgow would find it tough.

Yet again, it was experienced Lowther, assisted by the improving Byrnes, who were the only two to take the fight to the rampant Bears. This time the Tigers managed a respectable 28 in response to Bears' 56 in this league fixture. Lowther scored mine while Byrnes scored seven. None of the rest scored more than Bears' second lowest scorer, Bill Wilson. The Tigers had no real answer to Frank Hodgson, Wilf Plant and Kid Curtis as the powerful Bears took the flag in 12 of the 14 heats. Middlesbrough were unbeaten at home in the league, but on their second visit Glasgow got much closer to a match win.

Left: Keith 'Buck' Ryan had three seasons with the Tigers, from 1947 to 1949. The fans were disappointed that he decided to stay in Australia rather than return to Glasgow.

Below: Programmes from the 1947 season. The one for 6 August is Britain versus Overseas. The picture of Ian Hoskins on the right shows him wearing one of his famous hats. They were frequently burned by his riders to celebrate victories.
(Programme covers courtesy Duncan Luke)

July

After a long break, Crowther had a try out on Tuesday 1 July before declaring himself fit for a Challenge match with First Division Bradford the next day. He managed to score 5+1 and had two last places.

The Boomerangs arrived three men short, including heat leaders Alec Statham and Ernie Price. Bradford borrowed Fairhurst, dropped to make way for Crowther, Bates and Shearer to make up the Tigers side. Bradford's two heat leaders, Ron Clarke and Oliver Hart had poor nights, so the Tigers won more easily than expected, 48.5–35.5.

Lowther scored yet another maximum, while Bainbridge scored 7+3 and followed home his team partner in all his races. Glasgow could have won by more, but lost Garland. He was heading for a paid maximum, but fell heavily after contact with Ryan in heat 13, injuring his arm. He was taken to hospital, but went home after treatment.

In the second half, Norrie Isbister hoped to demonstrate leg trailing. He wanted to race fellow pioneer Jimmie Pinkerton, who rode in the first event at White City in 1928, but Jimmie declined to return to the track.

Crowther's return seemed to boost the Tigers in their home league match with Bristol on 9 July. He contributed 10+1. Lowther scored another maximum and, with Byrnes and Bainbridge starting to give support, they won 48–36. Fairhurst, in the side covering for Garland, scored a reserve's maximum six from two rides, another notable contribution.

The Bulldogs fell behind in heat three, and managed only one heat victory, which was when the meeting was beyond them.

Lowther had an almost unbeaten run but Byrnes beat him in the qualifying races for the Glasgow Tigers Club Trophy. Lowther had the last laugh. He qualified for the final as the fastest loser and completed his night by winning it.

The Tigers put on a good show the next night at Middlesbrough in the league. Bainbridge posted a good score of 10 to top the Tigers' score chart. He took a couple of notable scalps, Frank Hodgson and Wilf Plant. Only Lowther, who scored nine, made any significant contributions to Tigers total in a 46–38 defeat. The Tigers certainly rattled their hosts with an opening heat 5–1 and had heat advantages in four more races. This was not expected by the home fans. Only Sheffield scored more at Middlesbrough than the Tigers' 38 points.

In 1947 Wigan speedway was on Saturday nights at Poolstock Stadium. Sadly, it didn't catch on and closed until 1960 at the end of the season. On 12 July, the Warriors gave Glasgow a good beating. The Warriors had Jack Gordon and Norman Hargreaves unbeaten by a Tiger. Dick Geary, an immaculate looking rider with Brylcreem shinny hair, and Percy Brine on the ball. The 56–27 result reflected the margin between the two sides.

Lowther was Glasgow's top scorer with seven points. The Tigers had only three race winners. Behind from the off, the Tigers fell further behind as the match progressed. It was Wigan's biggest home win of the season.

The Warriors visited Glasgow on a wet 16 July and, on a track with liberal sprinkling of pools of water, times were 20 seconds slower than usual. However, the tables were well and truly turned. After 14 heats Glasgow won 56– 27, the same score to the home team as in Lancashire. Fairhurst was promoted to the team over Ryan who responded with a reserve's maximum. Paired with Lowther, Fairhurst had a tough spot to fill, but scored 4+2 as he followed Lowther, who scored 11, home twice. Crowther scored 10+1. It was the Tigers' biggest home win of the season. Maybe both teams were not familiar with the other's tracks. Wigan was 321 yards compared to White City's 430.

Norman Hargreaves beat Lowther in the opening heat, despite Lowther's efforts to pass him. The Tigers had a good pay night. Wigan's Don Houghton had a tough night, crashing in three of his rides. In one his bike appeared to be pulled from under him and he followed it sliding for a distance before somersaulting a couple of times. Thankfully he got up and walked away.

Ian Hoskins, concerned about the Warriors' drawing powers, booked Alec Statham and Oliver Hart for the second half.

Glasgow faced old rivals Newcastle Diamonds on 23 July in a British Speedway Cup match. The weather was no better than the week before and the wet track produced some thrills and spills. Despite track conditions, Newcastle gave the Tigers a run for their money, nullifying an early Tigers lead to be level by the end of heat nine. After drawing heat 10, the Tigers pushed ahead and a couple of 4–2s in the last two heats clinched the match 51–44.

Lowther, who had been at Wimbledon on Monday, where he rode poorly in a British Riders' Championship round, played an important role for Tigers. He shepherded Fairhurst home in heat 10 for a vital 5–1 This moved Tigers ahead at a vital juncture.

Crowther was taken to the Glasgow Royal Infirmary following a rib-breaking fall in heat five. His fall effectively handed a 5–1 to the Diamonds, but it may have stirred Lindsay into one of his best performances. He was the top scoring Tiger with 11+1. His best support came from Lowther on 10+1. Byrnes was consistent with four second places. Shearer and Ryan took extra rides, replacing Crowther, but they could not replace his fire power.

Lowther had been racing on the continent at Marienbad (Marianske Lazne) in Czechoslovakia where he finished runner-up. He returned to White City on 30 July, but was without his bikes. He was flown up to Scotland in a Tiger Moth by West Ham's Malcolm Craven. The pair got lost a couple of times, but eventually made it to Renfrew Airport. His borrowed equipment let him down badly but, thanks to the second strings, Tigers managed a 55–41 victory over Norwich.

The Tigers had Lindsay, Byrnes and Fairhurst to thank while Phil Clarke and Paddy Mills were the twinkling Stars. Lindsay with 10 did well while Byrnes did a little better with 11+2.

In the second half, Gordon McGregor beat established team riders from both teams, letting Ian Hoskins know that he was almost ready for a team spot.

August

A crowd of 23,000 watched Britain defeat an Overseas side including English born Phil 'Tiger' Hart and Fairhurst, in Glasgow on 6 August. It had an unusual format, raced over 20 heats with two reserves races in the body of the match. Normally an international is raced over 18 heats. Britain won 68–52. It was a one-off international match, not recognised as a 'test match' and not part of a series.

The star for the Overseas team was Australian pioneer Max Grosskreutz who lost his unbeaten record due to an engine failure in heat 11. He scored 15 points and featured in the best race of the night, heat 16. He and Oliver Hart raced for four laps neck-and-neck. He had an unhappy experience when winning the second-half Empire Trophy. His bike spewed out methanol over his leathers after the fuel cap fell off.

The Tigers' Lindsay was second highest Overseas scorer with 10 points while teammates in the Overseas team were Byrnes, Ryan and Fairhurst.

For Britain, Lowther top scored with 16 and his partner Crowther scored right, following Lowther home in four of their six outings. The other two heat-leaders for Britain were

Wembley's Bill Kitchen with 14+2, who always scored well at White City and Bradford's spectacular leg-trailer Oliver Hart with 12, who knew the track well. Bill Baird and Bert Shearer were reserves for Britain.

The Tigers continued their winning ways in Glasgow on 13 August with a 47–37 league victory over Sheffield. The Tigers dominated the heat winners but Sheffield, despite a dearth of first places, often filled the minor placings and made the score look respectable. Despite being dry the track conditions were reported as 'poor'. The Tigers took until the end of heat 12, when Bainbridge and Shearer posted a 5–1, to put daylight between the teams.

Lowther did not have things all his own way. Both Tommy Bateman and Len Williams beat him before he won two races for another double figure score of 10. Crowther, on nine, and Byrnes, on eight, were his main backing, but Ryan, on another reserves' maximum six points, showed he was ready for elevation to the team.

Wembley riders Split Waterman and Horatio 'Bronco' Wilson rode in the second half. Waterman beat Lowther in a match race and in the heats and final of the St Enoch Trophy. Bronco, who was fatally injured at Harringay two days later, beat Byrnes in a match race. Bronco Wilson was the only Wembley rider to be killed in a track accident after the Second World War.

On Friday 15 August, the Bulldogs again ripped the Tigers apart at Bristol. Only Lowther offered any real resistance with eight points. He was Glasgow's only heat winner, beating Billy Hole and Cyril Quick in heat seven. The Bulldogs won 57–27 and had the league points effectively sown up by heat 10. Again, Glasgow had a lengthy tail.

Had Roger Wise not had a miserable night, the Tigers would have been lucky to top 20. However, to be fair, Tigers were not the only team that took big beatings at Knowle Stadium.

Another big defeat for the Tigers came at Birmingham the next night. This time the score was 59–24 to the home team. The Tigers might have done better, but for an injury to Lowther in a crash, in which he wrecked his bike. He was contesting the lead with Bob Lovell in the opening race when the crash occurred. He also sustained a badly cut face and badly bruised thigh. Without his scoring power, it was always going to be an uphill struggle. Byrnes was also out of luck because he was pushed off line and parted from his machine by Phil Hart in heat seven. Hart was excluded, but the third place point was lost with Byrnes lying on the track. A suspected broken nose ruled him out of the rest of the match. Glasgow could only field one rider in the last heat.

This match saw the Tigers debut of Gordon McGregor, who replaced Shearer at second reserve. He managed just one point as the Tigers' lone representative in the last heat. The best Tiger was Crowther with eight while Fairhurst scored six.

Led by Lowther with 14 points and Byrnes on 12+1, the Tigers repulsed the hard riding Bristol Bulldogs on 20 August. Lowther was again on a borrowed bike, but this time top scored. Byrnes was impressive with 12+1 and Lindsay scored 8+1. Bainbridge was still scraping a few points, but his time would come.

The Bulldogs led briefly after heat 11 and were in with a shout until the end of heat 13, but the Tigers scored 12 in the last three heats to win 54–42 in the British Speedway Cup.

In the second half, Gordon McGregor raced against Lancastrian Jock Shead. The Linlithgow born Scot won. Jock was based at Bradford and was probably present on Johnnie Hoskins's request to compare the two riders.

Glasgow faced Birmingham in the British Speedway Cup on 27 August and sent them home on the wrong end of a 62–34 scoreline. Lowther scored an immaculate 15-point maximum, but it was Shearer who shone with 11 points.

Left: Gruff Garland, a Glasgow Tigers stalwart of the early post-War era.

He had greatness 'thrust upon him' because he had to deputise for Ryan who crashed in heat one and was advised by the track doctor to sit the night out. Thankfully his injuries only ruled him out for the rest of the meeting. Shearer was entered in the nominated heat where he repaid Ian Hoskins by taking third. Byrnes continued his good form with 10+1; fellow Australian Lindsay scored nine and Bainbridge also had a good night on 7+1.

The Tigers management must have considered the Brummies might be poor fare so the second half featured match races between First Division Australians Max Grosskreutz and Aub Lawson. Grosskreutz won by two races to one and went on to win the Silver Sword.

The Tigers were back in Wigan on Saturday 30 August for a league meeting. Jack Gordon set a fast time in the opening heat as he beat Lowther. Glasgow sparkled briefly in heat two with Bainbridge and Byrnes, who rode spectacularly, combining for a 5–1 which put Tigers ahead. Their advantage lasted until the end of the next heat and Wigan levelled the scores in heat four. The Warriors went on to win 45–39. This was a considerable improvement on their last visit to Wigan.

The Tigers had a run of four race winners late in the meeting, but without support they counted for little. Wigan secured their win with a last heat 4–2 by Dick Geary and Norman Hargreaves over Lowther and Crowther. A Tigers 5–1 could have secured a draw. Lowther and Bainbridge were the top Tigers on eight points each

September

The home meeting on 3 September saw Glasgow beat league leaders Middlesbrough 48–36. It was the Tigers' first league win against the Teeside team since the War. The Bears were a bit more subdued than usual. Lowther top scored with 10 and had good support from Crowther and Bainbridge, both on 9+1. In the second half, the fans enjoyed the appearance of top star Vic Duggan who defeated Max Grosskreutz in a couple of match races. Duggan was enticed by a couple of rounds of golf at St Andrews. Fellow second half star, Harringay's Australian Jack Arnfield, also visited St Andrews. He took home a souvenir tartan shirt home from Glasgow.

Sadly, both Duggan and Grosskreutz had bike problems in the Trophy event. However, the presence of the top stars saw a 25,000 crowd attend.

Saturday 6 September saw the Tigers in East Anglia scoring 33 points in reply to the Stars' 63 in the British Speedway Cup. Ryan was the top Tiger with 8+1 while Lowther scored seven and Byrnes 5+1. Ryan and Lowther rode together in the opening heat and emerged with a

4–2 win. However, by heat four the Stars were in front and stretched their lead in all but three heats. The Tigers had one race winner, Ryan in heat one, in 16 heats. Glasgow's Australians, Lindsay and Bainbridge did not manage well on the Firs track.

Norwich came to White City on 10 September seeking League points. They found the Tigers in good form and returned to East Anglia defeated 50–34.

Without Spencer, the Stars were not as strong as usual. However, this does not detract from the Tigers' fine win over their hard riding opponents. Lowther, Crowther and Byrnes gave Glasgow a platform for victory. Lowther delivered another maximum and cleaned up the second half. Crowther and Byrnes scored nine points each. The Stars only won one heat, the 12th race, when Bainbridge fell.

Ken Le Breton had an outing in the second half winning a match race event against Ryan two to one, but bombed out of the second half trophy heat.

The next home meeting on 17 September saw a good result for the Tigers, but the racing was quite poor in an almost run-away home win for Tigers. Birmingham were beaten 54–29. The Tigers' win was driven by maximum man Lowther and Bainbridge, who won three races then collected a third place. Ryan and Byrnes were involved in crashes. Ryan collided with Brian Wilson and was carried off, but came back for his last outing to complete a three-point return. The accident happened when Wilson's machine snapped a chain as he led Ryan in heat eight. Wilson stopped in front of Ryan who could not avoid him. Byrnes scored 7+2 from his three completed rides and reached the second half trophy final.

Around this time, Bainbridge was stopped by a Glasgow speed cop. Worried he had done something wrong, he approached the officer with some trepidation. However, things turned out fine as all the speed cop wanted was Junior's autograph.

The Northern Match Race Challenge Cup event, instigated by Ian Hoskins, featuring Will Lowther, who had been nominated as the first holder, and Sheffield's Tommy Bateman. It was a forerunner to the Silver Helmet competition. Lowther's good form had secured the nomination to face Bateman and he won with ease twice in this first round.

The Tigers arrived in Wigan on a wet and miserable Saturday, 20 September. The fixture attracted 8,000 hardy souls who watched what turned out to be a tight contest.

Tigers' Lowther and Crowther opened with a 4–2 and held the lead until heat four when Jack Gordon and Ron Hart combined for a 5–1. Wigan forged ahead to an eight-point lead by the end of heat 10. The Tigers rallied and were just two down going in to the last heat.

Dick Geary and Norman Hargreaves faced Byrnes and Lowther in the final heat, but sadly for the Tigers the home duo scored a 5–1 giving the Warriors a 51–45 win in this British Speedway Cup fixture.

On 24 September, the Bears blew a big hole in the 14-match unbeaten home run the Tigers had built up over the last few months. The visitors showed the form that justified their league winning credentials. Glasgow were without Ryan who was travelling south to catch the boat home to Australia. However, fellow countryman Byrnes, booked to sail on the same boat, stayed and faced the Bears. He scored 11, dropping his only point to Wilf Plant.

The regular top rider on each side, Tigers' Lowther and Bears' Frank Hodgson, both had an off-night scoring seven and 5+1 respectively, but the Bears had more riders in form than the Tigers. At the end, the score was 48–36 for the Yorkshire outfit. They had taken the lead in heat four and widened the gap from heat seven onwards.

Crowther injured his leg in a heat 11 crash and was replaced by Fairhurst. However, by that time the Bears were six ahead and the 5–1 they scored gave them a 10-point lead. McGregor made his home debut, scored 1+1 and again won the Reserves Promotion Race.

Will Lowther did well at Wigan on 27 September, defeating Dick Geary in a track record time to retain his Northern Match Race title.

Glasgow travelled to Tyneside to face the Diamonds in the league on Monday 29 September. This was a hard-fought contest with the Tigers getting the better it from heat three onwards. The Tigers, without Ryan and Byrnes, called up Maurice Stobbart but the race rusty Cumbrian failed to score. Shearer had one of his best away showings with eight. Lowther, the doyen of Brough Park scored 11 – Wilf Jay headed him home in heat nine. Lindsay scored 10.5. In heat three he and Jay crossed the line together and the Steward could not split them. Doug McLachlan prevented Lindsay from completing an unbeaten return. The Tigers took a well-earned 44.5–39.5 victory.

Newcastle could have salvaged a win in the last heat, but Lowther took the vital race win.

October

The win at Brough Park should have given Tigers a boost going into their match against the Diamonds two days later. Instead, their home defeat fired up the visitors to take the league points. Newcastle took the lead in heat two and Glasgow could not get back into the match. The Diamonds were set for a draw by the end of heat 12 and could not lose after heat 13. A Tigers' 4–2 saw the final score as 44–40 for the Diamonds.

Lowther was best Tiger with a below par eight and the level of support that should have come from Crowther, Lindsay and Bainbridge, never materialised. Best supporting rider was Shearer with 7+2 as partner to Lowther. He included the scalps of Wilf Jay and Norman Evans – no mean feat. McGregor recorded his first race win for Tigers. Glasgow gave a first outing to East Anglian Nobby Downham who scored a couple of points from reserve.

Will Lowther retained his Northern Match Race Championship thanks to his 2–0 win over Wigan's Dick Geary, who won the Friendship Trophy from Bainbridge, Jay and Lowther.

A challenge match against the North of England on 8 October produced some good racing and a 46–38 home win. The visitors would have done better, but for bike problems. Bradford's Ernie Price was a late replacement for Kid Curtis and he was the only real star in the scratch visiting side which included three Scots – Baird, McGuire and Bates. Even then, he fell to Crowther in a two-lap match race.

Lowther had another poor night and Lindsay on 11 and Crowther on 10+1 rode well, Lowther and Bainbridge each contributed 7+1.

Sheffield's incentive of a £200 prize for the League second place spurred them on to beat Glasgow on 9 October. Lowther, a last ride faller, on seven points and Crowther, on the same score, put up stout resistance but lacked support. Crowther started poorly, then posted two of Glasgow's three race wins to make his contribution more respectable. Sheffield won this battle of the Tigers 57–27.

Always a hard place for visitors, the Norwich riders again showed their supremacy on Saturday 11 October. The Stars made amends for a crushing defeat at Middlesbrough earlier in the week and the Tigers were unfortunately in the wrong place at the wrong time. All 14 race winners in this 61–32 league defeat wore the green and yellow of Norwich.

Crowther was the best Tiger with seven points, while Lindsay scored five and Fairhurst 4+1. Crowther nearly won heat 11, but was overhauled on the last lap by Powell who scored a maximum. The Tigers had completed their second League campaign and for the second time collected the wooden spoon.

Whatever the reason, familiarity with the track or local rivalry, the Tigers who raced at

Brough Park on Monday 13 October were much better than they had been at Sheffield and Norwich. In this curtain closer in the British Speedway Cup, they kept the Diamonds within striking distance for most of the match before losing 50–46.

Norman Evans beat Lowther in the opening heat, but he was the only Diamond to do so. Lowther showed his liking for the circuit and won his remaining four rides. Crowther, another familiar with Brough Park, scored 12 and Lindsay took a respectable nine points.

A seven-man Tigers, boosted by Alec Statham of Bradford, took on a side skippered by Belle Vue's Jack Parker. Hoskins juggled his assets and put out a couple of reasonable sides which brought down the White City curtain for 1947 on 15 October.

Statham was an excellent guest with a maximum. This included a couple of wins over Jack Parker, who was no slouch at White City. Statham then beat Parker in a match race and went on to annex the Silver Sword Trophy. The Tigers won 45–38.

Bainbridge, who decided to winter in Britain, had fun in the last meeting at Bradford. Dressed as a woman he gave the crowd a few heart stopping moments as he played his part in another Johnnie Hoskins stunt. The "lady's" identity was revealed at the end of the stunt which had fooled a lot of people including the local track announcer.

9. 1948: Improving

Since 1947 had, like 1946, been a wooden spoon year, the Tigers were determined not to repeat the experience in this season which saw the revival of the great inter-city contests of the past. The 1948 campaign feature the National League Division Two and the Anniversary Cup which celebrated the birth of the sport in 1928. The Cup format was the same as the National league fixtures up to heat 14. Heat 15 featured the reserves and heat 16 was a nominated riders race.

The Second Division was still predominantly based in the English midlands and north and Scotland, along with Bristol. Fleetwood replaced Wigan and Edinburgh's return made it a nine team league. The return of Edinburgh, based at Old Meadowbank, meant that derby matches were another attraction.

The First Division still had seven teams, five in London plus Belle Vue and Bradford. Twelve teams competed in Division Three, mainly in the English south and midlands, with Hull and Wombwell providing a northern presence.

March

The Glasgow folk must have relished the prospect of taking on their capital city rivals for the first time since 1939. The season opened with Glasgow facing their old rivals, Newcastle Diamonds, in the league on Wednesday 31 March. They won 47–37. Will Lowther was in the line-up along with Fairhurst, Crowther, Bainbridge, Lindsay, Ryan, and McGregor from the 1947 squad. The Tigers added Australian Jack Martin, also known as Raymond Urquhart. Lowther scored 9+1, but had been considering retiring due to pressure of work. Lindsay scored the same and Harold Fairhurst added 8+1. Jack Martin made his debut, but failed to score with a last place and a fall. Crowther also fell a couple of times, through trying too hard and entering the bends too fast.

The meeting was nearly postponed because it had rained during the day. However, the rain stopped and the sun allowed the track to dry. Wilf Jay was the Diamonds' best and was unbeaten by a Tiger, but the other riders, Norman Evans and Alec Grant apart, fared poorly.

The 14,000 crowd saw non-smoker Crowther win a gold cigarette case, the first of his many second half trophies in 1948.

April

Glasgow experienced their first defeat in 1948 from the powerful Middlesbrough team at Cleveland Park on 1 April. The Bears, seemingly as strong as they were in 1947, had four riders with paid maximums and reserve Bill Wilson was also unbeaten by a Tiger. It resulted in a 61–22 home win. The Bears, on the basis of this display, looked like carrying all before them again.

Lowther challenged some of the home riders. The Tigers did not have a race winner. Jack Martin rode and was excluded in heat eight. Gordon McGregor was given his rides. The Bears scored five 5–1 heat wins and the score was 25–5 before Tigers managed to limit the damage. Herby King was lucky to escape serious injury in heat eleven when he was flung over the handlebars when Bainbridge fell just in front of him

The Tigers raced a team branded as Wigan at White City on 7 April. It was a wet night and many regular fans stayed away fearing a rain-off. There were still hopes that Wigan's race night problems would be resolved and they would again ride at Poolstock. Unfortunately, that did not happen. The team moved to Highbury Avenue Sports Stadium in Fleetwood.

Australian Frank Malouf made his debut for Wigan, thrilling the crowd with his efforts. He came from the back before his chain locked up first time out. Then he ended up in the fence, after scraping round it in his second outing. Crowther was the Tigers' hero with his never-say-die efforts. He collected a maximum in this 49–34 Tigers' league win. Lindsay scored a paid maximum and the main support came from Ryan and Fairhurst who scored 8+1 and seven respectively. Jack Martin opened his account for Tigers with 2+1 in heat eight.

The Warriors opened with a heat win, but fell behind after heat three and a couple heat wins apart, did not set the heather alight.

The visiting Tigers did not relish the slick granite racing surface at Owlerton and it showed in their performance the next night. Sheffield, who seemed to have the correct machine gearing, won 55–28. Lowther and Crowther, the old hands in the Scottish side, both scored 6+1 to head their team's scorers. The Tigers' riders were fined five times for tape breaking.

Crowther ran into bike problems before his first outing at White City on 14 April and had to use the track spare. He later returned to his own mount to complete his paid maximum 11+1. Glasgow seemed to be cruising, but a late fight back by Birmingham made the score a respectable 48–36. Bainbridge had the ride of the night coming from last to first in heat 12. In his opening ride, he had set a near track record time, striving to stay ahead of team mate Crowther. He broke the tapes at the start of heat nine and was excluded.

Graham Warren, 'The Blond Bombshell', a recent arrival from Australia, made his White City debut. He took two races to get the hang of the track before winning twice. He topped the visitors' scores with 10

The second half featured Wilhelm Szeja (pronounced Sheya) from Silesia in Poland where he had earned a reputation as a wrestler. He was around for a couple of seasons, but never made it beyond the second half. R. McIntosh had an outing – presumably Alf – along with Eric 'The Bishop' Liddell.

The opening of the new Edinburgh team at Old Meadowbank took place on 17 April before a crowd of 14,000 to watch an encounter between the two rival cities. It ended with the Tigers taking the league points and a Tigers' track record holder. Lowther's time in heat one was the best of the night.

The Monarchs' misfortune started in heat one when Bill Maddern and Lack crashed together, allowing Fairhurst to nab third spot. Crowther gave Lowther good support with 10+1. Lowther scored 11. There were no other star performances but it was a solid showing from the rest, Bainbridge and Martin excepted, who scored 1 and 1+1.

Glasgow led from the off and, apart from conceding a couple of 4–2s, they stretched their lead to 44–39 win. The Monarchs could have won it near the end but Lowther and Crowther team-rode with Crowther guarding his team mate for the vital 5–1.

Maddern and former Tiger Bill Baird were best for the Monarchs. The other former Tigers, Eddie Lack and Bert Shearer scored 6+2 and 2+1 respectively.

The Tigers may have been depressed before the start on 21 April. Bat Byrnes had decided to stay in Australia due to pressure of work. The Tigers dropped Martin and re-introduced Angus (William) McGuire, but the Hamilton man failed to score.

The league match against Norwich went to a dramatic last heat decider with the scores tied at 39–39. Bert Spencer led and the Tigers tucked in behind. Freeman moved in on

Crowther and in the last lap knocked him off. Freeman finished third with Crowther on the track, but the Stars' Australian was excluded for dangerous riding and Crowther was awarded third. Under new rules, the meeting official was unable to award a point as in 1947, because Crowther could not finish the race.

By awarding Crowther a point, the match result was 42–42. The score was later amended following a Norwich protest to the Speedway Control Board. The Steward's decision to award Crowther, who was reported to have remounted to complete the race, the point in the last heat was set aside. The heat became a 3–2 to Norwich giving them the match, 42–41. Crowther's points were revised to 6+1 from 7+1. Rough justice to say the least. It was foul riding by the Norwich rider that prevented Crowther from legitimately finishing the race yet it was Norwich who benefited. Despite this, Crowther's unbeaten second half run continued.

The Tigers, despite fighting a losing battle, put up a good show for the Norwich fans three days later. Praise for their efforts were heaped on Crowther, Lowther, Fairhurst and Ryan but they and the other Tigers did not do enough to stop the Stars winning 53–31. Crowther scored 9+1, Fairhurst 6+1 and Lowther six. The reserves – the two Macs, McGregor and McGuire, failed to score.

As so often in previous years, the visiting Middlesbrough Bears won 47–37 at White City, but had to fight all the way. The last four heats decided this match on 28 April. The Bears took a couple of 5–1s and a 4–2 to stretch away from Tigers. Uncharacteristically low returns of three from Crowther after a fall and 4+1 from Lowther spelled disaster for Tigers. Lowther's cause wasn't helped by arriving late arrival due to a car crash. Lindsay had bike problems, pegging him back to 3+1. The top two for the Tigers were Fairhurst with nine points and Ryan on eight.

Bainbridge's best bike blew when he was leading and he used the track spare in his last race which saw him finish last. In the second half he used his spare engine and that seized up, throwing him into the fence. He suffered concussion and ended up in hospital.

Like so many other teams the Tigers were swept aside by the solid top five display by Bulldogs in Bristol. On 30 April Bristol won 53–31. Glasgow were always behind and the Bulldogs rose to the occasion in the second part of the match.

Tigers' only star was Crowther who scored nine points in a brilliant style. He won a couple of races while Fairhurst was the Tigers' only other rider to take the flag. Lowther had a miserable night with one point from four outings and Bainbridge, on four, still had trouble gathering points on the road. His efforts weren't helped by the concussion two days before.

May

The weather was dismal in Birmingham on May Day. The Brummies fans who braved the rain saw Glasgow's second strings, Fairhurst excepted, who won a couple of heats, fail to support their heat leaders. Also, Lindsay and Ryan came in for criticism as they did not put up much of a fight. The Tigers scored the same on the sweeping athletics track as they did at Bristol, going down 53–31. It was a track on which they should have done better.

Again, Crowther did most to keep the score line respectable with two wins and two second places for 10 points. He spoilt Graham Warren's maximum hopes, keeping him in third place in heat 11. Lowther scored 6+1 while Fairhurst scored six.

Bristol's Fred 'Friar' Tuck cut a swathe through the Tigers' ranks in posting a maximum at White City on 5 May. The Bulldogs had another five race winners in a match that went their way from the off. The Tigers were given a lesson in team riding, never mounting a serious challenge to counter the Bulldogs' onslaught.

Crowther and Lowther were, again, the best Tigers, but only managed nine points apiece. Next best were Bainbridge with 5+1 and Lindsay on five. The Tigers took a couple of heat advantages, too little and too late. Their last heat 4–2 came when the match was lost, making the final score 48–36.

The Tigers' Wednesday nights were briefly under threat from the greyhound racing fraternity. However, the status quo was retained with the canines staying on a Tuesday night.

Aware that their big problem was gating ahead of the opposition, the Tigers spent some time doing practice starts before their match with Edinburgh Monarchs on 12 May. It seems to have paid off. The Monarchs fought hard and the whole Edinburgh side showed some fight and kept the Tigers within striking distance for part of the match. The Monarchs were close until the end of heat five when the Tigers eased away from their big rivals. It was the first time Edinburgh had ridden at White City. A last heat 5–1 for Crowther and Lowther made the final score 49–35.

The Tigers fought hard and their efforts resulted in two full maximums for their men and another man just short of the full house. Ryan scored his first maximum and Lowther let Crowther take a full maximum as he eased over the line in heat 14. Bainbridge ended his outings with a race win, but his five points showed he was still not yet the big scorer that had been expected. Similarly, Lindsay was seen as under-performing as he collected 5+1. The Macs at reserve were still not doing much.

A side called Glasgow raced a team called Hamilton on Saturday 15 May at Hamilton Palace Recreation Grounds as part of the Lanarkshire Agricultural Show. The score was Hamilton 41 Rest of Glasgow 37. The event featured a few Tigers riders including Bainbridge, McGregor and Lindsay. Bainbridge scored two for Hamilton while McGregor scored nine. Lindsay scored 11 for the Rest of Glasgow. This event was described in the programme as 'grass speedway', but those taking part confirmed it was a shale surface, typical of many football pitches known as 'blaes parks' in the West of Scotland.

As well as the league meetings, the Second Division teams staged a celebration of the sport's 20th birthday, the Anniversary Cup, using a 16 heats formula. Glasgow started out on their Cup quest with a narrow 51–45 win over Birmingham on 19 May.

Using a former Vic Duggan machine, Graham Warren led the Brummies' challenge but, despite their solid scoring throughout, they lost. The hard dry track caught some riders out and caused a few falls. The Tigers' tail was poor, but the main riders, despite some early bike problems, did enough. Crowther was top scorer completing a five-ride paid maximum 14+1. Next best Tiger was Ryan on 10 and then Bainbridge on 9+1. An opening ride engine failure pegged Lowther back to seven.

The Brummies could have taken a draw by winning the last heat 5–1, but Warren fell leaving Crowther to win from McLachlan and fellow Tiger Ryan.

Stan Dell and Charlie May gave the visitors a good start with a 5–1, and it took Glasgow until heat five to get ahead. Heat six saw the visitors ahead again, but Lowther and Lindsay countered in the next heat and thereafter the Tigers eased ahead. Birmingham's reserves, Dick Tolley and Buck Whitby, combined for a 5–1 over McGuire and McGregor to reduce the gap to four points, but the last heat was won by the Tigers.

Rained off the night before, the Tigers team stayed in Newcastle and took on the Diamonds on Tuesday 25 May in the league. The day in Newcastle must have done the trick. The Tigers rose to the occasion and posted a good win. The Diamonds were never out of contention on a slick track, but Glasgow just had the edge and had the meeting sewn up by the end of heat 13. The last heat Tigers 5–1 from Lowther and Crowther made the 46–37 score look comfortable.

The second half final was an all Glasgow affair, a little bit of Brough Park history as this was the first time no Diamond had made the second half final.

The Diamonds' leg trailer, Wilf Jay, started with two race wins before tailing off. He had not stayed in Newcastle overnight, but drove home to Sheffield and back to visit one of his children who was unwell. In the pre-motorway days this trip was not easy.

Boosted by this away win, Glasgow took on their Sheffield namesake on 26 May in a league fixture and won well, 55–29. Stan Williams had to be in London the next day and his mind was obviously on the trip south. The bulk of the Sheffield team were also as good as being posted missing.

Glasgow veteran Garland was back, having passed a late fitness test, and, at his request, he started at reserve. After a pointless opener, Garland, who displaced McGuire, won his second outing. Lowther went well and set a new track record in the last heat of the match while completing a paid maximum. Most track records are set in the opening heat or early in the meeting. This shows the track was standing up well and Lowther was going some.

Bainbridge was down on power due to bike problems, but Crowther, who matched Lowther, Ryan and Lindsay, who both scored 9+2, and Fairhurst, on eight, all scored well.

Sheffield featured Belle Vue loanee Ken Sharples who soon become a major force in Manchester. Glasgow managed to spell his name correctly; at one track he was programmed 'Ken Shuffles'.

A win at Middlesbrough's fortress Cleveland Park the next night was not expected, but Glasgow got stuck in. Crowther impressed as he went through the card undefeated with 15 points. This was no mean feat facing Frank Hodgson. The Bears scored solidly from one to eight with only Hodgson reaching double figures. The Bears' team effort was enough to win this Anniversary Cup match 54–42. It was wrapped up at the end of heat 14. The Bears' youngster Bill Wilson, who was fatally injured at Norwich in early July, impressed taking Lowther's scalp. This was no means feat even though he was shepherded round by his partner, Jack Hodgson.

The Tigers had bike problems and in seven instances a Tiger failed to finish due to engine failure. Lindsay scored zero, as did McGregor. Had they chipped in a few points, the match might have been closer. Supporting Crowther were Lowther on 11+1 and Bainbridge on 7+1.

June

The Tigers made their first visit to Fleetwood on league business with Johnnie Hoskins. He made favourable comments about the track and the racing. However, with Wilf Plant and Dick Geary in fine fettle, the Tigers ended losing 48–36 on Tuesday 1 June. Crowther was top Tiger with 10 points. He took time to get the hang of Highbury Avenue Sports Stadium and its daunting corrugated iron safety fence before winning two heats. He also burst from the back to split the team-riding pair of Cooper and Geary to come second in his second outing.

Glasgow had Fairhurst and Ryan on eight points while Bainbridge was not impressed with the track and had three last places. Gritty Garland was riding with handlebars specially designed to make riding easier following his recent injuries. He scored two points. Lowther only scored five but won one of his races in a track record equalling time. Alterations to the track in the winter of 1948 meant that the track record was revised.

About this time a contemporary Glasgow statistician pointed out that Tigers had not won a match on a Tuesday, Thursday or Friday since the War.

Middlesbrough came to White City on 2 June and left with a big 55–40 Anniversary Cup win. Glasgow started by holding the Bears level but the visitors moved ahead in heat six and were never headed again. The Bears gave a reserve outing to Derrick Close – his first in Glasgow. He scored in a couple but fell and had an engine failure in the others.

Despite not being well Crowther rode but he and the others expected to score well performed poorly. Perhaps it was the Bears' firepower that kept Glasgow's scores down. Crowther only scored five points, falling in one ride, while Ryan and Lindsay could only manage four and two respectively.

Only top form Bainbridge rode well to score 12+1, but he alone could not halt the rampant Bears. He completed a good night by winning the second half final. It was an improvement on his display at Fleetwood the previous evening. McGregor deserves a mention with his five points from three outings.

Glasgow's biggest win of the season was on 9 June when they eclipsed the Norwich Stars 63–32 in the Anniversary Cup. After weeks of struggling, the Tigers took a big win – the up side – and the Glasgow public complained that the racing was too processional – the downside. The Glasgow promoters later described Norwich as having caved in like a paper bag. Lowther was back in the maximum groove; Crowther and Bainbridge were paid for a maximum. Ryan and Lindsay worked well, scoring 10+1 and 8+1 respectively. McGregor made his top six debut, but only scored two points.

Norwich may have put a better fight but for Bert Spencer dropping out after an opening ride bike failure. However, Geoff Revett gave a fair display as a substitute for the veteran Australian. Phil Clarke fell after two race wins and thereafter struggled. Norwich soon had three bikes out of commission and had to share equipment. One was used for three races on the trot.

Oliver Hart was in town. He beat Lowther and Crowther in match races and collected the Goddess of Speed Trophy. Oliver also brought a new frame for Will Lowther, an exact copy of his own and one owned by Crowther. Crowther used it to advantage on 12 June when he won the Fifty Guinea Trophy with a maximum at Edinburgh.

The two Scottish sides met in the opening National Trophy Second Division round. Was there some seeding? The first leg at White City on 16 June was won easily by the Tigers. Their 70–38 victory could have been greater, but for bike problems. Bat Byrnes, making his 1948 debut, lost out on a paid maximum in heat 11 when his bike failed when he was leading only 25 yards from the flag. Fairhurst also had bike problems and Lowther's hopes of a five-ride maximum ended when he fell in heat 16.

With five out of the eight Tigers on double figures, this was a comprehensive demolition of the Monarchs. The visitors only had two riders on double figures, Dick Campbell and Bill Maddern. Former Tiger Eddie Lack was plagued by bike problems and had only one scoring outing, in his last ride. The Monarchs did not reach double figures until heat seven.

Despite the pundits predicting that the Tigers were through to the next round, nobody told the Monarchs and on Saturday 19 June they tried to achieve a home win over Glasgow for the first time and claw back the gap. They started reasonably well, but the Tigers came back into it. Glasgow lost 62–46 on the night, but took the tie 116–100 on aggregate.

Two of Glasgow's Australians scored well: Ryan with 13+2 and Byrnes on 12+1. Crowther was down on power and fell in his second outing. A major shock was Lowther's three last places, a rare occurrence for him to have zeros beside his name. Bainbridge only scored one point, but his scoring fluctuated with the odd bad meeting.

The Tigers squared up to Birmingham in the next round on 23 June. They did well until heat seven, then the roof caved in as the Brummies started their powerhouse display which carried them to a 61.5–45.5 victory. The track was in superb condition and Lowther knocked a bit off the track record in heat one, only for Crowther to lower it in heat two to 81.2 seconds. However, only Byrnes put up a fight with 13+1.

A fall saw Crowther score only seven points after a couple of wins. Bainbridge had another night to forget with four last places after a bright opening heat second. Ryan also had an off night with a fall and two lasts restricting him to five points. Garland was beginning to struggle at reserve. Bainbridge also fell.

After the meeting, Lowther tried a bike he was buying from First Division rider Max Grosskreutz, but crashed when, unusually, the front wheel spindle broke.

Around this time, Lindsay headed to Birmingham by train for to take part in a British Riders' Championship round. He was let down and failed to arrive in time.

The Tigers made their second trip to Fleetwood. On Tuesday 29 June, they sought Anniversary Cup points, but the Flyers flew at the Tigers and, Crowther apart, Glasgow were routed. The score was 62–34. The Flyers were too good and – except for Crowther – all apart from Percy Brine soared more than the Tigers. Dick Geary opened with a new track record. Crowther scored 12 for Tigers while Ryan added eight, but next best were Lowther and Fairhurst on four each. Not a performance to send a postcard home from the seaside near Blackpool about for sure.

Crowther had a chance of winning this British Speedway Riders' Championship qualifying round at White City on 30 June, but fell in his last ride. The meeting was dominated by the three First Division riders, Bill Gilbert (Wembley), who won with an unbeaten 15, 'Iron Man' Joe Abbott (Bradford), a veteran who rode at White City in the pioneer days, scored 13 and Bill Pitcher (Belle Vue) was third on 12. Many lower division riders were unhappy facing the Division One entrants at this stage of the competition. Gilbert could not stay to celebrate, and rushed off to catch a train south. He was riding for Wembley the next evening.

Ian Hoskins had been critical of the inclusion of First Division riders, albeit not star heat leaders, in the Second Division round. His fears that they would dominate were borne out.

Crowther was involved in a bit of controversy after heat 12. The race was stopped when Wilf Jay fell. A dazed Jay turned the blameless Crowther away as he approached him to see how he was. Thankfully, Wilf came back out of the pits to apologise when things became a bit clearer. Unfortunately, the crowd turned on Jay for his apparently unsporting response and were not placated by Wilf's belated apology.

July

Birmingham's recent win in Glasgow suggested that the Tigers might find things a bit difficult at Perry Barr. On Saturday 3 July, they exited the National Trophy after losing 80–28. The aggregate score was 141.5–73.5. The Brummies took 11 5–1 heat wins. Only one home rider scored less than eight. The Tigers won a single heat as race winner Bainbridge and Crowther scored a 4–2 in heat three. The 'top' Tiger, on a night best forgotten, was Lowther with eight. Byrnes scored seven and Bainbridge 5+1.

Left: Gordon McGregor. Right: Junior Bainbridge. Both riders had long careers in British speedway.

The 1948 Glasgow Tigers: Keith Buck Ryan, Angus McGuire, Junior Bainbridge, Will Lowther (on bike), Ian Hoskins, Norman Lindsay, Joe Crowther, Harold Fairhurst and Gordon McGregor.

White City Programmes from the 1948 season. (Courtesy Duncan Luke)

Desperate times call for serious measures and to field a reasonably sound eight-man side Ian Hoskins had to think about bolstering his team

Byrnes rode in the Anniversary Cup match at White City on 7 July with an outsize boot covering a large plaster. The Tigers beat Newcastle 54–42. The twin spearhead of Lowther and Crowther scored 13 each and next best was the patched up Byrnes with 8+1.

Despite the efforts of Wilf Jay, Second Division Match Race Champion at the time, and Ken Le Breton, the Diamonds failed to outshine Tigers. They kept the pressure on the Tigers to the halfway stage, then gradually fell by the wayside.

As a break from league action, Ian Hoskins lined up a challenge which probably promised more than it delivered on 14 July. A Glasgow Select, in essence the regular Tigers with Frank Hodgson facing a team with two Tigers, Graham Warren and Edinburgh's Clem Mitchell, Dick Campbell and Eddie Lack led by legend Vic Duggan. Vic agreed to come north not for appearance money, but for the chance of playing golf on the famed Old Course in St Andrews. After his round of golf, Vic had a good night at White City. He was only defeated by Hodgson in the match after a close race and by Warren in the second half qualifier. In the second half final he tangled with Crowther and wrecked his bike. A sporting Ryan loaned Vic his bike on which he won the rerun.

Ian Hoskins said that Duggan usually only rode his own bikes, and wanted to withdraw from the final. But thousands of fans shouting 'We want Duggan' persuaded him to change his mind.

Vic's Select were reduced in fire power as Warren had engine failure in his first three outings and a win in his last ride was his only contribution. The score of 46–37 for the Glasgow Select also saw a return to form for Bainbridge on 7+1 from three rides.

Duggan scored 11 showing the Tigers faithful just how good he was. Vic opened with a new four lap track record of 81 seconds. Only Byrnes, who top scored for Tigers with 11, got anywhere near his time but was 1.4 seconds adrift.

Back to the Anniversary Cup and, again, the Tigers failed to perform at the pacy Firs Stadium. They were competitive without producing the results. The result on Saturday 17 July was 64–32 for the Stars. For the Tigers the best rider was Crowther, with 10 from five rides. He scored in four rides and in his second ride pulled out of the race. Byrnes chipped in 8+1, but he was the only Tiger to give Joe any real support. These two won three races between them. The Tigers collected 11 last places.

Glasgow totally outclassed their capital city visitors on 21 July, with a 71–24 win over the Monarchs. Such was the margin of the Tigers' superiority that their poorest rider was better than the Monarchs' top two of Bill Baird and Dick Campbell. The Monarchs were hit for 11 5-1s and managed one race winner. The Monarchs were Baird's second Scottish team.

Despite their superiority, only the Tigers' Lowther had a full maximum, but Bainbridge scored a paid maximum. McGregor scored a paid maximum from three rides in a reserve berth. Ryan was one short of a paid maximum thanks to Dick Campbell, as Tigers worked as a team. It must have had Tigers' fans in raptures, but for the Monarchs' fans it must have been pure purgatory.

Glasgow's Tigers came to earth from their big home win the night before with a sobering defeat in an Anniversary Cup match at Owlerton. The stadium was another fast raceway that was so different from Glasgow's circuit. Ironically Owlerton was built by pioneer Glasgow man, George Cummings. The visitors went down 69–27.

Sheffield had three riders unbeaten by a Glasgow rider. Early season Tiger Jack Martin had an outing replacing Lindsay, but failed to score. Crowther was best Glasgow rider on nine points, and Byrnes was one short on eight. Garland's poor run continued, a sad state of affairs for the pre-war Glasgow Lion and pioneer Tiger. Like many Tigers away matches, they slipped behind early doors and went ever further behind.

Lindsay was back scoring seven at Newcastle and the fans who watched on Monday 26 July saw the terrible twins, Lowther and Crowther excel. Garland, after his poor show at Sheffield, was replaced by McGregor who did marginally better on 2+1. The Tigers appeared to run Newcastle close in this Anniversary Cup fixture, but the match was wrapped up before the Tigers' 'twins' took a last heat 5–1 to make the final score 50–46.

Yet again Lowther showed his liking for Brough Park, dropping only one point to a Diamond as he powered to 13+1. Crowther scored 12 and would have scored a full 15 had he not fallen in his second outing. The Tigers were not helped as three of their Australasians were still struggling away from Glasgow to establish any degree of consistency.

The big difference was that Newcastle had a slightly more solid line up and the final score made the match look a closer run thing than it was.

The improvement in Glasgow's performance at Newcastle continued apace. Fleetwood took a beating in a lack-lustre night of Anniversary Cup action at White City on 28 July. When the bikes went silent for the interval, the Tigers had grounded the Flyers 68–28. Crowther with 15 points and Lowther on 12 were unbeaten. Bainbridge won only one of five of his rides, but followed home his teammate in the other four for a paid maximum. Ryan and Byrnes also had a good pay night with 9+2 and 9+1 respectively.

Wilf Plant, rapidly transferred from Middlesbrough in May, following a reportedly night long transfer negotiation, to bolster an under-performing team did reasonably well. He took Fleetwood's only race wins.

In the second half. Airdrie's Alf McIntosh fell in front of Irvine's Dave Galloway. Alf injured his collar bone. Dave's trip over the handlebars it was reported cost him a broken arm, but he rode at Santry a few days later. Alf returned to become a popular Tiger.

August

On Sunday 1 August, a Glasgow team visited Dublin's Santry Stadium. The visitors, with four Glasgow juniors, McGuire 5+1, McIntosh 5+1, Joe Arlet 3+1 and Dave Galloway on nine, plus three Tamworth juniors won 42–30 against a side that included Glasgow rider Jack Martin and some Irish juniors bolstered by Canadian Mike Tams and Belle Vue's Ron Mason.

Tuesday 3 August took the Tigers to the seaside again and they came home with a narrow 44–40 win over a struggling Fleetwood side. This broke the Tigers' record of failing to win a post-war meeting on a Tuesday. The team worked well without anyone being outstanding.

Crowther was set for a maximum, but blew it when he fell in the last heat. Lowther took his only race win of the night to seal victory. Crowther scored nine points, Ryan 8+1 while Fairhurst on 7+2 had one of his better nights. The teams shared the heat wins seven apiece but the Tigers had a better share of the second places and fewer lasts. Glasgow nudged ahead in heat nine and held the lead to the end.

In a very tight finish to the last heat, Lowther narrowly beat Bristol's Fred Tuck on 4 August. However, it did not matter as the Tigers had the match sown up by then. The Bulldogs, so often a real test for the Tigers at White City, had their teeth pulled. Glasgow's win might have been bigger but Ryan had to pull out after injuring his foot in a heat seven fall after scoring one in his first ride. Most popular win of the night was rising reserve McGregor's victory in heat 15 to give him 5+1 points.

Lowther was top Tiger on 13 in this Anniversary Cup 56–40 win. Crowther added 12 and Byrnes collected 9 points.

Bristol won the contest of the gaters two days later in the return fixture at Knowle. The wet track gave fast starters an advantage and this was usually the Bulldogs. No surprise then that they won this Anniversary Cup contest 55–39.

The Tigers produced five heat winners with Bainbridge, who impressed the locals, and Lowther taking two wins each and Crowther the other. The Lowther-Bainbridge pair took a 5–1 win in the last heat, but by then, the match was lost.

Lowther's 11 points from five rides was the best scorer for the Tigers. Bainbridge had a good 9+1 return. A few falls were recorded, but nobody was badly hurt.

Bristol on a Friday was followed by Birmingham the next day. The home men won this Anniversary Cup fixture easily. The margin of victory, 69–27, could have been larger but for Birmingham using at least one reserve in the nominated rider heat. The Brummies did this regularly and it would cause concerns for the Tigers' fans in the future. The home team won every heat bar one for 15 race winners,

Crowther was the Tigers' top man with nine points, a third of the team score. He was the only Tiger to win a race, heat 16, when he combined with Byrnes, the second best Tiger on seven points, for Tigers only heat victory.

Glasgow demolished Edinburgh at White City on 11 August. The Tigers fired on all eight cylinders while the Monarchs' octet stuttered. Lowther flew to a maximum, Byrnes scored a paid maximum, as did Fairhurst. Lindsay scored a reserves' paid maximum in his two rides. Former Tiger Eddie Lack was the top Monarch on six. The final score was 63–21 in this Anniversary Cup match. Three visitors scored a duck in a poor show.

Thankfully, promoter Ian Hoskins had booked Oliver Hart to take on his riders and, even on borrowed equipment, the leg trailer put on a show. Oliver did not win any races, but gave his match race opponents, especially Crowther who won yet another second half, a run for their money.

Scotland, with one home born rider, two Englishmen and five Scotland-based Australasians, beat England at White City on 18 August in front of a 20,000 all ticket crowd. Optimistic fans without tickets who turned up were out of luck. Crowther must have been surprised when handed a bunch of flowers by a lady supporter after winning his opening ride. He collected 13+1 for his adopted country. Popular Lindsay, replacing Dick Campbell after two pointless rides, collected 5+2.

At least the native-born Scot top scored, even though he had been claimed by his adopted country, Australia, as one of its top test stars. Ron Johnson, who always did well on his returns to Scotland, scored 17 and was the outstanding rider.

England was led by Jack Parker with 14 points. Frank Hodgson with 9+2 was the next best English rider, but the Scots clinched the match 59–49.

A trip to Newcastle usually meant a Lowther benefit, but on 23 August he met three determined Diamonds bent on sorting out the Tigers. Charlie Spinks and Kiwi Jack Hunt each scored a full maximum while Alex Grant only just missed out when he was beaten by Lowther.

The three Diamonds scored one more point than the combined efforts of the Tigers in this 50–34 league defeat. The Tigers never won a heat and their best were 3–3s as they packed in behind the race winning Diamonds' rider.

Glasgow's best were Lowther and Crowther. Both scored seven but Crowther had a bonus point. Byrnes scored 6+1 and Bainbridge 5+1. A Lowther maximum would not have saved the Tigers as they only had a paltry two race winners.

Bainbridge played a starring role in Tigers' first defeat of Middlesbrough this season on 25 August. The Tigers got stuck in and the league points were won 55–29 win. Crowther had bike problems and the track spare was a poor replacement. He ended the night with a poor 3+1. Bainbridge scored an immaculate maximum and he had the support of four of his team mates: Lindsay 10+1, Byrnes 9+2, Fairhurst 9+1 and Lowther 8+1. This Middlesbrough team were not as strong as in 1946 and 1947, and finished third in the final league table.

The Tigers nearly did the double at Middlesbrough the next night in what was the last Bears – Tigers encounter until 1964. Unfortunately, they could not hang on to win after leading at the end of heat 11. The Bears went in to the last heat 41–37 ahead. The Crowther and Lowther pairing, so potent in the past, did the business to put a 5–1 over the normally unbeatable Frank Hodgson to grab a 42–42 draw. The Tigers could take pride from a league point from Cleveland Park. Lowther scored eight and Crowther returned 9+2.

September

On the crest of a wave, Glasgow faced Sheffield at home on 1 September in the Anniversary Cup. Early on, it looked as it was all going Sheffield's way but Glasgow turned things round to win 51–45. It took Glasgow until heat 11 to draw level before moving ahead. Byrnes was the best Glasgow rider with 10 points from five rides. The rest had a solid haul of points as no other home man reached double figures.

Downham was back in the second half, returning after a loan spell at Edinburgh. He waited to get his chance for Tigers.

After a close meeting at White City the previous night, Glasgow ran away with this league fixture at Owlerton the next night. Unbeaten Bruce Semmens was the only home rider with any answer to Glasgow's efforts spearheaded by Byrnes, Bainbridge and Fairhurst. Sheffield had a long tail with three riders scoring one apiece.

Glasgow had a 10-point lead by heat seven, lost a bit ground in the next two heats, before piling up points again in heat 11 to end up worthy 50–34 victors.

Bainbridge was beaten by Semmens in his opening ride, then completed the match unbeaten to score 11. Fairhurst and Byrnes each managed 10 and Crowther gathered 8+3. A below par return from Ryan, who had bike problems, was more than compensated for by his team mates, McGregor apart. This one result that probably would never have been predicted even by the most ardent Glasgow fans. The Sheffield crowd must have gone home shocked as their men were mauled by their namesakes.

Glasgow's good form continued at White City against league champions-elect Bristol on 8 September. Crowther maintained his run of second half victories taking his 22nd prize. In the match he had opened with a zero before going on to record 8+1. The Tigers won this league fixture 46–38. Byrnes top scored with 10+1.

The Bulldogs clung on tenaciously to the Tigers for much of the match and it was only in the last four heats that Glasgow put daylight between themselves and Bristol with a 4–2 in heat 11 and 5–1 in heat 13.

The Tigers had been the first night visitors and this time they were the first visitors to race under the new electric lights that illuminated Old Meadowbank. Yet again, the Monarchs were beaten by the Tigers as they took yet another away win on Saturday 11 September. It was not as convincing a win as some, but they did enough to take the Anniversary Cup points back to White City. The Monarchs had been 29–19 up by the end of heat eight, but by the end of heat 15, the Tigers had levelled the scores at 45–45. Crowther and Fairhurst were the Tigers' heroes, their 4–2 win over Danny Lee and Clem Mitchell gave them a 49–47 win.

The four men for the nominated heat 16 had more or less picked themselves. It must have been a hard choice for the Edinburgh manager who could have been tempted to try Dick Campbell who had been unbeaten before his last race fall. Crowther scored 12 from five rides, including a last place. Fairhurst scored 10 before his last race, which added a point to give him 11. The real surprise in the Tigers ranks was McGregor on six with two wins from three rides.

The Tigers' winning home run stretched to 10 after sending Diamonds back home pointless on 15 September. The only Diamond to sparkle was Ken Le Breton in this 54–30 Tigers' win. Norman Evans, Wilf Jay and Maurice Stobbart, a former Tiger, also did well.

Byrnes was the star for the Tigers with a maximum while Lowther, back on form, collected 11 after losing to Le Breton. Crowther contributed 8+1 while Ryan used his reserve slot to advantage scoring 7+1 from three rides. In his extra outing he replaced an off-form Lindsay.

In the second half Downham created a stir by making it to the Final of the Diamond Lap-Dash Cup. He finished last, but was not too far off the pace.

The other noteworthy event was the first public outing for John McKinlay. Following the Hoskins tradition, John became much better known as Ken. It took a few years for the new second halfer to blossom and become arguably the best ever Scottish rider. For the record, Ken did not finish the race, falling as he contested it with Downham, McIntosh and Martin.

With the Monarchs away, stay-at-home Edinburgh fans seeking their weekly speedway fix on Saturday 18 September went to Old Meadowbank to see the battle of the Tigers and the Glasgow variety won. Unusually, 12 out of the 14 heats were drawn and Glasgow's 5–1 against Sheffield's 4–2 was the deciding factor. Sheffield were designated as the home team, but Glasgow made themselves at home and won 43–41.

Glasgow had no outstanding rider. Fairhurst and Crowther were best with 7+1 while Ryan scored seven. Glasgow's strong team performance clinched it. This was Ryan's last meeting for Glasgow for 1948 before he headed back home to Australia.

But for Byrnes falling, Norwich may have gone through the match without a race winner at White City on 22 September. The Tigers dimmed the Stars with a solid team effort to win 60–24. Fairhurst was the top Tiger with a paid maximum. Lowther scored 9+1, losing to Paddy Mills in the first heat. Lindsay ended with 10+1.

Bainbridge was in maximum form, but his bike failed in his last outing while Downham made his Tigers 1948 debut, scoring a reserve's maximum six. McGregor scored a reserve's paid maximum. Crowther's bike packed in twice whilst leading.

After a good display against Norwich, Tigers almost suffered a whitewash at Bristol two nights later. The 65–18 trashing was not quite a whitewash, but the Tigers' octet managed four points more than the minimum score possible on a track described by Ian Hoskins as a 'saucer'. Heat two was rerun after Bainbridge fouled the rising starting tapes. Wise was lucky as his wheel seized just after the race was halted and he made it back to the rerun. As it was, Bainbridge beat him for second spot, one of only four that evening for the Tigers.

The Tigers had their first 5–0 heat loss of the season when McGregor fell and Bainbridge was excluded for boring a Bristol rider.

Lightning struck twice on successive nights, but this time it was at Birmingham's Alexander Stadium on Saturday 25 September. The Brummies showed no mercy to almost repeat the score at Bristol. This time Tigers went one 'better' in a 65–19 defeat. Again, the Tigers did not win a heat, but at least they had two race winners. Bainbridge won heat 13, while Crowther's opening ride race win was taken from Stan Dell as Crowther raced through from the back. This was his only contribution as an engine failure and a fall pegged him back.

Not content with taking the stuffing out of Tigers in Birmingham, the Brummies came to Glasgow on 29 September and ended the Tigers' good home run with a 45–39 league win. They went ahead in heat four and gradually opened up a gap. Only Byrnes, 10, and to a lesser extent, Bainbridge with 7+2, Fairhurst on 6+2 and Crowther with six points get some credit.

Graham Warren won the second half final which featured Wimbledon's Norman Parker. The other First Division guest, Ron Johnson, won the mini tournament programmed as the Scottish Match Race Cup, but failed to make the second half final.

October

Fleetwood were not seen as a strong side, but drew 42–42 with the Tigers at White City on 6 October. The two Tigers in heat 14 had to work hard for the points and come from the back to take a 5–1. Fleetwood had started the last heat four points ahead. Crowther scored 11+1; he completed his paid maximum in the last heat. Fairhurst rose to the occasion in that race, winning it to finish on 8+2.

Bainbridge had a miserable finale to the season, drawing a blank before he set off for home. Lindsay also had a poor night with one point from three rides. The Australian duo's lack of fire power probably cost the Tigers the league point.

The scores went the Tigers' way for much of the meeting, but by heat 11 the Flyers were two points ahead. A fall by Downham in the penultimate heat allowed the Flyers a 4–2 and the chance of a win. It was a rare good away display by Fleetwood who often performed badly on the road.

Glasgow had another poor night at Norwich on Saturday 9 October. The 66–18 result was their biggest defeat on the road. Lowther top scored for Tigers with five points. Byrnes was next best with four while Lindsay and Crowther had to settle for three each. This was another away display that did Tigers no credit.

A wet track resulted in slow times as the weakened Tigers, without Bainbridge and Ryan, brought down the home curtain with a 42–42 draw in the league against Sheffield on 13 October. This was their second draw in two weeks, and for the second time in two weeks a Glasgow last heat 5–1 was required to tie. Glasgow were lucky to secure a point as at one stage they were 12 points behind Sheffield. In heat 14, the match seemed to be going away from Glasgow, but Semmens' engine gave up as he held the lead. This allowed Lowther and Lindsay to take the vital 5–1.

A couple of heats before this, Crowther's bike stopped before he reached the tapes. However, the replacement one kept going and with Bates, drafted in to make up the side after Bainbridge had gone home, keeping out the only other man in the race, Glasgow nabbed a 5–1 to keep them in with a chance.

Byrnes and Lindsay left immediately after the meeting to dash south to catch a ship back to Australia. Lindsay signed off with 7+1 while Byrnes ended with six. Crowther was top for Glasgow with 7+2.

Alarming rumours that Lowther wanted to leave the club were doing the rounds, but he would be back for the start of the 1949 season. The White City season ended with Tigers burning two symbolic wooden spoons to shake of the bad vibes of 1946 and 1947.

Over 16,000 turned out as the Tigers ended Edinburgh's season on Saturday 16 October. Unfortunately, the Tigers could not repeat the wins they had taken in the opening fixture in April and the Anniversary Cup. Much had to do with their weakened side.

The Tigers had three regulars in the side, Lowther, on seven, Crowther who suffered from bike problems, added five points and Fairhurst, who top scored with eight. McGregor and Downham were promoted to the side along with returnee Shearer, while Bates and McIntosh filled the reserve berths. This was Alf's debut as a Tiger in an official match and he scored two points thanks to a second in heat eight.

The Monarchs' fans must have been delighted to beat the Tigers for only the second time having suffered so many times at Tigers' claws in their opening season.

The Tigers ended 1948 on a losing note but at last they had risen from the wooden spoon spot and were the best team in Scotland. The wooden spoon passed over to Edinburgh.

In *Stenners' 1949 Speedway Annual*, Archie McCulloch said that the Tigers' tail had got stronger, which made them more of a threat. He noted Crowther's improvement, and that he had won at least 25 second-half trophies. However, it was disappointing that he had not been given a chance in the Second Division Match Race trophy.

He also mentioned the potential of Ken McKinlay, and concluded his report by saying that Ian Hoskins had done a good job as promoter.

10. 1949: Powerful at home, weak away

The 1949 season saw an enlarged National League Division Two. The Tigers had new rivals in Glasgow. Ashfield Giants were based at Saracen Park in Hawthorn Street, Possilpark. The new team were promoted by Johnnie Hoskins and managed by Norrie Isbister.

Other newcomers were Coventry Bees, backed by Jack Parker, Midlands side Cradley Heath Cubs, Southampton Saints, and London based Walthamstow Wolves. Middlesbrough had closed and Newcastle were now the 'Magpies'. The teams still rode twice at home and away against all the others, so the league programme was a massive 44 meetings.

Of the proposed new tracks for Scotland at Stepps near Glasgow, Falkirk, Aberdeen, Motherwell and Stenhouse Stadium, Edinburgh, only Stepps happened. Stepps was used for trotting and, in 1953, for midget car racing. It has also been reported as staging unconfirmed speedway bike practices.

The Tigers new mascot, Sheila, a tigress at Glasgow Zoo, was sponsored by the speedway promotion. Sadly, at the end of the season she mauled a keeper and was shot.

Reports indicate Sheila was to be stuffed and preserved in the Glasgow Art Gallery. Before Sheila, Ian Hoskins had a Tigers' head, affectionately known as Timothy, mounted on a board on his office wall. Before this he appeared on the track tractor on meeting nights. Legend has it he lost a tooth and it was re-discovered by Alec Grant who fell and landed on it. Timothy was almost kidnapped by Norwich riders, but did disappear for a week in 1948 after Edinburgh visited. He re-appeared later mounted on the Edinburgh tractor with a red and white doll in his mouth. Timothy was soon repatriated to Glasgow.

The Tigers fans were reminded of the team name spelled out in centre green lights. The riders had a new outfit, red and white vertical striped jumpers with their number on an arm band on their right arm. Some jumpers had a tiger's face on them. These were soon discarded in favour of conventional race jackets.

The potential problem of the 'three colonials' rule – no team was allowed to have more than three riders from Australia or New Zealand – was eased as Wigan born Harold Fairhurst and Norman Lindsay were classified as British. Fairhurst moved to Edinburgh in mid-season anyway.

Rumours that Will Lowther was joining Newcastle and Norman Lindsay heading for Walthamstow were false at that time. Both rode for Tigers opener against Monarchs at White City. Lowther moved towards the end of the season following a bust up when passed over for a place in the Scotland side against England at White City.

This brought Jack Hodgson from the re-named Newcastle Magpies to the Tigers. Dick Seers came to Glasgow from Fleetwood. He was recommended by Oliver Hart, but did not shine at White City. The other Australian hopeful, Jack Martin, rode in the second half for most of the season. Harold Fairhurst brought back the New Zealand Championship and fellow Kiwi, Frank Boyle. He had a few outings without progressing before moving to Oxford later that year.

The Tigers missed out on Willie Wilson, who performed well in the opening meeting second half. He signed for Ashfield. However, Ian Hoskins later snatched Alf McIntosh from under the Giants' noses later in the season. Ken McKinlay, hailed as a great find early on, gained experience as the season progressed. Gruff Garland joined Ashfield, as did start marshal Norrie Isbister and mascot Jimmy Cramb.

April

An impressive 20,000 fans came to the opener at White City on Wednesday 6 April and watched the Tigers win 50–34 against Edinburgh in a league fixture.

The Antipodeans – Bat Byrnes, Buck Ryan and Harold Fairhurst – were still on their way, so the Tigers had a makeshift appearance. Dick Seers, who had trained under Oliver Hart at Coppul, came second in his first outing then fell in his next. Ryan was nursing a broken arm sustained in Sydney on 18 February.

The Tigers might have scored more had Gordon McGregor not been baulked when Seers fell in heat 13. Crowther dropped points in his first ride when his engine failed as he led the heat. He collected nine from his other three rides. Bainbridge was down on points, with 7+1, due to the after effects of a vaccination. The Top Tiger was maximum man Lowther, who was riding on a new frame he had worked on in the winter.

The Monarchs were without sensational Australian debutant Jack Young, hospitalized with appendicitis. Eddie Lack rode spiritedly and his last outing saw Bainbridge gave him a wide berth fearing Eddie would steer him into trouble.

The 'Up and Comers' race featured Jack Martin, whose father had left Scotland for Australia changing the family name from Urquhart. The aspirants for the berth had included a woman, Pat Russell, 26 years old from Dumbarton. She impressed, but did not progress because of the ban on women riders.

Three days later, the Monarchs beat the Tigers 43–41 at Old Meadowbank watched by 22,000. The visitors took the Monarchs to a last heat decider. The score at after heat 13 was 39–39. Lindsay and Seers could go no better than a 4–2 loss. Seers was not far from former Tiger Bill Baird.

Lowther had an opening ride second place behind Eddie Lack, who went on to score a maximum. Lowther won his remaining rides. Crowther on 10 was the next best Tiger and a last race blip deprived him of a maximum for his crowd pleasing efforts. The Tigers should have won – they had the Monarchs on the ropes throughout.

Ryan was back from Australia with a new machine for the meeting on 13 April. He tried it out the day before and was pleased. He came in at reserve and scored 4+2. This relegated Seers, who was considered a bit inexperienced. He wasn't as bad as Martin who was given a free transfer.

The Tigers faced Coventry Bees for the first time and sent a relatively weak side back to the Midlands with a 59–25 league defeat.

The big star was McGregor with his first full maximum. He missed beating Crowther in the second half April Cup by half a wheel. Crowther had scored 7+2, short of a maximum due to a rare fall in heat five. Lowther had four unbeaten races and Bainbridge was unbeaten by a Bee. The meeting was not exciting because Coventry failed to provide a heat winner.

It was nip and tuck all the way and only in the last few heats did this league match at Southampton on Tuesday 15 April, slip away from Tigers. Ryan's fall in heat 10 was expensive as he lost the lead, giving Saints a couple of extra points. The match had several fallers, most of whom remounted.

The Tigers had the match in the bag when Bainbridge and Lowther took the lead in heat 14. However, home hero Jimmy Squibb forced his way through from the back, passing Lowther on the inside to win the race. The Tigers lost 43–41.

Glasgow Tigers 1949: Back: Nobby Downham, Harold Fairhurst, Will Lowther, Norman Lindsay, Ian Hoskins; front: Keith 'Buck' Ryan, Gordon McGregor, Junior Bainbridge and Bat Byrnes.

Ian Hoskins's plan to keep Ryan at reserve against newcomers Walthamstow Wolves was sunk by the Speedway Control Board. They said he was too experienced, and was forced to move into the team proper. He did not fare well at number one with 5+1.

Despite this, the Tigers outclassed their London opposition on a White City track made heavy by rain on 20 April, winning 52–32. Lowther dropped his first home point of the season to Charlie May in heat seven. He scored 11. McGregor, on 9+1, beat May and Wilf Jay. Lindsay, on 8+2 was next best. They had support from Crowther and Bainbridge.

Making his debut in the second half was Jack 'Red' Monteith. He entertained the fans with his 'never say die' approach. In the 1990s, Jack helped the fans save the Tigers. He predates Arnold Schwarzenegger with the catch phrase "I'll be back." The *Speedway Gazette* quoted Jack after his track debut at the 1949 trials.

Norman Lindsay was now no longer single. He had married local girl Helen Dalbeck the previous Tuesday.

A piece of Scottish speedway history was made when two Glasgow teams met for the first time at Ashfield Giants' Saracen Park on Tuesday 26 April. The Tigers won 46–35 in the league. The best race was the Giants' Ken Le Breton's win over Lindsay in heat seven.

Earlier Le Breton had been excluded for dumping Lowther from his machine after the Tiger had beaten him from the tapes. The Giants' Alex Grant was excluded in heat 14 for unseating Ryan. The race had only one finisher due to a fall, an engine failure and an exclusion. The Tigers, who stuck to the white line, had it wrapped up before the last race. Their top scorer was Crowther with 10+1. The colour coded Giants had red leathered Merv Harding, Keith Gurtner used blue leathers, Ken le Breton in his famous white leathers and Willie Wilson in black and yellow.

A new team takes time to knit together and the inexperienced Willie Wilson and veteran former Tiger Maurice Stobbart failed to give the boost needed from the reserve berths.

Newcastle were now known as the Magpies and the Tigers plucked their feathers on 27 April 53–31 in the league. The White City tapes caused problems and some heats were started with a flag. Bainbridge and Crowther scored full maximums. The Tigers' only other big scorer was Lowther with 10. This trio scored more than Magpies put together.

Newcastle included former Middlesbrough Bear, Frank Hodgson who only won one race. Rising star Derrick Close impressed.

Bainbridge's second half engine failure displeased him greatly. He kicked his crash helmet into the air. Ken McKinlay was progressing well in the second half but was not ready for a team place. The Magpies provided a singer, Son Mitchell, who sang *I will remember* – then forgot where he had left his helmet.

Despite the score, the Tigers and Norwich Stars presented some good speedway on Saturday 30 April. The home fans were happy with a 57–27 victory.

Bainbridge was the best Tiger with 10, but had support only from Lowther on seven points. The Tigers' tail was very long as the scoreline suggests. Their cause was not helped by falls and bike problems. Norwich had 12 race winners.

May

The Tigers took the Newcastle Magpies to the last heat, but lost a 4–2, going down 43–40 on 2 May. Lowther failed to best local hero Derrick Close, and Crowther did not start the rerun. His last heat fall and exclusion made the match secure for the Magpies. At least he would not damage his knee because he always wore a special knee brace as pioneered by 1938 World Champion Bluey Wilkinson.

The Tigers came back from 24–17 down after heat seven, but it wasn't enough. This was rated as the best meeting of the season by Magpies' fans. Lowther collected 11, just short of a maximum. Bainbridge was the Tigers' next best on seven while Fairhurst scored six from three rides.

Two days later, back at White City, the Tigers' equipment worked well. However, the visiting Belle Vue Aces had bike problems and falls in a challenge match. Their bike troubles started in heat one with Jack Parker's machine. He had a miserable night and at the end Tigers won 47–36. A heat nine breakdown left him close enough to the flag to push for home.

The Tigers borrowed Giants' Keith Gurtner, using him at reserve, replacing Fairhurst who had chipped a shoulder bone at Ashfield the day before. Crowther's last heat win was thanks to daring racing. He slipped between Dent Oliver and the fence to pass the Aces' star. Bainbridge's good form continued with 10 points, while Crowther collected nine. McGregor was back to form with 8+1. Maybe Ian Hoskins should have given a second halfer an outing – he had Ken McKinlay or Alf McIntosh available.

Second halfer Frank Boyle was a Kiwi on trial. He missed the start but raced through from the back to win his race by a good margin. He didn't stay in Scotland and moved south.

Two days later, the Tigers were poor side and failed to challenge Cradley Heath in most races at Dudley Wood Stadium. Cradley won 56–27. Only Crowther and McGregor put up a fight, scoring nine and 4+2 respectively. Ryan broke his toes when he fell in heat 14, which ruled him out for a few weeks.

The Tigers set a record in their 64–20 league win over Southampton in front of a 20,000 crowd on 11 May. They only had one last place. McGregor's high scoring run was ruined by a faulty plug lead preventing five of the Tigers scoring maximums. Fairhurst returned despite still suffering from injury and scored 3+1 at first reserve. Second reserve, an Ayrshire man who would be given the choice of plumbing or speedway by his father, Billie Bates, scored two. He chose plumbing. Nobby Downham was restricted to 7+3. Lowther, Bainbridge, Lindsay and Crowther were unbeaten by an opponent.

Bainbridge set the fastest time of the season in the Scottish Match Race opening heat against Ken Le Breton. He then had two bouts of bike trouble and lost the tie 2–1.

The following night the Sheffield Tigers were bigger and stronger than Glasgow Tigers. The visitors lost 59–25 at Owlerton. The best Glasgow Tiger – and only race winner – was Crowther on eight points. Sheffield's high speed circuit has been a problem for visiting teams over many years. Even with Ryan there is no guarantee Glasgow would have done better.

Joe Crowther was injured at Newcastle on 16 May which ruled him out until July. A challenge match at White City on 18 May had a few stars, including American Wilbur Lamoreaux. He replaced Jack Parker in the Atlantic Lions line-up which included Cradley's Alan Hunt, Newcastle's Derrick Close and Edinburgh's Dennis Parker. The opposition was the Kangaroos, who included Australian sensation, Graham Warren. He thrilled the Glasgow fans with a faultless 18 point maximum and set a new track record. In the record-breaking race, he and Lamoreaux traded first place over the four laps. The Australian team used mostly Scottish based riders, but along with Warren came Jack Arnfield, a team mate of Alan Hunt.

McGregor had problems in heat 10 and narrowly missed Fairhurst as he struggled to gain control. Lamoreaux and Lowther who were the top Lions both on 12+1 with Close on 12.

For the Kangaroos, Bainbridge equalled Lamoreaux and Lowther, but the next best Australians were Keith Gurtner on eight and Ken Le Breton with five. The solider Lions team won 58–50 from the Kangaroos.

Paddy Mills raced to a maximum for the visiting Norwich Stars on 25 May, but his team-mates did little to achieve a league win. The Tigers all round strength won the day, 48–36.

Bat Byrnes returned and featured in the race of the night, heat two. The lead changed hands frequently over the four laps with the Tiger shading it at the line. He scored 9+1, top-scoring for the Tigers. Bainbridge scored nine, while Lowther scored eight. He blamed his lower than usual score on using a 'lash up' bike which he thought might not even last a race. Tigers lead from the off and slowly pulled away.

A 25-year-old Gateshead novice, Fred Rowe, a farmer spotted riding on grass by Lowther, made his debut. He never progressed to the team. Also new was Navy lad George Taverner, stationed at Rosyth. Stoker George, a Rye House trainee, was another Hoskins 'find'. He disappeared into speedway oblivion. William (Jock) Gordon, also called Willie or Bill, had occasional outings with the Tigers, Edinburgh and Stoke. He starred at Dunmore Speedway in Belfast in 1950 before fading from the scene. He also rode in the second half against Rowe, Taverner and Martin.

Ian Hoskins could not get the Control Board to sanction an appearance for aspiring woman rider Pat Russell, who was aged 26 and a market gardener, due to the ban on lady riders.

June

Every member of the Bristol Bulldogs team recorded at least one bonus point in their scores in their match at White City on 1 June. In later times when bonus points were part of the payment package, the Glasgow promotion would have paid out 13 bonus points, 12 to the Bulldogs and one to the Tigers. The Bulldogs rode the white line which, at White City, generally paid dividends. The Bulldogs defeated the Tigers 57–27, their fourth successive away win.

The Tigers looked tired, and only Byrnes on nine and Bainbridge on seven looked anywhere near the pace. Byrnes missed a maximum through a fall. Bristol went on to win the league comfortably.

In the next home meeting, the Tigers had a relatively easy win despite an opening heat set back against Cradley on 8 June. Alan Hunt was visitors' chief threat, but even he could not beat Byrnes who out-gated him in heat nine. Byrnes completed a maximum. Bainbridge settled for 10+1 while Lowther added 9+2. The Tigers had a relatively easy 54–30 win. The next month, the Cradley Heath Cubs became the Heathens.

A new second half novice, 23-year-old Rob Fisher appeared. Recommended by well-known TT rider Johnny Waddell, Rob previously tried out racing on sand in India. Meanwhile, Fairhurst had his last meeting as a bachelor and celebrated with a paid maximum.

He married local lassie Catherine Dalbeck, a sister of Norman Lindsay's wife, on 9 June. Harold and his bride were introduced to the Glasgow crowd and walked under a ceremonial arch of flags and a brush held up by his team-mates. The brush bearer was Crowther.

Norwich Stars visited White City on 15 June in search of points to give them a cushion for the return leg of this National Trophy tie. The Tigers won 67–41, setting up an interesting trip to East Anglia.

Unfortunately for the Stars, Paddy Mills came off quite badly from his heat five accident caused by a chain break while leading. He reportedly sustained a slight fracture of the skull and a broken leg. He refuted this when he got back to Norwich. Downham was also involved in the heat five crash because he could not avoid Mills. He wrecked his bike and was forced out of the meeting.

Byrnes had a spectacular spill after a spin in heat three and Fred Rogers ran into the fence in heat four but gamely got up and continued. Amid this mayhem Bainbridge raced to a spectacular 17, while Lowther gathered 14+1.

Around this time, Ian Hoskins had a tough decision to make about his Australians and decided to let Ryan go to conform to the Speedway Riders' Association three Australians rule. This was not an immediate problem as he was out injured. The Tigers hoped Lindsay would be classified as a UK rider because he had been in the country since before the War.

The legendary Joe 'Whaler' Ferguson made his debut alongside Lazarus and McKinlay. Joe was never a star, but his style entertained the crowd and wrecked umpteen bikes. The Whaler, who later settled down and become a harbour master, returned to sea to fund his speedway activities. He is also famous for appearing on the big screen in *Moby Dick* doubling for film star Alan Ladd.

Norwich were well ahead of Glasgow in the National Trophy second leg at the Firs on Saturday 18 June. Lowther was reported as saying that they went round the turns faster than the local riders. The fans were impressed by the Tigers determination. Unfortunately, it did not bring the deserved result. Norwich won 71–36 to secure an aggregate 112-103 win and place in the next round.

Byrnes continued his run of form with 12 points from six rides. Fellow Australian Bainbridge added nine points.

The Giants first visited White City on Wednesday 22 June for a league match. Despite the potential for this meeting to be a real thriller, it never did because the Tigers comprehensively reduced the Giants to size, winning 52–32. Lowther and Byrnes scored 11 points each, while Lindsay and Fairhurst backed them with 7+2. Bainbridge, on six, had bike problems.

Ken Le Breton scored 10 points and was supported by fellow Australians Keith Gurtner and Merv Harding. The other Giants, mostly veterans, did not perform well. They included former-Tigers Maurice Stobbart and Gruff Garland.

The second half final was eventful with bunching at the first turn, but it developed into a Le Breton versus Bainbridge duel. Le Breton won in a relatively fast time.

Newcastle came to White City and went home defeated 51–32 on 29 June. Bainbridge and Byrnes were in fine form, each recorded maximums.

Heat four saw a coming together of Son Mitchell and Downham. Both fell, but neither was excluded because they both dropped out of the race. Derrick Close also fell in heat four and remounted to take second place. Lindsay had problems too, nearly falling in heat 10 and ending up with both legs on the right hand side of the bike as he fought to regain control. He did and came third.

Best race of the night was heat eight as Magpies newcomer Wilf Jay and McGregor traded places all race before McGregor won by half a wheel. Second halfer Bob King was a 35-year-old Australian newcomer. The former boxer never progressed to the team.

July

BBC Radio Scotland covered the World Championship third round meeting at White City on 6 July. A report was broadcast a few days later. They reported on a triple run off for the podium top spot. Swede Olle Nygren tumbled near the start and Birmingham's Geoff Bennett gradually overhauled Cradley Heath's Gil Craven to win the big prize money. Olle complained about being pushed wide by Craven, but his complaints were ignored by the steward. Only the first two qualified for the next round, so Olle's interest in the championship was over. He was peeved and recalled his feelings to the author very much later. Edinburgh's new Australian sensation, Jack Young, made his White City debut and did well, scoring 10.

Despite big efforts from returnee Crowther and Bainbridge, the meeting at Brandon on 9 July proved fruitless for the Tigers. Bainbridge produced some exciting racing with his heat seven burst from last to first the highlight. He also featured in a cracker with Lionel Levy in heat 11 when Levy just held on the win over 'The Flash'.

Heat three was unusual – Bert Lacey was the only rider who looked like finishing. McGregor dropped out with an engine failure and Jack Gordon's machine developed a fault which reduced his speed. Bainbridge fell, but remounted to pass Gordon and would have lapped him had Bert not shielded his partner from Bainbridge's attentions. Crowther top scored for the Tigers with 10+1 and Bainbridge scored 10. The Bees won 45–39.

The return to the saddle of Ryan, at the end of his Speedway Riders' Association 'ban', saw the end of Fairhurst's time with the club. The Anglo-Kiwi moved east on Wednesday 13 July to join Edinburgh for a £600 transfer fee. Of course, the 'curse of the ex' saw him beat all his former team-mates except Crowther on his debut as a Monarch on a soaking wet White City track. The Tigers scored solidly and won 48–34.

Disillusioned Cambridge based Downham came into the eight to replace Fairhurst. He was impressive in his first ride, coming from behind after the Monarchs' pair had tried to shut him out before drifting wide on the last bend. Jack Young, who had ridden in an individual meeting before at White City, was taking his first outing as a Monarch at the stadium and did not impress. For the Tigers, Crowther top scored again with 9+2 while Lowther collected nine points.

Byrnes missed the Tigers' meeting at Ashfield on 19 July. He had a nasty injury to his knee from a freak accident in an open meeting at Newcastle the night before. The accident happened after a race when Frank Hodgson hit him, causing his chain to break and flail about. McKinlay was drafted in at reserve and Ryan moved up into the team. As it turned out, the Giants' top riders gave the Tigers a hard time and held them to only two race winners. The Giants won 51–33. The Glasgow derby drew a crowd of 24,000 despite being in the Glasgow Fair Fortnight local holiday.

Lowther was the best Tiger with seven points, while Bainbridge contributed 6+2 and Ryan six. The main scorers for Ashfield were Ken Le Breton, Merv Harding and Keith Gurtner.

The demonstration of a bike fitted with a 'Jetaway' rocket developed by chemical giants ICI. proved to be a damp squib on the rain-soaked track on 20 July.

The times recorded in the demonstrations were much slower than those recorded in the match against Sheffield, well adrift of the track record. The track was poor. Bainbridge scored just two points, and had to use the track spare for three races.

Byrnes did not ride because he had to received penicillin injections to cure the injury he sustained at Newcastle. However, Tigers still won 45–39 win. Lowther with 10 points was well supported by McGregor on 9+1 and Lindsay on nine. Crowther also did well with 8+1.

Ian Hoskins signed Alf McIntosh, an Airdrie joiner, on a full contract. Alf had a novice contract at Ashfield but, as this expired after 31 days, Hoskins exploited the rules to recruit him. McIntosh was immediately taken under McGregor's wing. He did well in his second half race, just losing out to Len Williams on the line.

The Tigers had no answer to a fired up Monarchs side in Edinburgh on Saturday 23 July. They only produced two race winners and four second places. Lowther and McGregor were the best Tigers on six points each, more than half of the team's 23 points. The Tigers had all but one of the last places as Danny Lee suffered an engine failure. They were on the wrong end of 5–1s in seven consecutive races. This was a big change from 1948 when the Tigers dominated their east coast rivals for most of the season.

Joe Crowther was unlucky in one race to seize his motor a few yards from the line, gifting a win to Dick Campbell but his speed carried him over for second. The Monarchs topped 60 against Tigers for the first time ending with a 61–23 league win.

The main event did not feature a Tiger at White City on 27 July. Jack Young met Ken Le Breton for the Scottish Match Race Championship. Le Breton won the first race from the tapes, but Young won the second. In the decider the two raced neck-and-neck for two laps before Young pulled away to win.

In the match, the Tigers dominated their city rivals with another solid display. This included a maximum for Bainbridge who also had wins in the second half. The Tigers ran out comfortable 49–35 winners. Ryan and Crowther were next best on nine points each while debutant McIntosh contributed his first point. McKinlay had a good night with four points.

The only Scots in the Giants' team, Eric Liddell and Willie Wilson, failed to score. This was Gruff Garland's last appearance at White City. Riding at first reserve for the Giants, he scored 2+2. He was a big part of the early Tigers years and retired to Australia at the end of 1949.

A wet night in Edinburgh on Saturday 30 July saw the Tigers do well to take second in a four team tournament also featuring the Monarchs, Newcastle and Sheffield. Jack Young and Crowther both fell in the first heat, but went on to score well. Crowther gathered seven points. McGregor top scored for the Tigers with 10, but Bainbridge confirmed his dislike of wet tracks with just three points, one less than Lowther. The Monarchs won with 30 points; the Tigers scored 24; Newcastle collected 22 and the wooden spoon went to Sheffield on 19.

August

The Tigers gave a solid display at Fleetwood and, despite the Flyers having top end fire power, took the league points on Monday 1 August. The arrival of a black cat in the White City offices earlier that day was seen as a good omen. Maybe the absence of Wilf Plant from the Fleetwood side was more significant than the feline visitor.

It was a wet track, caused by the meeting-long downpour, that upset Fleetwood leg trailer, George Newton, who failed to score. The Tigers, Bainbridge apart, adapted to the conditions better than the Flyers. In a solid team showing, the best Tigers were Crowther, McGregor and Byrnes all on 8+1. Ryan took four rides, twice replacing out of sorts Bainbridge, and scored seven.

The Tigers eased ahead in heat three and were never headed thereafter. A 5–1 from Byrnes and McIntosh in heat 13 secured the league points and Ernie Appleby's maximum securing win in heat 14 was academic. Glasgow won 46–38.

Two days later, Byrnes lost a chain in one race and had a fall in another against Walthamstow at White City. His score was pegged back to 4+1. McGregor had a poor night, scoring 1+1 on a slick track. He was replaced in his last ride by Ryan who scored two points to make his total 6+1. McGregor came good in the second half once the rain had dampened down the surface. Bainbridge mastered the conditions for a home top score of 11. Unfortunately, most of the Tigers had problems with the track could not come from the back, so the Wolves won 45–39. The visitors went ahead on heat five and never lost the lead.

Jock Hill, a Glasgow novice who had ridden the Army speedway circuits with McGregor in Germany, was given a chance by Ian Hoskins in the hope of finding a star in the making. Hill's opponent in the second half, Joe Ferguson, kept the crowd amused as he cut the white line a couple of times before being excluded.

With Glasgow's Giants at Southampton, the Tigers and Monarchs met at Ashfield on Tuesday 9 August to settle the difference of opinion between East and West supporters on the strength of the sides.

The 56–28 win over the Tigers, albeit not at White City, was a good result for the Monarchs' fans. Few people owned cars, so their attendance was thanks to British Railways special trains which travelled to Springburn Station.

The Tigers were never at the hunt. The Monarchs opened at full throttle and their onslaught had the Tigers well and truly tamed before halfway. The Monarchs probably had an advantage because Ashfield was more like Old Meadowbank than White City.

Crash of the night involved two Tigers. McGregor came off and Ryan, just behind, also hit the cinders in heat six. Both rode again, but McGregor had another fall in his last outing.

The best Tiger was Crowther with nine points. Bainbridge, now at reserve, scored three points due to a race win in his first ride.

There was a big pay night for the Tigers back at White City the next night. The Fleetwood Flyers were grounded by a rampant home side which won 68–18, the best win of the season. Only Norman Hargreaves and Cyril Cooper, who both managed a second place in their five points total, stood between the visitors and a whitewash. The track was very, very wet. The Flyers often made the gate, but were soon overhauled by the home riders. Only Lowther and Ryan dropped points for the Tigers.

Bill Longley made up for the lack of competition in the match by showing his First Division skills, including a drive from the back to beat Crowther in the second half. Earlier Bill had been beaten in triangular events by both Dick Campbell and McGregor, but he relegated them to second and third respectively while winning the Ben Nevis Cup.

Despite appearances earlier in the season, the 'all new' novice race included Larry (John) Lazarus who became a Tiger in 1953 and 1954 after learning his trade at Ashfield. John, another renamed by a Hoskins promotion, was a motor mechanic working for 1928 Scottish 500cc Champion Jimmy Valente. He had been a sand racer pre-war and a Japanese Prisoner of War with West Ham's Howdy Byford.

Wilhelm Szeja, a 1948 novice, made his public debut. Silesian Wilhelm had been a champion wrestler, an all-round motorcyclist and distinguished war veteran. He made seven escapes from prisoner of war camps and was run over by a tank. According to Wilhelm, speedway racing was a 'push over'.

The Bristol Bulldogs demolished the Tigers at Knowle on Friday 12 August, winning the league fixture 62–22. The Bulldogs only had two last places and took eight heats 5–1. The Tigers secured a 3–3 twice. They did not have a race winner on the small, tight Knowle bowl.

The next night, the Tigers' travels yielded little reward at Coventry. The home side won 52.5–30.5 in the league. The Tigers were handed a 5–0 in heat two when Lionel Levy laid down to avoid Crowther and Les Hewitt fell on the last lap when leading. Crowther remounted to take second. but then was injured in his next outing.

Byrnes, who dead-heated with veteran Les Wotton, was the top Tiger on 7.5. Bainbridge scored seven. Apart from the dead heat, the Tigers only won three heats.

The Tigers promoter, Ian Hoskins, pre-empted a poor display by Southampton Saints on 17 August by booking West Ham's Aub Lawson to draw in wavering fans who may not have been impressed by the opposition's potential. The Tigers overpowered the Saints 58–26. Bainbridge was unbeaten in the match. Lowther scored a paid maximum. His good performance was on a machine with had a frame built by Ashfield mechanic Vic Kermond.

Aub Lawson finished one three lap event behind Bainbridge and ahead of McGregor. He then beat Byrnes and Ashfield's Keith Gurtner in the next race. He won both his heat of the Hillington Trophy and the final.

A 48–34 home win for Walthamstow did not indicate how close the action was on 22 August. The Tigers put on a good display once they got to grips with the small Chingford Road track. The score does not reflect the racing; Wolves steadily outpaced the Tigers as the match progressed. Bainbridge was the pick of the visitors with 11 points. Crowther fell in heat eight. He injured his shoulder and wrecked his machine, which ruled him out of the rest of the meeting. He had won his previous outing.

International meetings at White City had always been very popular, and estimates of the crowd for the Scotland versus England match on 24 August were between 25,000 and 27,000. Some fans were locked out. England won 55–52; the Scots had falls and threw away points. Even Jack Young, who scored 14 points, fell when trying to pass England's Norman Parker. The only Scot in the side, McGregor, had two falls. Ken Le Breton was best for Scotland. The injured Crowther had two starts but, having failed to score, was withdrawn.

England included four First Division riders: Wimbledon skipper Norman Parker, Malcolm Craven, Geoff Bennett, and Howdy Byford. This showed how seriously England took these contests. The match went to the last heat and Byford and Byrnes went all out for it. Byford just crossed the line ahead. However, the pair clashed beyond the flag and Byrnes flew off the track.

Lowther was bitterly disappointed to be left out of the Scotland team and immediately applied for a transfer away from White City, blaming Ian Hoskins for not ensuring his selection.

More international action followed. The Glasgow-based riders had a weekend in Holland 27 and 28 August. They raced under the Scotland banner in Amsterdam on the Saturday. Scotland won 38–34. On the Sunday, the action moved to the Feyenoord Stadium in Rotterdam. The meeting appears in the *1950 Stenners Annual* as Feyenoord Tigers versus Glasgow Tigers. The Dutch Tigers won 45–39. Photos show the track grafted into the stadium between the stands and a football pitch, heavily protected by barriers.

Lowther rode in the home meeting against Cradley Heath on 31 August under a cloud. He was looking for a transfer and submitted his request in writing. His score of 6+2 probably reflects his disillusionment. Fellow veteran Crowther also had a poor night because he was still suffering the effects of his injury at Walthamstow. He pulled out after two rides. McGregor rode with strained ligaments in his right ankle. The Tigers won 51–33.

The track had been wet at the start, but dried out later on. Track conditions probably had little to do with the Tiger Cub Scurry. First, Ivor Smith dropped out due to bike problems, then Jock Hill fell on lap two and Joe Ferguson did likewise on lap three. Wilhelm Szeja was the only finisher. He crossed the line without power after his chain came off. Smith made his debut in the second half and had a brief spell as a Tiger later in the season.
The newly named Heathens only had four heat wins.

September

Sheffield took full home advantage of the Owlerton track to roast Glasgow 68–16 on 1 September. Only Byrnes had any answer and he alone prevented the home team from posting the full score. His two second places, ahead of Tommy Bateman and Guy Allott held the line. Large wins like this, while occasionally enjoyable for the fans if against old rivals, did not increase the quality of the sport as entertainment. It showed the uneven nature of the league, particularly when the weaker team was away from home. Five Sheffield riders had maximums. The only interest for the home fans up to heat six must have been whether their men could post a record score. Len Williams set a new track record in this match.

After two good rides to score 5+1, Bristol's Fred Tuck pulled out of the meeting at White City on 7 September for an unusual reason. He was suffering from fibrositis, and is reported to have collapsed in the pits.

Bainbridge was the Tiger's star, but without support could not stop the title-seeking Bulldogs winning 49–35. He was unbeaten, but only Byrnes and, to lesser extent, Lowther, gave him any support. The normally dependable Ryan's zero from four rides was a major factor in this defeat.

Bristol had a passenger in Mike Beddoe, who had three engine failures in a row, but their all-round strength from the rest was enough. Bristol moved ahead in heat three and pulled away as the meeting progressed.

A meeting in the Midlands two days later was the first for the Tigers after it was announced that Lowther would be moving on. It was 10 years since he first raced for Glasgow in the immediate pre-War era. He managed a poor two at Cradley Heath on Friday 9 September and the Tigers lost 59–25. Byrnes and Bainbridge were the best Tigers with seven each, but not enough to make any inroads. Reports suggest that there was little fighting spirit from the Tigers except in heat 11 when Bainbridge and McGregor challenged Gil Craven and Phil Malpass. Glasgow only had one race winner, McGregor in heat 14.

The meeting at Norwich the next night was the end of an era because Will Lowther rode his last races as a Tiger. He went to Newcastle and Jack Hodgson moved to Glasgow in a swap deal.

It was also the end of the road for Byrnes who was involved in a crash on the first bend in heat 10. He sustained a fractured skull and never returned to race in Britain again. He was a big loss for Glasgow. Arguably, he still had scoring power as he was just about to complete his third season with Tigers. Unfortunately, the crash helmets of the day, known as 'pudding basins' or 'skid lids' did not provide the protection given by modern helmets. Serious head injuries were not uncommon in this era.

Bainbridge was the leading Tiger yet again, this time with nine points while Byrnes was next best on five from his three completed races. The home side won 58–26, with only two Tigers winning a race.

Jack Hodgson made his Tigers debut at White City on 14 September chipping in with 7+1 after a pointless first ride. He was matched by McGregor. Crowther, returning from injury, had his first outing as the new Tigers' skipper but only scored 5+1. Top Tiger was Bainbridge with nine, thanks to a last race engine failure. His side had a comfortable 45–39 win over Sheffield. Lindsay's return was reduced when he fell in the last heat after touching Allott's back wheel. Pre-match adjustments to McKinlay's knee hook cost him points in his first race, but this was resolved before his next race.

Glasgow pulled away from Sheffield steadily through the match although the visitors did not give up without a struggle. Tommy Allott's four rides produced heat wins for the visitors. Bainbridge and McGregor lowered Tommy's colours in the second half. Tommy Bateman crashed in the second half and was taken to hospital with concussion.

The second half also featured Ken Le Breton who had two races with Bainbridge on standard machines and a third with Bainbridge using a machine fitted with rockets. Le Breton won the opening four lap race with Bainbridge winning both two lap races, with and without the assistance of a rocket.

Bainbridge was the star of the meeting at Newcastle on Monday 19 September, winning all his races in the match by a large margin to record a maximum. McGregor also rode well for 10 points, but Crowther had an off night and failed to score. His last race fall left him badly shaken. He was described as playing 'roly poly' with his bike and ended up pinned under it. The Tigers' long tail again failed to wag and they lost 49–34.

Will Lowther scored 7+3 against his old club while Jack Hodgson managed only two for the Tigers. However, when Jack met his brother Frank he did finish ahead of him.

After a bright start, which saw him win his opening ride two nights later against Norwich at White City, Crowther dislocated his shoulder in heat four, which ruled him out for the rest of the season. According to the local press, Hoskins tried to fill the gap with either Ron Green or Jack Mason of Hull but both were ruled out by injury. 'Ron' was really Johnny and 'Jack' was really Eric.

Heat four took three reruns to complete. The first attempt was stopped when all four riders crashed. In the first rerun, Crowther crashed and retired from the meeting. In the second rerun, McKinlay and Johnny Davies crashed ahead of Norwich's Fred Rogers, who was ruled out of the meeting with a broken jaw after hitting the fence, avoiding the other two. With McKinlay excluded, Davies and Ted Bravery eventually completed the race for a Stars 5–0. However, the Tigers rode with some conviction to beat Norwich 47–36.

McGregor was the Tigers hero with a full maximum, while Ryan sprung back to form with a paid maximum. He benefitted greatly from his partner, Jack Hodgson's team riding skills. Bainbridge, for weeks a consistently good scorer, had a poor night with bike problems and settled for two points. Hodgson was third top Tiger on nine.

The second half novice event featured the White City debut of Tommy Miller. He finished third behind Ivor Smith and Joe Ferguson and ahead of Gordon Mitchell, who was also making his debut. Tommy later emerged as the hottest prospect in British speedway. Ian Hoskins said that Miller "was gifted with natural throttle control. He would slide his bike gently into a corner, blip his throttle a few times and come out of the bend, leaving the rest of them for dead." Mitchell did not develop as quickly, but rode for Motherwell's Golden Eagles in 1958, Edinburgh in 1960 and Newcastle in 1961. He also rode at Glasgow when it re-opened in 1964.

On 26 September, the Tigers visited Walthamstow in the league. They held their own in the early heats, but a 5–0 in heat four due to Ryan and Smith falling and failing to complete the race, was the turning point. McGregor and Hodgson scored over half the Tigers' total in a 56–27 defeat. McGregor scored 10 and Hodgson nine. It was a weak Tigers side with three juniors although McIntosh, newly elevated from reserve, scored three points despite his lack of experience. The Tigers' debutants, Smith and Ferguson in the reserve berths, replacing McKinlay and McIntosh, failed to score.

Yet again, it was solid rather than spectacular scoring opposition that beat the Tigers who often found it hard to adapt to tracks which differed from the long straights and tight bends of White City.

Southampton, so poor at White City, turned the tables on the weakened Tigers and took revenge the next night at Bannister Court. The Saints won 52–32. The Tigers had two novices in Smith, who scored his debut point, and Ferguson. The riders in the team should have done more. The Tigers top scorers were Bainbridge, Hodgson and Ryan all on eight points.

With no Tigers in the line-up, Ken Le Breton was hot favourite to win the Glasgow Gala Cup at White City on 28 September. However, he had bike problems which left him out of the frame. His bike packed up in heat 10, so he borrowed Merv Harding's for his next outing. That bike also let him down, but his last outing, on another borrowed machine, saw him win. Ken had to settle for nine points. Another pre-meeting favourite, Edinburgh's Jack Young, ended joint third with 11. Equal with Jack was fellow Australian, Norwich's Bob Leverenz.

First Division competitors were Wilbur Lamoreaux, who performed poorly for six points, and Ron Clarke, who did better for 14 points, giving him joint top spot with Alan Hunt. In a run-off for the trophy, Clarke overtook Hunt to win.

Fleetwood, rarely successful at White City, turned the tables on the Tigers on the same night as the Glasgow Gala Cup meeting. Fleetwood won 56–28. The Tigers were up against it from the outset. Ryan rode his last ever away match for the Tigers, bowing out with seven points. Lindsay scored six while Bainbridge and McGregor were next best on five. Ivor Smith picked up another point, but Joe Ferguson was still looking to make his mark.

October

The Glasgow Tigers joined with their namesakes from Sheffield to form a Select side to race the Edinburgh Monarchs at Old Meadowbank on Saturday 1 October. It was billed as a 'Grand

Challenge Match'. Glasgow men who scored were Ryan 2+2 and Lindsay 2+1. Bainbridge failed to score. McGregor crashed into the fence in front of the stand in the opening race and was hit by Don Cuppleditch. He then hit the starting gate rendering it inoperable.

It was not a classic for the Tigers' fans at White City on 5 October. However, the management recruited Graham Warren and Bill Kitchen for the second half, giving the fans no excuse to miss this meeting. Fleetwood were beaten 51–33. Bainbridge signed off for the season with an immaculate maximum. Hodgson and McGregor scored eight each. Ryan was next best while McKinlay, back in the side at reserve to replace Ferguson, scored 7+2, a paid maximum for his three rides.

Buck Ryan rode his last ever match for Tigers and scored 7+3. It was also his last in the United Kingdom. He had intended to come back, but could not before the start of the 1950 season because his wife was unwell. He never returned to British speedway

A late addition to the programme was a special race between Alf McIntosh and Dutch riders Piet Van Aartsen and Arenid Hartman who were members of a Dutch team preparing to race Scotland at Ashfield the next day. The fourth rider was D McAteer. Both Hartman and McAteer fell and the rerun was a match race with McIntosh beating Van Aartsen.

The second half also featured Wembley star Bill Kitchen and the Brummies' Graham Warren, who were the counter attraction to make up for the unattractive Flyers.

What can be said about a record defeat for the Tigers who lost 5–1 in every heat? The final score at Bristol on Friday 7 October after 14 heats was 70–14. The grand slam must have been something for the home fans to talk about rather than Tigers' woeful performance. To be fair Tigers were not at full strength, without a heat leader, but the Bulldogs' display was wheel perfect. It was the first whitewash of the post-War era and a record that stood for many years. Hodgson and Lindsay were the 'best' Tigers with four points each. Hodgson was the closest to preventing the record defeat, but Salmon snatched second place in heat eight. Malcom Riddell made his Tigers debut.

The side whitewashed at Bristol represented the Tigers against Coventry in this last meeting of the season at White City on 12 October. However, home fans had something to shout about. The Tigers fans were not happy with Bees' Derrick Tailby who they believed skittled McGregor by forcing him wide in heat four. Was it by way of retribution Lindsay and Tailby had a coming together in Tailby's next outing? Both stayed on to finish the race, with Tailby second. With five relatively inexperienced riders, it was always going to be hard for the Tigers who lost 49–35.

Hodgson scored 11 while McGregor and Lindsay added nine points each. The long tail of McKinlay, McIntosh, Smith, Malcolm Riddell and Ferguson all struggled against more experienced riders.

According to one report the annual mechanics race was won by George Downes who was timed at 25.4 for a single lap. Favourite for the race, Mark Black, who was a mechanic for Junior Bainbridge, had engine trouble. The finishing order was Dick Stewart, Mark Black, Joe Baker, and Downes. McGregor and Lindsay rode together on Ian Hoskins' mascot bike from a five yards handicap.

Tommy Miller won his first race at White City, taking the Consolation Scurry from Niven McCreadie, Mark Black (replacing Red Monteith) and Gordon Mitchell who retired.

In their report on the Tigers, *Stenners 1950 Annual* said that they were "Powerful at home but weak away". It also noted the amount of injuries the team sustained. From a Scottish speedway development point of view, it noted that Gordon McGregor was now heat leader class, and that the team fielded six Scottish novices in team line-ups.

11. 1950: So close

A new innovation was the concrete grid starting gate area designed to ensure uniformity at all tracks. The Tigers installed one and had it made locally. The savings on transporting a grid from England were put into the stadium terracing, increasing the capacity to 26,000.

The starting grid wasn't the only innovation – new tyres were introduced. Many riders were against this because they were considered to be of inferior quality. They were expected to last only a few meetings against the more than 20 some of the old tyres lasted. The authorities soon had a change of heart and riders soon returned to the old tyre.

Another innovation proposed for 1950 was a Scottish League. Ambitious plans to run the length and breadth of the country, fronted by Jimmy Valente, the first ever Scottish 500cc Dirt Track champion, never got off the ground.

The Tigers management wanted their riders to be fit and in early April announced that the riders would train at nearby Ibrox Stadium with the Glasgow Rangers footballers.

Glasgow had Joe Crowther, Jack Hodgson, Norman Lindsay, Junior Bainbridge, and, Gordon McGregor back in the line-up. They gave outings to Willie Gordon. He was back after a break due to a leg injury.

Also, the Tigers added new signings: Johnny Green, Tommy Miller, Peter Dykes, Peter 'Gundy' Harris – a 23-year-old rugby league playing Australian from Bathurst, New South Wales – Duncan Hendry a 17-year-old Scot, and Jack Morris. Morris, reportedly originally selected by Ian Hoskins using astrology from 200 applicants, was a flyweight boxer. The Tigers also had Ray Harker, but soon transferred him to the Giants. Newcastle's Joe Arthur joined the Tigers for a reported £200 transfer fee, but did not stay long.

Englishman Johnny Green came for a fee of £100 from under the nose of Fleetwood. Green from Burnley, a Hull Angel in 1949 soon moved on and was replaced by Ken McKinlay. He was wanted by Johnnie Hoskins, but eventually moved to Sheffield before returning to Scotland for spells as a Monarch and a Lanarkshire Eagle.

Tommy Miller rose to fame in spectacular fashion as the season unfolded. The Tigers' management obviously believed he would do well as they were reported to have supplied him with a new bike. Ian Hoskins was approached mid-season about selling him, but turned down Edinburgh's advances.

Kiwi Peter Dykes came from Taita Speedway and proved to be a popular signing and was a regular fixture in the team. Waiting in the wings on Tigers books were Alf McIntosh and Ken McKinlay. The latter started showing signs of progress in midseason and got better as the year went on. Joe 'Whaler' Ferguson was on the high seas at the start of the season and returning to continue to ride. Unfortunately, he never graduated to the team after his brief spell in 1949, but his daring kept the crowd entertained after the match.

Nobby Downham retired, Ivor Smith suffered a neck injury and was advised to quit. Jack Hodgson wintered in South Africa and flew back without his luggage just before the season. The trip back took almost five days, ending with a train trip from London to Newcastle. With his bike in transit, Jack used his brother Frank's new bike for the first meeting. Jack would be joined by Frank who, at the time, became Tigers' record signing. Frank never hit the form he had showed with Middlesbrough, but was, none-the-less, a dependable scorer.

Veteran Joe Crowther became the Tigers' captain. He had spent the winter nurturing new talent at Bothwell. Unfortunately, after an up-and-down season, he was axed in September, ending his lengthy association starting with the pre-war Lions and post-war Tigers.

During the season Tigers tried to sign Hanley Potter Frank Evans after he had shown up well in a second half. Trials were held each Wednesday from 1 March until the start of the season at White City. The trials were behind closed doors and only involved invited riders.

White City were again in the National League Division Two. There were 15 teams, and in the league, each raced against the others once at home and once away. It really was a national league, with three teams in Scotland and two – Southampton and Plymouth – on the south coast of England. Walthamstow again represented London, and Norwich were joined in East Anglia by Yarmouth. The other teams were from the midlands and north of England. The league matches started in June, before then there was the North Shield competition.

Bristol and Birmingham were now in the nine-team First Division. The Third Division had 10 teams, all from the south or midlands of England except for Liverpool. Bonus points became a scoring feature in 1950. The riders benefitted, and maybe it encouraged team riding, but did not affect the match scores.

April

The opening meeting of 1950 was against Newcastle in the North Shield on 5 April. It saw the Tigers debuts of Peter Dykes, Johnny Green, Willie Gordon and Blantyre's Tommy Miller. The latter had a quiet start scoring one point, but became the best of the lot. Junior Bainbridge was in form with 11, while Gordon McGregor and Joe Crowther both scored 7+1. McGregor had a new set of leathers in which he set a new track record in heat one. His old leathers were stolen from a car along with Johnnie Hoskins' camera. Dykes's debut earned him 6+1 and Green scored 1+1.

Unfortunately, the Tigers just lost 43–41. They led by eight points at the end of heat eight then two 5–1s allowed Newcastle to level. The Diamonds drew ahead in heat 11 and so it stayed until the end. The match went to a last heat decider, but a tactical ride by Diamonds' Derrick Close and Tommy Bateman shut out the inexperienced Bill Gordon as they followed Crowther home.

The Tigers had hoped to benefit from their team riding, but it was the Diamonds who gave lessons to the home riders. Will Lowther was back as a Diamond, but scored less than the man he had swapped with, Jack Hodgson. Newcastle may have made the trip north with some trepidation as the Speedway Riders Association recommended that visitors to Glasgow be vaccinated against smallpox as the city was in the grips of an epidemic.

Norman Lindsay returned from Australia where he and fellow 1949 Tiger Buck Ryan had been capped. Lindsay cut it fine as he had only arrived in Glasgow on the morning of the meeting against Fleetwood on 12 April in the North Shield. Lindsay scored eight points, and lost points for crossing the inside white line and being excluded in heat 11. McGregor scored a paid maximum while Hodgson on 9+2 and Dykes on 9+1 gave excellent backing.

Tommy Miller showed the fans a glimpse of what was to come when he came from the back in heat eight, passing George Newton and Fred Yates to gain a paid win. The Flyers were beaten 55–28.

Foreign visitors featured in the second half. Crowther's win over Swedes Bertil Carlsson and ice racer Stig Pramberg was thanks to a last bend outside burst. Swede Olle Nygren, seen as a rising star, beat Bainbridge in the other international race, before winning his heat and the second half final. A Fleetwood rider is reported to have been reprimanded at Stoke for trying to use a doctored tyre. His defence was that he had used it at Glasgow and had not been challenged.

Four heats were raced at Newcastle on Monday 17 April before the meeting was abandoned because of the rain soaked track. The score was 12–12.

Two nights later, the Tigers came down to earth with a bang at White City. The Hanley (Stoke) Potters came and won. The margin, 50–34, left the home fans stunned. McGregor was on the way to a maximum when his bike failed in the final heat. By then, the heat result was academic because the Potters had the points wrapped up. Bainbridge, now free from worrying about his old car known affectionately as the 'Bomb', but now suffering from dental trouble, was the best Tiger with 11 points. However, McGregor apart, the home riders had no answers. Dykes, so good the week before, had two lasts before being replaced by Green who fared no better. Crowther needed a physiotherapist to help him with an injured shoulder.

It was back on the old tyre at White City on 26 April as the Tigers faced Edinburgh Monarchs in a North Shield match. At last, it seemed that the blend of old Tigers and new blood were starting to gel. Lindsay and Crowther were pleased with the switch of tyres and it showed in their form. Crowther had a new motor and used it to good effect, beating Jack Young in his second half heat. Lindsay and Crowther scored 10 each. This and 8+2 from McGregor helped the Tigers win 47–37. Tommy Miller, with five points, was seen as a new hero. Bainbridge lost points when he fell in heat three. Despite the Monarchs' two misfortunes, the Tigers had the upper hand and only Green failed to contribute.

Young had clutch troubles in his first outing but bounced back to set the fastest time of the season in his next. He had bike troubles again in his last ride. The Monarchs management took advantage of a stoppage to fix a burst light and sweep up broken glass to sort out their man in yellow and black in heat 12. Programmed Ron Phillips, was eventually announced, but he was still in the pits having a cup of tea while Danny Lee was out on track. Maybe Ron was in need of a 'cuppa' to recover from his earlier push home.

Ian Hoskins gave a trial to a Spaniard, Emanuel Bua, who wrecked the track spare. He wasn't given a public airing. Australian Clive Gressor, brother-in-law of Bat Byrnes, did ride, but moved to Motherwell later in the season where he sustained career-ending injuries.

The Tigers had no answer to the Monarchs in the North Shield return match at Edinburgh on 29 April. Only McGregor with eight points emerged any credit in a 63–21 defeat. Crowther and Hodgson were dismal; both managed one point. Lindsay and Bainbridge scored four apiece. Four Tigers only amassed 3+1 between them. The Tigers did not hit double figures until heat seven. Pointless in the match, Miller shone in the second half. He won his second half heat and the final from the back, passing Allott, Lack and Lee.

May

Back on home shale on 3 May, the Tigers beat Sheffield Tars 47–37. The former Tigers were known as the Tars for most of the season. The winning margin might have been larger, but for a last heat Tars' 5–1.

Even at this early stage in the season, Miller was making people take notice. He set the fastest time of the night, took a paid win in his second ride. He had an engine failure in heat 10 when he replaced Dykes. He fell in his second half heat as he tried to round Guy Allott. McGregor scored a full maximum while Lindsay collected 9+1. McIntosh made his comeback in the second half.

Jack and Frank Hodgson during their time at Glasgow.

Meeting the management: Joe Crowther with Ian and Johnnie Hoskins.

1950 Glasgow Tigers: Ken McKinlay, Joe Crowther, Ian Hoskins, Jack Hodgson, Gordon McGregor; front: Peter Dykes, Junior Bainbridge, Tommy Miller, Norman Lindsay.

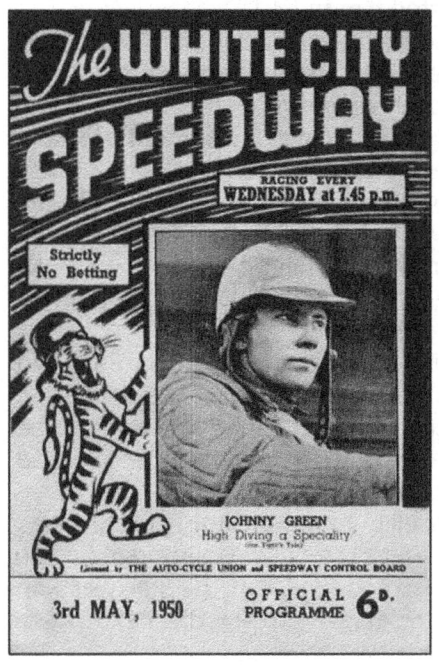

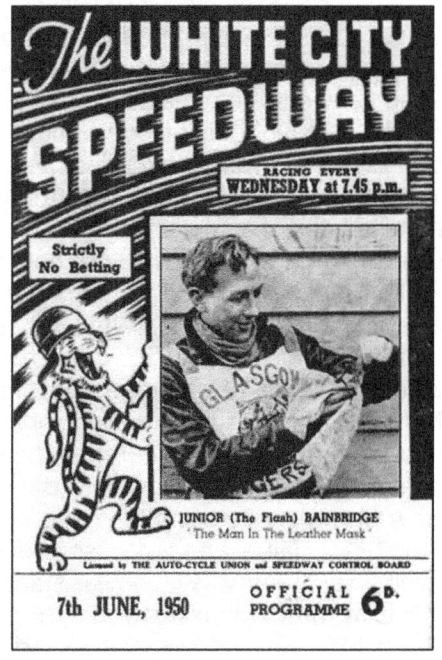

Sheffield were not stars so their score was creditable. Second reserve, Australian Jack Lasagna, was an Edinburgh signing who had a few outings for Sheffield before retiring. He never returned home, seeing out his days in Edinburgh.

A bit of Glasgow Tigers history was made at Sheffield on Friday 5 May in an otherwise forgettable match lost 53–31. Miller moved into the top six for the first time, but only managed one point. The Tigers' top two had bike problems which did not help their cause. McGregor was leading heat six when his bike failed and the track spare let him down in heat nine. He scored five in his other two rides. Bainbridge and Lindsay were the best Tigers with eight and seven respectively. The Tigers were close until heat five, then concede four 5–1s in five heats. The Tars were much tougher proposition than at White City. The top three Tars scored two more than all eight Tigers.

The Hanley management welcomed the Tigers to Sun Street the next night with the Clan Stewart Ladies Pipe Band. However, the music failed to inspire them. Glasgow lost 55–29 in front of 16,000 fans. The bright spot was Miller again showing progress with a well taken eight from three rides after a fall in his first. McGregor was the best Tiger on 9+1. Banbridge had withdrawn after two rides after a fall and engine failure.

A 20,000 crowd watched a keenly contested local derby at Ashfield's Saracen Park on Tuesday 9 May. It went to the wire. Unfortunately, Crowther and Hodgson couldn't grab the 5–1 needed to take the points, but Crowther did split the Ken Le Breton and Keith Gurtner pairing, both of whom came to the tapes unbeaten by a Tiger. Green, who had bike failure in his opener, skittled Baird in heat 13 and was excluded, thereby reducing the Tigers' chance of a win. After a short stretcher ride Baird, now with his third Scottish team, took third. Green had drifted wide on the bend, collecting Baird before injuring himself as he hit the fence.

McGregor and Bainbridge were outstanding with 10 points each while Lindsay scored 6+2. Crowther collected five while Miller's last outing win boosted him to 5+1.

It was a close match throughout and the teams were never separated by more than four, but the Giants prevailed 44–40. While the races that featured Ken Le Breton were cut and dried early on, the remainder went to the wire after a closely fought four laps.

The next night, first blood went to the Giants at White City. The match went to the visitors thanks to a 5–1 from the flawless Ken Le Breton and the often less than perfect Keith Gurtner. The latter rose to the occasion after an indifferent previous three races. The sides were well matched and the contest was close. The Tigers were two up going into the last heat, but Crowther and Lindsay could not hold the Giants who won by two points.

Le Breton completed his second maximum against the Tigers in two days. Willie Wilson, a Scot who had started in White City second halves, gave support.

McGregor continued his good run for the Tigers with 11 while Hodgson on 8+1 and Bainbridge with 7+1 gave reasonable support. Green who had the reserve berth, replacing McKinlay, was excluded for bringing off Eric Liddell in heat 13. Eric, despite appearing to be injured, returned for the rerun and collected the third place point. The Tigers lacked second string and reserve fire power on the night

A Glasgow Tigers and Giants Select rode against Bothwell Bulls at Hamilton Showgrounds on 13 May. Miller and Dykes scored 11 points each and were the only league riders in the joint side. Green was of similar status for the Bulls. He scored nine, but the star was Ken McKinlay with a maximum 12. He was rewarded by a reserve berth for the next Tigers meeting. The Select lost 48–35 to the Bulls.

Halifax Dukes visited White City on 17 May, and lost heavily 51–33. The Dukes held their own until heat seven, but fell apart in the last seven races. Green moved out of the team.

He was replaced by Ken McKinlay, who rose to the occasion, scoring a reserve's maximum, including a win over Arthur Forrest. Ken looped at the start of the second half final robbing him of the chance of facing Vic Emms.

The Dukes had been expected to beat the Tigers. Bainbridge scored 11 – his maximum hopes were spoiled by Vic Emms who scored a maximum. He also cleaned up the second half. For the Tigers, McGregor scored 9+1 while Miller took 6+4. Crowther managed only 3+1 and fans grumbled about his performance.

The Black Prince (because of his immaculate black leathers) – Arthur Forrest – did well for the Dukes but Emms and Forrest apart, the Dukes struggled on the Glasgow circuit which was quite unlike their banked high speed track. Harold Booth fell in heat 12, but his bike continued on and demolished part of the safety fence. Ashfield's new Australian, Sydney bus conductor Noel Watson, made his White City debut and won the Tiger Cub Rally in the second half. His chances of a senior team place were sorely hampered by the restrictions on signing more than the quota of 'colonial' riders.

The return North Shield match at Halifax's The Shay two nights later, produced few thrills for the fans. The Dukes comprehensively beat the Tigers 50–34, despite the Tigers scoring three 5–1 heat wins. The Dukes' win sealed their successful campaign for the silverware, just pipping Edinburgh. After two heats it looked like the Tigers would give Dukes a fight, but it never developed, despite a mini revival mid match.

Hodgson scored eight points while McGregor added 7+1, Norman Lindsay had a run of last places which was unusual for him.

Fleetwood's track was not everyone's favourite and the Tigers didn't do much on Saturday 20 May. They lost the North Shield match 47–37 to the bottom of the table side. Hodgson top scored on eight; McKinlay scored 6+1 while Bainbridge and Crowther added six each.

The Tigers started brightly, but the Flyers soon took control and a penultimate heat 5–1 made the scores look better. The Flyers' Alf Parker thrilled the crowd with his win from the back in heat five. He missed the gate, but soon rounded Miller. He then set off in pursuit of Hodgson. He stalked Hodgson before capitalising on him moving slightly wide on the last bend. Parker squeezed through on the inside and grabbed second almost on the line.

On the road for their third away fixture in four days, the Tigers suffered a 56–28 defeat at Newcastle on Monday 22 May. Bainbridge, with eight points, probably enjoyed stopping Derrick Close recording a maximum. Their race in heat 14 was a great tussle with Bainbridge just getting the verdict on the line. Miller was the next best Tiger on 4+1, including a from-the-back win in heat five. Former Tiger Will Lowther secured a paid maximum. The Tigers were well adrift by heat four and kept on falling further behind. They only managed two heat wins and were pretty poor. Former Newcastle rider Jack Hodgson struggled to get to grips with his old stamping ground.

The Tigers took a break from team action and Ian Hoskins staged the Glasgow Gala Cup on 24 May with a guest list including the First Division's Eric Chitty and Ron Clarke and top Second Division riders Forrest, Le Breton and Hunt.

Despite some poor team performances, Crowther was still the rider to beat at home when an individual trophy was at stake. He beat Clarke, who had earlier set the season's fastest time, in a run-off for the trophy after they had tied on 13 points. Hunt took third place with 12 and McGregor, Keith Gurtner and Forrest ended on 11. West Ham's Chitty had been a star at White City in 1945, but had a miserable night and pulled out after three races.

Tommy Miller was sacked by his employers for taking so much time off work. He bowed to the inevitable and became a full-time speedway rider.

A rain-soaked track in the Potteries helped give the Hanley team an advantage on Saturday 27 May. The 65–43 defeat was bad, but it was a National Trophy fixture, The Tigers could make amends at home. The only Tiger to stand up to the Potters was McGregor with 16 from six rides. Bainbridge, with just two points, still had bike problems which did not help as he also did not like wet tracks. Lindsay had a good night on eight while Crowther scored five. The Tigers on the road could still be fragile. The Potters heat leaders had reasonable support and they won twice the number of races Tigers did. While they had seven last places to the Tigers' 11, they had most of the second places.

The second leg was at White City on 31 May. The Tigers won 70–38 win to go through 113–103 on aggregate. The fast-improving Miller opened the night in a track record time, 78.6 seconds, wiping 0.6 seconds off Graham Warren's record.

Miller scored a career best 13+1, one short of Bainbridge who scored a maximum 15. In order to avoid three rides in a row for Junior, Miller and Crowther were given extra rides in the nominated heat. Crowther, along with the veteran Lindsay were the Tigers' trump cards with 10+2 and 10+1 respectively. McGregor only contributed 6+1 due to a faulty – recently welded – frame which now lacked flexibility.

Before the meeting, Ian Hoskins was unhappy about the Stoke line-up with Brian Pritchett in the team and John Fitzpatrick at reserve. Fitzpatrick had outperformed Pritchett before, but this time round the reverse was the case. Stoke were two down at heat three then a run of Tigers' 5–1s decided the outcome. The Tigers had secured the tie by heat 14.

June

The Tigers built up a big lead on 7 June to take to Norwich for the second leg of the National Trophy tie with a 70–38 win. They had four riders in double figures: Bainbridge with 14, Miller on 12, Hodgson on 11+1 and McGregor on 10+2. Reserves Dykes and McKinlay both scored 5+1 from two rides. Norwich were 20–4 down after four heats. Apart from a Phil Clarke and Fred Rogers 5–1 in heat seven, it was one-way traffic for Tigers.

Visiting stars Ken Le Breton and Jack Young vied for the Silver Helmet. Young won the first race from the outside, but Le Breton won the other two. In the second race he locked up in front of Young who slowed to avoid him. This let Le Breton to regain control and win.

However, the Stars outclassed the Tigers three days later at The Firs to bounce back from the big defeat in Glasgow. They won 78–30 in front of crowd of over 12,000. This meant they won the tie 116–100 and progressed to the next round.

Only Bainbridge, with 11 points, was on the pace. Dykes managed five from four reserve outings while Crowther took four points. The rest of the visitors was poor.

On a wet night in Glasgow, it was uncertain whether a crowd would turn out on 14 June, but the programme was promising. Top Australian Vic Duggan fronted a select side which had Graham Warren the only 'imported' star. The rest of Vic's Team were Scottish based. Duggan was beaten by to fellow Australians Jack Young and Ken Le Breton who had been drafted in to the Scottish Select team. Duggan avenged his opening heat defeat by outpacing Young in the last heat. Vic, who was at an advantage because of the special frames he made, used the track spare. This was not to his liking, but he was stuck with it as he had wrecked his own machine at Ashfield the night before. He still managed 10 points, but his Select side lost 51–33. Le Breton scored an impressive maximum, winning each race by a big margin while Jack Young scored 11. The best Tiger was Bainbridge with 9+1.

Warren had an off night with a fall reducing him to six points. The Giants' Keith Gurtner scored eight for Duggan's team. Miller was getting faster and set a new track record plus he beat both Young and Duggan. Le Breton cleaned up taking the second half final from Warren, Miller and Duggan.

The Tigers went to Ashfield on Saturday 17 June with a new mascot. Miss Dorothy Lamour, a well-known Hollywood film star, agreed to accept the role. While she never saw the Tigers in action, maybe she helped inspire them to this 56–52 Border Cup first leg win. The Border Cup was the forerunner to the Scottish Cup. For the record Dorothy replaced the 1949 mascot, Sheila the tigress.

McGregor scored 14 points from six rides. Bainbridge added 9+2 while Hodgson scored 9+1. McKinlay had a good night with eight.

On the wet night in north Glasgow the track was not good early on. The Tigers were without Miller – on his way back from Exeter – and the Giants were without Willie Wilson. Both riders were stranded at Bristol when their car broke down en-route from their World Championship round in the south west.

The Hanley Potters were up against it at White City on 21 June in the league, but were handed a heat win in the 10th race when McGregor fell, Les Jenkins had engine failure and Norman Lindsay struggled to turn his machine. The race was won by reserve Ray Harris. He was the only Potters race winner as they struggled to a 60–23 defeat.

Miller took his first maximum, albeit a paid one, with 11+1. Bainbridge and Dykes also had paid maximums with 10+2. With Lindsay on 11, and Crowther with 9+1, the. Tigers had a big pay night.

Unlike at Ashfield the night before, the wet weather in Glasgow missed White City, but the threat of rain kept the crowd down. Localised rain is unusual in a city the size of Glasgow, but before television weather forecasts and the internet it was not easy to find current information.

A Glasgow Select, mostly Tigers with a couple of Giants thrown in, faced a Monarchs side in Edinburgh without Jack Young who was riding in a test match on Saturday 24 June. However, on the wet track the visitors scored well below their potential. The Select side led for much of the match, but let things slide towards the end. The Monarchs won 44–40. The Tigers had Miller on 10+1 and McGregor on 9+1 as top scorers.

The Tigers won 60–48 at White City on 28 June in style to clinch their place in the Border Cup Final 116–100 on aggregate. Ashfield had the two top scorers on the night, but did not match the Tigers' strength in depth.

The Giants' Australian trio took the match to the Tigers. While the top Giants, in dark blue and white, were the best riders on the night, it was the more solid team in red and white that won the day. Four Giants, half the team, only gathered three points between them. The Tigers took 10 bonus points to the Giants' one. Bainbridge and McGregor both scored 12, while Miller – emerging as third heat leader – scored 9+1.

The Tigers would now face Edinburgh in the final after they had knocked out Newcastle in the other semi-final.

A Glasgow Select team rode at Santry Stadium in Dublin on Friday 30 June. Only Alf McIntosh was a Tiger and of the rest, only Willie Gordon – an occasional Tiger – had any real experience. Gundy (Peter) Harris was a junior at Ashfield, Allan (McQueen) Robertson was a Scottish novice. Tony Murphy was probably Tommy (Spud) Murphy an Irish novice who had rides in Scotland. Nothing is known of Harry Briggs but he may have been a better known junior Alan Briggs. Glasgow Select lost 33–27 to the Santry Saints.

July

The Tigers visited Coventry in the league on Saturday 1 July. A 16,000 crowd enjoyed the action. Coventry Bees' Stan Williams injured a knee first time out and withdrew. A spectacular fall and crash into the fence in heat six saw Derek Tailby score just six points.

Unfortunately, the Tigers could not capitalise on Bees' problems. Crowther and McKinlay both failed to score in a 47–37 defeat. Miller, who moved to Coventry in 1954, scored nine and McGregor scored 8+1. Dykes took extra rides to replace Crowther.

Sadly, this night was not be remembered for this fixture, but for fatal accidents. At Odsal veteran Joe Abbott was killed, and at Norwich where Jock Shead died.

On a lighter note, around this time some of the Tigers were being lined up for membership of the Handlebar Club. Nothing to do with motorcycles, this was a club for gentlemen who sported moustaches. Prime candidates were 'The Tash' McGregor, Crowther and Hodgson. Potential members were Dykes and second halfer, Glasgow born 'Buffalo Bill' Bill Byford. The subscription was £1 a head.

Byford was a friend of Gordon McGregor, a former Army dispatch rider who had ridden for Hanomog in Germany. He was a rolling stone, who worked in Canada after demob. The then 24-year-old gave speedway a go. but never made the grade.

The meeting of the 'other Tigers' went to the Irish side which was staffed by First Division Wimbledon riders or their reserve league side. Sunday Speedway was frowned upon in Britain, but was the norm in Ireland. Glasgow Tigers met Shelbourne Tigers at Shelbourne Park, Dublin on Sunday 2 July. The home side won 55–28. Shelbourne featured a father and son pairing in Les and, Ronnie Moore. For Glasgow, McGregor top scored with nine, which included Glasgow's only race win. Hodgson contributed 5+1 while Miller scored five. Dykes nearly didn't make it, having left his passport in his car at White City. However, he forgot his boots. With borrowed boots, he then had bike problems which restricted his tally.

A drawn heat at the start did not signal the trouble ahead for Tigers who were comprehensively beaten by Southampton at Bannister Court on 4 July. Only McGregor and Lindsay won a race, and these were too late on to make much difference.

The Sporting Saints' fans cheered McGregor's win from the back on the last bend in heat 11. Crowther was best Tiger on 6+1 while Lindsay, Tigers only other race winner, scored five points. The Saints won 56–28.

Newcastle's Frank Hodgson took the £30 cheque after keeping lone Tiger Crowther into last place in his last race in the World Championship round at White City on 5 July. Crowther had to settle for joint runner up with Leicester's Cyril Page and Johnny Carpenter. He must have been worn out with traveling back from Southampton, a daunting trip at the best of times. Fourth place was also shared between Swede Bertil Carlsson and Len Read. A second ride fall reduced Johnny Carpenter's return to nine while Charlie May suffered bike problems after a bright start.

A weakened Cradley Heath side missing Alan Hunt and Jack Arnfield were no match for the Tigers at White City on 12 July. The Tigers raced to an easy 50–34 win. This meeting saw Miller's first full maximum and his first second half trophy. McGregor, with a now almost perfect bike frame, scored a paid maximum. Lindsay had a good night on nine. He could have had a maximum but for an engine failure. Dykes's contribution was pegged back due to bike problems. Crowther also had bike problems and changed an engine in 12 minutes. The Heathens kept things close early on but Tigers pushed them aside in the second part of the match.

Frank Young, brother of Edinburgh's star Jack, fell after performing a spectacular somersault in his opening ride. He was ruled out thereafter. Eric Boothroyd, then a young rising star, rode for Cradley. The Heathens were lucky to have had their machines as they had a bit of Cooks' Tour of western Scotland before a British Railways clerk phoned White City, thereby averting a crisis.

Ken McKinlay won the opening round of the Dorothy Lamour Progressive Match Race beating Willie Gordon.

The Tigers' trip to Fleetwood on Saturday 15 July was fruitless. The weather prevented any speedway.

On 19 July, the Tigers raced to a record, if not entertaining, 68–16 home win, two points short of a whitewash, over Yarmouth Bloaters. They were on their first visit to Scotland. Only McGregor and Dykes dropped points; the rest cruised to full or paid maximums. Gordon lost control for long enough in heat two to let Fred Brand past for second spot.

The highlight of the night was Tommy Miller's challenge to Jack Young for the Scottish Match Race Championship. Miller took the first leg but Young rallied to win 2–1. Bainbridge and Miller relegated Young to third place in the 'Handlebar' Trophy final.

The annual Press Sports at Edinburgh's Old Meadowbank on Thursday 20 July included some speedway. An Edinburgh Juniors versus Glasgow Juniors event was event 10 and the home side won the four heat match 15–9. Dykes took two wins for a maximum six but he did not have much support.

A late burst by the Tigers beat the Flyers at Fleetwood on Saturday 22 July, giving them the match 44–40. Fleetwood might have won by taking the last heat, but Bainbridge completed his paid maximum and Miller's third place just made sure.

The Tigers recovered from 10–2 down and 5–1s in heats 12 and 13 gave them the advantage before the last heat. McGregor and Hodgson with seven each gave Bainbridge the most support. Ian Hoskins put the win down partly to a female Tigers fan carrying her bit of coal for luck – a superstition he had not heard of before.

Halifax were expected to be a tough test for Tigers on 26 July. It turned out to be easier than expected as only Arthur Forrest, Vic Emms and Al Allison resisted the Tigers. Their only heat win, 4–2 in the last race, only made the 56–28 score look marginally better.

Miller set a new track record, 78.2 seconds, in heat one and went on to score a full maximum. Bainbridge matched this while McGregor scored 10. Crowther's run of poor form continued and he only managed two points. The second half saw round two of the Dorothy Lamour Progressive Match Race with Dykes beating McKinlay.

The long trip south to Plymouth on Thursday 27 July did not help the Tigers chances, but they made the Devils fight all the way. In the end Plymouth won 54–30. Miller was again top Tiger with eight points. This was the Tigers' only visit to the track at Pennycross Stadium which was later redeveloped and is now the site of a primary school.

On Monday 31 July Bainbridge rode for Australia in the test match against England at Wimbledon. As first reserve, he had a couple of rides, scoring one point. The Giants' Le Breton and Harding and Edinburgh's Young were also in the Australia team. Bainbridge was unsure about riding for Australia as it looked as though he would have to forgo the World Championship Qualifying Round at Newcastle. However, the Speedway Control Board switched him to Stoke and allowed him to win his first cap. Even better for Bainbridge was that he won the Stoke round.

August

The Tigers faced city rivals the Giants on 2 August at White City and, watched by a record 25,000 crowd, won this league encounter 49–35. Heat one had to be rerun after Miller fell on the first turn as Ken Le Breton, suffering motor problems, took him wide. Bob Lovell could not avoid the fallen Miller and Dykes hit both fallen riders. In the rerun Miller took off and won clear of Dykes and Le Breton. The latter got his revenge in the last heat beating Miller, who was slowed by a rear tyre puncture. The two had ridden shoulder-to-shoulder for much of the race. Miller also won the Dorothy Lamour Match Race event, beating Peter Dykes.

Bainbridge steered clear of trouble to record a full maximum while McGregor was again the third heat leader with 8+1. Bainbridge also cleaned up the second half. Crowther was missing due to an injury picked up at Cradley Heath two days earlier.

The Tigers gave a debut to former Newcastle Diamond Frank Hodgson, signed for a Tigers' record transfer fee of £875 on Wednesday 9 August. The Tigers appeared to struggle to defeat Walthamstow Wolves 43–41. However, the score looked close thanks to the Wolves' last heat 5–1. The Tigers had the match won before the start of heat 14.

Frank Hodgson arrived to replace Bainbridge, injured in international action for Overseas at Sheffield. His arrival coincided with an upsurge in the fortunes of his brother Jack, who matched Frank's score ride for ride. Jack rode even better in the second half and won the main final from a field that included Miller.

Miller scored a full maximum while the Hodgson brothers scored 10 each. McGregor had an off night with just two points. His problems were blamed on a new bike that seemed difficult for him to master. Miller progressed in the match race event beating Jack Hodgson.

Ian Hoskins was becoming agitated about the new promotion at Motherwell borrowing his riders. He was happy for them to ride in meetings against nondescript opposition, but when he found out they would be facing a full league team like Cradley Heath, he went ballistic. As it was, Miller, who had broken the Wembley three lap record the night before, did turn out for the Lanarkshire Eagles with McKinlay. He was given a big welcome, but his five points had the fledgling Eagles fans giving him 'the bird'.

Bainbridge, who had turned down bookings at Motherwell because he wasn't happy with the track, missed out racing on a rough track which caused Tigers' junior Ferguson to fall on the straight causing a chipped bone injury.

On their small Chingford Road track on Monday 14 August, Walthamstow showed Tigers the way round. The Wolves were sharper from the gate and the Tigers managed only three race winners and one heat victory. The result was a 53–31 win for the Wolves. Jack Hodgson rode well for 7+1 while Miller scored 6+1. Frank Hodgson scored six. Without the injured Bainbridge, the Tigers lacked bite at the top end as McGregor's run of poor form continued.

The next night, at Yarmouth's Caister Road, a tricky track for visitors, the Tigers came close to winning. They lost 43–41. The Tigers secured an opening heat 5–1 as Yarmouth's Reg Morgan fell and Fred Brand had bike problems. The Bloaters levelled in heat two, then it was nip and tuck to the end. The Tigers could have snatched it, but Reg Morgan and Johnny White shut out McIntosh preventing him linking with Miller for a positive result.

Miller completed a paid maximum. He had fair support from McGregor on nine and Frank Hodgson on 7+1, but the lower order didn't do enough to take the match and league points.

The Tigers' management were annoyed that Yarmouth used a new rule on substitution of the second reserve to their advantage. The rule said that provided the second reserve was present and ready to ride, he did not have to do so.

Back home on 16 August, the Tigers faced Coventry. Another fine display from Jack Hodgson, who had a new lease of life after Frank's arrival, helped the Tigers win 47–36. Jack Hodgson and Miller scored full maximums. Lindsay scored eight, but McGregor was down on power again and limited to 5+1.

Tommy Miller swatted aside Norman Lindsay in the Progressive Match race. Will Lowther was back in Glasgow and took part in the second half. He beat Frank Hodgson in a match race, but had an engine failure in the second half trophy.

Perhaps it is unfair to bill the side as Glasgow Tigers because they had only three regulars. However, the records show the Tigers rode at Dunmore Stadium in Belfast on Friday 18 August. They were beaten 39–32 by Dunmore Bees. On a wet night the match was only completed thanks to reducing the last few heats to three laps.

Regular Tiger Lindsay scored a full maximum while Dykes rose to the occasion to collect 10. McKinlay, the third Tiger scored four with two second places either side of the race in which he fell. The Tigers' Alf McIntosh, who, like Willie Gordon, rode regularly in Belfast, was appearing as a Belfast Bee.

Bainbridge was the hero at White City on 23 August as Tigers defeated the Sheffield Tars 45–39 in the league. He had his injured shoulder (or collar bone according to another report) strapped up, allowing him to ride. He earned a paid maximum. Miller dropped a point for the first time in weeks to young Tar Guy Allott. However, he kept his best display for the second half match races when he beat Wimbledon star Norman Parker 2–0.

The Tigers roasted the Tars in the early heats and, while Tars had a mid-match fight back, it wasn't enough to win the match.

Old hand Joe Crowther, returning from injury, created the thrills for Glasgow fans at Edinburgh on Saturday 26 August. He had a couple of race wins in his seven points, including the scalp of Dick Campbell, before fading in his last two outings with bike problems. A strapped-up Bainbridge scored eight and Miller scored seven. McKinlay and McIntosh were replaced by Crowther and Dykes. With the Monarchs going well the final score was 49–35. Two 5–1s in the last two heats for the Monarchs made the score look better for them.

It was unlucky 13 for the Plymouth Devils, who were making their debut in Scotland, as the Tigers completed their 13th straight home win in a row on 30 August. The Devils only won one heat – heat 13 – as they lost 61–23. While the score suggests a poor meeting, the races often featured overtaking as the Tigers came from the back.

Miller and Bainbridge spearheaded the Tigers' attack, both scored full maximums. McGregor shook off his problems to score 9+2 while Lindsay did well with 8+2. Crowther did well as first reserve with 5+1 from two outings. In the second half, Miller won the £100 Regent Gold Casket when he beat Ashfield's Merv Harding 2–0 in the second leg of the final. Bainbridge beat Miller and Harding in the second half final to complete an unbeaten evening.

September

The Tigers' first visit as a team to Motherwell was on Friday 1 September. Bainbridge, Miller and the Hodgson Brothers were absent and the team was billed as a Glasgow Tigers Select. Bainbridge was not fond of the track when he'd tried it earlier in the season. McGregor, who would move to Milton Street during the winter, top scored for the Tigers with 11 while McKinlay scored 9. Crowther, who became an Eagle in 1951, equalled McKinlay's score.

The makeshift Lanarkshire Eagles were best served by their own Noel Watson. Their guests included Newcastle's Ernie Brecknell, Don Wilkinson, Will Lowther and Don Lawson.

The home team was not strong enough to prevent the Tigers winning 47–37. Motherwell were known as the Lanarkshire Eagles. The Motherwell Eagles was the local motorcycle club.

The match at Stoke the next night marked the end of an era. Joe Crowther raced his last match as a Tiger. He bowed out with a lowly one point after a career in which he had held some poor Tigers sides together.

Most of the luck went to the Tigers as they took the league points from Hanley with a 43–38 win. Two successive 5–0s in heats seven and eight put Tigers well ahead and two Potters 5–1s were too late. Miller fell in his opening ride when half a lap ahead, but scored nine. Jack Hodgson crashed out of the match in heat five and Dykes crashed out of the meeting in heat 12. Bainbridge completed his four rides and was unbeaten by an opponent. Lindsay with 7+1 and McGregor on seven both did well for Tigers.

Les Jenkins had his bike wrecked beyond repair when he was hit by Jack Hodgson as he rebounded off the fence. Gil Blake was reportedly knocked off his bike by a Tiger who, for some reason known only to the steward, was not excluded.

Bainbridge was in the wars again, this time at Dudley Wood Stadium, on Monday 4 September. Cradley Heath defeated the Tigers 52–32. His fall in heat two, as he raced with Brian Shepherd, resulted in a broken wrist and another few weeks on the fence in an injury littered season. The Heathens were without skipper Alan Hunt on World Championship duty at Wimbledon. However, the Tigers, similarly handicapped by the absence of Miller who was in the same meeting as Hunt, failed to capitalise. The faster gating Heathens piled up the points. McGregor was the top Tiger with 9+1 and McKinlay, taking two extra rides covering for Bainbridge, was next best on 5+1. The Tigers had opened with a 5–1, but Cradley struck back in heat two before achieving three 5–1s, stamping their authority on the match.

The Tigers' first home rain off since the War meant that the match against Southampton on 6 September was postponed. However, the partially flooded track only delayed action for one day. The Saints were up in Scotland for a few days so it was easy to re-stage the fixture. The depleted Tigers, without Bainbridge, Crowther and Jack Hodgson, won 51–33.

An odd event in heat two saw the starter's flag hit Tom Oakley as he waited for the tapes to go up. Oakley let the clutch go and stalled his bike just as the tapes rose. Miller expected a rerun and cruised away from the start before realising that the steward was allowing the race to continue. Miller finished third but scored 10 in the meeting.

Lindsay, who just got on with it in heat two, recorded a – rare for him – paid maximum. McGregor, yet again, was third heat leader on nine and Frank Hodgson had a good night with 8+1. The Tigers gave a 1950 league debut to Willie Gordon who scored a point. The Lamour Trophy was still in Miller's sights as he beat Frank Hodgson.

Despite being staged on Monday 11 September, which was notable for miserable weather, a 24,000 crowd watched Scotland, using a stack of Australians and a Kiwi, beat an England side 67–41. A busload of Harringay fans and thousands more were locked out, according to Ian Hoskins. Jack Young, Tommy Miller and Ken Le Breton were outstanding up-and-coming riders, along with England including some First Division stars.

It had rained so much in Glasgow on the day of the meeting that the fire brigade was called in to help dry out the track. Needless to say, the rain-soaked track did not facilitate great racing, but the slower gating 'Scots' came from the back a few times.

The only Scots in the side were Miller, who recorded a full maximum 18, Gordon McGregor and Willie Wilson. Willie had four rides at reserve and was only beaten by one English rider, Jack Parker. McGregor managed a point from three rides. Ken Le Breton missed out on a full maximum with an engine failure in his penultimate ride. Jack Young scored 14+1.

Jack Parker had a good night for England and top scored with 11, while Belle Vue's Louis Lawson scored 10. The rest of the English Lions were poor. The pick of them was Halifax's Vic Emms. Arthur Forrest, his teammate, fell in heat 14 and broke his arm.

The Tigers took full advantage of a wet track and torrential rain on 13 September to pile on the agony for their rivals from Edinburgh. The Tigers were happy in the wet, while Edinburgh Monarchs, Jack Young excepted, never got to grips with the track. Young took the Renfrew Supporters Trophy from Frank Hodgson, Miller and Lindsay. McGregor had the highest individual score with 10, while Frank Hodgson scored 9+2. McKinlay also managed a good pay night taking a bonus in every ride boosting his pay packet to 7+4. Reserves Dykes and McIntosh were unbeaten by a Monarch. The Tigers gave the Monarchs a lesson in wet track riding and won 60–24. In the second half, Ron Phillips and Jack Hodgson were involved in a spectacular pile up but, rather than asking for the meeting to stop, they asked for it to continue.

A week later, another wet night in Glasgow on 20 September saw the Norwich Stars a bit washed out after 14 heats. The Tigers won their 16th successive home match by a convincing 61–23. Heat seven ended any slender hopes the Stars had of challenging the Tigers when Paddy Mills contacted Frank Hodgson's back wheel and somersaulted into the fence. He was carted off to hospital, somewhere familiar to him, to have his dislocated shoulder fixed. However, Norwich, despite this set back, went on to win the League.

Feeling unwell, McKinlay pulled out of heat nine but took his last ride and won. He was replaced by Dykes. However, both Dykes and McKinlay rode in heat 12 in a red helmet cover. Dykes was given the win before the crowd reaction alerted the officials that something was amiss. The corrected result gave McKinlay credit for the win.

Ken Le Breton retained his Scottish Match Race Championship by beating Tommy Miller after setting up a first leg advantage at Ashfield the night before. Miller had his own success in the Dorothy Lamour trophy. He beat Gordon McGregor 2–0.

Miller continued his maximum ways while Frank Hodgson scored 10+2. Frank's brother Jack was paid for 10 as was Lindsay.

Before the match at Norwich on Saturday 23 September, the Tigers' fans marched round the track headed by a piper. Unfortunately, the riders were not so inspired and only McGregor showed any class in another wet meeting. He scored an impressive 11, one of the better showings by a Tiger there. Miller had a couple of poor efforts before two great wins for six points. The Tigers lost 54–29.

Paddy Mills had recovered from his prang in Glasgow and lead Stars to their win. The Stars did not pull ahead overly fast, but steadily opened the gap between the two sides.
About this time Norwich tabled an unsuccessful £2,000 offer for Tommy Miller as he would have boosted their promotion efforts.

The Tigers were ahead for most of the league match Newcastle two days later. Derrick Close looked great when he came from the back to win heat seven, but an engine failure blunted his returns. However, he could not beat Miller in the final heat and the Tigers shared the heat, enough to win 43– 41.

This win placed the Tigers near the top of the Division, ready for the run in with Norwich to the flag. Miller led the Tigers' scoring with 11. No other rider managed double figures, but it was a solid display that produced the goods. McGregor took eight points while Dykes added 6+1 and from reserve McKinlay produced two wins. With hindsight, the Tigers' management should have used him to replace out of form Lindsay and Jack Hodgson.

The Tigers entertained Fleetwood on 27 September on a track described as the best for some time. The Flyers flew from the gate in most heats, but the Tigers had their fans roaring as they reeled in and passed the visitors. Fleetwood lost advantage after advantage due to poor team riding. Former Tiger Angus McGuire had a flash – his motor spectacularly blew in heat 12. He failed to score.

Miller and the Hodgson brothers dominated in this 56–28 win. Miller scored a paid maximum. His second place was behind Jack with 11. Frank, on a paid maximum until his last outing, was beaten by the Flyers' Australian, Graham Williams, and settled for 10+1. Lindsay, a largely unsung Australian, scored 9+2.

October

A 56–28 win against Newcastle at White City on 4 October allowed the Tigers to draw level with league championship rivals Norwich on points in their very close run in to the title. While the Tigers won the match, the Diamonds' Derrick Close was top man on the night with 11 points. For the Tigers, Miller scored 10, but with McGregor on 9+2, Jack Hodgson with eight and Frank Hodgson on 7+2, the Tigers had strength in depth. Their reserves, Dykes and McKinlay, were unbeaten by an opponent. Bainbridge was back from injury and he added 5+1. Alf McIntosh was dropped to make way for him.

Australian star Aub Lawson featured in the second half. In the Match Races he beat both Bainbridge and Miller in the qualifying races and beat Miller again in the final to collect the White City Match Race Cup. Miller had been ahead in the final, but allowed the First Division star to get past. In the Linthouse trophy, Lawson was surprisingly beaten in his heat by McKinlay who overhauled Lindsay and Lowther before passing him in lap three.

However, Miller won the final and in so doing confirmed victory in the season-long Duncan Edward Trophy, named in honour of Ian Hoskins' son, just ahead of Bainbridge.

The Tigers tore into the lead from the start at Saracen Park on 10 October. The Giants fans watching their favourites must have been wondering which was the home team. The 47–37 win gave the Tigers a slight lead over Norwich in the league table. The prize for the league title was £400, double the purse for second.

Ken Le Breton had a subdued night. He was only the third highest Giant as Bruce Semmens had three unbeaten rides after an opening ride engine failure. This was Le Breton's last appearance at Ashfield. He was tragically killed in a track accident in Australia a few months later, and is still fondly remembered by Scottish speedway fans.

It was a solid display from Tigers, with Miller, who matched Merv Harding on 10, receiving sound support from all the other Tigers. McGregor took eight points, and Jack Hodgson got 6+1. Dykes was unbeaten by a Giant at reserve.

Fresh from a win over on the north side of the River Clyde, the next night the Tigers fans who came must have been confident that their team would send the Monarchs packing. However, Edinburgh gave Tigers their first defeat of the season at White City. Too many Tigers men had an off night and they couldn't afford that against their old rivals. The 62–46 defeat made the second leg of this Border Cup Final academic.

Miller scored 10+1 from six rides. Lindsay, McGregor and reserve Dykes each scored six points. McKinlay took 5+3 while Frank Hodgson scored five. It was a poor performance all round. The Monarchs led from the start and drew away steadily as the meeting unfolded. Jack Young dominated with a maximum. The three top Monarchs scored 43 points.

The Tigers needed a win to boost their league championship hopes. However, defeat at Sheffield the next night dented Glasgow's aspirations. Bainbridge had a wrist injury and both Lindsay and Dykes had engine troubles which reducing their scores. Bainbridge failed to score while Lindsay only scored one. Jack Hodgson scored nine while McGregor added eight. Miller was subdued with 7+1. Sheffield – once again Tigers – won 48–36.

The first leg result made the Border Cup Final second leg two days later a non-event for the Tigers fans. Only Miller with 12 from six rides stood up to the rampant Monarchs. The Tigers lost 71–37 on the night and 133–83 on aggregate.

The Tigers went to Halifax on 18 October with the possibility of winning the league if they could beat the Dukes. However, the match finished in a 51–33 defeat thereby ending the Tigers title hopes. McGregor and Miller could not match the Dukes, but each won a race in compiling their seven points apiece.

The title dream was over, but second place was in their grasp, the best Scottish League team showing to date. Had Bainbridge raced the full season they may have gone one better. In the end Norwich won the title with 37 league points from 28 meetings. The Tigers were a point behind on 36. The Tigers were unbeaten at home, but only won away four times. A two-point defeat at lowly Yarmouth was notable, a win would have taken the title to Scotland.

Glasgow ended the 1950 season with an open event at White City including Scottish based riders, Bradford's Ron Clarke and Oliver Hart and former Tiger Will Lowther. The top prize was the Gold Medallion, presented by the Lord Provost – equivalent of Lord Mayor – of Glasgow, Victor Warren. He had only recently taken an interest in speedway and both Glasgow teams. Miller's opening race engine failure cost him the top prize. This went to the Monarch's Dick Campbell who scored 13, one more than Miller. Miller settled for joint second with Ashfield's Keith Gurtner. Ron Clarke took fourth spot with 11. The other Tigers were McGregor and Dykes on nine each, Lindsay with six, and McIntosh four.

Tommy Miller had been invited to ride in the second half of a Wembley Lions meeting. The Lions often did this to assess potential signings. Ian Hoskins said that Miller set a new three-lap record at Wembley. He was phoned by Wembley manager Dave King, who offered a £5,000 transfer fee for Miller. Hoskins turned the offer down, saying that he would be 'lynched' by the White City fans if he had taken it.

The season ended with the retirement of the track tractor "Growling Gerty", replaced by a new machine for 1951. The Tigers fans in the supporters' club were all sent a Christmas card from Ian Hoskins which had the following verse. "If you press on regardless and are full of good cheer, You may, like the Tigers, be on top next year."

Stenners 1951 Annual noted the Tigers' progress, they "succeeded beyond Ian 'Mac''s optimistic expectations. Miller backed Bainbridge and Co stoutly to elevate the Tigers to a previously unattained position in the league. After floundering disappointedly around the foot of the Northern Shield table, Hoskins junior decided he was fed up with mediocrity and in early August opened up the Ibrox moneybags to secure ... Frank Hodgson. Hodgson's experience helped place the team on its soundest footing to date ... White City supporters can look forward to a 1951 start in top gear."

Tommy Miller – Glasgow's top rider in the 1950s.

12. 1951: "Somewhat disappointing"

The Tigers retained their top two riders, Tommy Miller and Junior Bainbridge. They were supported by Frank and Jack Hodgson, Norman Lindsay, Alf McIntosh, Ken McKinlay, Jim Blyth and a new find, Eric Davies. Eric, a Paisley based mattress stuffer, did not live up to expectations and was soon relegated to the second half.

Jim Blyth was on loan from the Giants. Buck Ryan decided to remain in Australia. He had been on a boat for Britain, but disembarked because his wife was seriously ill. Peter Dykes, who had finished third in the New Zealand Championship, was back home in New Zealand and unable to return.

Early on Ian Hoskins tried to sign Johnny Carpenter from Leicester but, despite a fee of £200 being agreed, the deal faltered. In early May, he tried to sign 26-year-old 'Slim' Irvine from Dunlop, Ayrshire. Slim had been perfecting his skills on Bob Lindsay's training track. He turned Hoskins down because he felt too inexperienced.

The Tigers did add a newcomer: Newcastle's Len Nicholson. Marine engineer Nicholson, like Joe Ferguson, spent his winters on the ocean.

For the new season, the First Division had nine teams. The Second Division had 16, so each faced the other once, home and away. Motherwell's inclusion meant there were four Scottish teams. Otherwise, the league was geographically spread. However, Plymouth had moved to the Third Division, which had 10 teams in the south and midlands of England, plus Cardiff. Southampton quit after riding seven league meetings. Sheffield also pulled out of the league before riding any league fixtures.

March

The practice day on 21 March was unsuccessful for Miller and Bainbridge who were unhappy with their new equipment. It was as much a washout as the wet weather. Bainbridge was trying out a new home-made frame with the fuel tank under the saddle. The rationale was that it would alter the weight distribution, placing more weight over the rear of the bike. The only rider happy was new recruit Eric Davies, who was trying out new equipment too.

Apart from the departed Gordon McGregor, the Tigers' line-up that opened the 1951 season, in front of the biggest opening night crowd on record, on 28 March against Fleetwood, was similar to that of 1950.

'England' tourist to Australia in the winter, Tommy Miller, opened his new season where he left off with a maximum in the Tigers' 56–28 North Shield win. Jack Hodgson was unbeaten by an opponent while brother Frank was one point adrift on 9+2. The only weak link was the new reserve, Davies, who failed to score. He had a jammed throttle in his opening ride which caused him to fall.

Bainbridge's new bike didn't propel the new captain to a big score. McKinlay and Lindsay also used new machines, but they performed better than Bainbridge.
Fleetwood included former Tiger Angus McGuire and a very short-term Tiger who never wore the red and white, Ray Harker.

Miller ended the month by winning the Edinburgh Spring Handicap on 31 March. He scored 14 which, with his two points handicap, saw him tie with Monarchs' favourite and 1946 Tiger Eddie Lack. Miller won the run off with ease, leaving the Monarchs fans bemoaning his 'gift' of extra points.

April

The Tigers had their North Shield meeting against Newcastle on 4 April tied up when disaster struck in the last heat. The Tigers won 47–37. Tommy Miller was chasing a maximum and, in trying to pass Derrick Close, he fell and went over the handlebars. Jack Hodgson was close behind and couldn't avoid the fallen Miller. Thankfully, the early diagnosis of a fractured skull and pelvis was inaccurate. However, his injuries ruled Miller out of action for a few weeks. Another version of events suggested that Jack Hodgson had hit Miller's back wheel and knocked him off.

Tail-ender Davies went through the fence in heat eight which ruled him out of the rest of the meeting. The injuries meant that McIntosh had two extra rides, but he only added one point to his two programmed race wins. He fell in one after Ernie Brecknell took him wide and was pushed wide by Derrick Close in the other. In the second half he was also in the wars, this time it was Son Mitchell who carted him off.

Frank Hodgson was the best Tiger with 9+2, missing a maximum for the second week running, while Miller scored nine and Jack Hodgson seven.

The Tigers entered the derby with the Monarchs at White City on 11 April without their star, Tommy Miller. Concussion the week before meant the doctor stopped him riding. The Tigers were reduced to a seven-man side with the inexperienced Jim Blyth at number seven. Eric Davies was listed at number eight, but did not ride. Blyth, signed from Ashfield, did not let the Tigers down, and his 5+3 was better than both Monarchs' reserves. He rode so well in his opening heat that he was given Davies's rides, an unusual move at this time.

Ian Hoskins was just 'bursting' with delight at his team's 42–41 victory. A solid display by the weakened Tigers gave them a deserved win when for much of the match it looked like they were out of it. Two 5–1s in heats 11 and 12 put them in the driving seat and a 3–3 effectively sewed it up in heat 13. The Monarchs took the last heat 5–1. So the final score looked closer than it actually was. The Monarchs had trouble staying on their bikes, especially junior Harry Andrews, which helped the Tigers. Lindsay top scored with 10+1 and McKinlay was next best on seven points. Bainbridge was still having bike problems and scored six.

The second half included Slim Irvine, Bill Hosie and Scott Hall. Only Hall moved to team action when he rode for Motherwell.

The Tigers' nominees for the World Championship were announced. They included Miller plus the team riders except McIntosh who was specially recommended by Ian Hoskins to fill any available gap.

Considered to be best meeting at The Stadium in Motherwell so far, the home riders had the better of it on 13 April. The Tigers lost 46–35. This was partially due to bike problems including chain breakages, punctures and falls. Frank Hodgson's zero did not help. Only Bainbridge performed well for the Tigers with 11. Blyth on six points was the next best Tiger.

Former Tiger Joe Crowther made his comeback against his former colleagues after eight months out of action. After finishing last in his first ride, he reeled off three straight wins. Gordon McGregor also scored well, but over-slid while trying to pass Bainbridge. The Eagles also had former Tigers in Will Lowther and Bill Baird, riding for his fourth Scottish team.

Making his debut as the Diamonds' skipper on 16 April, Derrick Close showed his team how to ride Brough Park. Former Diamonds in the Tigers' ranks, the Hodgson brothers, did not have a happy return to Tyneside. The Diamonds won 47–37. Jack scored four points and Frank managed 2+1. Tommy Miller was back and scored 10, as did Lindsay. The Tigers were never very far adrift, but could not close the gap.

The Tigers' fans welcomed back Miller to White City on 18 April and he rewarded them with another maximum. The Tigers beat Motherwell's Lanarkshire Eagles 51–32 in the North Trophy. The rest of the Tigers gave a solid rather than spectacular show. Miller missed out on a clean sweep to McGregor in the second half. The Hodgson brothers came back to form with Frank on 8+1 and Jack with 7+1.

The visitors, with four former Tigers, never reached the heights, but at least those riders showed they still could negotiate the sometimes tricky White City strip. McGregor, Crowther and Lowther all scored eight, but the other five only managed eight between them.

A victory over the Tigers is always savoured by Monarchs fans and vice versa. This meeting was one-sided. The Monarchs won easily, 61–23 at Old Meadowbank on 21 April. The Tigers often made the gate, but were soon being passed. They had to wait until heat 12 for a race win. Lindsay, the Tigers' most consistent rider, scored seven, and took their only victory that night.

Bainbridge had a difficult night as, after being unplaced in his first race because of a fall, he over-slid at the second bend in his next outing. He was badly shaken and took no further part in the meeting. Reserve McIntosh stepped in collect six points. The Tigers were not happy with the state of the track and considered it to be overwatered and hard to ride.

Miller came to grief at the same spot as Bainbridge at the end of heat two when he appeared to be going too hard in trying to hold off Don Cuppleditch. He only scored six.

The Tigers' top two, Miller and Bainbridge, were in brilliant form with 11 and 10 respectively as the Tigers beat the Ashfield Giants at White City on 25 April. After an opening heat setback, Bainbridge won all his other races from the back.

Miller's bike sustained a broken fork as he won one of his heats. However, handicapped by using the track spare, he lost to Bruce Semmens in his third ride. Frank Hodgson backed Miller and Bainbridge with 9+1 in this 57–27 demolition of their local rivals. The fans turned out in large numbers and their colourful ranks contributed to the meeting's sense of occasion.

A heat seven crash between two Tigers, Bainbridge and Jack Hodgson, resulted in Hodgson hitting the fence. This ruled him out for the rest of the meeting at Fleetwood on 30 April. McIntosh took his place in the rerun and went on to score 7+1. The crash was adjudged to be Bainbridge's fault and it prevented him from completing his maximum. He ended the night with nine and the top Tiger was Miller with a paid maximum. Lindsay went well, contributing eight, the same as McKinlay who was paid for nine points.

McKinlay's last place in heat nine was caused by his newly acquired face mask blowing up in front of his eyes. He had to pull up to restore his vision. Needless to say, he did not use it again. Despite these problems, the Tigers ran away with the match 49–35 for the North Shield points. The Tigers were second of a triple Scottish whammy for Fleetwood who lost to the Monarchs, Tigers and Eagles in the space of three meetings.

May

The Tigers were due to race at Ashfield on 1 May but rain ruled out proceedings. Bainbridge had a poor time the next night and, after two poor last places, withdrew from the rest of the meeting. The visiting Newcastle Diamonds did not take advantage of this and lost 51–33.

Ernie Brecknell had a bad luck in heat 11 when his frame broke in two and he shuddered to a halt in front of Don Lawson. Lawson could not stop and ploughed into him. This crash left the Newcastle pair in hospital, Brecknell with a broken leg and Lawson with concussion.

Derrick Close missed a maximum when his motor stalled at the start of heat six. Don Wilkinson was a big Geordie in the Diamonds team who became a Tiger in 1952. The Diamonds made a match of it early on, but ran out of steam.

Miller had an easy maximum. McKinlay's rise continued with an 8+2 return while Frank Hodgson matched the young Scot. Dependable Lindsay scored seven points.

Sheffield's closure left the Glasgow Tigers with a blank date on 9 May so they invited Division One Belle Vue to White City. Bike failures pegged back the Tigers' score in a 45–39 defeat. Bainbridge fell in his opening heat efforts to beat veteran England star and 1949 World Championship runner-up Jack Parker. However, he had the satisfaction of beating the old maestro in the last heat to score eight points.

Miller had a bike failure, but managed seven points while Jack Hodgson scored 6+1. Miller had beaten Parker in a match race. The Aces took an early lead and edged away from the Tigers to record their expected victory. Falls and engine failures pegged back the home team. Most of the 20,000 crowd probably went home disappointed, especially as the Aces filled the top three spots in the Rider of the Night event. However, they had seen some class riders.

Bainbridge opened with a win in a new track record time and with Jack Hodgson third, as the Tigers took the lead at Liverpool on 14 May. Reg Duval equalled Bainbridge's time in the next heat and the Chads pair levelled the score. From then on it was downhill for the Tigers, the Chads eventually won 47–37.

The Chads' reserve, Peter Craven, who rose to fame with a World Championship title win four years later, took a couple of falls and failed to score. The Tigers had two stars in Miller and Bainbridge with 11 points, but next best on the big Stanley Stadium track was Lindsay on five. The Tigers longer track travel sickness was again all too apparent.

With the destiny of the North Shield settled, Edinburgh having won it, only local pride was at stake, and Tigers won 44–40 at Ashfield the next night. The match went to a last heat decider and Jack Hodgson was the red and white hero with McKinlay putting the icing on the cake in third place. Miller missed out with a fall in the second half final after scoring a maximum. Jack Hodgson backed him with nine while Bainbridge added 8+2.

Visiting Walthamstow's Jim Boyd caught the eye on 16 May, even though he was unfortunate enough to meet Miller and Bainbridge in his races. Both Tigers were on fire and beat Boyd while scoring full maximums.

The track suffered from a very strong dose of afternoon sun and was unpredictable, making racing difficult. The Tigers adapted better in the earlier heats and the Wolves did better in the second half. However, by then, the visitors were losing. The Tigers had built up a big enough lead to secure a 49–35 win.

Tommy Miller defeated arch rival Jack Young in the Scottish Match Race Championship, but his clean sweep bid faltered at the gate in the second half final. Bainbridge made sure the trophy stayed at White City.

Despite Stoke missing Les Jenkins and Bill Harris the Tigers could not capitalise on the weakened Potters team at Stoke on 19 May. The home side won 53–31. The match had its share of thrills with passing and re-passing. For the Tigers, Miller shone with a maximum, but the remainder were not at the races. Pick of the rest were the Hodgson brothers and Lindsay who all scored four.

The Tigers hoped for a big lead in the first leg of the Scottish Cup First Round to take to Motherwell. However, the meeting on 23 May didn't go to plan and they had to be satisfied with a 57–51 win. The former Tigers in the Eagles' ranks made sure it was close and the fans enjoyed some great racing. The Eagles were in front until heat five before the Tigers nosed ahead in heat seven. Had Noel Watson been fit, the Tigers could have struggled more.

Miller notched his usual big score with 17, losing only to Gordon McGregor in heat 16, while Bainbridge, somewhat enigmatic, blew it in one race as he missed the gate, but pitched in with 13+2.

The Eagles' recent recruit, Bill Dalton, made a rare top score. Former Tigers Gordon McGregor, Joe Crowther and Will Lowther all scored well as did former Giant Keith Gurtner.

Around this time, the Tigers signed Len Nicholson, a North of England based junior, to boost their tail end strength. He had his moments before a head injury ended his career.

In the second leg, the winning margin the previous Wednesday was academic. The Tigers produced a great show in Motherwell before a record crowd two days later. They went through with a 61–47 win at The Stadium. The aggregate score was 118–98. The Tigers showed what they could do on the road when they did not go very far. The Eagles were let down by below par showings from Gurtner, Lowther and Crowther. Only McGregor and Noel Watson, including wins over Miller, put up a good fight.

Blantyre born Miller opened his account with a new track record for The Stadium and scored 15. McIntosh had a very good meeting with 10 from a reserve berth. Bainbridge, not always a fan of this track, scored a paid maximum while McKinlay had a good night with 10. The Tigers dominated and pulled ahead as the match progressed. A revival by the Eagles fizzled out and the Tigers re-established their supremacy towards the end of the night.

The Tigers were in trouble at Norwich on 26 May in a National Trophy tie, but the meeting only lasted three races before it was abandoned. The Tigers were 14–4 down. Bainbridge, never a wet track fan, had two rides before it was called off.

Two days later, the Tigers could have expected more from Newcastle skipper Derrick Close at Brough Park on 28 May, but he was excluded from two races. He fell in one and was excluded for exceeding the two-minute time allowance in the other. Earlier he had lost his Second Division Match Race tie with Jack Young 2–1.

The unlikely stars for the Diamonds were former Tiger Johnny Green and future Tiger Don Wilkinson. Many of the Tigers' problems could be put down to poor track conditions, but the racing surface was the same for both teams. Newcastle took the league points 45–39. Miller had an opening ride third then three wins for his 10 points. Bainbridge contributed 8+1. Former Diamonds Frank and Jack Hodgson scored 6+1 and five respectively.

But for bike problems, the Tigers' margin of victory over Norwich Stars in the National Trophy at White City on 30 May might have been greater. Bainbridge seized an engine in his second outing, which pegged him back to 13+1 from six rides. Miller's fuel tank come adrift in one race, but he kept it in place to win, part of his 18-point maximum. Frank Hodgson rode well for 11+3 while Jack added 8+2. Phil Clarke, who injured his arm the night before, pulled out after one pointless ride leaving Australian Bob Leverenz to fight the Tigers on his own. The Tigers sped to a 64–44 win. With any other team, it might have been enough. However, the return at The Firs would be a daunting task.

June

Saturday 2 June saw Tommy Miller at Edinburgh for the second leg of the Scottish Match Race Championship contest with Jack Young. He lost 2–0, but his first round win meant a further clash at Motherwell. The same night Bainbridge top scored with 11 points for Overseas in an international against Britain at Stoke.

Jim Blyth, who had injured his shoulder at the Hamilton Showground meeting in May, showed that the unusual cure of a game or two of tennis worked a treat on 6 June. He took a reserve's paid maximum against Leicester who were seen as poor opposition at White City as they lost 53–31. Miller helped Blyth in his first outing, but he won the second from the gate despite being a bit erratic. Miller went on to complete yet another maximum. He was joined on 12 by Bainbridge while Lindsay scored 10+1. Frank Hodgson had bike troubles and only scored 2+1. In the second half Len Nicholson did well – pressing for a team place.

The Tigers travelled to East Anglia on Saturday 9 June to face Norwich. The Stars dominated with an 81–27 National Trophy win. Norwich earned an aggregate 125–91 victory. Not for the first time the sweeping curves of The Firs proved a hard venue for Tigers to master. Their cause was not helped by the weather because, after a week-long dry spell, bang on 7.30pm the heavens opened to soak the track. It was so wet that the Tigers' management wanted the meeting abandoned.

Every Norwich rider finished placed in every race. Bainbridge had a single win in his seven points haul from six rides while Miller managed a poor – for him – five. Lindsay and McIntosh tied for third best Tiger with four. It was another night to forget for Tigers on the road.

A break from league business at White City on 13 June gave the fans a chance to see Division One riders representing England as they faced a side billed as Scotland. The 'Auld Enemy' won this one, but the Scots did not disgrace themselves with a 58–50 defeat.

Bradford's fast starting Eddie Rigg kept his polished leathers clean by wearing overalls over them the night before. He had an incentive to keep them clean as the track was wet. He scored 16 points. Only Jack Young and Tommy Miller prevented the Bradford rider from completing a maximum. Australian Jack, who always raced wearing a tartan scarf, scored 17 while fellow Australian Bainbridge added 15. Miller was the best native Scot with 10+1, Willie Wilson scored four and Gordon McGregor 2+1.

The wet weather detracted from the encounter and the track was quite slippery. Sadly for the Scots fans, the visiting English riders made the best of the conditions. However, their win was not as big as the star-studded line up was expected to achieve. Rigg's main support came from Jack Parker with 15 and his brother Norman collected 9+1, as did Derrick Close.

Halifax had problems in the opening heats on 15 June. In the first heat, the Dukes' Welshman, Jack 'Bluebell' Dawson, reared at the start and crashed into Jack Hodgson. Dawson was trapped under both bikes but, despite being shaken, rode again. The crowd, wrongly, was unhappy with Dawson's exclusion thinking because the riders had not reached the 30 yards board, they should be allowed to get up and continue. The Halifax promoters supported the Steward. They explained the rules in the following week's programme. At that time, riders suffering problems at the start could be pushed up to 30 yards to continue to race, but only if they had not broken any other rule e.g., causing the race to be stopped.

The heat was rerun and drawn 3–3 after the Dukes' skipper Arthur Forrest passed Bainbridge who had made a good start. The Tigers took a two-point lead after heat two, but from then on, the home riders dominated. Only Miller had an answer to the Dukes, but even he had to wait until the last heat to post a win. Bainbridge had bike problems and used the local track spare with little effect. Miller scored eight in a 55–29 defeat.

Cradley Heath Heathens' birthday boy Laurie Schofield celebrated his coming of age –21 – at Dudley Wood two days later with a win over Miller and another win from the back before disaster struck in his third outing. Trying to pass Miller, he drove too hard under the Tiger, and, as he was adjudged to have bored out Miller, was excluded.

1951 Glasgow Tigers: Ken McKinlay, Norman Lindsay, Jack Hodgson, Alf McIntosh, Johnnie Hoskins; Front: Jim Blythe, Frank Hodgson, Junior Bainbridge and Tommy Miller.

Unfortunately, the out-of-sorts Tigers, Miller and Bainbridge apart, did not provide the Heathens with any real opposition and the Midlands side won 55–29. Miller and Bainbridge both scored nine while Frank Hodgson, scored five points.

It was lucky 13 for the Tigers on 20 June as they reached this milestone of home wins when they sent Stoke home pointless with a 60–24 defeat. Stoke did well in the first heat with a 4–2, but could not contain the Tigers. The home riders were keen to make up for some lack lustre away meetings.

Bainbridge set a new one lap record and won the Kirkintilloch Supporters Cup in the second half. He scored 11 in the match, but was bettered by Miller and Frank Hodgson who both scored paid maximums. Blyth scored a paid reserve's maximum. Len Nicholson improved his team prospects by winning a heat in the second half from Jack Hodgson, Brian Pritchett and faller McKinlay.

On 27 June Glasgow comfortably beat Yarmouth, who were often uneasy on the White City track. Just like the previous week, the Tigers lost an opening 4–2, but soon overcame that hiccup.

The Tigers' management expected the poor show that the 57–27 score reflected because they booked Birmingham star Graham Warren to race against Junior Bainbridge in the second half. Bainbridge did not let the fans down and won the series 2–1, but critics were not impressed by the event. The only Bloaters to win a heat were Bob Baker and Tip Mills and they were last in 10 of the 14 heats.

Miller tried to team ride with McKinlay in heat 10, but Bob Baker's dive under McKinlay made Miller realise that he had to speed up or drop points. He went on to score a full maximum, one point better than Junior on 11. Frank Hodgson collected 9+3 as he continued his good run of home form.

Two nights later, in what was considered to be the best match of the season at Fleetwood, the Tigers went down 45–39. The racing was of a high standard, often with three riders crossing the line in close proximity. The Tigers held a narrow six points lead for a time, but 5–1s in heats six and seven put the Flyers ahead and the visitors just could not catch them.

Dropped to reserve, McKinlay had a poor night and failed to score. Miller faded after a promising start. He had bike problems and had to use the below par track spare. However, he did take eight points, one less than Bainbridge who fell in his opening ride before winning his next three outings. He did not have things all his own way. He had a bit of a scrap with Wilf Jay in heat five and had to come from the back to take the flag.

July

An unofficial international between a team of native Scots and a New Zealand team went to the wire at White City on 4 July. It was a fine decision as the match Steward gave the final heat to Ronnie Moore handing the Kiwis a 42–42 draw. A late burst from Miller pulled him so close to Moore that many fans thought the Tiger had won. The verdict went to Moore who had an estimated six-inch lead on the line. He went through the second half unbeaten to collect The Empire Trophy, ahead of top Scots, Miller and Willie Wilson with Junior Bainbridge thrown in for good measure.

Miller and the Eagles' Gordon McGregor each scored 11 points, while the Giants' Willie Wilson scored 10. The other five, McKinlay apart, didn't have a great night.

Moore, who had been beaten by Miller in the opening heat, scored 11, while Ron Johnston, from Belle Vue, not be confused with the Scots Australian with the similar sounding name, scored 8+1. The next best Kiwi was a future Glasgow promoter in the 1960s, Trevor Redmond. He scored 7+1.

Miller continued his good form by winning the World Championship round at White City on 11 July. He was unbeaten for a 15-point maximum. The track record was lowered three times in the first three heats which must be some kind of a record. At the end of the night, it was Miller's, reduced by 1.8 seconds from the old time of 78.6.

It was unusual that this meeting had three reserves who had two rides each. Fourth placed man, Wimbledon's Dennis Gray, had been programmed as part of the very first Tigers team which visited Newcastle in 1946.

Jimmy Gooch pulled out after cracking his collar bone and wrecking his bike in a heat nine crash which also involved Reg Reeves. Reeves, who damaged a finger, did not have another ride after heat nine either. Poole's Tony Lewis had a miserable night, and withdrew before completing his five rides. The meeting featured the veteran rider Lloyd Goffe who was near the end of a long career. The runners up and third place cash was split between Bainbridge and Birmingham's Ron Mountford as both scored 13.

Coventry Bees just managed to take a point from their encounter with the Tigers at Brandon on Saturday 14 July against a somewhat skewed Tigers side. The individual brilliance of Miller and Bainbridge – both scored 12-point maximums – and the long tail compared with the solid throughout Bees. The Tigers were 10 points up after heat eight, but let it slip and settled for a draw. It took two Coventry 5–1s and a drawn heat in the last three to save their unbeaten home record. It was close as the Tigers were on for a match winning 4–2 in the last heat before Stan Williams managed to relegate Frank Hodgson to the back. In addition to the Tiger's league point Miller collected the Coventry track record.

Miller's fine form was not unnoticed, and he was about to be nominated as challenger to Jack Young for the Second Division Match Race title. Miller kept up the pressure with a fine full maximum against the visiting Liverpool Chads on 18 July.

It was very one sided. The Chads only had two race winners, Reg Duval and Bill Griffiths, but a string of second places helped avoid a rout. The Tigers won 54–30. Reg's win in heat 13 was achieved after a race long tussle with Jack Hodgson.

Jack's brother Frank matched Miller's efforts and Bainbridge was the third Tiger to score a maximum, albeit a paid one with 11+1. Len Nicholson made his Tigers debut, replacing an off form McKinlay and had to work hard for his 3+1. McKinlay showed his disgust by winning a second half trophy heat and the reserves race.

In the pipeline were proposals to take the Tigers to race in Sweden, although this never materialised.

A crowd of 11,000 attended the annual charities event organised by the Edinburgh newspapers on Thursday 19 July. A Glasgow Select beat Edinburgh 19–11 in a five heat event. Speedway was just one of several sports featured that night. Ken McKinlay, the only Tiger in the quartet, scored a maximum nine.

The Tigers racked up their 14th home win of the season on 25 July. Miller suffered an unusual home defeat as Coventry's Johnnie Reason beat him in heat nine after Dick Stewart and other Glasgow mechanics repaired the footrest on his bike. Nevertheless, Miller won his other three races to collect 11. Bainbridge, on nine in the match, took the Scottish Match Race Championship tie 2–1 against Jack Young. Unusually, the event was staged in the second half as Bainbridge hated riding in the opening heats of a meeting and Young was prepared to wait until after the interval to race the Tiger.

Jack Hodgson scored 7+4 as he followed home a Tiger in all his four races. Reserve Peter Brough won two of his three outings, but a flat tyre in his third outing meant he wasn't given another ride.

The Tigers were 12 up going into heat 12, but a couple of Coventry 5–1s made the score respectable. A last heat 5–1 for the Tigers opened up the gap between the teams to eight points so the Tigers won 46–38. Maybe they were in a hurry to see the half-time attraction of a re-enactment of a ride by Lady Godiva.

Ian Hoskins recalled that interval attractions "... did provide light relief following a tame meeting, or let the public forget that the team had just been scalped by the opposition ... On a visit from Coventry, I once decided to produce Lady Godiva for their benefit. I hired a model who agreed to ride on a big white horse clad in a skin coloured bathing costume with a wig that flowed down her back to her waist." She then did a circuit of the track. Hoskins was criticised by a Sunday newspaper reporter, but pointed out that the reporter's paper often had photos of near-naked women!

Jack Young took part in the Second Division Match Race Championship with Tommy Miller prior to the start of the match at Old Meadowbank on Saturday 28 July. Young was pushed to equalling the track record of 65.6 seconds held jointly by himself and Miller. He beat the latter by about 35 yards in the first heat. Young won the second heat from Miller with about 25 yards to spare in 66.6 seconds.

The Edinburgh captain was deprived of scoring a maximum 18 in the first leg of the Scottish Speedway Cup when in the last heat he finished third to Glasgow captain Bainbridge and clubmate Dick Campbell. Young, pushed out on the first bend, was in a duel with Campbell for most of the race, but Bainbridge had plenty to spare at the finish. The Monarchs won 66–42.

The Tigers' best was Bainbridge who scored 13, the only visitor to reach double figures. Miller was down on scoring power and settled for nine. He failed to score in his last two outings, his cause not helped by breaking his frame in heat nine so he used a spare bike for his remaining outings.

On 31 July Jack Young had ended Bainbridge's interest in the Scottish Match Race Championship by winning the decider 2–0 at Ashfield.

August

Tommy Miller set out his stall to take Jack Young's Second Division Match Race crown with a 2–1 tie victory at White City on 1 August. Young won the first heat, then Miller won the second from the gate. In the third race, Young took Miller's front wheel after he had momentarily lost control. Down went the Tiger, the Monarch was excluded and the race was awarded to Miller. Tommy managed to repair his bike to ride against Norwich, but Jack's bike was wrecked.

The Tigers gave another strong home display, winning 53–30 thanks to a solid team effort led by Miller and Bainbridge on 11 each. Miller's chance of a full house was spoiled by Bob Leverenz, while Phil Clarke, who had an opening race engine failure, deprived Bainbridge of his maximum. Yet again, the Hodgson brothers were influential in a Tigers win with Jack on 8+3 and Frank with 7+2.

The Tigers made a big effort, giving the fans a thrilling meeting, to take the Scottish Cup against Monarchs on 8 August. They won 64–42. After 36 heats, only two points separated the two sides on aggregate. The Monarchs just shaded it, 108–106 to collect their coveted first Scottish Cup.

Edinburgh lost Don Cuppleditch in heat two. Hitting the back wheel of his team mate Eddie Lack, he vaulted over the safety fence to receive a broken collarbone. Heat eight saw a rarity, a fall by Jack Young who spun out of control when chasing Miller after he had been overtaken by the Tiger. The Monarchs were unlucky in heat 12 when both Campbell and Jimmy Cox fell. They remounted and finished, only to be disqualified giving the Tigers a 5–0 thanks to McKinlay and Jack Hodgson.

In the last heat decider Young just got clear of Bainbridge, but Miller made a hash of the gate and spent the race trying to catch up. To be fair, Miller was not far from Young at the flag and Bainbridge blew it by trying too hard and almost running out of track. Wet weather had thrown the meeting into some doubt but then the sun came out. Miller made a huge 17 points contribution to the Tigers' total while Bainbridge added 11+1. McKinlay scored 9+1 and Len Nicholson who rode above himself to score seven points from three outings at reserve. For the Monarchs, Young had five unbeaten races.

Young beat Miller at Old Meadowbank on 9 August, winning the Scottish Open Championship by a point. Former Tiger, now with Motherwell, Gordon McGregor completed the podium line up.

The Tigers took a trip across Glasgow to Saracen Park on Saturday 11 August and the Giants did not make them welcome, sending them back south of the river on the wrong end of a 55–29 defeat. The Tigers' cause wasn't helped by the lack of Bainbridge, out due to injury, and Miller's total was reduced to seven, as he blew a motor forcing him to use the track spare. Even with a maximum, Miller could not have closed the big gap between the local rivals. The other seven Tigers were out of form.

The Giants ripped into the Tigers from the off and their march to the victory was only stemmed momentarily by a 5–1 from McIntosh and Jack Hodgson in heat six. Otherwise, the match was one-way traffic.

The stinging defeat at Ashfield a few days before made the return local derby at White City on 15 August about pride. It brought out the best in the Tigers and the Giants were again cut down to size south side of the Clyde with a 56–28 defeat.

The meeting saw the first of what would be many full maximums for Ken McKinlay and he was joined on that score by acting skipper Miller. Jack Hodgson was a point shy of a paid maximum with 9+2, but brother Frank was down on power with 4+1. Lindsay recovered some of his missing form with 8+2.

The Giants were as poor as the Tigers had been the meeting before and only managed three race winners and a solitary 4–2 heat win. The Giants were making the starts, but the Tigers were flying from the back. The Giants included Scots Australian pioneer Ron Johnson, but he failed to score. The second half featured Bob Serrurier, one of the five brothers, Alan, Jack, Harry, and Doug, from South Africa who rode speedway. The last-named, Doug, did best and rode for Liverpool.

Miller and McKinlay led the Tigers again but they didn't have the support on Friday 17 August. The Scots duo could have scored more than eight each but both had a fall. It was rare for either to fall but for both to do so on the same night was unusual. Leicester Hunters took the points with a 51–33 win.

The East Anglian air did not suit Tigers. The next night saw them give a poor away display, losing 59–25 at Norwich. Only Miller, with 10 points that included three race wins, saved them from a complete rout. McKinlay scored six but the next two Tigers, Jack Hodgson and Jim Blyth, combined to match his return. The Stars were the masters of The Firs and were pressing for promotion to the First Division.

The Tigers' fans welcomed the new Second Division Match Race champion home after Tommy Miller won the decider against Jack Young at Ashfield. He went on to show them just how good he was and picked up the Festival of Britain Trophy on 22 August at White City. The Trophy was a silver quaich – a Scottish two handled drinking vessel – to add to his Silver Helmet. Despite the presence of two First Division stars, Aub Lawson and Louis Lawson, it was the Division Two riders who dominated. Aub scored nine points while Louis scored six.

Miller crashed with Nicholson in the opening heat, but won the rerun on a borrowed bike before going on to record a 15-point maximum. Realising the scale of the bike damage, the Steward ran the second heat before ordering the rerun of the opener.

Second place went to Derrick Close with 14 who collected the second quaich on offer while Gordon McGregor scored 13 to take third. The top three met in heat 14 and it effectively determined the finishing order.

The solid Motherwell team repulsed the Tigers at The Stadium on Friday 24 August to win the Lanarkshire Cup. The Tigers had only Miller on top form and yet again he showed his liking for this track by scoring a full maximum. His appearance was in doubt, but he made it despite problems from his Wednesday night injuries. He defied an order to rest to take part in the meeting. Bainbridge was back from injury but was off the pace as his four outings netted only four points. McKinlay continued his second heat leader role with seven, while the Hodgson brothers each returned 5+1 as their form started to slip. The Tigers opened with a 5–1 and it was heat five before the Eagles levelled the scores. They moved ahead, then the Tigers pulled back within a couple of points at the end of heat 10. The Eagles won 46–38.

Big things were expected from Halifax but they never hit the heights at White City on 29 August. They lost in the league match 52–32. Oddly enough, the Tigers had only one rider with a maximum against a team that had only three race winners in 14 heats. Needless to say, it was Miller with 12. McKinlay had two wins and two seconds for 10 points; Bainbridge rode three unbeaten races for nine before his maximum hopes went on the last bend with an engine failure.

The Dukes were below par on a track very different from their Shay strip. The meeting ended in the rain, rounding off a dismal night for the Dukes.

The Tigers gave Third Division Poole rider Dick Howard a try out in the second half and he won the Consolation Race. The Scottish Riders' Championship for the Regent – a petrol company – sponsored £100 Gold Casket began in the second half with the Giants' Willie Wilson defeating Ken McKinlay two races to one. The second half featured Fred Chalmers who practiced at the obscure Craigmiller Trotting Track in Edinburgh. He had a bad crash at Edinburgh the following Saturday and never returned to the track.

The rain-soaked track was tricky at Oxford's Cowley Stadium the next night. The start of the meeting was delayed for half an hour to allow for track preparation work. While it gave a few heart stopping moments for the riders, it provided thrills for the fans. The Tigers were in the hunt until heat 11, but the Cheetahs pulled away, winning the last three heats to take the match 47–37. Miller was the best Tiger with 9+1. Frank Hodgson managed 7+1 while Bainbridge scored seven points.

September

The Eagles came to White City on 5 September with their new heat leader, signed a few weeks before from Newcastle, Derrick Close. His fire power gave them the edge and they won 44–40 to end the Tigers' unbeaten home run. Tigers' old boys McGregor and Lowther showed up well, but the other former Tiger, Joe Crowther, did not.

The Tigers were never ahead and only Bainbridge scored a maximum. Miller dropped a point in each of his first two races before completing his night's work with two wins to score 10. The next best Tigers were the Hodgson brothers with 5+1 each. McKinlay had an off night with 2+1, but he was not the only Tiger who should have done better. He alone cannot be blamed for the home reverse.

Bainbridge faced Miller in the Second Division Match Race Championship. It went 2–1 in Miller's favour after the Blantyre man was declared fit to race following his hip injury.

The challenge match between the Rest of Scotland and the Scots Australians at White City on 12 September was a mouth-watering prospect for fans, not only because it set up the battle of the big two in Scotland, Miller and Jack Young. Yet again at White City it went the way of the Scot. They met twice and Miller showed Young his rear wheel both times. The notoriously slow gater Young out-gated Miller in heat 10, but Miller made ground on the corners to pass Young and win. Miller's other win came in the final of the second half trophy. The match went 46–38 to the Rest of Scotland with Miller unbeaten on 12. Frank Hodgson came back to form and scored 10. They support from McGregor on 7+2 and Willie Wilson with seven points.

Young scored 11 and his main support came from Keith Gurtner on 8+1. Home Tiger Bainbridge was not up to his best with 6+1. The Rest of Scotland, with five native Scots and three Anglos, started to edge ahead in heat four and opened the gap as the meeting progressed.

Left: Norman Lindsay.
Below: Alf McIntosh.

Both riders were important second strings for Glasgow in the 1940s and early 1950s.

The Lanarkshire Eagles did the double over Tigers comfortably two days later, winning 50–34. Miller showed his liking for The Stadium track again with a 2–0 defeat of Junior Bainbridge in the Silver Helmet, a maximum 12 in the match and the second half trophy. He lowered the track record yet again. Unfortunately, the rest of the Tigers didn't do much. Bainbridge only managed seven points while McKinlay scored 6+1. Lindsay failed to score while Nicholson was injured when he crashed after the race had finished.

Joe Crowther crashed out of the meeting in heat four while trying to overtake McIntosh on the outside. He suffered a knee injury after scoring in his opening ride. Derrick Close repaid his transfer fee with a big score. Bill Dalton at reserve was probably the most vital Eagle with a superb effort. The match was close contest the end of heat six, then the Eagles pulled away to record a convincing victory for the league points.

Lindsay's return to top form on 19 September saw him take a 10+2 paid maximum against the Cheetahs at White City. Miller had an uncharacteristic fall to dent his unbeaten record but, despite that, the Tigers scored solidly to win 57–27. The Cheetahs were not helped by having six fixtures in seven days and their machines were showing the strain too.

The Tigers had to do it the hard way, from the back, as the Cheetahs gated well. McKinlay was second top Tiger with 10+1 after an opening ride defeat by Roger Wise. Frank Hodgson scored 9+2 while Miller and Bainbridge both returned 8+1.

The Tigers travelled to London and Walthamstow Stadium on 24 September. The Tigers gave a good account of themselves in the second fixture of this double-header meeting, but still lost 49–35. Walthamstow staged a few more meetings and completed the season before withdrawing from speedway permanently.

One report suggests McIntosh collided with Archie Windmill who was excluded from the race. Another suggests Windmill laid his bike down to avoid a teetering McIntosh. As it was, Windmill was injured and withdrew from the meeting. However even without the lanky Windmill, the Wolves had the better of the Tigers. Miller and Bainbridge, who both scored 11, were only matched for the Wolves by Jim Boyd, but another long tail did not help the Tigers. Next best Tiger was Frank Hodgson with five points.

The next night saw one of the Tigers better showings at Great Yarmouth, a track they found hard to master. Their 46–38 defeat was a good result in the circumstances.

The Tigers' heat leader trio had a fair return for their efforts. but the second strings made heavy weather of it. Lindsay had a good evening and why he didn't have his full quota of rides is not clear as he could have added to his 7+1. Miller scored 10 while Bainbridge and McKinlay both collected eight points.

'A good result'. This comment was one which, unfortunately, summed up all too few performances delivered by Tigers away from home in 1951.

Back in Glasgow, there was another defeat for Edinburgh at White City on 26 September. It meant that Edinburgh had yet to win a league match at this track, but the 44–40 defeat was a good show.

This time the Monarchs faded after a promising start. Jack Young, the new World champion, failed to find the maximum form expected and was beaten by both Miller and Bainbridge who both scored 11. Young was second to Bainbridge in the final of the Trophy event. The Monarchs' programme said that Young's throttle trouble cost the Monarchs a draw. Young did have a win over Miller, so maybe that excuse is not valid.

Another excuse was that Dick Campbell had engine trouble. This was valid as he produced one of his worst efforts at White City. Excuse three was Bob Mark's injured thumb which handicapped him, but Bob scored well. By way of a consolation, Bob beat Ashfield's Willie

Wilson in two straight races and qualified to meet Miller in the final of the £100 Gold Casket Scottish Born Riders' Championship.

The truth is that Tigers had three good heat leaders as McKinlay rose to the occasion to score 11. This meant Tigers top three scored 33 points between them against Monarchs top three with 26.

The teams met again at Old Meadowbank on 29 September and the Tigers were given a bit of a going over, 55–29. Consolation for the Tigers was that Miller won the first leg of Scottish Born Riders' Championship. He had luck on his side as Bob Mark took the lead after entering the second lap and held it until the final bend when his engine seized allowing Miller to win by two straight runs.

The decisiveness of the Edinburgh victory can be seen from the home side winning 10 heats to the visitors' one. Miller was the best Tiger scoring 10 points. His two defeats came in the first and last heats by the new World Champion.

Once again, Bainbridge disappointed away from White City with two points. McKinlay, who had bike problems, took three rides on the track spare, and did well to score seven. Third best Tiger was Lindsay with 4+1.

October

The Tigers biggest win, a whopping 65–19, came on 3 October against Fleetwood, who were competing in one of their last league fixtures. The Flyers pulled out of league action at the end of 1951 and, after a 1952 season of open meetings, closed for good.

It took until heat seven for the Flyers, on what looked like very slow machines, to have a man above third. Norman Hargreaves displaced Len Nicholson to halt the rot, but only momentarily. McIntosh was the only Tiger to score a last place when he was excluded in heat 11.

McKinlay and Bainbridge scored full maximums, while Miller with 11, Lindsay nine, and Frank Hodgson eight all had enough bonus points to pay them for 12. Jack Hodgson scored a paid reserves maximum. Alf Parker took the Flyers only race win, beating McIntosh and Nicholson. The visitors gated well with the Tigers coming from the back.

Miller won the Scottish Born Riders' Championship with a 2–0 win over Bob Mark to collect a cheque for £100 and the Regent Gold Casket.

The second half mini four team tournament was won by Scotland, from the Tigers, Giants and Flyers. The format saw one rider from each team in the heats, but if all four from one team had qualified for the final their team could have collected six points.

The Hodgson brothers bowed out of 1951 on 10 October with a flourish. Both were only a point short of a paid maximum. Frank scored 9+2 while Jack scored 10+1. Also saying goodbye to the Tigers for good was their veteran Australian, Norman Lindsay, who had given the team five good years of service since his arrival from Harringay in 1947. He settled for 7+1 which ended a career in which he had been a solid rather than spectacular scorer.

A powerhouse show from the Tigers left Cradley Heath battered and bruised and beaten 60–23. Miller sped to yet another maximum.

Both McKinlay and the Heathens' Schofield were out for the night after their heat 10 coming together. McKinlay was concussed and missed out on facing world number two Split Waterman in a match race. Also in the second half, Waterman showed both Miller and Bainbridge a clean pair of heels in the match races, but Miller turned the tables on Waterman in their second half trophy heat. The pair dead-heated in the second half final.

The Tigers riders raced in a full-blown version of the experimental six-a-side team challenge as the Motherwell promotion piloted the format at The Stadium two days later. The original idea was that substitutions could be made quite freely, but that a rider could only score a maximum of 12 points. Clearly, this format was yet another version with each man taking five or six rides. Miller had five rides for the Glasgow Select scoring 14, while Bainbridge scored 8+3. McKinlay rode for the Eagles and scored 9+1.

The six riders team idea was being seriously debated by the promoters who were looking at possible money saving options.

Fresh from his win the night before at Ashfield, the Monarchs' Harry Darling was favourite, but he had problems and only managed a single point in the Novice Championship at White City on 17 October. Experienced Tiger Jim Blyth was top scorer with nine points from three rides. Scott Hall won a run-off against Niven McCreadie after both had scored eight from three rides and earned the right to race Alf McIntosh. Scott, who went on to race for Motherwell, lost to McIntosh. In a farewell match race, Lindsay lost to McKinlay and Miller beat Bainbridge in the exhibition match race.

The season ended with Tigers in the lower half of the league as the worst Scottish side of the four in the league. Norwich were promoted to the top flight in a sport which had no automatic promotion and relegation. Had the Tigers done a bit better on the road they might have picked up the plaudits in the league.

The review of the season in the *Stenner's 1952 Annual* said that White City were "somewhat disappointing". It continued: "They had two of the Division's best in Miller and Bainbridge, and men of experience in the Hodgson brothers, yet the team did not succeed away from home, as on paper, it should have done." It added that, apart from Miller and Bainbridge, the riders were good at home, but mediocre away. Only one league point was won away from home – the draw at Coventry. It concluded that Ian Hoskins needed to "draft in additional talent."

13. 1952: Scottish Cup winners

The Tigers started 1952 with Peter Dykes back in the fold after a year away. Tommy Miller was back and for this season had three bikes at his disposal for each match. It was clear that he had done more than dance away the winter as he had suggested. Junior Bainbridge was back as were Alf McIntosh and Ken McKinlay. Jim Blyth returned to city rivals Ashfield.

Ian Hoskins decided to experiment in an attempt to get the balance of the side correct, likening the exercise to playing with a yo-yo, pulling up and letting down riders between team and reserve. He added former Newcastle Diamonds riders Don Wilkinson and Len Nicholson and gave a chance to Scottish prospects Stuart Irvine and Jim Steward.

Hoskins kitted his team out with jerseys, with the exception of Peter Dykes, who, as a Kiwi, would be better as an all black. Miller was pleased with the jersey idea as it would help keep his leathers clean. Not that he was on the receiving end of anyone's shale very often.

For the new season, Norwich had been promoted to the First Division, which now had 10 teams. The four Scottish teams, including White City, were in the Second Division. This now had 12 teams, with Poole, who had been promoted from the Third Division, on the south coast of England, and the rest in the English midlands or north. Each team would face the others twice at home and away, for a programme of 44 league matches. The Third Division was replaced by the Southern League, which started the season with 11 teams, but Long Eaton pulled out halfway through the campaign.

March

The Tigers foursome dominated a four-team event at Ashfield on 25 March which opened the season. To be fair, the Giants split their better riders into their two sides, but even pooling the best Giants riders, they still were no match for the Tigers. The Giants 'Blues' side gave the Tigers a run for their money. The Giants 'Reds' might have done better but for Bruce Semmens falling, remounting, then falling spectacularly again in the first heat.

Miller, who was reported as saying that running more than one bike was a waste of time, was pleased with his efforts. So was his promoter Ian Hoskins, who Miller affectionately called the 'Big Yin', long before Billy Connolly used this nickname. Miller was paired with fellow wee man Len Nicholson and the pair scored well together.

It is said that Tigers' mechanic Dick Stewart re-bored Ken McKinlay's engine in the White City workshops between heats eight and 11. If true, it did the business for him. Certainly, Miller was impressed by Stewart's mechanical abilities and his willingness to help the team.

Miller was unbeaten while McIntosh scored eight points, Len Nicholson six and McKinlay, who had two engine failures, scored five. The Tigers' 31 points was three ahead of the Ashfield Blues, 12 better than the Eagles quartet and 13 better than the Ashfield Reds.

Cold weather at White City the next night did not deter the fans, and the new team, without Dykes and Bainbridge, just won 44–40 against the 'Ex-Tigers' in a reunion challenge match. No one could stop Miller recording his first maximum in 1952 at White City.

Both McKinlay, noted as an after the meeting singer who fancied himself as the Scottish version of Perry Como, a laid-back American singer of the time, and McIntosh shone scoring 11 and 10 respectively. Unfortunately, some riders did not do so well, especially Don Wilkinson, who had bike problems.

The 'Ex-Tigers' came close and may have won as Wal Morton dropped points when he reared as he raced with McIntosh. He capitalised on Morton's loss of control, and took the lead while Morton was focused on his bike. Some in the crowd blamed McIntosh for boring out Morton, but the steward took no action. The best Ex-Tigers were Gordon McGregor on nine points, Harold Fairhurst eight, Joe Crowther 6+2 and Will Lowther 6+1.

April

The Tigers' opening league match at Ashfield's Saracen Park on 1 April fell victim to the weather. The next night, Miller opened his home league account with his third full maximum in three meetings. He led the Tigers to a 56–28 win over the Liverpool Chads. His two Scottish compatriots, McKinlay and Alf 'Tartanic' McIntosh weighed in with double figures with 10 and 11 respectively. 'Tartanic' was a nickname made up by Ian Hoskins.

Dykes eased himself back in with 4+1. Back in Scotland for his second season, Dykes sported a natty shirt he'd acquired in the USA. He gave a colourful display against the Chads, scraping the fence, losing good positions in the process. Peter blamed his lack control on a weakness in his arm, a hangover from a crash in his native New Zealand when Belle Vue's Ron Johnston had run over him. However, it was possible that he was suffering the after effects of a recent vaccination. Peter was too sore to contest the second half. Still, the Tigers' fans must have been pleased by the performance without Bainbridge, on his way back from Australia. Jim Steward had his only match for the Tigers in this meeting, scoring one point.

Liverpool were without heat leader Len Read who had a stomach upset, but he would have had his work cut out against the rampant Tigers. The match was won by the Tigers when Alf Webster fell in heat nine, ruling himself out of the rest of the meeting. He went to hospital as it was suspected he had fractured his skull. Glasgow fans saw a small Liverpool reserve who would become a twice world champion, Peter Craven. The press described Peter as a 17-year-old leg trailer.

The word in the dressing rooms before the meeting was that the riders should check their leathers for itching powder as Dykes was a bit of a practical joker. He had been up to tricks on the boat back to Scotland by swapping hair gel for shampoo and blackening a cabin mate's set of dentures.

The Tigers took until the middle of the match at White City on 9 April to establish their superiority. They won 47–37 after losing the lead to Coventry Bees in heat five which saw Miller end his unbeaten run. Many thought that he was pushed wide by Les Hewitt and Miller ended up in the fence on the second bend of lap one rather than tangle with Les. The Steward disagreed and Miller was excluded. The fans let the Steward know they were not happy with the decision.

Bainbridge, back from Australia, scored a maximum and saved the Tigers. He had ordered a new frame before leaving Scotland at the end of 1951 but, on the strength of his maximum decided he didn't want it, and sold it to Dykes. McKinlay was pushed wide in his first ride and excluded after he fell. This reduced his return to seven points. McIntosh took the rerun, passing both Bees on the last bend. Frank Hodgson was back from his broken rib injury but had to settle for a second half outing, such was the strength of the Tigers. Around this time, one-time Tiger Ivor Smith was killed in a building site accident.

Yarmouth came to Glasgow on 16 April with only seven riders. The Tigers' offered the Bloaters Jim Steward for the meeting, but were turned down. As it turned out, Glasgow did loan Steward to the visitors, but not until after Vic Ridgeon was injured in heat nine. Ridgeon and fellow Bloater Tip Mills both had a trip to hospital. Mills fell in heat 13. The Bloaters were slow from the gate and paid the penalty. Their cause wasn't helped by Johnny Chamberlain making his British debut. The Australian struggled to find a way round White City.

Miller's second half final fall was put down to the effects of 'flu'. He wasn't the only one under the weather. Dykes was riding with an ongoing medical problem and was trying to master his newly purchased frame.

Miller scored yet another maximum while Bainbridge and McKinlay scored 11 and 10 respectively as the Tigers won 58–26. Miller was reported to be pleased that Ian Hoskins was intending to buy new jerseys, but he scarcely needed one to keep his leathers clean.

Bainbridge won the second half final. After missing the start, he had to give it all to pass Miller, McKinlay and Brand. He was concerned that the 26 shillings (£1.30) per point for this event was inadequate given the standard of the opposition. In 1951, a prize of £10 was shared between the riders in addition to the points and start money. Bainbridge was also reported to have said that his mechanic had earned more in 1951 than he had.

The Edinburgh Monarchs registered their first success of the season in no uncertain manner against the Tigers at Old Meadowbank on Saturday 19 April. All the home riders scored in every race they rode in, but Miller was the only visitor to accomplish this.

He managed to score 11, missing out on a maximum to Bob Mark in his last ride. Reserve Nicholson was the second best Tiger on seven from four rides, while Bainbridge had a poor night with 5+1. The main difference between the teams was the reserves. The Glasgow pair collected 9+1 between them. The Edinburgh reserves scored two points from four rides. However, the Tigers' main six were down on power and the Monarchs won 53–31.

Probably the biggest cheer of the evening was for Bob Mark when he beat Miller in the last heat. He made a good start and hugged the white line all the way to romp home despite all the wiles of Miller to get past. The Tigers took a big contingent of supporters with them, enough to fill a train and 30 buses, but the team disappointed their traveling support who formed a good part of a 13,000 crowd.

The newly promoted Poole Pirates, with skull and crossbones flying, visited White City for the first time on 23 April. The Tigers had stars and tailenders while the solid scoring was left to the Pirates who all rode well with a distinct degree of skill at the starts.

The Tigers' top guns, however, held all the aces and they won 49–35. They often had to come from the back. Bainbridge missed out at the gate in heat 10 and appeared to be pegged back by the legendary team riding of Lewis and Middleditch. However, the Poole pair drifted from the white line and Bainbridge took his chance to sneak past and beat them to the finishing line with little to spare.

Miller equalled the track record in heat one, thanks to the push he had from Ken Middleditch in the early stages of the race. Miller had another perfect 12 and excellent support from Bainbridge and McKinlay with 11 points apiece.

Nicholson suffered concussion and facial cuts in a heat 10 fall. He put his fall down to trying too hard. Jim Steward sustained a broken knee cap and arm injuries in a second half fall in a fraught Tiger Cub race that was eventually abandoned.

'The Nipper' – 17-year-old Brian Crutcher, whose efforts impressed Miller, kept his team mates amused as he hunted for a haggis bird. Crutcher found the tight bends of White City difficult to master.

It was a windy night and Ian Hoskins' plans to release 500 hydrogen filled balloons was abandoned so the children were given them as a present as they came in to the stadium.

Three days later, the Brandon circuit was very wet, not because of rain, rather because of an over-zealous track man who soaked the track anticipating the sun would dry off the excess moisture. The state of the track for this league fixture favoured the Bees, Miller apart. He did well from the gate. Once the mud had settled, the Bees won 48–36.

Miller followed Vic Emms home in heat one, then had three wins for 11 points. Veteran Jack Hodgson scored eight and Bainbridge was next best with five points. He had two last places before picking up his points in his last two rides.

Bainbridge and Dykes were lucky to arrive in one piece. Their van was knocked off the road after colliding with a lorry near Catterick in Yorkshire. On the way home, the gearbox gave up and they were rescued by Jack Parker who put them up for the night before sending them home by train.

The trip to Coventry saw Tommy Miller tie up his winter plans by accepting Jack Parker's invitation to tour Australia.

Back at White City, Miller took another maximum and Bainbridge was paid for the lot, 11+1, in an easy win over the Potters on 30 April. Stoke did not put up a great fight going down 53–31. Dykes gave a good show scoring nine points from three rides. Frank Hodgson returned from injury. He had been easing himself in by riding in the second half. He scored 4+1.

For the second time in three weeks, the visitors were a seven-man side with Ron Peace missing due to suspected appendicitis. The Potters were offered Stuart Irvine, but chose to use their seven and give each man four rides.

May

The Tigers were expected to do better than a 53–29 defeat at Oxford on May Day. Much to the surprise of the home fans, the Cheetahs mastered the wet conditions better than the Tigers.

The Tigers were unlucky. In heat three McKinlay was the innocent victim of Bill Kemp's machine losing power as Kemp was about to pass him. Neither was injured or awarded a point. Wilkinson fell in heat 13, but it was teammate Jack Hodgson who ploughed into him and came off worst. Thankfully they walked back to the pits after some medical attention.

For the first time since 9 April, Miller failed to record double figures. The Tigers lost McIntosh, who fell and injured his leg after losing control on the wet and greasy surface. Bainbridge had a good night with a heat eight last bend win after swapping the lead with Frank Boyle for much of the race. This was the highlight of the meeting. Miller and Bainbridge scored nine points each while McKinlay added seven. Cheetahs reserves Frank Boyle and Jim Gregory took 11 points out of 12. They outscored three of the Tigers' tail who failed to bag a point.

The Tigers were again fragile away from home the next night. Miller again failed score double figures in a 56–28 league defeat at Cradley Heath. Home star Harry Bastable faced Miller twice and twice came from the back to beat him. Yet again rain played its part in the Tigers' downfall, although many fans expected the wet track to disadvantage the home team.

McIntosh rode after his injury the night before. He scored four points, but this set him back and he was forced to miss the team's third meeting in three days at Stoke. Frank Hodgson didn't make it and was replaced by Nicholson. Miller managed eight while Wilkinson was the highest paid Tiger with 6+3.

The next night saw another wet meeting and the Tigers' third defeat in a row. This was at Stoke and the Tigers lost 53–31. Miller's scoring touch returned and he showed the Potters fans why he was so popular at White City with a brilliant maximum. McKinlay returned to form with eight while Bainbridge chipped in with five points. The other five riders had a night to forget. The Potters' hero was Reg Fearman, but he could not beat fast-gating Miller. Despite running Miller close in heat seven for a few laps, Fearman lost ground in a big over-slide and his challenge was over.

While doing three away meetings in the midlands in three days might have saved travel costs, it did not do the Tigers or the fans any favours.

An 18,000 crowd watched the two Glasgow teams fight out a 42–42 draw at White City in an incident packed match on 7 May. Heat 13 was rerun after both the Giants looped and fell at the starting gate. It was seen as an unsatisfactory start. The Giants got the benefit of the doubt and took part in the rerun when the Tigers' fans felt they should have been excluded.

The Tigers levelled the scores in the rerun thanks to Don Gray, riding the machine damaged as he looped, and Dick Howard who was suffering the effects of a bruised back. However, Frank Hodgson and McIntosh could not stop Cyril Cooper winning the last heat to secure a share of the league points.

Miller, pleased that he had been appointed captain of the Britain side to face Overseas at Stoke on 15 May, scored his usual maximum. Bainbridge, down to lead the Overseas, scored 9+1 while next best was Dykes with five points. The biggest gap between the two teams was six points.

New Australian at Ashfield, 'Cowboy' Bob Sharp and Scot Jimmy Tannock made their White City debuts in this meeting. Nicholson was also trying to get his place back with the Tigers, but was team ridden out of it in the second half Reserves Race by mentors and position holders, the Hodgson brothers.

At this time, McKinlay and Ron Phillips were two of the eight Second Division riders nominated to race abroad. The third Scottish rider, Don Cuppleditch, was reluctant to ride on a Sunday and relinquished the nomination. Bob Mark took his place. The Scottish promoters were not happy their riders should have such a share of the nominations with Jim Gregory, Tony Lewis and Reg Morgan from Oxford, Poole and Yarmouth respectively.

Next up was another local derby for Tigers, but this time, thanks to superior heat leader power, they beat the Lanarkshire Eagles on 9 May. The Tigers were never headed at The Stadium on two days after the Ashfield meeting and held a narrow lead winning 44–40. The veteran Hodgson brothers in the reserve berths helped cover the rides that should have been taken by McIntosh and Wilkinson.

Gordon McGregor recorded a maximum and beat Miller twice. However, his teammates, especially Noel Watson and Keith Gurtner, had an off night with bike troubles. The Eagles other heat leader Derrick Close was down on power.

The Tigers top riders were Miller and McKinlay with 10 points each, but McKinlay added a bonus point to his tally. Bainbridge managed nine points. His win in his last outing effectively secured the match after three second places.

The Eagles visited White City on 14 May bent on revenge but, despite scoring more than at The Stadium by a point, they lost 43–41. The Eagles could have taken a league point in the last heat, but Miller settled for second place after he passed Gordon McGregor, enough for the win. McGregor had bike problems in heat six and pulled out when leading. This turned the destination of the match. In the same heat Noel Watson, who had been beside McGregor on the way to a 5–1, hit a bump and fell. So, a 5–1 to the visitors became a 5–1 to the Tigers.

This match showed that the Tigers' tail was very vulnerable. The Hodgson brothers, Nicholson and Wilkinson were all struggling and contributed only five points between them. McIntosh was missing due to his ongoing knee injury.

Miller and Bainbridge were equal top with 11 each, beaten by Close and Gurtner respectively. Dykes had another good performance when it mattered and scored 9+1. Gurtner was injured in a second half crash into the fence compounded by being hit by the following Jack Hodgson.

The second half featured two hopefuls from Ernie Appleby's Newton Heath training track, Roy Peacock and Frankie Corrie. Jack Monteith was added to the Tigers' books after a good display in the Discovery Race. Ian Hoskins also expressed interested in former Eagle Bob Lindsay.

Watched by a 16,000 crowd two days later, the Leicester Hunters took until heat four to get in front on a dusty Blackbird Road track. When they did, the Tigers' challenge faltered. Miller showed his skills with a maximum, but Leicester had the all round strength. Not for the first time away from home, the Tigers' heat leaders failed to produce big scores. This, coupled with another poor return from the Hodgsons, Nicholson and Wilkinson spelt disaster. Miller's main backer was Bainbridge and future Hunters' hero, McKinlay. Both scored seven points. The home side won 48–36.

For some reason, the Glasgow men could not master the Caister Road track in Great Yarmouth. To be fair, many riders found this track challenging and 17 May was no exception. Even Miller had a miserable night, falling in his opener and recorded a poor, for him, six points. Dykes fell in his opening ride too and withdrew from the meeting after another outing. The Bloaters had no problems even when the Tigers left them at the gate. After 14 heats the score was 56–28 to Yarmouth. Bainbridge was the best Tiger with eight and Miller and Wilkinson on six were joint second best.

Yet again, the Tigers were poor travellers as the prospective 1952 Second Division Champions, Poole Pirates, gave the Tigers a 61–23 pasting on 19 May. The Pirates were solid, from one to eight. Miller scored almost half the Tigers total with 11 points. Dykes and Bainbridge each scored five, taking the tally for the three to 21. Also, Miller and McKinlay had to leave their waterlogged car and bikes 40 miles from the track and continue the journey in Bainbridge's car. The two riders used the Glasgow track spare for most of the meeting which did not help McKinlay much.

A local derby in the National Trophy saw an exhausted Tigers team, still weary from their travels down south, establish a fair lead to take across the Clyde on 21 May. The Tigers put inexperienced youngster Stuart Irvine at number one and, after he was ruled out following a fall in his first ride, the Hodgson brothers took his remaining rides. If it was a deliberate ploy to pull Irvine out after a ride, it certainly worked to Tigers' advantage. The Tigers piled up a 65–43 victory. Also, the Tigers had noted the Giants' ploy of fitting new rear tyres and did the same, much to their visitors' surprise.

Irvine, who had been signed by Ian Hoskins on the strength of his Leo birth sign as much as his riding ability, replaced Nicholson who decided not to ride until he had fully recovered from injury.

Miller lost his maximum to Cyril Cooper in the last heat. Cooper was normally a steady second string, but on his night he could beat the best, particularly at White City. Miller piled up 17 points while Bainbridge was the only other Tiger on double figures with 12+1. Jack Hodgson scored 9+1.

The Tigers were in the market for a new and experienced rider. Attempts to sign Son Mitchell for £500 failed. On the junior front, Jimmy Tannock was impressing Ian Hoskins who rated him highly.

In the return National Trophy match, the Tigers knocked the Giants out in spectacular style. The crowd of 20,000 expected the home riders to do much better three days after the White City first leg. A 56–52 win for the Tigers made the aggregate score Giants 95 Tigers 121. Dykes pulled out of the meeting following his crash into the safety fence in heat 10 which resulted in a cut arm.

The Tigers had come out fighting. Miller's opening race win was the fastest time of the season. Despite the attentions of Willie Wilson in heat eight, he scored a maximum while Bainbridge was one point short of a paid 18 return. Stuart Irvine took three rides and scored 1+1. The third best Tiger was McKinlay with 9+2.

On 28 May, Scotland met England at White City. The three Scots in the side gathered 35 points and the balance were contributed by two Australians and an Englishman. All those representing Scotland were Second Division racers while England used a mixture from the First and Second Divisions. Yet again, it was Miller who was the hero with an immaculate six ride maximum. His last two wins were from the back and he left it until the last bend to beat Billy Bales. He took another 0.4 seconds off his track record to leave the new one at 76.0 seconds. Bainbridge scored 11+1 for Scotland while Bob Mark and Derrick Close both added 10 to the Scotland total of 61. Keith Gurtner rode with a special plaster cast and scored 5+1.

Billy Bales had a great night for England scoring 14 points, while Ken Sharples scored 9+1. Arthur Forrest scored seven from four rides as he replaced team mates from the reserve berth. England's eight scored 46 points.

A makeshift Tigers team met their fellow big cats, a non-league cobbled together Wigan Panthers side, at Woodhouse Lane on Friday 30 May. The Tigers won 43–41. Jack Hodgson was injured after falling in heat 10 and Ron Hart was excluded for unseating him. Jack was out for the rest of the meeting. He had cuts to his foot and leg and did not return to action until August. Miller was excluded in heat eight for crossing the inside white line which spoilt his maximum hopes. The Tigers' youngster, Jim Russell, fell in heat 13 after clipping the safety fence. Bainbridge scored a maximum while McKinlay and Miller both scored eight. McKinlay also had a bonus point.

With the Giants away, stay at home fans at Saracen Park had a local derby between the Tigers and Eagles for their weekly speedway on Saturday 31 May. Both sides included juniors, but both had their top riders as they faced each other in the Scottish Match Race Championship before the match.

It was a big enough challenge to be facing Miller, but Derrick Close discovered he had lost his leathers between home and the track and the borrowed suit did not help his cause. Miller won the tie 2–0. In the first race he came from behind, but in the second raced away from the tapes to the flag.

In the Lanarkshire Cup, the Tigers were more at home and won 50–34 easing ahead as the match progressed. Miller took a customary maximum and McKinlay did likewise. Wilkinson, Dykes and Bainbridge all scored seven points and all except Bainbridge added bonus points.

June

Despite three Tigers suffering bike problems, the team beat visitors Cradley Heath 49–35 on 4 June. Frank Hodgson, Dykes and Bainbridge all blew engines in this meeting. The Heathens proved hard to shake off at first, but the tide turned in heat eight when the Tigers posted a 4–2. The continuing rise of McKinlay, with 10 points, was starting to pay dividends for the Tigers. Not far behind him was comeback man McIntosh with 8+1 after an engine failure in his opening ride. The two Macs rode well as a pair and both had to come from the back in each of their outings together. Needless to say, however, the top Tiger was, yet again, Miller with a maximum.

The second half final prize, an electric razor, was coveted by Bainbridge. As circumstances turned out, a rare Miller engine failure cleared the path for him to win it.

Yet again, the Tigers showed their liking for Saracen Park and three days later, they routed the Giants 48–36. Miller's maximum took him to an average of 10.22 from 18 meetings. He had scored 184 points – without any bonus points – out of 216 on offer. Fellow maximum man Bainbridge had an average of 8.24. McKinlay scored nine with two wins.

The Giants matched an opening Tigers 4–2 in heat two, but thereafter it was all Tigers who pulled ahead steadily. It was not until heat 13 that the Giants managed another heat win, but by then their 4–2 was merely a consolation for their fans as the match was lost by heat 12. The Giants' efforts, especially against the Tigers, did not bode well for the future. None of their riders scored double figures.

The Tigers saw off the challenge from Leicester on 11 June, despite the visitors showing the Tigers how to gate. However, in return the Tigers showed Hunters how to come from the back. The Hunters' only heat win came thanks to McKinlay's fall in heat eight which allowed them to snatch a 5–1 over Stuart Irvine. Les Beaumont had his moments, including a win over Miller, a rare feat at White City.

Miller's return was reduced to 11 and Len Williams stopped Bainbridge's maximum, restricting 'The Flash's' return to 10+1. McKinlay managed 8+1.

Stuart Irvine continued to hold his place pending the return of Nicholson, who was keen to ride again after his head injury. He scored one point in the Tigers 49–35 win over the Midlanders. Fellow reserve, Wilkinson, notorious for running into car problems on his way north each week, scored a reasonable 4+1 from two rides.

Despite the Lanarkshire Cup fixture being staged on Friday 13 June, neither the Tigers or the Eagles could claim to be unlucky. The result had something for the two sets of fans. Two evenly matched teams, with the home side just shading it with a last heat 5–1. The Cup, however, travelled to Glasgow. The Tigers won 90–78 on aggregate.

Miller took the individual honours with a maximum. He also retained his Scottish Match Race Championship by seeing off Edinburgh's Harold Fairhurst. Miller treated Fairhurst with respect and shattered the Motherwell track record to win the first leg. In the second race Miller took a bit more time to win this leg 2–0.

Nicholson was back for the Tigers, but only managed one point. His return was not expected to yield a lot of points, but the Tigers management must have been disappointed by five points from Bainbridge and 3+1 from McIntosh.

Leicester's trip to White City the week before stood them in good stead for the National Trophy tie. This time, on 18 June, they pipped the Tigers by a couple of points to put themselves in the driving seat to win on aggregate. On the basis of the previous result, few would have predicted the Hunters' 55–53 win. A wet home track, which normally aided the

Tigers, worked against them this time. The home team also lost points through bike problems and falls. Their usual slowness from the gate did not help. Miller, however, rode well despite the track to score 17+1 while Bainbridge, not always a fan of wet tracks, scored 13+2.

Wilkinson nearly missed the meeting when his car broke down in Edinburgh. Acting swiftly, he pushed his bike to Waverley Station and arrived at White City at 7pm. His cars were less than perfect.

Surprise packet was Nicholson, who rose to the occasion with a superb 9+1. It could have been more, but for a last race fall. He had extra rides after Dykes withdrew with bike problems. A massive over-slide on the wet surface led to his fall.

The match was tied 45–45 after heat 15. Leicester took the advantage with a couple of heat wins to go six points up. The Tigers' last heat 5–1 made the score look a bit more respectable.

Two points down from the first leg and faced with the daunting prospect of visiting Blackbird Road, few would have given the Tigers much of a chance two days later. However, the Hunters turned into the hunted as the Tigers dominated the home men in spectacular fashion, winning 62–46 to take the tie 115–99 on aggregate. The Hunters must have assumed they had the tie won, but they were wrong.

Miller scored a full maximum and had superb support from Bainbridge and McIntosh who both scored 10. Only Joe Bowkis threatened Miller's supremacy, but that only lasted for a lap before Miller found a way past.

Stuart Irvine was given the chance, replacing an out-of-form Frank Hodgson. The youngster, who was like teammate Nicholson, a former merchant navy man, finally mastered the art of the power sliding and rose to the occasion with six points as a reserve. His points were a vital and unexpected contribution. He did it the hard way as he was not shepherded home by a team mate.

This was a memorable meeting for Tigers, a true red-letter day in their history. They led from the off, were pulled back level at the end of heat five, but thereafter forged ahead with only a couple of heat setbacks on the way to a great away win. The Leicester fans, sensing things were going wrong, had hoped the impending rain would arrive in time to save their side, but it held off until five minutes after the end.

Back in league action, Liverpool put their defeat by the Tigers, on Monday 23 June, down to the loss of Reg Duval who fell and suffered a serious leg injury in heat six. With Duval out, the Chads did not have the combined strength to repulse the Tigers who won 43–41.

The match ended in a dispute. The final race was stopped with the Liverpool pair on the way to a match winning 5–1. The Steward spotted a tapes infringement, but waited a full lap before ordering a restart. Despite the fans considering Nicholson the culprit, the original starters took part in the rerun. Miller took full advantage of the restart to complete his maximum and won the match for his team. He might have been joined on a maximum by Bainbridge, but for an engine failure spoiling his unbeaten run. He had to be satisfied with nine points, the same as McIntosh. The Tigers were without McKinlay, so Ian Hoskins gave an outing to Red Monteith at reserve. He scored 1+1.

McKinlay had been in Kumla in Sweden on 24 June for a World Championship qualifier. He was flown over and back to minimise any disruption. At this time, air trips to Sweden, or anywhere else, were an adventure. Ken borrowed a bike because his own did not arrive and failed to qualify after scoring five points.

A solid display by Tigers at White City on 25 June sent Oxford back south pointless on the wrong end of a 56–28 score. The result suggests that the Tigers had things all their own way, but they had only one rider on a maximum. The Cheetahs made a match of it and the Tigers worked hard to gather points and faced stout resistance throughout the match.

Needless to say, Miller scored a maximum and had strong support from McKinlay with 10 points, and Bainbridge on nine, who were both paid for 11. Dykes had four second places and followed home a team mate for a 5–1 in three of them, so scored 8 + 3.

The Tigers' second-halfer, Red Monteith, had a fantastic escape after being dragged the length of the straight hanging on to the handlebars. He eventually let go without injury and promptly returned to win his next race.

To say the Tigers let the Monarchs off the hook at Old Meadowbank three days later is an understatement. To put it in a nutshell, the Tigers blew it big style. At the end of heat eight the Tigers had an 18 points advantage. The Monarchs' fans had started to stream out of the stadium fearing the worst. A Tigers win at Old Meadowbank was bad, but the projected margin at heat eight must have been unthinkable.

Had the departing Monarchs' fans held their nerve, they would have seen one of the remarkable revivals since Lazarus and the Tigers' fans must have been rubbing their eyes in disbelief. At the end of 18 heats, the Tigers had lost by four points. This still set them up for the second leg of this Scottish Cup contest. The Monarchs could point to four bike failures and flat tyres by their top heat leaders as the cause of their early meeting slump.

The Tigers' decline started with Miller's engine failure in heat nine and in his next two rides, he could only manage two second places. The Tigers could have snatched a win in the last heat, but Miller and McKinlay could only manage a 2–4 which wasn't enough. Miller ended with 13 points while McKinlay added 11 to the Tigers' total. McIntosh scored eight while Bainbridge scored 7+3.

Bainbridge was the top Tiger, scoring 14+2 as the visitors set about the Pirates in faraway Poole on Monday 30 June in the National Trophy. Miller did not have things his own way, but his 13 was no mean feat against the Pirates. He over-slid and fell in the opening heat, but remounted to take a point. McKinlay scored 8+2 from four completed races. He dropped out of one with bike problems.

The Pirates lost Roy Craighead with bike problems, but reserve Jimmy Squibb made up for the former Wembley man's lack of fire power. The match ended 61–47 to Poole, who had a 14-point lead to take to Glasgow for the second leg.

McIntosh was in the wars with his trousers. He tore his first pair in the bike chain as he pushed his bike from the railway station to the track. He bought a new pair, put them on and went off the cinema where he sat on two lumps of chewing gum which did the new garment no good. To cap it all, his engine seized in his first race and he had to use the track spare for the night.

July

The ploy of fielding Irvine at number one and giving him a single ride failed at White City in the return leg against Poole on 2 July. Neither reserve, Nicholson or Wilkinson, rose to the occasion. Despite the Tigers winning 58–50, it wasn't enough to take the tie. Reserve Jimmy Squibb, on the other hand, was the winner for Poole taking rides for Lewis, Holden and Craighead. The aggregate score was 112–106 to the Pirates. The Tigers' dream of facing First Division opposition in the next round of the National Trophy was gone. Yet again, the Tigers' inability to gate cost them dearly.

An unusual tale from this meeting was the delivery of two roses for Ken Middleditch – a first at an away track – from a mystery admirer.

For the Tigers, McKinlay had a great night. He top scored with 16+1 while Miller managed an acceptable 15+1. Bainbridge continued 11+2. Lindsay Nixon, a young Australian based at Motherwell, had a rare outing in the second half but finished last in the consolation race.

On a wet afternoon in Dublin, the spirited riding of the Glasgow Tigers gave Irish speedway fans something to talk about on Sunday 6 July. The match was evenly balanced, but a Bainbridge and McIntosh 5–1 in heat 11 set Tigers up for at least a draw. The Tigers must have expected Miller to deliver three points in the last heat, but Cyril Brine and Dom Perry salvaged a 4–2 which saw Wilkinson second and Miller with a rare zero. The 4–2 wasn't enough and the Shelbourne Tigers won 37–35. The Tigers deserve credit for this win because most of the Shelbourne riders were from First Division teams. Perhaps if American Ernie Roccio had not had so many bike problems, the result would have been different. Miller and McKinlay scored nine apiece.

Louis Lawson and Fred Rogers were the First Division stars expected to do well in the World Championship round at White City on 9 July. In heat four, they started well, but Miller tore past them. Giving chase, they collided and hit the fence, tearing down 20 yards of it. Rogers ended up on the dog track and Lawson on the shale track. Both were excluded from the race, but were reinstated when Miller spoke on their behalf. Bent bikes meant using spare machines and both Rogers and Lawson were hampered with bike failures afterwards. Miller won the round pocketing £30 with Wimbledon's Cyril Brine and Norwegian Basse Hveem tied in second place with 13 points each.

Miller was impressed with Hveem and his hard riding style. He had wondered how much a threat he would be when they met. Miller beat the Norwegian, and put of his success down to Hveem's inexperience on the British style starting grids. Miller was also impressed by Larry Lazarus who turned out at very short notice to replace Ron Peace. Norrie Isbister sent a messenger to bring Lazarus back to Ashfield from his house while the track mechanics rebuilt his machine.

Back in league action three days later, the Tigers opened with a heat win at Brandon, but thereafter Coventry Bees edged ahead and eventually won 54–30. The Tigers had been on for a 5–1 in the first heat, but Charlie New overtook Wilkinson on the last turn to make it a 4–2. Only Miller gave the Bees a fight, but even he could only score 11. Vic Emms got the better of Miller in heat 10, but knew he had been in a race. More was expected of the Tigers, but none of the other riders shone. Biggest disappointment was Bainbridge who collected a poor, for him, 3+1. McKinlay was the second-best Tiger on six points. Once again, the Tigers struggled away from home.

Poole was becoming a Tigers' bogey track as they had their third try at beating the Pirates in Dorset. This visit on Monday 14 July ended with Tigers going down 56–28. The team riding Pirates collected ten bonus points.

The Tigers' best was McKinlay who scored 10 points, followed by Miller on eight. The rest of the Tigers contributed little while the home team scored solidly. Miller had two third places before getting the hang of the track and winning twice. He ended Ken Middleditch's maximum hopes in the final heat.

Peter Dykes was lucky to survive an afternoon yachting incident. Despite good advice, Peter had set his boat up to sail itself while he sunbathed. A gust of wind capsized it and Dykes had to be rescued. The other riders rescued him, but were almost blown out to sea. They only managed to get back to land when the wind changed direction.

Two days later, back at White City, the wet track surface, which was described as a quagmire, played into the hands of the fast-starting visitors from Leicester. Falls and engine troubles affected Glasgow most, and rendered McIntosh a virtual passenger. A 5–0 to Leicester in heat three put them on course for a win. The Tigers duo in the race, McKinlay and Dykes, both over-slid and fell. In the next heat, Bainbridge lost traction, locked up and drove off the track. Despite returning to the track, he was excluded.

Miller only managed a couple of wins and only scored nine points. Bainbridge and McKinlay both scored seven while the tall Geordie, Wilkinson, scored 7+1. Frank Hodgson returned for this fixture and Irvine was demoted to the second half, losing his team place. He did have a few other outings from time to time.

Les Beaumont was injured in the pits. A rider used a brick as a bike stand to warm his machine. Unfortunately, the brick was caught by the back wheel and flung at Les who ended up with a burst blood vessel in his leg.

Despite their poor performances prior to riding at Motherwell on 18 July, the Tigers still rose to the occasion and beat the Eagles. Miller opened with a win and took an amazing two seconds off his own track record. The score was close throughout, but with Miller in the last race, the Tigers always had the edge. Yet again, he scored a maximum at Motherwell. Bainbridge, using a new frame, returned to form with 10 points and McKinlay weighed in with eight.

Like the other Eagles versus Tigers matches, it was a close-run affair except after heat three when there was an eight-point margin in the Tigers favour. However, the Tigers had the edge over the last two races and won 43–41. The Tigers had nine race winners to the Eagles' five.

The Eagles' fans would have expected a home win, but Derrick Close had a poor night by his standards due to bike problems.

Having restricted the Monarchs to a four-point win at the end of June in the first leg, on 23 July the Tigers took this second leg 67–41 to win this Scottish Cup tie second leg on aggregate 119–97. The Tigers gave Australian Bob Sharp, known as 'Cowboy', his debut and he did not let them down. He scored 3+1 as second reserve. He had been released by Ashfield who were over their quota of 12 signed riders.

Miller raced to another full maximum and, with support from McIntosh with 11+1, McKinlay 12+1 and Dykes on 9+4, the Tigers raced away with the match. Only Bainbridge was out of sorts, his bike did not perform as it should.

For the Monarchs Dick Campbell, like Bainbridge, had bike troubles. Eddie Lack pulled out of his premature return from a wrist injury after a single pointless ride. Also, there was a poor show from Harold Fairhurst, usually no slouch round White City.

The Tigers missed Nicholson who injured his shoulder in a car crash near Carlisle earlier that day. He was traveling in Joe Crowther's car when it was hit by a bus.

The roller-coaster of being a Tigers fan took a nosedive again as they lost to Stoke Potters 54–30 at Sun Street on 26 July. Only Ron Peace could match Miller, who scored 11, but the rest of the Potters had the measure of the rest of the Tigers. Frank Hodgson, once the scourge of the Second Division, was last in both of his rides.

It was a bumper pay night for the top Potters. Peace achieved his defeat of Miller coming from the back in heat seven, a feat not many riders managed. However, Miller beat him in the last heat to level the score between them.

After Miller, the next best Tiger was McKinlay on six points. The Tigers had surrendered the match by the end of heat 11 and it was another poor away result.

Tommy Miller (left) and Junior Bainbridge (right) – two of the best riders for Glasgow in the 1950s.

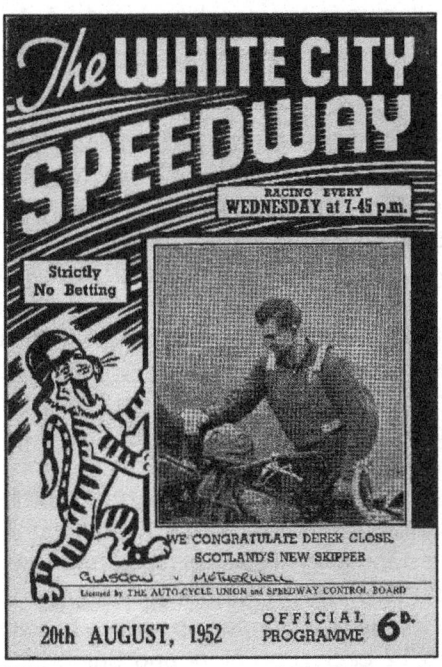

1952 Tigers programme courtesy Duncan Luke.

Yet again, Yarmouth was a graveyard for the Tigers as they all tried to master the tricky turns on 29 July. They lost 57–27. Fred Brand and Bob Baker were unbeaten, and both defeated Miller. Reg Morgan also best Miller. Miller and Bainbridge were the best Tigers on seven points each. The next best rider was Wilkinson with 4+1. The Tigers never managed a heat win and the best they did were four 3–3s. In two of them, Miller won the heat. Yarmouth were strong at home, only being beaten twice at home in 22 matches in 1952. They lost all their away league fixtures.

The Tigers' mid-season slump continued. Even at home they were failing to hold their own. Maybe the bumpy state of the track, which caused concern for locals and visitors alike, did not help. In any event, the promoters noted the concerns and made plans to dig up and relay the track.

The next day, visiting Cradley Heath took the league points from the Tigers with a narrow 44–40 win. Cradley's reserves did not score in their four rides. It was the other six who combined to outscore the Tigers. Cradley had the three Tolley boys in their team, Les, Jim and Dick.

The top two Tigers were McKinlay and Miller who scored 11 each. Bainbridge, who had earlier faced Miller in the Scottish Match Race, only scored six. The other five contributed 12 points between them and the blame must be with the long tail. To be fair, the Tigers' involved were not happy with their form and Dykes even contemplated packing it in and returning to New Zealand. He was so despondent that he sat out the second half.

The meeting had opened with Miller and Bainbridge facing each other in the Scottish Match Race Championship. Miller fell in the second heat when leading easily as his engine gave up the ghost. The fans, whose loyalty must have been divided, saw him use the track spare fitted with his own handlebars in the decider. He won 2–1.

August

On 4 August, the sporting Liverpool fans applauded McKinlay's heat five win from the back. They could afford to be generous as by then it was clear that Tigers were not shaping up to present a challenge to the Chads. After 14 heats, the Chads had won 47–37. Miller just missed out on a maximum as Harry Welch had a brilliant last ride to beat him. McKinlay and Bainbridge both scored eight points, but yet again the other five riders were not really at the races.

The big Stanley Stadium track should have been easier than the tricky smaller tracks for the Tigers, but yet again the riders stuttered on another away trip.

Disaster struck for Bainbridge on the next day when riding for Scotland against England at Ashfield. He was involved in a crash which saw him break his knee cap and damage ligaments. He was out for the rest of the season.

Every rider in Scotland had a chance to make it to the Scottish Riders' Championship as they contested qualifying rounds. White City hosted their round on 6 August. The rise of McKinlay was confirmed as he deprived Miller of his maximum. As it was, McKinlay could not beat Wilkinson and Ashfield's Willie Wilson, settling for second spot overall. Miller still won the round with 14 points. McKinlay was runner-up with 13, while Willie Wilson and Harold Fairhurst were joint third with 12 each. Bob Mark and Bainbridge had been included in the draw but were both out due to injury. Wilkinson had a good night and his 10 is worthy of mention given the opposition he faced.

The Giants faced the Tigers in the first leg of the all-Glasgow final of the Scottish Cup on Tuesday 12 August. On yet another wet night, the track conditions favoured Tigers for a change and Miller was particularly at home on a slippery surface. The Tigers were without Bainbridge, but the Hodgson brothers were back filling the reserve berths and scored four points each. McKinlay continued to show that he was a rapidly emerging talent with 11+2.

The Giants slipped behind early on, but managed to draw level by heat nine. After an exchange or two, Giants managed to lead by a couple of points in heat 13, but the Tigers levelled the scores in the next and then forged ahead to take the match 58–50 after 18 heats. The result effectively killed off Giants' challenge for the Scottish silverware. Their team, like the Tigers, had no real third heat leader to provide top end strength.

If the Tigers did not like the Yarmouth track, the Bloaters had no love for White City. So it was on 13 August that Yarmouth lost heavily in Glasgow. The meeting was almost all one-way traffic. The Tigers had two full and one paid maximum. The full houses were recorded, not surprisingly, by Miller and McKinlay but the paid maximum, 11+1, McIntosh must have pleased him and the Tigers fans after a run of unspectacular returns. The Tigers won 56–28 and collected two league points. Miller showed his skill by beating the popular top flight Wimbledon whizz kid Ronnie Moore by 30 yards in two match races.

The red and white ribbons were probably on the Scottish Cup before heat one of the meeting at White City on 18 August. The Tigers made sure of the cup in style. The Giants were blitzed 75–33. The aggregate score of 133–83 showed the Tigers' superiority. They had four riders on double figures, although only McKinlay was unbeaten by a Giant. He scored 17+1. Miller fell in the last race as he tried to come from the back when the result did not matter. He was carried off with mild concussion and had scored 15 through five race wins. McIntosh continued from the week before with 11+3 while Dykes also had a good night with 12+2. Only Jack Hodgson struggled to do much after an opening ride paid win behind Miller. His brother Frank took 4+2 from two outings and fellow reserve Nicholson showed better form with 7+1.

The Eagles from Motherwell could never be faulted for not trying at White City as they challenged the Tigers on 20 August before settling for a 45–39 defeat. The Eagles started with a 5–1, but the Tigers levelled the scores in the next heat and, after a drawn heat, moved ahead and were always ahead for the rest of the match.

Had Miller been in action, the margin would have probably been greater. Nicholson moved up to cover for him and Stuart Irvine rode at reserve, but failed to score. The Tigers top man was McKinlay on 11+1. He had sound support from Dykes with 9+1. The solid middle order of Nicholson, McIntosh and Wilkinson was the difference between the two sides.

McKinlay recorded yet another paid maximum as the Tigers took the league points from Stoke on 27 August with relative ease. Miller came back and scored 9+2. The Tigers pair of Wilkinson and Miller followed home Ken Adams for an opening heat 3–3. Thereafter, apart from three heat wins, the Tigers had things very much their own way.

Three Tigers dropped points due either to an engine failure or a fall. This reduced the margin of victory to 52–32. The Tigers rode as a team with eight bonus points to Stoke's one.

September

Nicholson was a hero by Tigers fans as he raced to paid 10 against the old rivals from the east on 3 September. The Monarchs had no answer to the Tigers – their riders won only three heats. Miller and McKinlay were the Glasgow big guns but Nicholson, together with Dykes and McIntosh, also contributed to the red and white glee which ended 58–26. The two Hodgsons, now firmly established as the experienced reserve department, contributed seven points to the comprehensive demolition. Miller nearly lost his maximum to Dick Campbell in a close fought heat one. Half a wheel separated the two at the line. As it was, he scored 11+1. McKinlay took 10+1.

Doug Templeton, a seasoned grass tracker who would go on to serve both the Tigers and Monarchs and Scottish speedway with distinction, made his speedway debut in the second half but did not return until the start of 1953 when the Tigers threw him in at the deep end.

The meeting was attended by Tommy Miller, Scottish Featherweight Boxing Champion and the speedway Miller took him round the track, but declined an offer of a sparring session.

A second one-sided meeting followed. The Chads were on the wrong end of the biggest score at White City in a league fixture this season. The 61–23 win against Liverpool was almost too easy and Peter Robinson was almost a one man show for the Chads, winning two heats. He featured in the only heats that Tigers failed to stretch their advantage. Unusually, not a single Chad scored a bonus point.

Yet again, Nicholson was a big scorer and narrowly missed out a maximum. He scored 11 and McKinlay matched him. Robinson prevented both their maximums. There were no problems for Miller who strolled to yet another maximum.

In sharp contrast to two days earlier at White City Tigers yet again stuttered on the road. This time the trip to Cradley Heath ended with another heavy defeat. The solid Heathens won 55–29. Miller produced his usual double figure score with 11, but his teammates were well down. McKinlay scored 6+1 while Dykes was the third highest on 5+2.

The Miller-Bastable races were the highlights of the meeting as they traded wins in the opening and closing heats of the match and both ended up with 11 points.

Back at White City, the Tigers' fans must have been worried early on as the Giants tore into them like men possessed on 17 September. By the end of heat three the Tigers were 13–5 down. However, a 3–3 in heat four steadied the ship and the Tigers were level by the end of heat seven. The Giants again edged ahead and it was not until the end of heat 11 that the two sides were level. It all went wrong for the Giants when Larry Lazarus had completed his rides. The Tigers fought back in the last three heats to win 47–37.

Lazarus showed his liking of the White City strip when he beat Miller in the opening heat and only McKinlay and Dykes lowered his colours in heat seven. For the Tigers, Miller and McKinlay both scored 11 while Dykes added 6+1.

Third Division Exeter's star Goog Hoskin travelled to Scotland for a couple of match races with McKinlay and a second half. He was considered by some fans to have modelled himself on Ken Le Breton with his white outfit and it may have given a few people in Glasgow the feeling of déjà vu.

At long last the Giants managed to put one over their Glasgow rivals. Three days later, the Giants took the league points with a 45–38 home win. The Tigers edged a single point ahead in heat three after Norman Hargreaves had fallen and been excluded. In the rerun, McIntosh stalled at the gate and Dykes got the better of Willie Wilson. However, the Giants eased ahead and kept their lead.

Miller and McKinlay on 11 each did well, but they needed support from the remainder of the team which did not come. Third best Tiger was Dykes on six points. Cyril Cooper ended Miller's maximum hopes and Willie Wilson completed his night's work with a win that deprived Ken McKinlay of his. Despite the short trip, yet again Tigers away form was poor.

In these pre-motorway days, Brian Crutcher got lost on his way to Glasgow on 24 September. As a result, a major part of the Pirates fire power was missing and the Tigers managed to subdue the rest of the side to win 45–38. With Crutcher, Poole could have beaten the Tigers but the home octet, Frank Hodgson apart, piled on the points. Even young Sharp at second reserve chipped in 3+1. Miller and McKinlay scored 12 and 11 respectively and Nicholson and Wilkinson each added seven each.

Poole stuck to the task and Roy Craighead was lucky to be reinstated into heat eight after he had been excluded by the Steward. The Steward changed his ruling when he was told that Roy had laid down to avoid the fallen Dykes. Heavy rain which made the track difficult brought the meeting to a premature halt before the second half final was completed. With an all Tigers line up, it was staged a week later.

Even allowing for Jim Gregory's absence and Oxford Cheetahs' woeful home record recently, they were no match for Tigers who had their best show on the road for a long while. The 49–35 win for the Tigers the next day effectively earned Cheetahs the wooden spoon. Yet again Miller banged in a faultless maximum and he was well supported by Wilkinson who followed him home for a couple of Tigers 5–1s. McKinlay and McIntosh ended on 8+1 and 9+1 respectively. It was a good night for Tigers who took a rare away win and the league points. It was one of the Tigers' two wins away from home in England all season.

The Cheetahs' Frank Boyle gave his all and his win over Wilkinson in heat four saw him flying past the Tiger on the line, failing to turn and ending in a heap. Despite taking another ride, he could not complete his programmed rides.

Twenty-four hours later, Leicester brought the Tigers back to earth with a bump. After a promising 4–2 start, the Tigers were blasted by the Hunters with four maximum heat wins in a row leaving the Scots an impossible hill to climb. Leicester's 58–26 win gave them the league runners-up spot.

Miller started brightly, but faded in the second half of the match to end with nine points. Only Dykes, in the unusual for him reserve berth, rose to the occasion and posted 7+1. McKinlay had a poor night on the track he would later join in 1954 scoring just four points.

October

Tigers could not withstand the solid Coventry Bees at White City on 1 October. The visitors eased themselves ahead over the match to win 46–38. It was downhill from Miller's heat one defeat, a decision booed by the crowd who thought the Steward got it wrong. Critics of the Tigers were outspoken in their condemnation of their failure to team ride in the face of a committed side looking to secure the league runners-up spot. Miller with 11 points and McKinlay on nine were the only Tigers to receive pass marks and McIntosh got an award for his six points. It was an all Bees second half final which showed how well they were going.

The East - West derby always raised the Tigers' sights and they opened brightly at Old Meadowbank on 4 October with a 5–1 over Bob Mark and Dick Campbell. They held the lead until heat five when the Monarchs levelled. The home team then gradually stretched away to win 46–38. Miller took a full maximum, but support for him was not solid enough. Dykes's evening was spoiled in his opening ride by an eye injury caused by a stone flung up from the track by Don Cuppleditch's back wheel.

The Tigers had only six race wins, four by Miller and one apiece by McKinlay and McIntosh. Miller managed a full maximum while McKinlay scored nine points and McIntosh seven.

Without a race win, Wilkinson managed a creditable 7+2. With Dykes and Nicholson as passengers it was always going to an uphill struggle.

It was a better evening for Tigers on 8 October as they made light work of Oxford who were nearing the end of a miserable season. It was a much better Tigers performance, but the 59–24 win was confidently forecast before any shale was shifted in anger.

Both Miller and McKinlay scored full maximums and Nicholson might have joined them but for a fall. He scored 8+1. McIntosh was excluded for knocking off Jim Gregory who then lost a gift point by falling in the rerun. Jack Parker was in town but an injury the previous night meant he was not the force he normally was. The Tigers' two maximum men both lowered his colours in match race contests.

What turned out to be the last meeting of the season was staged on 15 October and it was a joy for the Tigers fans. The men in red and white turned over the Monarchs 46–38 to take the league points. The Tigers did it the hard way with only six of the 14 race winners. However, speedway is a team sport and the Tigers combined better than Monarchs gathering seven bonus points to the Monarchs' two.

This was the last meeting for the Hodgson brothers. Frank signed off with one point and a fall. Not the most auspicious end to a career for him, for a while one of the very top riders in the Division. Jack took a second half outing, running a third in his heat to end on a downbeat note. Yes, they had a poor season to end with but don't consider their careers on this last year.

Miller closed his season with another maximum while McKinlay scored 9+1 and Dykes ended an up and down season with 8+3. Nicholson was seriously injured in his last ride of the match. He clipped Bob Mark's back wheel and was flung into the fence. This resulted in serious head injuries which effectively ended his career as a Tiger.

The meeting, the return of an event staged at West Ham earlier in the year, scheduled for 22 October was not staged due to dispute over pay rates. The Scottish team that had been due to race against West Ham in a challenge for charity was Tommy Miller, Don Cuppleditch, Bob Mark, Derek Close, Ken McKinlay, Willie Wilson, with Peter Dykes and Alf McIntosh at reserve.

The team finished in fifth place in the league, with 47 league points from their 44 matches. They were 16 behind champions Poole, but only eight behind second-placed Coventry. Given they had not had Bainbridge for a large part of the season, it was a credible outcome, although they struggled away from home too often. Tommy Miller was ranked as the best Second Division rider by the *1953 Stenners Annual*, with Bainbridge in ninth place. The *Stenners* review of the season pointed out that White City were the top Scottish team, but had "a seeming inability to do themselves justice away from home." The report also highlighted Miller's success, topping 1,000 points and riding for England against Australia. However, consistency from the middle ranked riders was necessary for the team to challenge for the league title.

14. 1953: "Terrific and terrible"

The Tigers started 1953 as the only Glasgow league side. City rivals Ashfield Giants had dropped out of the league. The Tigers signed Larry Lazarus from Ashfield. Back came Tommy Miller, Ken McKinlay, Bob Sharp, Junior Bainbridge, Peter Dykes, Alf McIntosh and Don Wilkinson. The Tigers had hoped to see Buck Ryan return, but he stayed put in Australia yet again. Joe Crowther turned down a move to White City and the Speedway Control Board refused to let Tigers sign Jim Blyth.

Miller, McKinlay and Bainbridge had wintered in Australia while Dykes had been in South Africa. The Tigers recruited a new 18-year-old Australian from Sydney, Arthur Malm, who had rave reviews in his homeland. Unfortunately, Arthur, who arrived in February to try to get some practice on the Scottish circuits, did not make much impact and spent most of the season in the second half. He had an injury scare when he damaged his wrist in a practice event just before the start of the season. Miller seriously damaged a pristine white boiler suit to the extent that he felt the wind round his nether regions.

Fife farmer, grasstracker Doug Templeton joined the Tigers but, after being flung in at the deep end in the opening fixture, he set about learning his trade in the second half, and improved enough to return to the Tigers line up towards the end of the season.

The Tigers accepted that Buck Ryan wasn't coming back to the Tigers or a Second Division provincial club, so the promotion placed a £600 price tag on the stay away Australian.

The First Division was intended to be 10 teams again, but the mid-season withdrawal of New Cross saw only nine complete the season. The loss of one of the 'big five' London teams was a serious sign that the sport had problems.

Similarly in the Second Division, 10 teams started the season, but the Liverpool Chads withdrew part-way through so their matches were expunged from the records. The three remaining Scottish teams had a journey to the South coast of England to Poole and to East Anglia to Yarmouth. The other four teams were in the Midlands. The league programme was the same as in 1952, so the Tigers had 32 matches, 16 at home and 16 away.

The Southern League started the season with nine teams, but Cardiff pulled out after 12 league meetings.

April

Ian Hoskins had a rider shortage and contemplated signing former Tigers Joe Crowther and Will Lowther to plug a short-term gap for the opening match at White City against Coventry on 1 April. Others approached included Frank Hodgson and Jim Blyth, but neither was available. However, the Tigers introduced Doug Templeton, a find by Larry Lazarus who could not live with Templeton on grass. Templeton, who had had a single second half outing in 1952, was given his team debut because Peter Dykes was still in transit from South Africa.

After the meeting Templeton, who had shown a lot of style and determination, slipped quietly out of the stadium and changed in his car before heading home for an early rise to milk his cows. He was not used to changing rooms, something of luxury for a rider used to changing alfresco for grass track events. He failed to score but, mounted on the track spare, did well in the second half. The Tigers also missed Bainbridge, who was fit again after riding in Australia in the close season. Arthur Malm (pronounced Marm) made his debut, but failed to score. Malm had first ridden at White City on 4 March along with Miller and Ron Phillips, who, at that time, appeared Glasgow bound.

The Tigers also introduced Larry (John) Lazarus from Ashfield. He had started riding before the Second World War on the beaches with 1928 500cc Scottish Dirt Track Champion, Jimmy Valente. After the War, Larry graduated to speedway via the grass tracks. He had been a prisoner of war in Burma and survived, together with fellow speedway man Howdy Byford of West Ham.

The Tigers nosed in front by heat six and stayed in front until the end of heat 10 but, lacking a third heat leader and sound second string support for Miller with a maximum and McKinlay with 10, could not hold their advantage.

The scores were level for a couple of heats, then the Bees edged ahead thanks to a 4–2 in heat 13. Charlie New won the final heat from McKinlay and Wilkinson, despite the efforts of the two Tigers to pass, and the match ended 43–41 to Coventry.

Speedway must have been a breeze for Miller after his wintertime swims in shark infested waters and visits to snake infested islands. Needless to say, he wasn't in Scotland.

The odds for Tigers were considered good for their fixture in Liverpool as the Chads, now coached by Oliver Hart, had not won an opening meeting since 1949. On Friday 3 April at Stanley Stadium, history did not repeat itself and the Chads won 49–35. However, the result, ultimately, did not matter as Liverpool closed and the result expunged from the records.

Liverpool fans loved Harry Welch's win over Miller in heat seven when the Tiger just could not catch him. In heat 14, Miller turned the tables to end Welch's maximum hopes. Miller was the top Tiger on 11 and next best was Lazarus on eight. McKinlay fell in his opening ride, then took three second places for six points.

Despite sharing nine of the 14 heats, the Tigers were well beaten by Coventry at Brandon on Easter Saturday, 4 April. Inspired by Les Hewitt, with a maximum, the Bees won 51–33. Charlie New shed a chain in heat five after passing both Tigers but, with Malm out soon after losing a chain, he was able to push home for a point.

A much subdued Miller scored seven points, but even with him on full song the margin would have still favoured the Bees. McKinlay, who top scored for the Tigers with nine, put in some thrilling rides which included his win from the back over Johnnie Reason in heat two and his less fruitful heat eight race with Jack Wright. Third top Tiger was McIntosh with 4+1. Doug Templeton did not ride and his place was taken by Jack 'Red' Monteith. He was only given one ride and the rest of his rides were taken by the reserves.

Wolverhampton Wasps were expected to make Tigers hurt when they visited Glasgow on 8 April. However, the Tigers, still without Bainbridge, had a relatively easy night and collected their first league win, 51–33. The weather probably did not help the visitors with cold biting rain falling throughout the meeting.

Wasps only had Brian Shepherd on good form and only Miller beat him. For the Tigers, Miller scored another maximum and had support from McKinlay on 9+1 and McIntosh on 8+1. There was also more second string support. Dykes, back from South Africa, made his first appearance in 1953 with a reasonable 6+1, but faded towards the end of the evening. Malm, now dropped from the team, ended up in hospital due to a fall in the second half.

Ian Hoskins had a couple of problems before this match with Stoke at White City. He had to decide who to drop and who would be the Tigers captain. He decided to return Templeton to the second half and Bainbridge, who had returned from Australia, did not resume as captain on 15 April. Miller, who had taken over in 1952 when Bainbridge was injured, kept the job. With Bainbridge back as a heat leader and scoring 10+1, the Tigers won 57–27.

Miller and McKinlay both recorded maximums while Lazarus was unbeaten by an opponent on 9+3. Only Potters' skipper Ken Adams put up any resistance on yet another cold and wet night in Glasgow and he ended Bainbridge's maximum hopes in heat 10.

The Tigers provided attractive opposition, but could not win at Leicester two days later. Len Williams thrilled the fans with his burst from the back in heat one to beat Miller. The Tigers could have snatched a draw, but Williams won heat 14 to complete a maximum and the league points went to Leicester. The final score was 44–40.

Bainbridge resumed the captaincy, but had four last places. Miller and McKinlay were joint top scorers on nine points apiece, and McIntosh took seven. Don Wilkinson scored a useful 6+1 from three rides.

Stoke turned over the Tigers to win their first match of the season the next day. Ian Hoskins blamed the Sun Street track for his team's 50–34 defeat, saying it was one of the slickest the Tigers had encountered so far.

McKinlay broke a finger in a heat 12 fall, but did not realise it was broken until he had it x-rayed the following Wednesday. Miller won his first two outings. He missed the start allowing Reg Fearman to get away in his third and spent much of the race dicing with Don Potter before hitting Potter's back wheel and falling. In the last heat Miller was defeated by Fitzpatrick. This pegged his return back to a team topping eight points. McKinlay had a poor night with only an opening heat win to show for his efforts while Bainbridge took three rides to compile the same score. Wilkinson with 7+1 from four rides, including a fall in his third and McIntosh with 5+1 rode with any real passion. When Wilkinson fell, he was second behind McIntosh, ruining his chance to be the Tigers' top scorer. Whatever the track conditions, the Tigers' display was not up to the standard expected.

The Tigers looked fragile on the road again and were a shadow of their White City persona at Poole on 20 April. The outcome was a 58–26 defeat for Tigers who, to be fair, probably had travel weariness from the long trip.

It was not until heat 10 that the Tigers got to grips with Poole. Miller, who had previously recorded a couple of third places, managed his first heat win and the Tigers took their first heat advantage. He had two wins in his 8+1 return and his only real support came from McIntosh with six points. Bainbridge, beset with bike problems, had two pointless outings.

The Tigers' slump in form followed them home to White City, where they had been producing the goods. They were lucky to snatch a draw against bogy side, Leicester, two days later. Eight points down with three heats left, they managed to take a league point with a 42–42 draw.

The failure of the starting gate gave the Tigers problems because they could not get the hang of the lights based starting system while the Hunters mastered the 'green light-go' approach.

Miller, who had an off night due to machine problems including a broken frame, scored 9+1 while McKinlay, riding with a broken finger, only managed four points. McKinlay had cut the plaster off before the meeting. Bainbridge also had bike problems and shared the track spare with Miller for part of the meeting. On their own equipment, the Tigers might have sneaked a win. Since the start of his season, Bainbridge had blown two motors, expensive for any rider. Her admitted that he experimented with his machinery. It was clear from his low returns that a back-to-basics approach was required.

Sharp managed a reserve's paid maximum and was involved in heat 13 that levelled the match, setting up the last heat decider. Len Williams snatched the last heat win from the gate, gathering a rare visitor's maximum to head Miller and Dykes to give Hunters their draw.

Poole disappointed on 29 April, but the Tigers' management and their 15,000 fans must have been happy to see their team win 49–35. The Tigers' win came from McIntosh's return to form with 10+1, after a spell in the doldrums and McKinlay's second maximum of the season.

With the starting gate working again, the Tigers worked their magic from the tapes against the 1952 League champions. For a change, Miller dropped a point as he was second to Ken Middleditch in his last ride. Miller blew it at the start and failed to catch the flying Pirate. Nevertheless, he scored 11, selflessly taking every opportunity to help his partner, Peter Dykes. McIntosh's upsurge was matched by a downturn in his partner, Bainbridge's fortunes. He was still having new bike trouble and was down on points. However, Lazarus had serious bike problems when his engine blew up in its third outing. Thereafter he used the track spare and collected only two points. Sharp grabbed his two points in the style that became his trade mark – a last bend dash to the flag. He was nicknamed 'Last bend Bob'.

May

The National Trophy draw brought the Tigers and Monarchs together again. The first leg was on 6 May at White City. The local derby with a place in the next round as a prize gave Tigers the impetus to dominate the Monarchs. The result, over 18 heats, was 75–33. Pundits had expected a close match, but the former Tigers in the Monarchs ranks had a poor night.

Miller collected a full maximum 18 and McKinlay was paid for 15. Dykes had a better night and was paid for 12 points. McIntosh was paid for 11. Bainbridge's bike again gave problems so he scored nine points.

Two days later, the Eagles made heavy weather of the match, but still beat the Tigers 44–40 in the Lanarkshire Cup match at The Stadium. The Tigers probably should have won, but the result had no decisive influence on the outcome of the league.

Miller started out with wins in the Scottish Match Race Championship over Derrick Close and then completed a maximum. Unfortunately, he only had strong support from McKinlay with nine points, and, to a lesser extent, Bainbridge with 7+1. His bonus point was earned when he followed home Sharp who made a superb start in heat eight. Falls by McKinlay and Wilkinson at vital times did not help the Tigers' cause. McKinlay fell in heat nine trying to pass Gordon McGregor, and Wilkinson slid off when leading in heat 13.

In the National Trophy, the foundations laid in Glasgow were not needed because the Tigers blasted the Monarchs for a second time in four days on 9 May. This time the score was 61–47. The tie was effectively already won for the Tigers and this was icing on the cake for their fans. The aggregate score was a huge 136–80. Miller scored 36 points over the two legs. His main backer was Lazarus on 10+1 as the rest gave solid support. Larry might have scored more, but he hit a bump in the nominated heat and fell.

By halfway the Tigers were 16 points up on the night. The Monarchs rallied to reduce the leeway to eight points after heat 13, but another Tigers 5–1 opened the margin to 12 and a short run of drawn heats plus another heat victory saw the win go westwards.

On 13 May, back at White City, a windy night followed a long dry day, one of a run of such days, saw a dry track send clouds of dust into the crowd. A water cart was called for to try and improve the conditions. Despite the dust, the action on the track suited the Tigers riders as they raced to a 59–25 win over Motherwell.

1953 Glasgow Tigers: Don Wilkinson, Bob Sharp, Doug Templeton, Ian Hoskins, Peter Dykes; Front: Ken McKinlay, Larry Lazarus, Tommy Miller and Junior Bainbridge.

Two stalwarts of Scottish speedway: Doug Templeton (left) and Ken McKinlay (right).

The teams had the attention of the Scotland selectors and the Tigers' Miller, McKinlay and McIntosh all rode well, scoring 12, 11 and 11 respectively. Bainbridge had bike problems and failed to impress the selectors with a poor 5+2.

The Eagles' riders did not impress the selectors either. With only two race wins from the 14 heats, it was a poor display. Even Derrick Close had a poor night which started with him rearing at the gate and falling in his first ride.

The Eagles' Joe Crowther, once a Tigers' stalwart, scored two points in his last appearance at White City. He ended up on the losing side, but won his last race at White City, the Consolation Race.

Liverpool Chads took a heavy defeat at White City on 20 May as three Tigers scored full maximums. Back to form Bainbridge and McKinlay joined Miller on 12 points. With 36 from three riders, the other five only needed seven points between them to win the match. As it was, they gathered another 21 and Liverpool lost 57–27.

Miller went through the card including a 2–0 win over Derrick Close in the Scottish Match Race Championship. Close reared at the start of both races and Miller led from tapes to flag.

If Miller was on a high, Lazarus was not as he ended up over the fence in his heat 12 fall while challenging Cyril Cooper for the lead. Lazarus, who developed a bit of an over-slide, somersaulted on his way over the fence.

The match against Liverpool is reported as having been a charity event staged for the benefit of the British Sailors' Society, and a number of heats were, according to the Rt Hon, Lord Inverclyde's notes, sponsored at a cost of £11.80 each. It was noted that the charitable acts did not extend to the track action. The result was later annulled when the Chads withdrew from the league.

Despite fielding a team comprised almost completely of First Division riders, England was given its biggest humbling by the Division Two riders for Scotland on 27 May. This time Scotland included five true Scots who scored 46 out of their team's 70 points, more than England's 38. White City specialists Miller and McKinlay led the Scottish charge.

England supporters could point to Split Waterman's engine failure in heat six, but that could be set against the bent frame on Cuppleditch's machine which caused him to withdraw. Close also suffered from a bent frame from his heat five fall. Unlike Cuppleditch, Close managed to borrow another machine and went through the rest of his outings unbeaten although he did miss one ride.

Scotland opened a four-point lead in heat one thanks to Miller and Cuppleditch then, after a few 3–3s, they managed another 5–1. Ken Sharples and Jack Parker hit back immediately with a 5–1 in the next heat, but that was the last of the English resistance. Thereafter Scotland pulled steadily ahead and ended the night well satisfied. Miller scored a maximum 18 while McKinlay scored 14+1. Next best for Scotland was the Eagles Close on 11.

The Tigers unbeaten run in the National Trophy continued at Wolverhampton's Monmore Green on 29 May. The Tigers' win was put down to smarter gating and they nosed ahead in heat four then pulled steadily away to win 59–49.

Miller racked up another impressive maximum 18, almost a third of the Tigers' total. McKinlay gave him support with 11+2. The Tigers' third heat leader, Bainbridge scored 9+1. Wilkinson one of the Tigers' reserves, did very well and scored 8.

Some fans put down his good return down to the Wolverhampton track being similar to Brough Park where he had learned his trade.

June

Miller celebrated the Queen's Coronation by winning the Skelly Trophy at Motherwell and was booed by the home fans.

The Steward inspected the rain-soaked track and called off the National Trophy meeting just as the Wolverhampton riders arrived at White City on 3 June.

The Stadium in Motherwell was, yet again, a happy hunting ground for the Tigers two days later. The Tigers, visiting on league business, had two maximum men in Miller and McKinlay. Their next best rider was Bainbridge with five points. The rest of the side scored modestly, but they did enough to win the match. The Eagles had three riders who failed to score and this was their team's downfall.

The Tigers were level after heat seven after the Eagles had eased ahead early on. Heats eight to 13 were drawn, keeping the scores level. With Miller in the last heat a draw was, engine problems aside, a banker. He flew out of the traps but Gordon McGregor and Scott Hall, deputising for an off-colour Bluey Scott, looked like securing a draw. Unfortunately for the Eagles, Hall lost concentration and Dykes pounced to pass him. The Tigers won 43–41.

The next day, the Tigers lost by the narrowest of margins at Old Meadowbank after a late rally earned them a last heat decider. Trailing 40–32 with two heats to go, a 5–1 gave them the chance of a draw. With the pairing that did the business at Motherwell the night before, the Glasgow fans in the 10,000 crowd were probably looking for history to repeat itself.

Unfortunately, it didn't happen. Miller won, completing another maximum, but former Tiger Harold Fairhurst separated the two Tigers for the vital two points. Fairhurst was carried from the track shoulder high for his efforts, sending Glasgow's fans home disappointed.

The Tigers had the bulk of the heat winners, 10 out of 14, but the Monarchs packed the minor places, and collected seven bonus points to the Tigers' one.

One Tigers' highlight was McKinlay's new track record in heat three. He rode an amazing 64.6 which was unchallenged until 1966. Local pundits were surprised as most thought he had not ridden a very spectacular race. However, as legendary track guru Alan Bridgett often said, a track record is never set by a spectacular ride. Records tumble when the rider puts in a steady performance. Ken had a zero and a fall between two wins for six points.

A solid display from the Tigers reserves tipped the match their way at Liverpool on 8 June. The Tigers were ahead from the off and the Chads had no real answer except for Peter Robinson. Even he could not stop Miller scoring a maximum. He traded wins with McKinlay restricting him to 11 points. The key riders for the Tigers were the reserves, Sharp and Wilkinson who scored nine between them.

McIntosh was injured when young Chads reserve Johnny Greenwood knocked him off in heat 13. There were no broken bones, but he had a bad shaking and mild concussion. In the rerun, the Tigers' Sharp and Wilkinson took the match winning 5–1. With heat 14 3–3, the match ended 47–37 for Tigers. Heats six and nine produced some exciting action. In heat six, Griffiths passed Dykes to unsuccessfully pursue McKinlay, Anderson chased and caught Dykes for third spot. Heat nine saw Robinson and Allott team ride to shut out McKinlay before the Tiger found a gap to drive through to grab the win.

The Tigers' troubles were doubled because Lazarus, who had scored 7+1, picked up a broken wrist in the second half. Ultimately, it all counted for nothing with the Chads failure to finish the season.

The Tigers' Yarmouth bogey appeared again the next day. This time, the seven-man Tigers were riding their fourth fixture in five days. They were too weary to put up much of a fight. Templeton drove down to Yarmouth to fill one of the spots vacated by the injured McIntosh and Lazarus.

The number one spot, which was to be occupied by Lazarus, was covered by the reserves but it produced few points. Without McIntosh and Lazarus, the Tigers efforts were blunted and Yarmouth won 57–27. Miller scored 10 at the tight Caister Road bowl. Bainbridge added seven while McKinlay contributed five points.

Back at White City, aware that the road weary and injury hit Tigers might be somewhat toothless, Yarmouth made the Glasgow riders fight for their 45–39 league win on 10 June. The Tigers fought for this victory. Sharp and Wilkinson moved into the team proper and responded by scoring seven and one point respectively. The reserve berths were filled by Templeton and Malm who both failed to score. Miller and McKinlay each scored a full maximum, but Bainbridge, once again with bike problems, was out of sorts with a poor five. Sharp kept his best for heat 11 when he came from the back to change a Bloaters' 5–1 into a drawn heat.

Home favourite Miller cruised to victory in the individual meeting at White City on 17 June which led to qualification for the Scottish Riders Championship Final in Edinburgh. Three riders were joint runners-up, one from each Scottish team: McGregor (Eagles), Cuppleditch (Monarchs) and the Tigers' Bainbridge. Each scored 13. Miller defeated Don Cuppleditch, suggesting his Scottish Match Race Championship was still in the bag. He left McGregor standing at the gate when they met as the only remaining undefeated riders.

McKinlay might have scored more, but was excluded in heat seven for pushing Edinburgh's Roy Bester wide, taking his front wheel and thereby causing him to fall. The exclusion cost him three points, but other poor races reduced his total to nine. Earlier in the race, the Tigers' man had been carried wide by Bester who burst through on the inside. Needless to say, McKinlay's loyal fans let the Steward know of their displeasure with his decision but, with Roy Bester failing to stay on, the Steward probably had little option. As it was the race continued and Bester did not score a point either. Lazarus had hoped to ride but his injury still ruled him out.

The White City track, which had been criticised, appeared to be returning to its former glories and repaying the promoters' time and money spent on it.

Normally a bit suspect on the road, Tigers found a destination that suited them. Despite still missing Lazarus and McIntosh, they did well in the Midlands. The Tigers' speed from the gate gave them a big advantage, which helped them win their second match at Wolverhampton. The missing regulars allowed the Tigers to give an outing to Templeton and Malm. The Tigers took the league points with a 44–40 win on 19 June. Miller completed yet another maximum and with sound support from McKinlay with 10 points and Bainbridge on 8 while the other Tigers responded well.

Glasgow were never very far ahead, the biggest margin was six points. However, it was all but won before the final heat. The Wasps could have snatched a draw, but faced Miller. As it was a 3–3 wasn't enough to stop the Tigers winning.

The Tigers breezed into the next round of the National Trophy with a 76–26 win at White City on 24 June over the Wasps. The aggregate score was 135–81. It completed an unbeaten run in the competition.

It was a big pay night for most of the Tigers riders as they won as they pleased. Miller took six straight wins for 18 points and Bainbridge had four wins and two paid wins for a paid maximum. McKinlay scored 13+2 from five outings.

McIntosh and Lazarus, who still had a broken bone in one hand, returned to the Tigers' ranks and the latter, despite his injury, won his two races. McIntosh came back to racing with four points from five outings.

Miller started the evening with a defeat as Don Cuppleditch lowered his colours in the opening leg of their Scottish Match Race Championship. However, Miller won the next two to take the tie 2–1.

July

Rayleigh Rockets, from the Southern League, came to Glasgow on 1 July in a National Trophy match. They rode well despite losing 69–39. The Rockets, who went on to win the Southern League title, never gave up despite the result. Gerry Jackson, son of Australian pioneer rider Jack, was the visitors' star. He made Miller work for his opening heat win and combined with Maurie McDermott in heat six to show Dykes and Wilkinson a quick way round White City. Later in the match he beat Bainbridge.

Peter Clark took second place behind Les McGillivray in the second heat after McKinlay was excluded for causing the race to be stopped. He had a nasty fall, but returned to be unbeaten by a Rocket to collect 13+2. Miller gathered a maximum 18 while Junior was third best with 11+2. The Tigers continued their unbeaten National Trophy run with a 30-point lead to take to The Weir Stadium in Essex.

Ian Hoskins used the second half to test his steel plate idea, staging a race which confirmed his theory that the plate would act as a handicap. He used three Tigers and invited Edinburgh's Bob Mark to join in. Mark was encouraged enough to suggest a full-scale trial of the idea, which fell by the wayside. Hoskins did suggest it again in the 1960s.

Miller's run of big scores in the National Trophy and the Tigers' unbeaten run in the competition came to an end at Rayleigh on 4 July. The Tigers made heavy weather of beating the Rockets. Miller started slowly in heat one, then built up speed to overtake the Rockets duo before his bike seized. Machine problems reduced his contribution. Bainbridge had bike troubles too while Dykes, who found the track tricky, and Wilkinson failed to have all their rides. McKinlay was the top Tiger on 11, Bainbridge scored eight while Miller settled for 6+1.

The second heat was full off incident. Bainbridge dropped out after scrapping for the lead with Les McGillivray. Ken, who probably couldn't see too well having been filled in, passed Frank Bettis. As he did so, McGillivray fell, which allowed McKinlay past and caused Bettis to fall. Both Rockets remounted to follow McKinlay home.

Had Maurie McDermott, who had scored a couple of seconds behind his partner, completed his rides, the Rockets could have pulled off a shock win. McDermott crashed into the back of McGillivray as they were battling with Lazarus. As it was, the Tigers secured an aggregate win, 113–103 to reach the next round after losing 64–44 that night.

Miller scored yet another maximum at White City on 8 July, making light of the wet track conditions. An afternoon of rain required many gallons of water to be sucked off the track to allow racing. Miller won the World Championship Qualifying Round meeting and £30 prize. Next to him on the rostrum was team mate McKinlay, who scored many of his points from the back. The Monarchs' Bob Mark was third. Bainbridge, who was expected to do well, had a nightmare with bike problems and effectively went out of the competition. He was leading his first race when his bike expired and that was repeated in his next three outings. Bainbridge, never one to hide his emotions, took a kick at the offending machine after he had pushed it onto the centre green following his last outing.

McKinlay blew his chance at the start of his heat with Miller and the result was cut and dried. Sweden's Stig Pramberg and Rune Sormander provided an international dimension, but neither seemed at home with the ribbed concrete starting area. The Swedes were slow away and took some time to weigh up White City. The fans also had a chance to view First Division riders, Howdy Byford, Malcolm Craven, Ron Johnston (the Belle Vue Kiwi), Eric Boothroyd and Eddie Rigg. Only Boothroyd showed his top form.

In the National Trophy, the Tigers were a one man show – Miller – when they faced First Division Birmingham Brummies at Perry Barr on 11 July. The wet track took much from the meeting and became worse as the evening wore on. It became a quagmire and racing was described as ever more farcical. However, the Tigers could be pleased that in Miller and Wilkinson, they had the only riders who risked and pulled off overtakes. Miller ended the night with a creditable 15 points and reserve Wilkinson scored an even more creditable eight. McKinlay scored six points, which included a win, in his first three outings, before twice finishing last.

The Tigers hung on in the early exchanges and after heat eight were only eight points down. In the remaining 10 heats, the Brummies moved up a gear and Tigers scored 18 points from those races.

The Brummies won 70–38. The result made the return at White City appear a formality and the Brummies showed their self-belief by giving the nominated rides in heat 18 to their reserves, Bob Roger and Ron Barrett.

Ian Hoskins always had new ideas. He employed an Egyptian Yogi called Kitao, who lay down on a bed of nails, to help will Tigers to victory in the return against Birmingham on 15 July. Kitao, who had six of the Tigers stand on him as he lay on the nails, is reported to have given each Tiger a good luck charm. Sceptics in the crowd were not convinced as both Lazarus and McIntosh dropped chains at the starting gate for the first time in their careers while Lazarus fell and had an engine failure. Hoskins knew his Tigers were on a hiding to nothing with little hope of progressing to the next round and needed something to draw in wavering fans. The Tigers won the match 56–52 they failed 122 to 94 over two legs.

The scores were level at 51–51 at the start of heat 18 and many in the 15,000 crowd were unhappy with the Brummies giving the nominated race to their reserves. Their tactic was greeted by a slow hand clap from the Tigers' fans who wanted to see the Brummies put out a couple of their big guns.

Yet again Miller led from the front scoring another superb maximum. He had sound support from fellow heat leaders McKinlay with 12+3 and Bainbridge on 10. McKinlay had a storming outing in heat five as he came from the back and passed Hunt and Boothroyd to partner Miller to a 5–1. Unfortunately for the Tigers, the Brummies picked off their second strings and assured their passage to the next round.

The Tigers' trip to Leicester on two nights later fell victim to rain. A solid display by Tigers at Stoke on 18 July laid the foundation for a 42–42 draw. Dykes on 4+2 from three rides was their hero. He held on to second spot behind Miller in heat 14. This gave the Tigers a draw while John Fitzpatrick buzzed his rear wheel for four laps. Dykes was in the last heat replacing Lazarus who had struggled all night.

The Tigers and the Potters dished up some good racing and both sides could point to off form riders as the cause of the draw.

For the Tigers, Miller continued his winning ways and McKinlay had only one blip, a third behind Hughes and Potter, on his way to 10. Wilkinson did well with 7+1.

Non-league action at Ashfield on 21 July featured teams representing all four Scottish tracks. Motherwell carried off the honours with 27 points. The Tigers had two passengers in Dykes and Malm. Scott Hall was the difference between the Tigers and the Eagles.

Between them, Miller and McKinlay, both on nine, and Bainbridge on six, scored all the Tigers points. The Tigers took second place ahead of the Monarchs on 20 and an Ashfield side with 11.

An all Scottish born team went down 64–44 to the team of Kiwis that included First Division riders at White City on 22 July. Scotland's stars were Miller with 16 and McKinlay on 11+2. McIntosh returned to ride after a first heat fall, not knowing he had broken his leg in a couple of places. He pulled out and this gave a chance to young reserve Doug Templeton who scored an unexpected 6+2. He was the third highest Scottish scorer. The Monarchs' Bob Mark and the Eagles' Gordon McGregor were in poor form, scoring four points each.

The New Zealand colours inspired the Tigers' Dykes who piled up 10+2. He joined Ronnie Moore 17, Geoff Mardon 16+1, and Ron Johnston 12+1 in double figures. Scottish based Dick Campbell and Harold Fairhurst had outings to replace a struggling Barry Briggs and returned zero and four respectively.

The Kiwis did not have things all their own way and Miller repaid Moore in heat nine, when, in a classic, he came from the back to win by a bike length. BBC Scotland broadcast a commentary from this match on radio, a rare event even then.

The annual Press Sports Gala in Edinburgh the next night featured speedway racing. A Monarchs quartet defeated a Glasgow Tigers foursome 20–10 in a five heat match. The Tigers opened with a race win and drawn heat thanks to Lazarus, but thereafter the Monarchs dominated. The Tigers' top two were Lazarus with six and Dykes on three. Doug Templeton scored a point while Bob Sharp failed to score.

A wet night in Motherwell on 24 July nearly caused the first ever rain off there, but both teams made a go of it. The track was described as a shambles and the riders ploughed through the mud. The last heat was won by Miller in 82 seconds, 10.2 seconds over his own record time. The track contributed to falls while the rain probably caused the engine troubles due to water in the electrics.

The Tigers were aggrieved that their top man, Miller, was thumped by a slightly out of control Noel Watson as he left the start in heat one. Miller retired from the race and the loss of these points proved vital. Saying that, Watson had only one other ride before withdrawing. The match was close. Early on the scores were tied. The difference between the teams was never over eight points, this at the end of heat eight. The Eagles then reeled the Tigers in and pushed ahead at the end of heat 12, which the Eagles won 5–1, thanks to Wilkinson and Malm falling at the same time. The former remounted to take a point, much to the annoyance of the Eagles' fans who were reminded of the rules by announcer Archie McCulloch.

The Tigers did have the opportunity to win the match, but the Eagles let Miller lead and tucked in together to block out Lazarus. This gave them the match 43–41. The Tigers' cause, weakened by McIntosh's absence due to injury, was not helped by Bainbridge being absent on World Championship business.

Promoter Norrie Isbister hired in the local league teams to give supporters an interesting match at Ashfield on 28 July. The usually dominant Tigers, missing McKinlay, were downed by the Eagles who raced away with this match after an opening heat reverse. The wet track saw racing continue to the end of heat 10 when the score was 38–22 to the Eagles and racing was abandoned. Miller scored a three ride maximum, but the rest of the Tigers were a bit toothless. Bainbridge scored five and next best was Templeton on three.

Reigning League champions Poole visited White City on 29 July. The Tigers broke the deadlock in heat three when Wilkinson and Bainbridge got the better of Small and Kidd. The Tigers kept their lead and won 46–38.

Only Ken Middleditch had the answer to the Tigers as Miller, fresh from winning his first Scottish Championship title at Edinburgh, led them to another home win. He took another maximum. McKinlay, who had gone to Norwich the day before to see Huck Fynn in an attempt to sort out bike frame troubles, had one less with 11. Obviously, the new frame helped. No other Tigers managed a double point score but, Dykes apart, they all scored.

August

Miller kept his mind on the track rather than his forthcoming wedding to score yet another maximum for the Tigers at White City on 5 August. With Bainbridge scoring 14+1 and McKinlay also on song with 11+3 Wolverhampton were out of the Queen's Cup by 71–37. The contest was, in the initial stages, a single tie tournament. The luck of the draw decided home advantage.

Bainbridge missed a maximum in his last outing. His motor stalled on the line and he was pushed off to restart the bike. Despite chasing for four laps, he failed by a few yards to gain any reward for his efforts. Lazarus scored an unbeaten nine from three reserve rides, one replacing Templeton, while the others all contributed to the Tigers' total.

In the second half Junior Scratch event, press reports tell of Malm falling and being run over by Red Monteith. Monteith then lost control, hit the fence and was catapulted on to the dog track. He broke ribs and had to go to hospital for treatment while the ambulance men had to deal with women in the crowd who fainted. It took several minutes to disentangle Monteith's machine from the safety fence. Red did not get back to the track for some weeks.

The Tigers yet again gave the Monarchs a run for their money in a league match at Old Meadowbank on 8 August in a meeting hailed as one of the best of the season. Bainbridge and Miller clawed their way to 11 each. The remaining six Tigers were just not solid enough to beat the Monarchs. McKinlay had bike failure in heat 11 and the loss of his points proved vital. His return for the night was just 6+1. Miller lost his maximum to the Bob Mark – Dick Campbell pairing in the opening heat. The wily Kiwi held Miller back for just enough time to stop him passing Mark. Bainbridge lost out to the team riding of Fairhurst and Bester in heat three. Thereafter the Tigers duo won the lot.

The Tigers had individual stars, but the Monarchs' team riding just gave them the edge. This was a close meeting with nine of the heats drawn. The teams traded two 4–2s each and the Monarchs took the only 5–1 when Fairhurst and Bester beat Dykes in heat 11 when McKinlay had an engine failure. The final score was 44–40 to the Monarchs.

12 August is the start of the grouse shooting season, but the Tigers had an Eagles shoot on their agenda. The main excitement in Glasgow was the heat two dead-heat. The Steward could not split Dykes and Ron Phillips. Gordon McGregor had a good night, but his team mates, Johnny Green apart, did little to worry the Tigers who won 52.5–31.5.

Miller had four race wins and was only pushed by McGregor. Bainbridge scored 11. Dykes, who had all but decided to retire from speedway because he said he could not make the sport pay, returned a sound 8.5+1. McKinlay had an off night due to motor problems and settled for 5+1. Lazarus had a quiet night on the eve of his wedding to Anna Bell.

Ian Hoskins booked in double World Champion Jack Young to race old rival Miller. Miller won their series 2–1, but Young made up for it, and won the second half final. The match race decider was a thriller as Miller just out-gated Young and this advantage was all that separated the two for four pulsating laps. Miller stuck to his favourite line on the bends, which made it difficult for Young to go inside or outside to pass. Winning the toss for gate positions, Miller had opted to start from the outer half of the track. The second half also featured two grass track riders, Perth's Don Adams and Roger Parry.

The Tigers' fans probably weren't bothered that Wilf Jay was missing from the Monarchs line up on 19 August. The visitors used Glasgow-based junior John Paul. For the red and white fans, it was another win over their eastern rivals and the home riders dominated. The Tigers' three heat leaders had things much their own way and the Monarchs had only one race winner. The Tigers raced to a 58–26 win. Miller, again, scored a maximum and Bainbridge scored 11+1. McKinlay lost to the Monarchs' only race winner, Don Cuppleditch, but still managed 11 points.

This was meant to be Dykes's last outing as a Tiger. The Kiwi was going to sell insurance in South Africa, appeared to have signed off with 6+2.

Former Liverpool rider Harry Welch made his Tigers debut at Ipswich on Thursday 20 August in a Queens Cup tie and his five points from reserve helped them beat the Witches. Welch could have been cup-tied had not Liverpool shut down before they were eliminated.

Miller provided the magic for the record 19,000 crowd with a full maximum. Bainbridge, had bike problems twice, added 9+2, and McKinlay scored 7+2. The latter was unlucky in heat three when his motor died and he was hit by a following rider. He was carried off but returned to ride and had bike problems a few heats later. Despite retirement plans, Dykes rode for the Tigers and scored four points.

The Witches duo of Dick Shepherd and Sid Clark had machine troubles in all their rides. The home side had a 10-point lead after heat five, but the Tigers gradually reeled them in and went ahead after heat 15. The two sides traded 5–1s in the next two heats and Miller shut out Edwards and Read for a match winning 3–3 to end the night 55–53 to the Tigers.

An engine failure in heat seven robbed Miller of a likely maximum at Poole on 24 August, but it probably would not have much influenced the result. The Pirates were well served by maximum man Terry Small, in their hard fought 47–37 league win.

Lazarus was a Tigers race winner. He caught the Pirates cold as he flew from the back in heat four. McKinlay continued to impress winning a couple of heats and was close in others to top score for Tigers on 10 points. Had the long tail of Harry Welch with a point and pointless Wilkinson and Sharp scored, the Pirates may have been a bit more threatened.

The Tigers held a small lead after two 4–2 wins in the opening heats, but the Pirates had the match all but won by the end of heat 12. Poole's team work was reflected in their scorecard with seven bonus points to the Tigers' two.

Yarmouth usually saw a poor performance by the Tigers. On 25 August a 5,000 crowd saw the Tigers lose 58–26. Even Miller could not cope with this track and his five points was his season's poorest display. He trailed in yards behind in his first two, won a race and then had a rare fall.

Wilkinson caused a talking point in heat six when he fell. He remounted, but fell again. This time as he tried to hang on, his throttle stuck open. A JAP full on delivers a formidable amount of power and he had to let his machine go. His bike crossed the centre green, scattering ambulance men and officials before crashing into the fence. Thankfully, the other riders had responded to the red lights and slowed, otherwise it could have scythed them down as it crossed the track. The bike tore down fencing then collided with a lamp post. The net result was a wrecked bike. For the Tigers, McKinlay was the best with nine points. Bainbridge scored seven.

With Miller away on World Championship business, the Tigers were left to get on with it at White City on 26 August. Wolverhampton failed to take advantage of the weakened Tigers line up and lost 49–35. McKinlay and Bainbridge both scored maximums and Welch repaid his transfer fee with 8+1. Bainbridge had a great ride from the back after being left at the start on the final heat.

Wilkinson wrecked a third bike in two nights. This time he wrecked a frame on a bike belonging to Sharp when he parted company with the machine on one of the tight White City turns.

The second half featured sidecars with the outfits piloted by Australians Jim Davies and Peter Speerin. Davies had arrived without his usual passenger, Johnny Glasbrener, and Bainbridge, onetime regular passenger for Davies, volunteered to fill the gap. In one race Speerin's handlebars caught him, thankfully without injury, but Speerin and his partner shot off the track and were flung from their machine which suffered a buckled wheel. The sidecar racers staged lap record attempts using the one serviceable machine but their times of 64.2 by Davies and 64.8 by Speerin were much slower than the solos over the same distance.

A talking point among the fans was the 50 percent hike in the price of the programme, up from 6d. (2.5p) to 9d (3.75p).

A fixture backlog meant that Tigers raced Edinburgh at Motherwell on 28 August when the Eagles were absent. The Monarchs held their own up to heat 13, then fell away badly allowing the Tigers to win in their Scottish Coronation Cup tie.

Miller scored a maximum, while Templeton also impressed for Tigers with seven from five outings. Miller produced several fast times to demonstrate his mastery at The Stadium. With Bainbridge on 11+1 and Ken McKinlay on 11, the Tigers had a sound platform. The Tigers won 61–47, but would it be good enough to give then the tie on aggregate?

Not many teams enjoyed a visit to the County Ground in Exeter, with its long, banked track and solid metal fence, and so it proved with Tigers on 31 August. The margin in the 69–39 score was probably wider than they hoped. However, the Southern League riders rode well above themselves. The Tigers, who had bike problems and falls, could not take it away from the Falcons. Goog Hoskin, who had impressed Ian Hoskins earlier in the season, led the Falcons from the front. The Tigers' top two were McKinlay on 11+2, and Miller on 10. Both had falls, while Bainbridge had a subdued night with four from five rides.

The Tigers were faced with scoring more than 69 points at White City, while the Falcons' target was over 40 to progress to the next round of the Queen's Cup.

September

Coventry Bees came to Glasgow on 2 September as League leaders, but the sting was taken out their tail by Tigers' heat leaders. They were given a boost by Lazarus partnering Bainbridge to four 5–1 heat wins. Lazarus scored 8+4.

To be fair, the Bees gave the Tigers a run for their money, but were handicapped by arriving without injured Charlie New. They then lost Les Hewitt who rode wide and crashed into the fence in his first race. He ended up on the dog track. He also had blown his motor as he warmed it up before the match and was forced to use the track spare.

Heat three, which saw Hewitt's demise on the first time of asking, was rerun and Derek Tailby split the fast-starting pair of Lazarus and Bainbridge, only to carry poor Lazarus into and through the fence. Tailby's muted show probably stemmed from his opening ride crash and exclusion, almost a repeat of the first staging of the race. Later on, Jack Wright over-slid resulting in him breaching the fence. The safety fence was damaged three times as the Tigers won 57–26.

Miller and Bainbridge both collected full maximums while McKinlay was only beaten by Coventry's sole race winner, Johnny Reason.

The first part of a double header went well for Tigers on 9 September as they saw off the Leicester Hunters 54–30. Confusion reigned over the score which was amended during the meeting. Heat two saw McKinlay and Charlie Barsby go down. Barsby remounted to complete the race, but was excluded. Later on, the steward found out that Barsby should have been awarded the point and did so, hence the confusion.

Yet again, Miller and Bainbridge raced to full maximums while Dykes had a good pay night with 10 points. Lazarus's good form continued with 7+3. McKinlay had a miserable night, a fall and engine failure pegging him back to 3+2.

The Tigers' management wanted to use the steel plate starting surface to give Stoke an advantage, but the Speedway Control Board ruled it out. A handicap for the Tigers men may have made this a more exciting meeting as the Potters in the second half of the double-header were a pale shadow of the Hunters. The Potters lost 64–20 to a rampant Tigers, in the groove from the first meeting.

Dykes notched his second 10 of the night, blowing his maximum in his last ride. Miller had another maximum while McKinlay bounced back to take 10+2. Lazarus scored another paid maximum, 9+3 and Bainbridge would have scored more, but for a first race engine failure. Templeton took a 'guest' outing for the Potters but failed to score.

It took Wolverhampton until heat 13 to confirm their 45–39 victory over the Tigers at Monmore Green on 11 September. The Wasps were smart out the gate and the Tigers could not get past them. Miller played his usual role, but lacked heat leader support. Eric Irons was the only home man to beat him. Ken McKinlay had to settle for 7+1 and Bainbridge ended up with 6+1. The Tigers were never ahead but after heat eight were within two points of their hosts.

The Tigers led early on, but once the Coventry Bees got ahead the next night, they left the defeated Tigers on the wrong side of a 51–33 result. Yet again, Miller was the lone star without any solid support. He was one short of his maximum. McKinlay with seven points won a couple of races, but their efforts did not inspire anyone else. Lazarus opened brightly with a win over Les Hewitt but faded later.

The Tigers staged another double header on 16 September. In the first half they brushed aside Yarmouth Bloaters 62–21. The Tigers had five riders unbeaten by a visitor. Yarmouth did not have a race winner.

The final heat had to be staged three times as Miller tumbled at the same spot in the first two starts. In the first attempt, Miller and Reg Reeves collided. Miller ended up on the centre green as his bike raced riderless over the grass. A rerun with all four riders produced a similar situation, but this time Reeves pushed Miller wide into the fence. The upshot was an exclusion for Reeves, much to the crowd's pleasure. After the match, the home fans closed in on Reeves who had to be escorted to the dressing rooms by his team mates.

The episode brightened an otherwise dull match. Miller and McKinlay scored full maximums; Lazarus scored 11+1 and Dykes and Bainbridge both collected 9+3.

Such was the confidence of the Glasgow management that they staged this double header with local rivals Edinburgh as the second act. The Tigers won with three men on full maximums with 36 points between them. They scored more than the Monarchs put together. The final score was 55–29. The maximum men were Miller, Bainbridge and McKinlay.

Over the 28 heats on the night, the Tigers provided 26 race winners as the Monarchs had only two men first over the line, Don Cuppleditch and Roy Bester.

Two days later, the Hunters scored solidly at Blackbird Road. Leicester accounted for the Tigers, although the visitors had the top heat leaders in Miller and McKinlay. Miller's contests with Len Williams were the top races. Each rider won once to continue a rivalry that developed each time they met.

The Tigers were in striking distance for much of the match, but Leicester's 5–1 in heat 13 gave the home side victory. With Miller on 11, McKinlay on 10 and Bainbridge on nine points, the top end worked well. However, the tail was woefully long.

The Exeter Falcons' first visit to Glasgow on 23 September was not a happy one. They had their wings well and truly clipped 72–36 and went home out of the Queens Cup with a 111–105 aggregate defeat. The Tigers had to work hard for this and it was in doubt until the last race. The Tigers nominated duo of Miller and McKinlay beat the Falcons' Goog Hoskin and Jack Geran to clinch the tie.

Yet again Miller scored a maximum. McKinlay had a paid maximum with 16+2. Lazarus completed a paid maximum with 13+2. The other five all scored, but none were outstanding.

Pundits put Exeter's problems down to over anxiety at the gate. However, they settled down and managed to pick up points by separating Tigers heat leaders and second strings. However, the early tapes offences were too much to carry the day.

Sharp bade farewell to the fans over track microphone before his departure home to Australia. McIntosh had hoped to make a comeback, but medical advice prevented a return this season.

The Tigers were down on power, but held the Monarchs to a 22-point lead with a 65–43 defeat in the Queen's Cup Final first leg in Edinburgh on 26 September. Miller was not as dominant as usual, but he cannot be blamed as his seven team-mates failed to rise to the occasion. Miller scored 11, while Bainbridge and McKinlay on 7+1 and seven respectively were also below par.

Miller showed that he was still the master of Jack Young as he beat the former Monarch 2–1 in a match race event. The Queens Cup Final return leg at White City on 30 September was rained off.

October

The contest for the Scottish Cup was over as Tigers flattened the Eagles on their home turf on Friday 2 October. The Eagles, without Noel Watson, had no answer to Miller and Bainbridge. They inspired the Tigers to a 58–50 win. They came from an eight-point deficit after 11 heats to win by the same margin. Two consecutive 5–1s pulled the Tigers level with the Eagles by heat 13 and a heat 14 4–2 put them in the driving seat.

Miller was again unbeaten at The Stadium and one-time hater of the track Bainbridge gave sound support with 15+2. McKinlay managed only one race win in his 11 points, but he was paid for two bonus points.

The Tigers could not erode the Monarchs' first leg lead by a big enough margin to take the Queen's Cup at White City on 5 October. Edinburgh took the tie thanks to a 56–52 defeat on the night and a 117–99 aggregate win.

The home riders had a fight on their hands and it was heat 13 before they managed to get ahead, but, by then, it was too late.

Miller raced to a six ride full maximum. McKinlay contributed 10+1 and Bainbridge 10 points – enough to win but not by enough. Most of the other points were gathered in heat wins but Dykes had an off night and failed to score. He wasn't helped by bike problems including a seized motor, a fate that also befell Bainbridge.

Tigers had their second Cup meeting in three days. This time, on 7 October, they made no mistakes and collected the silverware as Miller and McKinlay scored full and paid maximums respectively. They won the Scottish Cup 123–93 from the Lanarkshire Eagles on aggregate, a trophy they would not win for another 12 years.

This meeting was effectively the end of an era. The Tigers did run in 1954, but it was never going to be anything more than a token effort. It was, although no one knew it, Tommy Miller's last outing as a Tiger and he signed off with another splendid six ride maximum 18.

McKinlay was paid for the same total but had two bonus points. Lazarus and Wilkinson did reasonably well with eight and 7+3 respectively but, albeit he did not know it at the time, Junior Bainbridge signed off his Tigers career with a poor four points.

For the Eagles, an award for merit went to Guy Allott who had an acrobatic dismount in heat six when he hit the fence and was flung from the saddle before rolling along the track. He tried the same stunt a few races later but managed to stay aboard his bike.

The trophy was presented by *Speedway Gazette* correspondent, Barney Bamford, who went on to be a sports commentator with the BBC. He reported that Ian Hoskins had told him the attendances for the last couple of meetings had been the worst in the track history and suggested that crowds were averaging 7,000. This may explain the decision to run the two double-header meetings, sometimes a sign that a team wanted to complete their fixtures, but was losing money staging the meetings. Bamford was also critical of the track shape suggesting it did not make for exciting racing and the meeting against the Eagles was a poor affair.

He was not kind about the city's night life either, suggesting that it died at 9.30pm. Had he been around on a Friday or even Saturday night his views may just have differed.

Hoskins commented in his book: "The 1953 season saw Tigers at their strongest and their opponents, Birmingham apart, at their weakest. With Young and Le Breton gone, even the local derbies were predictable ... Our crowds began to fall and many fans began watching television at home on Wednesday nights ... We finished the season with an average gate of over 7,000 people a meeting." He concluded that despite a reduction in the entertainment tax, the promotion was no longer viable and the company was forced into liquidation. The speedway was taken over by the greyhound company who owned the stadium.

Needless to say the season ended with a blaze with Ian Hoskins' hat as the combustible material.

Speculation was rife on where Tommy Miller might move to during the close season. This was fuelled by him making guest appearances for Leicester. Other rumours circulating about this time were a move south for Tigers to re-establish a team in Liverpool.

Stenners 1954 Annual said that the Tigers were a rider short after McIntosh was injured, and their form varied between terrific and terrible. The Tigers finished fourth in a nine-team league, but only won away from home twice. It would be 10 years before league speedway was again staged in Glasgow.

Jack Young and Ken McKinlay riding in the Television Trophy at Harringay on 16 June 1954. When this photo was taken, there was no speedway at either of the Scottish tracks where they had been local heroes – both Glasgow and Edinburgh had closed. The meeting was an international best pairs. The meeting was won by England, represented by Split Waterman and Alan Hunt. Young and McKinlay, riding for Scotland, finished last with only four points. Jack Young was, of course, Australian, but had started his speedway career in the United Kingdom with the Edinburgh Monarchs

On occasions Ian Hoskins would use stunts to try to increase the crowds. Left: an Egyptian Yogi who was in Glasgow and used before the National Trophy match with Birmingham in 1953 to inspire the riders. Don Wilkinson is doing the hammering! Right: Lady Godiva, who rode round the tack for a visit by Coventry on 25 July 1951. (Both courtesy Friends of Edinburgh Speedway)

15. 1954 and 1956: Short seasons

Speedway was not in a good place at the start of the 1954 season and Glasgow was no exception. Although reduced, the Entertainment Tax was still drawing cash out of the sport and television was becoming a serious alternative source of entertainment.

The drop in crowd numbers everywhere had come to a head at many venues and after the 1953 failures like Liverpool, many tracks, including former Glasgow rival venue Ashfield, did not reopen. The First Division ran with eight teams. The Second Division was planned to have 15, but White City and Wolverhampton withdrew without riding a league fixture, and Edinburgh and Plymouth closed after riding four and two league fixtures respectively.

The White City owners decided to give it a go, but sold Tommy Miller to Motherwell and Junior Bainbridge to Ipswich. Peter Dykes did not return from South Africa.

With no disrespect to the Tigers of 1954, they only had one heat leader in Ken McKinlay. Larry Lazarus and Alf McIntosh were good scorers with potential to step up a gear to that level and potential laden Doug Templeton and Bob Sharp were capable of becoming able second strings. Arthur Malm had yet to prove himself and newcomers, Vern McWilliams and Scot Douglas Craig were unknown quantities.

April

The Tigers began the season at Edinburgh on 10 April in a North Shield match, and went down 47–36. Ken McKinlay shone with a maximum and Lazarus contributed 7+1. Bob Sharp chipped in 6+1, but the rest fared poorly. McKinlay set a track record of 66.4 in his first outing which stood for over 11 years. Engine failures and falls littered the score charts of both teams. Edinburgh had five engine failures while Glasgow had two and three falls.

The home season opened on 14 April and Tigers lost badly, 51–32 to Coventry Bees. This meeting was also a North Shield one, as were the rest of the Tigers' fixtures. McKinlay scored 11 having traded honours with Charlie New but his only backing came from Lazarus once more. Alf McIntosh was out of form and his two points was way below what he should have scored. Three Bees featured in the second half final and McKinlay could only manage third behind New and Emms. The showing probably did not enthuse the Tigers' loyal fans who were missing two of their favourites, Miller and Bainbridge.

The Tigers now faced a trip to Leicester two days later. McKinlay raced to his second away maximum. The promise from Lazarus was shown as he scored eight and Sharp gave a fair display also for eight points. After three heats, the Tigers were eight points up, but at the end Leicester won 47–37. McWilliams and Craig both failed to score.

The inexperience of many of the Tigers showed and their only other experienced rider, Alf McIntosh was having a poor start to the season.

The next night saw the Tigers meet up with Junior Bainbridge. Now an Ipswich rider, he was only beaten by McKinlay. The Tigers star picked up his third away maximum. Bob Sharp improved again with nine points, but the other six slipped back a bit, although the final score was 48–36. To be fair, the Tigers were respectable opposition away from home, no worse than the 1953 team. Their weakness was riding at White City and on 21 April, the Tigers succumbed to Edinburgh 45–38. Without Vern McWilliams, Willie Templeton was introduced to the side and picked up a point beating the Monarchs' Jimmy Cox.

Left: 1954 Glasgow Tigers: Larry Lazarus, Doug Templeton, Ken McKinlay, Vern McWilliams, Arthur Malm, Bob Sharp, Doug Craig and Alf McIntosh.

McKinlay scored 11, and was beaten only by Dick Campbell. Sharp scored eight and Alf McIntosh improved with seven points. The picture was not all bad. The other riders were below par and could not continue to be carried. This was the first time the Templeton brothers, Doug and Willie, rode in the same team.

The writing was on the wall when the Tigers travelled to Motherwell on 23 April. They faced Tommy Miller and his 12 was part of the Eagles' 58 points. Miller, with fellow Eagles Derrick Close and Ron Phillips, scored more than Tigers' 25. Ken McKinlay's unbeaten away record tumbled and he scored nine. Bob Sharp continued his reasonable run on seven, but even the re-introduction of McWilliams at the expense of Malm did nothing to boost the visitors' fortunes.

The upshot was that the results were so poor that the management pulled the plug and closed the speedway team down. The Tigers were no more as a league team and White City fell silent.

Ken McKinlay went to Leicester where he became a multi-world finalist and is acknowledged as the greatest ever Scottish speedway rider. Larry Lazarus and Bob Sharp went to Ipswich while Alf McIntosh and Willie Templeton crossed over to Edinburgh. However, Edinburgh's future was short-lived and Motherwell took Doug Templeton under their wings. Both Doug and Willie would return later to the Tigers.

Vern McWilliams went to Wolverhampton only for Wasps to close a few weeks later. He saw out 1954 at Poole. Douglas Craig drifted out of the sport as did Malm. Arthur Malm was in Edinburgh for the Monarchs practice in 1961 but disappeared without riding in a meeting.

May

The Tigers' 'last hurrah' was at Hamilton Showgrounds on Saturday 8 May, where, in the guise of a Glasgow Select, they beat a Hamilton Select 43.5–39.5, Doug and Willie Templeton top scored with 11 and 12 respectively while Arthur Malm managed just two points. For Hamilton, Douglas Craig scored 6.5. The rest of the riders were mostly second halfers except for Jimmy Tannock who had ridden for both Ashfield and Motherwell.

For the records a Glasgow Tigers Select lost 54–9 at Hamilton on 14 May 1955 with Doug and Willie Templeton top scoring for Hamilton and Glasgow respectively.

The closure of Glasgow White City, followed by Edinburgh's demise, left Motherwell as Scotland's only speedway team. The Eagles wanted to continue in 1955, but the English Second Division teams said that the travelling for only one meeting was unsustainable, and

Motherwell were barred from the league. This short-sighted action finished league speedway in Scotland until 1960 and the launch of the Provincial League.

1956

May

Tommy Miller and Junior Bainbridge took to the track at White City on 9 May to give a demonstration of the new tyre that the Speedway Control Board required all riders to use. The new tyre had very little tread and was introduced in an attempt to slow down machines in the hope that it would improve the racing. The new tyre was universally unwelcome and Bainbridge voiced his concerns after this demonstration. On 5 May, a meeting at Belle Vue between the Aces on the new tyre and a visiting Polish team on the old tyre turned out to be a rout for the Poles until the Aces reverted to the old tyre.

The promotion team of Tommy Miller and Junior Bainbridge must have been very pleased with the 18,000 turn out for an international fixture which saw Scotland face an England Select on 16 May. However, the riders were not happy with the bumpy circuit.

Larry Lazarus came in to the side to replace Bob Mark and had to use the track spare as his own bike was still down south. The track spare was never a machine to win races on. Willie Wilson came out of retirement to help the Scots. He started well, but his lack of match fitness showed as he tired later on. Like the other riders, he had to use the unpopular new tyre and had built a training track to try them out.

World Champion Peter Craven had an easy night and was happy to follow home Dick Fisher in a couple of his races. Craven was, however, not as fast as Tommy Miller who nearly beat his own track record in heat two. Craven collected a paid maximum of 16+2.

Next best English rider was Bradford's Arthur Wright on 12 while Arthur Forrest added 10+3. For Scotland, Tommy Miller with 13 was top scorer while Ken McKinlay scored 11. Tommy's co-promoter, Junior Bainbridge, scored 8+1.

The England Select were behind for only one heat when McKinlay and Gordon McGregor took a 5–1 in heat six. A last heat 5–0 to Scotland, when Charlie Barsby and Jim Lightfoot both fell, made the score look a bit more respectable. England won 57–49.

The Tigers were back and faced their old rivals the Birmingham Brummies on 30 May. The meetings against other teams were staged as Anglo-Scottish Cup matches.

While it wasn't used, both sides had the opportunity to use the recently introduced tactical substitute facility. Neither team fell six or more points behind so neither implemented the new rule. The match ended 48–48 as a Junior Bainbridge and Willie Wilson 4-2 in the last heat evened the scores. Bainbridge scored 14, while Miller, who had been on the wrong end of a 5-1 in the penultimate heat, scored 12. Bob Sharp scored 7+1 and Willie Wilson seven.

June

It was nip and tuck all the way as Britain faced an Overseas side on 13 June. Junior Bainbridge's engine failure in heat 17, when he never left the tapes, was the turning point. Britain's 4–2 left them one shy of the match winning total. Tommy Miller and Gordon McGregor bagged three points between them to win the Inter-Continental Challenge Match' match 56–52. Willie Wilson had been lined up as reserve for Britain, but with Charlie New missing he was pressed into service for the Overseas side.

The 'Tommy Miller' in the second half was the promoter's namesake, a local lad who had some grass track experience. Before the Tigers' Tommy Miller came on the scene, Glasgow had a prominent boxer also called Tommy Miller.

Bainbridge arrived in Glasgow before this meeting with his ribs strapped up to allow him to ride. He had been injured a few days before at Rayleigh. Wilson had bike troubles which he put down to a faulty timing chain. He is quoted by Ian Hoskins, who wrote a report for a local newspaper, as saying that he might as well have been riding a bicycle for all the speed the engine gave him.

Alan Hunt gave a superb performance for Britain with 16 points. Ian Williams, brother of Freddie and Eric, scored 12+1. Tommy Miller scored 8+2 and George White 8+1 for the British side. For the Overseas side, Kiwi Bob Duckworth started with a fall then raced on to a top-scoring 14. Bob Sharp scored a creditable 12+1 while Ron Phillips scored 10.

The Glasgow Tigers versus Bradford match on 27 June saw Ron Phillips don the race jacket of a fourth Scottish team. Bill Baird, however, was the only rider to compete for all four Scottish League tracks and his record is unique. Phillips was, in reality, a guest, as were all the others riding for the Tigers.

Bradford was the first team in Scotland to use the tactical substitute rule. The first rider in the role in Scotland was Ron Clarke in heat 13. Guy Allott became the first tactical substitute to win a heat in Scotland in heat 15.

Tommy Miller's fall in heat two was unusual. At the time he fell, Miller was winning easily. Gordon McGregor's contribution was reduced as he was suffering the effects of a bruised foot. Phillips top scored for Tigers with 12+2. The three former Tigers all scored 10; Junior Bainbridge Tommy Miller and Gordon McGregor who also secured two bonus points. The Tigers won 58–38.

An aspiring female rider, Cecilia Calder, who was a stock car driver, had hoped to ride at White City. However, the Speedway Control Board did not allow her to ride.

July

Norwich was a weakened outfit on 11 July. Geoff Pymar replaced the programmed Ove Fundin for the visitors in a match which was not a classic. Aub Lawson withdrew from the meeting as he had to ride at Bradford for Australia. Reg Trott was out injured and Fred Brand retired just before this meeting. For the Tigers, Red Monteith replaced Willie Wilson and Gordon Mitchell was drafted in as reserve.

The major talking point was heat 13 when Gordon Mitchell lost control at the start of the race. He hit Phil Clarke who fell from his bike and was injured. Thankfully, he just suffered a bit of a shaking. Peter Atkins replaced him in the rerun and fell.

Gordon McGregor was the top Tiger with 13+1 while Tommy Miller and Ron Phillips ended their careers in Scotland with 10+2 and 10+1 respectively. The meeting marked the end of the brief revival attempt. The lack of supporter interest ended the Tigers' return. However, the Tigers did go out with a win, 54–41.

The programme of meetings was not successful, despite a good start, and it would be 1964 before a Glasgow Tigers team returned to the track.

16. 1964: Speedway returns to Glasgow

The Glasgow Tigers had been hibernating since 1954 and the brief season in 1956. Hopes that the formation of the Provincial League in 1960 might see Tigers back did not materialise. There were glimmers of a revival in 1962 involving former Belle Vue promoter Alice Hart. However, White City was used for stock cars, but in speedway, nothing happened until 1964.

The sport had re-established itself in Scotland in 1960, when the Edinburgh Monarchs came back in the Provincial League. The sport had been in gradual decline in the second half of the 1950s, and at one stage there were only nine senior teams in the United Kingdom. In 1960, a group of promoters led by Mike Parker established the Provincial League, mainly through opening tracks where the sport had previously been staged. It was not as high a standard as the National League, but found younger or previously retired riders to join its teams. It attracted older fans from the post-war period and new, younger supporters.

The Hoskins family, who were in the background, established it was possible that White City Stadium might provide a home for their team if the Edinburgh Monarchs were thrown out of Old Meadowbank at the end of the 1963 season.

Obviously, the White City owners considered the stadium was ripe for speedway again, but given that Ian Hoskins was running the Monarchs, it would not have been a wise move for the Hoskins family to front up the new promotion.

Enter Trevor Redmond, who had been rider/promotor at St Austell, who was looking for a track for his team. He had recent expertise in promotion at Neath in 1962 and St Austell a few years earlier and in 1963. In the past, he had also promoted the sport in South Africa.

Redmond had come to Great Britain from New Zealand in 1950. After two seasons at Aldershot, he joined the Wembley Lions and stayed there until their closure early in 1957. He then rode at several different tracks, but was more involved as a promoter.

He had retained riders on his books from St Austell in 1963. Redmond, who had hung up his leathers at the end of 1963, was the man the Hoskins family preferred to work with. In his book, Ian Hoskins says that the promotion was owned between Redmond and the Hoskins family on a 50-50 basis, and that Redmond flew up to Glasgow every Wednesday to run the meetings. He brought Maury Mattingley with him, who had just been released by Wolverhampton, but was based in Southampton. He was the 1963 Scottish champion. Such a deal was very unusual at this time. Mattingley was noted as a hater of heavy tracks and also being habitually late to arrive. This would often necessitate him changing alone. However, early arrivals caused by the flights saw him enjoy dressing room gatherings and he changed his ways.

Before settling on White City, Ian Hoskins says that they had considered the Celtic FC stadium, which had briefly staged the sport in the 1920s. However, the club's rules forbad other sports being staged at the ground, so they decided to go to White City. The Tigers intent to run was confirmed by the application for membership of the Provincial League deadline of 31 December.

Obviously courting publicity, Redmond did not admit the Hoskins link and, when he announced the first Glasgow signing of Charlie Monk, he publicly refused any help offered by Ian by way of riders from Edinburgh. Effectively this cranked up the two 'rivals' which would help both to re-create a team loyalty before the Tigers turned a wheel.

In addition to match race Silver Sash holder Monk, Trevor brought in Cornishmen Ray Wickett and Chris Julian to the table. Ray was a reluctant recruit and did not stay long. Bill

McMillan and Jack (Red) Monteith did sign from Edinburgh. Monteith had ridden for the Tigers in the early 1950s. Two rookie Kiwis, Bruce Ovenden and Joe Hicks, were snapped up for the Tigers in February 1964.

The Tigers had also hoped to add Don Perry, an Irish rider who had done well at Wimbledon in the 1950s, but he never materialised. Redmond could not entice George Major, Ray Cresp, Glyn Chandler and injured Chris Blewett up north.

The opening night line-up did not last long and the Tigers team changed regularly over the season. Redmond was forced to return to the track as a rider to strengthen the team and postponed his swansong until the end of 1964.

A dispute over whether Wolverhampton should join the ailing National League saw the Provincial League run outside the sport's established structures. This meant that the Provincial League riders could not ride in the World Championship or on National League tracks. Fortunately, this mess was resolved at the end of the season, and the Shawcross Report into the sport saw the formation of the British League. Speedway had been in desperate trouble when the Provincial League started in 1960.

So, the Tigers became members of the 'blacked' Provincial League together with fellow newcomers Newport and Sunderland and the rest of the 1963 teams, old rivals Edinburgh, Newcastle, Middlesbrough, Sheffield. Long Eaton, Wolverhampton, Cradley Heath, Hackney Wick, Poole and Exeter. The teams faced each other once home and away. Sunderland dropped out of the league, so there were 12 teams and a 22-match league programme.

April

It was no April Fool as the Tigers woke up on 1 April to face Middlesbrough Bears in a Northern League match which drew in a crowd of 10,000. The three heat leaders, maximum man Charlie Monk, Chris Julian with 11 points, and Maury Mattingley on 10+1 became Tigers heroes overnight. Bill McMillan and Jack (Red) Monteith chipped in four each while Ray Wickett added 3+1. New Kiwi Bruce Ovenden was the only Tiger to score a duck, not helped by breaking his frame in his opening ride as result of a fall. Wickett was unlucky his handlebars worked loose in heat 8, an unusual event for any speedway rider.

One time Lanarkshire favourite Bluey Scott top scored for Bears, but the rest of his team mates produced solid rather than starring contribution and the Tigers won 44–34.

The second half Grand Opening Trophy was won by new track record holder Mattingley from Monk and the first lady on a Scottish Speedway track since the mists of time, Maureen Taylor, took 57.4 to cover a couple of laps. Mattingley set the new track record at 78.6 in heat one and equalled it in the second half final.

For some reason Bluey Scott was not given the opportunity to challenge Charlie Monk for the Silver Sash which should have been his right.

The following evening a Tigers team with only six riders journeyed to Sheffield to face their namesakes in Northern League action. Glasgow were slaughtered 59–19, losing the first seven heats 5–1. Trevor Redmond had to replace Monk and Ovenden as vehicle breakdowns prevented them from arriving in time for the start of the match. Sheffield held up the start by 20 minutes and could not wait any longer.

The problem was that Ovenden was carrying four bikes and other equipment which left the affected Glasgow riders scrambling about for kit. Varey arranged for Derek Jay, Gerald Goodwin and Ken Handscombe to loan bikes and leathers to get the meeting started. Only

Mattingley won a heat in his five ride eight points haul and this was after Ovenden had delivered his bike after heat seven.

The two missing Glasgow Tigers did arrive late, but the incident was still was referred to the League Management Committee. The promotion was fined £25 and Monk, Ovenden and, oddly, non-programmed Joe Hicks were given written warnings. £15 of the fine was paid to the Sheffield juniors.

The furious Sheffield promoter, Frank Varey, was heavily criticised by home fans for his comments on the tannoy. He apologised in the programme the following week, saying that he had not tried to be critical of Ovenden. He was being critical of the Glasgow management for giving a newcomer to the country the responsibility of bringing the bikes and kit and not taking care of the task themselves.

Oddly enough, Varey was not happy with the margin of victory as the missing men had lowered the quality of the opposition. By way of punishment dished out by Varey, Monk was 'stripped' of his Silver Sash by the Sheffield promoter.

The Glasgow Tigers took their revenge against Sheffield on 8 April at White City with a 49–29 win thanks mainly to Monk taking his second maximum and Mattingley his first home paid maximum. It was a solid show from the home riders. Ovenden opened his Glasgow account with a respectable 6+3. The Tigers' win could have been bigger but for McMillan having magneto problems. The absence of Clive Featherby, a Sheffield heat leader, did not help their cause.

Two days later, the Tigers were at Cleveland Park, Middlesbrough for the first time since 1948. The Bears gave a solid show to take the Northern League points 46–32. The Tigers introduced their first new rider in speedway enthusiast Terry Stone from Essex. He replaced Ray Wickett who got his desired move to Exeter. Stone scored 4+1. Monk top scored with 11 and Mattingley gathered seven. Monk dropped his point to Bluey Scott in heat 10 with the places reversed in heat 12.

Wednesday 15 April was the first local derby since 1954 when the Tigers and Edinburgh Monarchs clashed at White City. Stone had a reasonable home debut with 4+1. The Monarchs nosed in front in heats one and two and it took to heat five for the Tigers to level before moving ahead in the next race. In a tense finale, with all to play for at 37–35 after 12 heats, Tigers' heroes Monk and Mattingley took a 4–2 over Wayne Briggs and George Hunter to send the red and white fans home happy with a 41–37 victory. Monk added yet another maximum. Unsung hero McMillan at reserve scored 8+1 and Mattingley added eight. Jack Monteith had a fall and cut his forehead.

Edinburgh's Willie Templeton topped off the night by giving Charlie his first defeat at White City in the second half. Following Charlie Monk's failure to defend the Silver Sash on 2 April, Varey's claim was vetoed and Monk was required to defend it against the top Sheffield Tiger at the Sheffield versus Kiwis meeting on 16 April. He successfully did so by defeating Jack Kitchen.

Saturday 18 April saw Tigers in Edinburgh and this time the plaudits were earned by the Monarchs who won 56–21. The Monarchs had a good pay night with every race winner in a match described as producing processional racing. Monk had four second places in his eight points with former Monarch Bill McMillan next best on four. Monk lost to George Hunter who took the Silver Sash in the second half. Scottish Open Champion of 1963 Mattingley only managed 3+1 due to bike problems. Julian also had bike difficulties. Oddly, the Tigers did not elect to use a tactical substitute as the Monarchs relentlessly opened the gap between the two teams in all but one heat. Eric Hanlon a Glasgow junior who had guested for the

Bears in the opening night match replaced Monteith but failed to score. Glasgow were reviving a bad tradition of struggling away from home.

Glasgow fans saw a change of fare on 22 April with the first full international since 1953, discounting the one staged in 1956. Of course, it was under the Provincial League banner, and therefore did not include any riders from the National League.

Scotland, aided by Australian Monk, faced New Zealand boosted by Australians Scott and reserves Guasco and Airey, who did not ride. Monk and Scott scored 13 for Scotland and New Zealand respectively. Doug Templeton led the Scots' charge with 17 supported by brother Willie who matched Monk. McMillan and Monteith missed out for Scotland due to injury. Another genuine Scot in the home team was Edinburgh's Bert Harkins, who scored one point at reserve.

After 18 heats the Scots had lost 57–50. Newcastle's Ivan Mauger was the inspiration for the Kiwis with an 18-point maximum. He also set a new track record, His main assistants were Scott and native Kiwi Wayne Briggs who chipped in with 10+1. Alf Wells failed to give much support due to bike problems. However, the visitors were just a bit more solid than the Scots for whom George Hunter was a surprise poor scorer with two.

It was back to Northern League fare a week later at White City when the wind played havoc, blowing the riders across the track. This time the Tigers faced fellow newcomers Sunderland Saints in Glasgow. The weak Saints team lost 50–28. Monk and Mattingly scored a full and a paid maximum respectively. Newcomer Terry Stone scored seven. The remainder, including Redmond, standing in for Julian gave a solid show. Julian had injured his spine and a hand. Sunderland were level pegging at heat four but then the roof fell in. They only achieved two 3–3s in the last nine heats.

May

The Tigers made the trip to Tyneside to face the Newcastle Diamonds at Brough Park on 4 May. The solid Diamonds, fronted by maximum man Ivan Mauger, saw off the Tigers 46–29. Only Monk was on full power with 10 points. Mattingley, not a fan of Brough Park, was next best Tiger on six while Ovenden on 4+2 formed part of the long Tigers' tail. The Tigers may have done a bit better had they taken three points in heat eight. Only Goog Allen finished. The melee behind Allen was caused by Stone who fell and brought down Maury Robinson and Monteith.

Also, McMillan did not ride after an opening heat exclusion. The Tigers' failure to use a tactical substitute again seems odd. Monk failed to win the Silver Sash which was held by Mauger. It was an eventful meeting with falls, engine failures, exclusions and pile ups.

Two nights later, the Tigers exacted their revenge at White City with a 53–25 win over the Diamonds. It was the 'new' team's best win so far. Mattingley, Julian and Monk all returned double figures, 12, 11 and 10 respectively. Ovenden recorded an unusual and promising four bonus points return to post a score of 7+4. Apart from Mauger, who was excluded from heat seven after falling while chasing Mattingley, the Diamonds failed to sparkle. However, Mauger's nine included two defeats of Monk and a new track record. Mauger ended a poor night, by his standards, with a fall in the Boys Brigade Trophy final.

The Tigers visited Sunderland's East Boldon Greyhound Stadium on 12 May with some hope of gathering their first away points in the new era. However, the Saints were boosted by guest Pete Jarman and new signing Ken Sharples. Ken was a veteran Belle Vue Ace, who was making a comeback in the Provincial League.

1964 Glasgow Tigers: Bill McMillan, Charlie Monk, Trevor Redmond, Bruce Ovenden, Terry Stone; front: Chris Julian, Maury Mattingley and Red Monteith.

In addition, new Australians Jim Airey and Gordon Guasco were starting to find their feet. At the end of 13 heats Monk had posted another full maximum for the Tigers, but the rest were very poor and the net result was a 48–30 defeat.

This match was the end of the Northern League fixtures. The Tigers won all their home meetings and lost all their matches on the road. They finished fourth out of six teams.

Back home in Glasgow on the next day, the Tigers welcomed the first visit to Scotland of a Welsh league team. Fellow newcomers, Newport Wasps gave the Tigers a fright by levelling the scores in heat 12. Luckily for the Tigers, Monk was in heat 13. He completed his maximum with McMillan in third to ensure a 40–38 win for the Tigers' fans. Their other heat leaders Mattingley, who had engine failure in heat four, and Julian scored eight and six respectively. The match was nip and tuck with never more than four points between the teams. It was level after heats two, seven, eight and 12, but the Tigers were only behind once.

Exeter Falcons swooped into White City on 20 May and ran the Tigers close before going down 41–36 on a bumpy track caused by a stock car meeting. Yet again, Monk completed another maximum in heat 13 but the pressure was less intense than the week before and only a 5–0 to the Falcons would have given them a draw. The Falcons had veteran Jimmy Squibb, who was familiar with White City, in good form and he was backed by short term Tiger Ray Wickett.

The Tigers' three heat leaders did a bit better with Monk scoring 12, and Mattingley and Julian both on 10. The others all had a poor night which maybe rang warning bells for the promoters. McMillan broke his handlebars when he hit the fence in his opening ride and could not settle using a pair borrowed from Joe Hicks.

Changes were rung for the Tigers' visit to Exeter on 25 May. Out went Jack Monteith and in came promoter Trevor Redmond in a familiar role as rider-promoter. He scored six points and was an able replacement. Monk finished last after missing the gate in heat 13 and so only collected nine points. With Mattingley posting only 3+1, not helped by an engine failure in heat three, the result was a 41–35 win for the Falcons. Julian showed his familiarity with the fast, banked, track with a steel sheet safety fence by scoring 10 points.

It was close for most of the match with the Falcons just surging over the line with a 5–1 from Alan Cowland and Maurice McDermott, who had moved on from Sunderland, in heat 12. The wet slimy track meant it was uncertain whether the meeting would go ahead and it produced some processional races.

On the way home, the Tigers rode at Long Eaton the next night. It had been Monk's home track in 1963. He scored 14 points, losing to Eric Boothroyd in heat nine. Julian obviously enjoyed the pacey track with 11 points from five rides. The remainder, including guest Ken Vale, managed eight between them in the Tigers' 33 points. Had Mattingley ridden he might have helped the Tigers to a win.

As it was, the Archers won 45–33. A young Ray Wilson only lost to Monk and scored 11. Monk made the second half final but was excluded.

On 29 May, back in Glasgow, the Tigers dropped their first home Provincial League points, watched by the best crowd of the season so far. Poole Pirates forced a 39–39 draw. The match was unusual as the scores were level after eight heats and the next five were drawn. Had Monk not fallen in heat nine and Redmond stepped down from the team the home side might have won. Monk was second top Tiger with nine, a point behind Julian and one ahead of Mattingley. Ovenden took a good 7+2, but the rest were still not pressing home their track knowledge. Mattingley did especially well given that his bike did not arrive and he used the track spare.

The Tigers' hopes of fielding veteran Cyril Roger were still on hold and would, ultimately, come to nothing.

June

By way of variety, on 3 June the Glasgow faithful were entertained by a four-team tournament. Teams represented Scotland, England, Wales and Overseas in what was one of four legs. Scotland won with an almost all tartan team. England and Overseas were similarly staffed. Wales included a Dutch Australian and three Englishman. The home team surged ahead in heat three and collected 36 in the 16 heats. 'Wales' were second on 29, Overseas gathered 19 while a reasonably strong looking England team surprisingly trailed last with 12. The Tigers' Monk scored 10 and one-time Tiger Doug Templeton topped the charts with a maximum 12. Mattingley with five and Julian on four scored all but three of the English total. There were several fallers, including Julian – twice, Ivan Mauger, Bluey Scott, Eric Boocock and Monk. Boocock and Wayne Briggs also suffered bike failures.

It was a poor night for the Tigers on 10 June. Heat leaders Mattingley and Julian returned six and four points respectively. The team's unbeaten home record was finished by Wolverhampton who won 42–35. Monk rode to form with a return of 14, but the others stuttered. Mattingley started well with a win then only added three from his remaining rides. Julian packed up in his opener, won a race then fell. Monteith also fell after running into Harry Edwards. He knocked himself out but came round later in the dressing room. All three

Tigers heat leaders did well in the second half heading Jarman to the flag in the final, with Monk winning the Miss Scotland trophy.

A week later, Glasgow axed Monteith again, and replaced him with Redmond who rode at number one. Glasgow knocked fellow Tigers, Sheffield, out the Knock Out Cup 59–37 in a single meeting tie. This arrangement obviously favoured the home team. It was a much-improved team effort thanks to Mattingley scoring 12+1, Julian 11+1 and Monk 13, all from five rides. The team effort shows up with all but Monk scoring a bonus point. They picked up 10 between them.

The Sheffield riders soon extracted revenge on their Scottish namesakes. Glasgow were at Owlerton the next night in the Provincial League. Mattingley struck form and rattled in a maximum 12 to make it 24 against Sheffield on consecutive nights. With Monk on 10 points, the visitors had a good platform, but the other five, Redmond included, didn't rise to the occasion. The match ended 42–36 to the home side. Glasgow were close to Sheffield most of the way. It took a 5–1 from Kitchen and Jay in the last heat to put daylight between them.

Heat 11 caused fireworks. Alan Jay fell as the riders bunched on the first bend and Stone was excluded. Despite this, Jay attacked Stone and a bit of a battle ensued. It resulted in the police being called to restore order.

In the second half Julian crashed and was badly injured, fracturing his skull and his arm, which meant that he was out until mid-August.

The Tigers never got going at Newcastle on 22 June. The Diamonds outshone the Tigers 51–26. Monk gain demonstrated his good form with 14 points, swapping race wins with Ivan Mauger. He had another go at securing the Silver Sash, but Mauger won after Monk fell. Missing Julian, the Tigers brought in tailender Hanlon, who, together with Stone, McMillian and Ovenden, failed to score. Mattingley with three points and Redmond with nine added the other 12.

The team's misery was compounded two days later when the Monarchs visited on league business and left with the two league points on offer. The Monarchs led from the first heat to heat eight, when the Tigers' pair of McMillan and Hanlon's 5–1 levelled the score. Heat nine saw Tigers ahead, but Wayne Briggs and Willie Templeton snatched a 5–1 and the visitors hung on for their 41–37 win. The consistent Monk bagged another 12 points maximum, but again it was the Tigers' tail that failed. Mattingley and Redmond both scored seven. The former fell in one race while Redmond's bike failed in another which did not help their cause. Ovenden tangled with Bill Landels in heat eight. Landels ended up with a broken collar bone while Ovenden suffered leg and foot injuries.

July

Despite scoring 4+1 against the Monarchs, Eric Hanlon was dropped for the match at home to Long Eaton on 3 July, but with Ovenden missing they needed a reserve. The Tigers ran the Reserves Race before the match, making it what is known as a 'Vulture's Race', when the winner is given the reserve spot which was up for grabs. Gordon Mitchell, a 1960 Monarch doing well in the second halves, won from Eric Hanlon after Jack Monteith fell and was excluded. Mitchell was given the number seven race jacket and scored one point. In addition to Mitchell, the Tigers introduced former Sunderland rider Vic Ridgeon, to strengthen the team rather than replace the missing Ovenden, and he scored four points. The Tigers had planned to include Chris Blewett, but he decided that a 1963 arm injury had not healed enough to allow him to be insured to race.

The Tigers beat the Archers 44–34 with Monk returning another maximum. Redmond scored 11, showing he was back on form and Mattingley took nine points.

The Diamonds from Newcastle were next to face the Tigers at White City a week later. They sparkled with a 46–31 win against a Tigers outfit with a long tail. Both Monk and Mattingley had an engine failure, pegging Monk back to 9+1 while Mattingley only scored a single point due to bike problems. Promoter Redmond rode well with 13, but the others didn't follow his example. Guest Chris Blewett failed to score. Ivan Mauger was unbeaten in the meeting. He kept the Silver Sash after beating Redmond.

For the Knock Out Cup tie at home to Newport on 15 July, the Tigers introduced another former Sunderland man, Graham Coombes. They dropped Ridgeon and welcomed back Ovenden. They also welcomed back a heat leading Mattingley who scored 13. Monk scored another White City maximum with 15. Redmond added a respectable 10+1. He clashed with Jon Erskine in heat 12 and fell. Despite Redmond's protests, no rerun took place. Unfortunately, it was another poor night for the rest and the Wasps won 49–46 to knock the Tigers out. It was reported that Terry Stone had decided to retire as he was struggling financially.

Glasgow could have won the match in heat 16 with a 5–1, but Jon Erskine and Peter Vandenberg shut out Coombes and scored the three points they needed for the win.

The Tigers were looking to improve the squad, but Tommy Miller turned them down due to health problems and a spin at Edinburgh convinced Don Wilkinson it was not practicable for him to return to racing.

Surprisingly, two days later, the Tigers went to a rain soaked Monmore Green and headed the Wolverhampton Wolves into heat 13. After a poor start Pete Jarman won through and completed his maximum and Cyril Francis backed him to snatch a 5–1 and win the meeting 39–38. The Tigers had reinstated former Wolf Ridgeon to replace fellow one-time Wolf Terry Stone.

Another former Wolf, Mattingley, rose to the occasion with 10 points, one less than Monk on 11. Had Redmond, with six, managed a couple better than his last in heat 13 it would have given Tigers their first away win. As it was a race point, and possibly a match point, were lost when Coombes had engine failure in heat 11 when only two riders finished. There were other 'what if' moments, but they don't win meetings.

Without Bill McMillan, the Tigers added Chris Blewett at reserve and travelled to Poole on 22 July. He fell in his only ride and did not score. Riding at number 1, Ridgeon failed to score as did Ovenden and Coombes picked up a single point. The Tigers best two, Monk with a maximum 15 and Mattingley on 12+1, won eight of the heats. Redmond fell first time out before gathering 7+1. In theory it was possible the Tigers might have won with three scorers, but it did not happen. The Pirates were no pushover on their own strip and a 43–35 defeat at Wimborne Road was a respectable showing.

Monk used his visit to Poole to meet with Barry Briggs in an attempt to sort out some riding problems. The upshot was that Barry said that it should be Monk meeting him at Swindon to help him out.

Friday 24 July took the Tigers to Hackney for their first match in London since visiting Walthamstow in the early 1950s. They found the Hawks strong opponents. The home side steadily pulled ahead and the match ended 49–29 in their favour. As usual, Monk was the top Tiger, but he could not best Colin Pratt or Roy Trigg and only won one race. Fellow heat leaders Mattingley and Redmond, who fell in heat nine, were pinned back to seven points each. and the remaining four contributed four points between them. Terry Stone came back to help the Tigers turn out a seven-man team, but only scored three points.

The second half saw Rosita Mattingley race Mary Mansfield, but the Hackney lady won the race.

The Tigers turned the tables on Hawks a week later in Glasgow on 31 July. The scores were close until the last heat when a 5–1 for the Tigers made the score 42–36. It was a close match with the lead changing hands early on. Neither team could use a tactical substitute. Monk, Mattingley and Redmond all scored 10 with Monk picking up a bonus point. The margin might have been bigger had not Coombes lost a chain when leading heat eight. The Tigers, with McMillan and Hanlon back and without Vic Ridgeon, were well served by their heat leaders and again were a bit short on second string and reserve power.

August

In 1964 the Provincial League had its own Riders' Championship. The Glasgow qualifying round was staged on 7 August and produced a shock winner in Trevor Redmond, with 14 points. He was beaten only by Monk. Unfortunately for Monk, his bike let him down in heat 10 and he had to be content with 12 points. The Monarchs duo of George Hunter, who loaned Monk his bike for his last two outings, with 13 points, and Templeton, on 12, were second and third respectively. Templeton won heat 10 when he and Monk had met. Probably the biggest shock was Mattingley's duck, not a good showing against a field he should have been well capable of beating. The reason was a new frame, of his own making, which was a bit of a handful.

Sparks flew at Edinburgh round of the Provincial League Riders' Championship Qualifying Round the next night. There was a coming together of Monk and Doug Templeton as they clashed on a bend. Templeton had to be restrained and someone took things into their own hands, pulling Monk off his bike. The upshot was that Monk was excluded, Templeton won the rerun and things blew over.

At long last the injured Tiger, Chris Julian, was back in the saddle. He returned for the away fixture at Middlesbrough on 13 August and returned a creditable 3+1. It was another match in which the Tigers ran the home team close before letting it slip away. A 5–1 to win the match in heat 13 was maybe a tall order, but as it was Dave Younghusband and Bluey Scott took a 4–2 over Redmond and Ovenden to give the match to the Bears 41–37. Monk scored an immaculate 15-point maximum with Mattingley and Redmond on 7+1 each. The rest didn't deliver enough.

About this time Bruce Ovenden admitted his interest in flying and how it was an approach to photographer Alf Weedon that had pointed the way to his joining Glasgow.

The Glasgow fans must have been pleased that their men fought back from level pegging at the end of heat seven to put one over their rivals Edinburgh Monarchs 52–43 in the first leg of the Scottish Cup on 14 August. While the Monarchs' best outscored the Tigers' best, the rest of the Tigers put in a big effort to knock the crown off their peers. Monk lost three times to George Hunter, including a rare home fall in heat 13, for his 10 points. Mattingley returned to form with 12 including a win over Hunter and defeats by the Templeton brothers Doug (twice) and Willie (once). Promoter Redmond added 11+1.

Bert Harkins, a native Glaswegian, had bike problems all night and scored just one point. The big question was would this be enough to take the silverware?

The cup tie drama unfolded at Old Meadowbank the following night, 15 August. It was another nip and tuck match and after 15 heats it looked as though Monarchs had the cup in their hands, leading by a comfortable 51–39. It was tense for all as the tapes rose at the start of heat 16, but by the end of the four laps, the Monarchs fans managed a sign of relief as George Hunter had split Mattingley and Monk to get the two points needed to carry the Monarchs over the line by 10 points, 53–43 on the night. They won by one point, 96–95 on aggregate. Trevor Redmond led his team from the front scoring 14, only giving second best to Kevin Torpie, who had one of his best ever Monarchs performances. Mattingley with 13+1 again showed his liking for Edinburgh while Monk added 10. The Tigers' long tail was a telling factor away from home once again, but over 32 heats they did not let anyone down. Monk retained his Scottish Match Race Championship after beating Hunter in a best of three event.

The Tigers fans could set the Cup defeat behind them on 19 August and stand beside their rivals as they came to see Scotland take on England in front of a partisan crowd. With no disrespect to the Anglos, the team was not as star studded as it had been in the past. With three native Scots, the home team put the 'auld enemy' to the sword 73–25. Veteran Jimmy Squibb apart with 12+1, England did not put up much resistance. The home team had a bumper pay night and the natives, all from Fife, gathered over half the total with 40 points. Scotland's best was Charlie Monk, with 18, George Hunter scored 17 and was beaten by Squibb, and Redmond with 8+3. While it could be argued that Scotland was a bit of a hybrid team, the home fans were not bothered as the winning team sported their colours. Scotland probably could have put together a native born team, but it would have been almost Tiger free and poor box office material. England can't really take the moral high ground as they also had a record of using non-native riders over the years in this fixture, notably, Welsh double world champion Freddie Williams.

Back to league business on 28 August, and the visitors were Cradley Heath Heathens led Ivor Brown. It was another close-run meeting which saw the gap never more than six points after heat three. The Heathens narrowed the gap to 2 with two heats to go and might have narrowed it even further had Brown managed to join team mate Eric Hockaday in heat 12. As it was, he was last and heat 13 became a last heat decider. Thankfully for the Tigers, Monk won to complete his maximum and Coombes finished third behind George Major to clinch the match 41–37.

The Tigers should have been out of sight, but Mattingley had a night of machine trouble, including blowing his motor while warming it up in the pits. He contributed a single point using Gordon Mitchell's bike. Redmond scored a reasonable nine points and Julian took seven.

September

The Sheffield namesakes visited White City on 4 September. The home team were solid rather than a mixture of very good and very poor, a description that more aptly befits the visitors. After an opening race fall, Monk wasn't beaten by a visitor for his 8+1. Redmond was the best Tiger with 10, reeling off three wins after an opening race third on the wrong end of a 5–1. Redmond was in danger of being banned from the promotors group because he was riding, but common sense prevailed. He could have argued he was still promoting as his return to the saddle had helped draw in the crowds. He was still actively promoting stock cars at St Austell.

The enigmatic Mattingley that turned up this week scored 9+1. He also opened with a third place behind the ever-improving Julian, who scored 7+1. Glasgow had a poor opening spell, but levelled by heat five and got ahead by heat six. The Mattingley and Monk 5–1 in heat 13 was a final flourish. Glasgow won 44–34

In the second half Monk had another fall. This time he fell in the opening Champion of Champions Match Races with Ivan Mauger who won the tie 2–0. Mattingley lowered Mauger's colours in the second half heat, but the New Zealand star repaid the compliment in the final.

Heavy rain at around six pm ruled out the Scotland versus Rest of the World challenge match on 9 September.

Any Tigers fans wanting to see their team this week had to travel to Newport on 11 September where their team was beaten 48–30 by the Wasps. Once more the Tigers had a long tail and their best rider was Monk with 8+1. Old hands Mattingley and Redmond scored eight points each. The other four riders scored six between them.

The solid Tigers reverted to their former persona and it was a bit of a shock when the league lesser lights Middlesbrough Bears arrived at White City on 18 September and left with the league points. Maybe a final flourish to end their poor season. The Bears did it in some style. They started with a 5–1 and stayed ahead for the whole match.

The Tigers were not in great shape and their woes started with the late arrival of Julian because he missed his scheduled flight north. This kept his contribution down to five from two rides. Ducks from Ovenden, thanks to a blown motor in his opening ride, McMillan and Coombes, with a burnt out clutch, were also a big factor. Mattingley was poor due to bike problems. Effectively a two-man team, Monk on 15 and Redmond 11+1, could do no more than give their best without support.

With Julian missing, Coombes moved up to take his place with Mitchell slotting in at reserve. The referee probably accepted the revised line up and should have stuck to it. However, as he didn't the Tigers managed to use eight men once Julian arrived.

The sequence of events is a bit of a saga. Coombes replaced Julian and took his first two rides, in heats one and four. Monk replaced the by then present Julian taking a tactical ride in heat seven. Mitchell had replaced Coombes at reserve in heat four and also in heat eight where he was paired with Julian who rode in heat eight as a substitute replacing Ovenden. The last change was in heat nine when Redmond replaced McMillan as a substitute

The Bears clinched the match 41–37. They must also have been supportive of allowing the Tigers to use Julian as they were eight points up before the Coombes and Julian swap was made. There is no word of their objecting to this arrangement.

After this result, there must have been few people in either camp at Old Meadowbank on 19 September who would have predicted the Tigers taking a league point from this match. However, the Tigers regrouped and, after a shaky start where they were eight points behind after eight heats, they reeled in the Monarchs to level the scores by heat 12. The Monarchs fans must have been confident of taking heat 13, but Redmond showed his class taking the win from Monarchs icon George Hunter and new signing from a now closed Middlesbrough, Dave Younghusband. Trevor's partner Coombes almost made it an away win, but just failed to beat Younghusband on the line. Monk had competed his maximum in heat 12 and Mattingley scored 8+2, following Monk home in the same heat to draw the Tigers level. The 39–39 draw stunned the Monarchs fans, the author included, and the Tigers deserved their point over an injury weakened Monarchs without skipper Doug Templeton and Wayne Briggs.

After the lows and highs Tigers all but had the wooden spoon but before the season was completed the home fans had a couple of events to watch. On 25 September, the meeting was the Supporters' Trophy Best Pairs. Six pairs battled it out and Chris Julian and Willie Templeton took the trophy with 20 points. Hard on their heels were Dave Younghusband and Bluey Scott with 19 and next were Charlie Monk and Bill McMillan on 15. The Tigers could have probably produced a winning pair but chose to have reasonably fair pairings which is admirable to say the least.

Saturday 26 September saw the big Provincial League event of the year. The Provincial League Riders' Championship was surprisingly staged at National League Belle Vue. Belle Vue argued they were honouring a stadium booking made in 1963, but were then suspended by the Speedway Control Board. Belle Vue then arranged challenge matches with Provincial League teams. However, the National League could not afford to lose Belle Vue, and it became clear as the season finished that peace needed to break out in British speedway.

Anyway, Charlie Monk was the favourite but after an electric start to heat 2 he was overhauled by Bill Andrew and veteran Jimmy Squibb on the first bend and relegated to third. However, he went through the rest of the card unbeaten. Both Monk and Ivan Mauger finished on 13 points. In modern times, Monk would have won it on countback as he beat Mauger in heat 12. As it was, he faced the New Zealander in a run-off. Mauger gated and raced to the flag leaving Monk in his wake to take the runner-up spot.

The Glasgow promotion chose to bring the curtain down with a powerful Rest of the World team as opposition to a Scotland team boosted by Scottish based assets on 30 September. Charlie Monk, for his adopted country, bowed out with 17 points after trading wins with opposing number one Ivan Mauger. The best Scots were George Hunter with 13 and Willie Templeton on nine. The only other Scotland scorer was Trevor Redmond who gathered a Scottish swansong 7+2. At the end of the meeting, he was carried round the track by the Rest of the World team – aboard a stretcher. With the other four in the Scotland team all failing to score, the Rest of the World took a handsome 61–47 victory. They gathered 12 bonus points over 18 heats to Scotland's two, but the Scots had more heat winners. Mattingley missed the meeting because he could not get a flight north and Doug Templeton was out due to injury. Julian crashed out in heat 15 and ended up in the fence on the first bend resulting in a badly gashed thigh.

October

The Scottish Open at Old Meadowbank on 3 October was to be Monk's second runner-up spot. He and George Hunter tied on 14, but the Fifer managed to pip him in the run-off.

The Tigers ended their league season at Cradley Heath on 17 October. Monk signed off with another maximum. Mattingley did well with 9+1 and promoter Redmond hung up his leathers after taking six points. However, the Heathens won 42–36.

The Tigers received the wooden spoon after a roller coaster season. The consistent Charlie Monk became a Tigers hero. The gamble of flying up Maury Mattingley did not work as he did not show the anticipated consistent high scores. Chris Julian's injury disrupted season and long car trips to Glasgow took their toll. Bruce Ovenden showed flashes of his potential without being consistent. Bill McMillan had his moments, but the others brought in then discarded never coped with speedway at this level. Thankfully, the Tigers had Trevor Redmond. He was a big asset on the track; originally, he had only intended to promote and manage. Without his contribution, the Tigers would have been further adrift at the foot of the table. As it was, they finished 12th in the table with six wins and two draws from their 22 league meetings. They were two league points behind Long Eaton.

17. 1965: The British League

At the end of the 1964 season, teams in both leagues realised that a new start was essential for the future of the sport. The Speedway Control Board asked Lord Shawcross to do a report on the state of British Speedway, and by December, it was agreed that there would be one league for the 1965 season.

So, the 1965 campaign saw the Tigers as fully fledged members of the new British League, an amalgamation of the National League and the Provincial League. Sadly, National League Norwich bowed out as the stadium had been sold for redevelopment. Provincial League Middlesbrough had folded as a league venue and in their place, Halifax emerged after 13 seasons of inactivity.

A bright spot on the Scottish horizon was a new track at Cowdenbeath in Fife. It became the most northerly track in the United Kingdom. It staged eight speedway open meetings and a few training sessions before closing. It became a stock car venue.

The teams from the top flight kept a lot of their riders from 1964 with only a handful moving to former Provincial League teams to level up the strength of those teams. The opportunity arose for some European and Commonwealth riders to ride in Britain, although the former top flight teams had a distinct advantage in riding strength.

The other saving grace for the former National League promotions was the variety introduced by the new rivals. This meant that the fans were not seeing the same old teams every few weeks. The benefit for the Provincial League teams was their fans would see the top stars in the sport at least once a season. Rider control emerged in an attempt to level team strengths. In the author's opinion, it did little for the Provincial League teams, but was the start of a process which has, by and large, kept team strengths in check since then.

Glasgow retained Charlie Monk, Maury Mattingley, Bruce Ovenden, who rode part of the season with broken toes, and Graham Coombes. Monk won the prestigious Internationale and missed out, some would say very unfairly, on a World Final place at the last hurdle.

Glasgow signed hotly tipped returnee Monarch Willie Templeton who had been at White City in 1954. Templeton, an expert in throttle control on tricky circuits, had shown up well as a visitor in 1964, but as only on loan. For Bluey Scott the closure of Middlesbrough and his family links, via his wife Anne, to Scotland, made Glasgow a good choice for him.

The Tigers then entered the foreign market and added Norwegian Nils Kristian Paulsen. He had some highs and lows over the year, including a broken collar bone and back problems. Nils, another to ride through the pain barrier with broken toes, literally missed the boat and failed to arrive for the first fixture of the season and at least one other fixture.

It was, on paper, an interesting team and Glasgow must have wondered about bringing back Maury Mattingley after such an up-and-down 1964. He remained an enigma for most of 1965, sometimes brilliant, sometimes unexpectedly poor and sometimes just the victim of rotten luck with engines and oddball injuries.

Overall, the 1965 Tigers were potentially a much better proposition than 1964. Chris Julian, winner of the 1964 *Speedway Star and News* Mr Courage award, did not return and, winner of the Mr Veteran award Trevor Redmond, now a sweet shop owner, retired from riding for good.

March

With practices starting in March, Charlie Monk was among the first back and he had a mid-March Sunday morning spin at a very wet Ipswich.

April

The Tigers first venture into the British League came on 2 April as they faced Hackney at White City. Chris Julian rode as a guest for Paulsen and the Tigers ripped the Hawks to bits. They won 59–19 on a heavy track. The score could have been wider had Julian and Monk completed all their races. Such was the home supremacy they had no third places and only three ducks.

Bluey Scott took the only full maximum with Templeton and Mattingley both on paid maximums. Mattingley was un-fazed by a type of track he didn't like. Julian, Monk and Ovenden were all paid for nine points and Coombes, 4+2, was unbeaten by a Hawk. The meeting was filmed by Scottish Television (STV) and screened the next day.

A rain-soaked White City saw the fixture against Halifax on 9 April rained off. It had been anticipated as the acid test for the 1965 Tigers. The weather did not affect Tigers' financially as it was reported they had insurance protection.

The Tigers had to wait until 16 April for their first test against former National League opposition, Coventry Bees. The 56–22 Tigers win was not expected. They raced to an 18 points lead in the first five heats. Over the next eight heats, the gap was opened up to 34. The Bees had little answer and held Glasgow in only three heats. Monk scored his first full maximum of the season, while Mattingley scored his second paid maximum. Templeton and Scott dropped points, but still returned 9+1. New Norwegian Nils Paulsen chipped in 4+2 in a steady debut. Monk won the second half. His prize was a giant chocolate Easter Egg which was presented to the Glasgow children's hospital.

In heat nine, Nigel Boocock chased Monk to set a new track record time of 76.4. For the rest of the Bees, it was a night to forget.

The following night, the high-flying Tigers travelled to Edinburgh and set about demolishing the Monarchs. The home riders were reeling as the Tigers opened up a 12 point lead by heat six. A couple of Monarchs' heat wins in the last three heats brought the deficit back a more respectable six points, but it certainly showed that Tigers meant business in the new league. In reality, Glasgow had the match won by heat 11.

Both Monk and Willie Templeton scored 11. Monk added the Old Meadowbank track record to his CV. Scott added eight. The 42–36 result does not mark the Tigers' superiority in this match.

Sheffield must have steeled themselves for the visit of their fellow Tigers on 22 April given Glasgow's results so far. The visitors came back to earth as the Owlerton riders gradually overcame them. After 13 heats they had secured a 42–36 win. Again, Monk and Templeton who led the charge with 10 each while Mattingley added a respectable eight. The rest of Glasgow's Tigers were relatively poor with two failing to score. The Tigers used three tactical changes, but they had little effect.

If the Monarchs thought they could exact revenge at White City on 23 April, they were wrong. After holding their own for seven heats, the Tigers moved up a gear and won 48–30. Monk gathered a maximum while Willie Templeton remained on the pace with 10. Nils Paulsen showed he was getting the hang of White City with a maiden race win in his 7+2.

So, with the famous former National League Wimbledon Dons as visitors, the Tigers must have been reasonably confident of another win even without Mattingley who only had a standby ticket to get him north. Bill McMillan came in and Coombes moved up to the number one race jacket, so the Tigers were marginally weaker. As it turned out on 30 April, Templeton scored a reasonable eight. However, a duck from Coombes, caused by bike problems, and only 2+1 for McMillan didn't help. An exclusion for Monk in heat five after a fall was another loss of points when he really needed to score. A looping at the gate fall for Scott in heat 12 ended his maximum hopes. This allowed Dons to nose ahead. With the Dons' best rider, Trevor Hedge in heat 13 alarm bells must have been ringing and the Dons' 4–2 allowed them to clinch the match 41–37 and take the league points south.

May

The famous Belle Vue Hyde Road track was the venue for Tigers' third crack at former National League opposition on 1 May. The legendry home of the Aces was normally a banker for a home win. It must have been a shock when the Tigers took the lead in the opening heat and then kept daylight between them and the Aces for the rest of the 12 heats.

Once again, Monk was unbeaten by a home rider with a paid maximum. He and Mattingley combined for a 5–1 in heat 12 over former Tiger Gordon McGregor to secure the win. A final heat 4–2 to the Aces made the final score 42–36. Scott continued to show he was a good signing by the Tigers with 10 points.

The Tigers were back home on 7 May for the visit of Exeter Falcons, who included former National League rider Colin Gooddy. Used to their big banked fast track, the White City track was probably tough for the Falcons. As it was, Monk again notched another home maximum. Paulsen won both his two reserve rides. Monk had good backing from Scott who was paid for the lot. The Tigers onslaught on yet another rain-soaked track was almost relentless with 10 heat winning margins and all the race winners. The Tigers won 54–24.

The next night, the Tigers were in Coventry and went down 51–26. They were lucky as normally reliable Jim Lightfoot fell, interrupting his winning run. Only Scott, with nine points, took a bit of a fight to the home team. Monk, with five points, had his worst ever showing for the Tigers on the very wet Brandon track. Bill McMillan, replacing Paulsen who was in Norway on World Championship business, scored a couple and it is doubtful if Paulsen would have done much better. Coombes managed to break bike forks in heat five and Templeton's clutch countershaft broke as he rode round to the tapes in heat one. These were not common bike problems.

On 12 May, Monk was at Poole facing Barry Briggs for the Golden Helmet. This was big honour for him. He won the tie 2–0 but wasn't happy it had been more or less a walk over as Briggs had trouble with two ESOs and a JAP. He had his bikes sorted by the second half and cleaned up, beating Monk in the second half final. The second leg was at Sheffield on 13 May. This time Briggs won 2–0 with very fast times.

The fixture planners had given Glasgow a hard run of former National League teams and next up on 14 May were the Swindon Robins. Against a trio of great heat leaders, Briggs, Mike Broadbank and Martin Ashby, the Tigers were up against it. However, the Robins tail didn't quite deliver and a last heat 4–2 from Monk and Mattingley over Broadbank and Bob Kilby gave the Tigers a 40–38 win. Monk's win saw him completing another White City maximum while it was Mattingley's only point after a bout of bike trouble. Scott and Templeton again provided the steam for the boiler with nine and eight respectively.

Briggs, the 1964 world champion, dominated everyone except Monk, who equalled the track record to beat Briggs in heat nine. Briggs's 5–1s with Mike Broadbank and Martin Ashby in heats 11 and 12 levelled the match for the Robins. The Tigers' fans must have breathed a sigh of relief after this win and had smiles as wide as the Clyde.

The British Match Race Championship to give the Golden Helmet its official name was decided at West Ham on 18 May. In heat one, Briggs gated and pulled ahead. His bike started to stutter and Monk caught him. However, a big handful of throttle saw Briggs go over the line just ahead. In race two, Monk gated but Briggs passed him after a lap and made it to the flag to win 2–0 and retain the Gold Helmet. The two met in the second half final with Ken McKinlay and the race was a cracker with Monk winning from the back, passing McKinlay on the outside.

A week after the Swindon match and yet again the visitors were a former National League side. This time they were London east enders West Ham, led by former Tigers favourite Ken McKinlay. He stalled at the gate in his first ride. He then lost to Monk in his next before showing the Australian the way round in heat 13. Monk still managed 11 points and had his best support from Templeton, on 10 and Scott with nine.

The Tigers opened up a 16 point lead by heat seven, widened it to 20 at one point then settled for a great 46–32 win. While they did not know it the time, the Tigers had just beaten the team that would go on to win the League, Knock-Out Cup and London Cup. True legends of London speedway.

Buoyed by their big win over the Hammers, the Tigers set off for Halifax the next day. It went to the wire. In the penultimate heat, the Tigers levelled the scores. Then in heat 13, they took a 3–3 to secure a 39–39 match draw. This was thanks to Scott winning that heat. Scott, Mattingley and Monk all posted a return of nine, but Mattingley had five rides and secured a bonus point. Monk fell in heat seven and, but for that, the Tigers may have won. He was booed for a hard move on Bryan Elliott, but the referee ordered an all four back rerun. The rest of the Tigers gave their all, taking points from the Halifax second strings and reserves. Another remarkable away trip given the fast, very highly banked, Shay was not a favourite of many visiting riders.

The next match for the Tigers was against a poor Long Eaton team on 28 May. Without star Ray Wilson, the Archers withered under the Tigers onslaught and slumped to a 60–18 defeat. Without Mattingley, the Tigers had Monk, Templeton and Scott on full maximums and both Ovenden and Coombes took maiden paid maximums. Only Paulsen and McMillan dropped points, saving the Archers from a whitewash. The Tigers' second halfer Red Monteith took the reserve role for the Archers, but failed to score.

June

With former Archers in their ranks in Monk and Scott, the Tigers must have hoped for a win on 1 June. The march was described as the most exciting to date at Station Road. However, the Tigers did not factor in Terry Betts in the home pits. The new signing was a former Norwich rider who was making his debut, replacing the injured Ray Wilson, and displacing short term stand in and one-time favourite Eric Minall.

Glasgow Tigers 1965: Bluey Scott, Charlie Monk, Nils Paulsen, Trevor Redmond, Bruce Ovenden, Willie Templeton, Graham Coombes and Maury Mattingley (on bike).

Left: Nils Paulsen. Right: Former Motherwell star Bluey Scott.

Charlie Monk just ahead of Swindon's Barry Briggs in a Golden Helmet match race.

Charlie Monk with Alan Foster after winning the 1965 Internationale at Wimbledon.
The shiny new bike was the main prize.

Left: Willie Templeton – another stalwart of Scottish speedway.
Right: Maury Mattingley – a key rider for Glasgow in the 1960s.

Monk found Betts and Ray Cresp a handful and settled for 10. Scott excelled with 11+2, only giving second best to Cresp. Templeton added eight, but with Mattingley still absent the other Tigers struggled and they lost 41–37. They had been level after heat seven, but once behind could not close the gap.

The Scotland versus England test match, the third in the series, on 2 June saw Scotland with the only adopted Scot being Monk in their team take on a strong England line-up, all of whom had visited White City earlier in the season. Ken McKinlay skippered the Scots and set the tone with an inspirational 18 point maximum. He was well backed by Monk and George Hunter on 17, which gave the Scots a big platform for their 62–46 win over 'The Auld Enemy'. The Templeton bothers struggled, as did another one-time Tiger, Gordon McGregor. Despite the Scots' dominance of the chequered flag, three English riders took double figure scores.

Back to league business the next night, the Tigers were in Oxford to face the Cheetahs. The home team had taken the 1964 NL by storm after years of being the league's also-rans.

The 1964 promotors had changed the Cheetahs overnight. Most of their team stayed and were formidable opponents. No surprise then that the home team won 48–30 due to a superb show by their heat leaders.

For the Tigers, only Monk gathered double figures with 10 but unusually did not win a race. Paulsen scored six, but the rest, including returnee Mattingley, struggled.

Despite claims it was hard to find, all the Tigers turned up at Cradley's track in Dudley Wood near Birmingham on 5 June. The Tigers did reasonably well, but lost 43–35. Their cause wasn't helped by an unusually poor show by Scott and a disqualification for Monk in his last ride for a contentious overtake. Monk scored 10 and his next best support was from Templeton and Paulsen on seven each.

Former Tiger Chris Julian faced his old team, but did not perform well. Apart from a slip that allowed the Tigers within two points after a 5–1 in heat nine, the Heathens edged ahead and had won before the start of heat 13.

The fixture planners sent the Tigers to faraway Exeter on 7 June. Even more unusual was the start time – 11am, but it was a regular Exeter bank holiday Monday start. Yet again, Scott had a poor meeting, as did most of his team mates. The Tigers slumped to a 46–32 defeat on the intimidating County Ground track. However, it did not phase Monk who only dropped a point to Colin Gooddy on his way to 14 points. Scott improved as the meeting progressed. He started with a fall, then a last, followed by third then a second place.

The same evening, the 7.30pm start time was reserved for the big FIM Internationale meeting at Wimbledon. The strong line-up included Barry Briggs, Ove Fundin, Gote Nordin, Sverre Harrfeldt and Bjorn Knutson, but the trophy was won by Charlie Monk. He was beaten by Nordin and Briggs, but won his other three heats to gather 13 points, two ahead of Nordin and Knutson.

This result was probably the career pinnacle for Monk and acknowledged by him at the time. Some detractors said it was a lucky win. The prize was worth winning, a brand new speedway bike paid for by cigarette giants of the day and sponsors WD & HO Wills.

Back in Glasgow, the Tigers faced Oxford, who arrived without a manager on 11 June. Yet again Monk was top Tiger with 11. He only had real support from Templeton with nine points. Without Mattingley, Ovenden again moved to number one and Bill McMillan returned at reserve. The Tigers never built a lead and the Cheetahs got ahead in heat 11 and held on to win 40–38.

The meeting had its fair share of controversy, starting in heat two when Scott fell pursuing Arne Pander and Paulsen laid down. The race was stopped and a rerun was intimated. The Cheetahs septet refused to take part in the rerun and after 20 minutes referee Taylor declared the heat void and moved on to heats three and four. Oxford then agreed to a rerun, but Paulsen's win did not give Cheetahs an advantage.

In heat six, Paulsen followed Gooch home, but he broke his footrest which caused him to fall after the race as he reached the pit gates. He was taken to hospital. In heat seven, a 3–3 position was lost when Ovenden's engine blew. This left him out of things for the night with nothing to ride. The Tigers decided to replace Ovenden in heat 8 with their reserve, Coombes, but the 'barrack room lawyers' in the Cheetahs ranks argued that he could only replace an injured rider and the referee agreed, ruling the Kiwi out.

The meeting came to an unhappy conclusion for the Tigers. Trevor Redmond was unhappy with the Oxford riders for employing delaying tactics and threatening to pull out of the meeting at one stage.

World Championship business returned to White City for the first time since the 1950s the next week and Monk topped the charts with a flawless 15 points maximum. Next best was bang back on form Bluey Scott with 14 who only ran a second to Charlie in his last ride. The third man was Ivan Mauger who only managed 12, after being beaten by Monk, Scott and Coventry's Jim Lightfoot. The other Tigers in the field, Mattingley, Templeton and McMillan scored two, five and two respectively. They did not progress beyond this round, unlike their team mates.

On 19 June, Monk cleaned up the Cradley Heath Round but he nearly didn't. Somehow his leathers had fallen out his car and were handed in at White City. Trevor Redmond recognised them by a patch in the seat and managed to contact Monk before he left for the

Midlands. After a trip to London by plane with Redmond and run up to Cradley Heath by Eric Hockaday, the leathers and owner were reunited.

It was back to league action on 25 June with a visit from the Poole Pirates. The Tigers produced the goods. Monk scored a full maximum and his team mates give a solid display to back him up. Nils Paulsen, despite his injury the week before, had another good night with eight. He bravely rode with his broken toes strapped up. Mattingley and Templeton added 7+1 and 7+2 respectively. After an opening shared heat, the Tigers widened the gap over most of the match and won 49–29.

The Tigers fans had a view of a possible new Monarch, Austrian Alfred Sitzwohl who had somewhat unfairly been hyped by Halifax. His last place behind the regular second halfers Monteith, Hicks and Leo Ramm did not bode well. His stay in Scotland was brief.

July

The Knock Out Cup draw was kind to Glasgow as they faced Sheffield at White City on 2 July. Monk and Mattingley were joint top scorers on 14 points. Both riders dropped a point to Jack Kitchen and Monk repaid the complement twice. With Scott on 10+4 the win was never in doubt. All the home Tigers struck form and the early season performance levels were returning. Coombes fell in heat eight and remounted to repass Sheffield's Bob Paulson. The Glasgow Tigers progressed to the next round with a clear 64–32 win over 16 heats.

A week later, the Tigers continued where they had left off with another solid showing, this time against Cradley Heath who were without their star riders Ivor Brown and George Major. Monk, riding with a wrist injury, scored another maximum. But for an opening race second in heat two, Nils Paulsen would have had his maiden maximum; his 11 points equalled his previous best showing. Scott and Templeton added eight apiece. The Tigers won 11 of the 13 heats, and took the match 53–25. Concerns were being expressed about the home big wins, but it would not be the margin rather the way opposition folded that was a concern.

Around five miles separated Cradley's Dudley Wood from Wolverhampton's Monmore Green, but the Wolves were much better than Heathens when they visited White City on 15 July. At last, Nils Paulsen recorded a first paid maximum. Monk didn't finish heat three, but then gathered nine from three wins. Scott and Templeton added eight apiece. Mattingley failed to score in four rides. The final score, 43–34 to the Tigers, was the best from a visiting team since Oxford's win on 11 June. Bob Andrews retained the Silver Sash, defeating Nils Paulsen in the match race.

A trip to Newcastle held no fears for Monk on 19 July. He followed Diamonds star Ivan Mauger home twice, but spoilt the Kiwi's maximum in heat 12. Monk totalled 13 but, Paulsen apart on eight, the rest of the Tigers were outshone by the Brough Park men on a rough and deep circuit. With Ovenden out, McMillan, who was known to be unhappy with the way Glasgow were using him, had another outing but he and Mattingley failed to score. Coombes wasn't helped by a heat one fall which curtailed his contribution to a single point. The solid scoring home team never lost a heat advantage, but seven heats were drawn. Despite this, the Diamonds won 48–30.

With no home match due to the local holidays, the Tigers headed south on 23 July to face Hackney. Unfortunately, rain prevented any racing.

All was not lost as the Tigers team moved north the next day to face a team representing King's Lynn at the recently launched open licence venue at Saddlebow Road. The new Stars were from a mixture of tracks and combined well to beat the Tigers who were losing situation after 11 heats. Two 5–1s made the score look a respectable 40–38 in this challenge match. The track was very wet and with nothing really at stake it would have been daft to risk injuries. The Tigers' fans could be pleased that Monk scored a maximum, Scott scored 10 points and Templeton seven.

World Championship aspirations were achieved and lost on 30 July at White City. The Tigers fans saw their idol, Charlie Monk, progress to the next round in this British Semi Final with a flawless maximum 15. Eric Boocock on 14 took second and Brian Brett with 13 were also on the podium. Ivan Mauger had to settle for number four on 11 points, with a single race win. The Tigers' only other competitor at this stage, Bluey Scott, was eliminated after a poor show at Poole. Monk's victory was by no means plain sailing – he missed the gate in every race and had to come from the back.

August

A week later, Ivan Mauger was back with his Newcastle Diamonds facing the Tigers at a flooded White City. He and Monk finished honours even on 11 points each. Nils Paulsen was again in fine form with another great 11 points return. The rest of the Tigers did enough to take the points with a 42–36 win. Surprisingly, experienced grass-tracker Templeton did not manage more than two – wet tracks often favoured riders with grasstrack experience. Ovenden was back, but only managed four points.

The Diamonds had the best of it until heat eight when the Tigers levelled the scores. After a 4–2 to each team over the next two heats, the Tigers moved up a notch to press home their advantage.

Ivan Mauger finished his night with a second half defeat by debutant Bernie Lagrosse. He never did it again and went home at the end of the season, reinventing himself as Roy Williams at Berwick in 1968.

In the third round of the Knock Out Cup, the Tigers set superstition aside on Friday 13 August and just beat a determined Swindon Robins team. Without Ovenden, a victim of a car breakdown on the way north, Tigers gave Jack Monteith a rare team outing and his four points did not let them down.

Monk led the line with superb 15 points maximum and Scott came back to form with 11. Without his uncle Willie Templeton, suffering from flu, in the team, Bill McMillan made a telling 6+3 contribution. Monk beat Barry Briggs to secure the points needed in the last heat to take the tie 49–46. To add to the Tigers' woes however, Paulsen broke his collarbone and Mattingley blew an engine in his opening ride.

The Robins headed the Tigers up to heat eight, then, as before, the Tigers got ahead and stayed there to the end. Swindon's top end fire power wasn't given enough backing and the Robins tumbled out the competition. The Glasgow fans had an extra treat as the promotion staged the opening leg of the Golden Helmet, featuring Briggs and Nigel Boocock, before the match. Briggs won the tie 2–1.

On 17 August the Tigers visited London's cockney east end. West Ham hosted the Tigers at the Customs House Stadium, not very far from a pioneer motorcycle racing oval at Canning Town. West Ham, as expected, picked up the league points with a 47–30 victory.

After running second behind Monk in his opening ride before racing to 11 points, Sverre Harrfeldt was the top Hammer. Mattingley had a sadly rare good night for Glasgow, with 10 points. This gave Monk his only meaningful support because the rest struggled on the fast, sweeping track. The Tigers gave a league debut to New Zealander Bernie Lagrosse at reserve as they had to cover for the injured Paulsen and unwell Templeton, but he failed to score.

Sverre had solid backing from Norman Hunter and Malcolm Simmons both on 9+1. Ken McKinlay had bike problems pegging back his score.

The Tigers headed further south the next night, to Poole on the English Channel coast. The home side won 49–26. Monk accounted for all the home riders except Bill Andrew in his 14 points. He and Andrew traded wins. None of the rest of the Tigers, again without Paulsen and Templeton made a noteworthy contribution. Bike problems were another big factor in their demise – faulty motors meant gift 5–0 scores in heats five and 13. In the opening heat, falls saw it finish 3–2 to the Pirates.

Back home, the Tigers faced Edinburgh Monarchs in the Scottish Cup on a wet 20 August. Scott returned to form with 12+1, Monk managed 11 taking second in one race and falling in another. Mattingley was paid for 11, showing he knew the importance of the fixture to the Tigers fans. Coombes and McMillian also did well, but Willie Templeton had a night to forget, failing to score because he returned too early from his bout of flu. The big question was the reasonably comfortable 55–41 win big enough for the return leg to achieve an aggregate victory. This would be answered 24 hours later.

The Tigers, without still recuperating Willie Templeton, travelled east the next day to find out. It was a nail biter for both sets of fans and it looked as if the Scottish Cup would have blue and gold ribbons by heat 12. The Tigers reduced the deficit to 13 in heat 13. Monarchs restored their lead to 17 in the next heat. The Tigers duo of Coombes and Scott cut it back to 13 points in heat 15.

The stage was set for a last race aggregate decider of 32 heats in the cup

Hunter took the flag, but with Monk, completing a haul of 11 – which could have been more but for a fall – and Mattingley finishing third for his 7+1 contribution, the 3–3 was enough to produce the red and white ribbons. Poor old Kevin Torpie, who had done well up to heat 16, could not grab a point and Tigers won 96–95 on aggregate.

The teams were pretty even and the Monarchs fans did have the consolation of a 54–41 win on the night. So, the Tigers' tenacity showed that they were up for the Cup and Edinburgh Festival fireworks over Edinburgh Castle were, effectively, a salute to the Tigers.

The euphoria of the Cup win boosted the Tigers' confidence. The following Friday, they beat Newport Wasps 43–35. Monk was back on the maximum trail. Coombes was growing in stature and scored 9+1. Scott and Ovenden both added seven points. Mattingley was off the boil again, but this can be attributed to an eye injury caused by him being hit by a piece of flying shale. Templeton still had not returned to action, and Red Monteith had a couple of rides, scoring two. Bill McMillan replaced Paulsen, and scored three points.

The next day, the Tigers were in Wiltshire facing Swindon Robins at Blunsdon. The top Tiger was Monk with 10+1 and Scott contributed seven points. Without Mattingley, whooping cough sufferer Templeton, and Paulsen they used McMillan, Lagrosse and Joe Hicks without much effect, even though all three and Ovendon gave their all. The Robins won 54–24.

The riders had a day off on the Sunday and then went into Wales to face Newport at Somerton Park. The Wasps exacted revenge on 30 August with a 50–28 win. Monk stood between the Tigers and slaughter with 13 points. The same supporting cast as at Swindon struggled again, not surprisingly on a track which was known to be difficult to master. Scott crashed and broke a toe, adding to the Tigers' problems.

Strongly tipped to make his World Final debut, Charlie Monk arrived at West Ham for the rearranged British Final on 31 August. It had been postponed from 24 August because of torrential rain. He was carrying the hopes of the Tigers' management and fans. The start was delayed for the nearly 20,000 strong crowd by the riders seeking additional payment. The top six would qualify for the World Final at Wembley. Rain staring to fall after heat two, which was won by Monk with Briggs third. Monk gathered a two second places in his next two rides, then a third. This gave him eight going into his last ride. An 'alleged' tangle with Ken McKinlay resulted in an exclusion and the irony that Ken and rerun heat winner Jimmy Gooch scored enough to make the Final at Wembley. Monk ended up one point adrift of last qualifier Mike Broadbank who was on nine.

It was no comfort to Monk that many were critical of the referee, especially when footage of the race seemed to support the critics. However, to be fair to the referee he had no access to the footage on the night and called it the way he saw it. Trevor Redmond hoped to use the BBC footage to support his appeal to the Speedway Control Board that the race should be rerun at West Ham. The *1966 British Speedway Handbook* said that "... it was only the decision of the [British Speedway] Promoters Association that prevented the RAC from completely rerunning heat 20 at West Ham only four days before the World Final – a rerun that could have affected the chances of qualifiers McKinlay and Gooch. The promoters made it clear that such a rerun would not be in the best interests of speedway."

Charlie Monk never did ride in a World Championship final, but did ride later in the season for Great Britain in the World Team Cup final.

September

As the season moved into its penultimate month, it was clear the team's bright start had tarnished. On 3 September the Belle Vue Aces came without really challenging the Tigers as they had done with Glasgow teams in the past. Mattingley returned to good form. He contributed 10 points, one less that Monk. Coombes again was third best on nine. The Tigers missed Paulsen. He was fit, but beset by travel problems and stuck in Norway. Templeton was back and 'eased' himself in as Monk's partner, scoring two points. The Tigers won comfortably 46–32. The Belle Vue team included former Tiger Gordon McGregor.

The strange fixture schedule saw the Tigers at Wimbledon on 4 September. Originally, Monk was due to have been practicing for an international event abroad on the day after, but what would the Tigers have done without him? He rode at Wimbledon and his 13 points ensured the Tigers were not almost whitewashed. Mattingley added seven points from five starts. The rest did not make a meaningful contribution as the Dons had the league points in the bag by heat 11. They won 49–29. It was another away trip for Tigers to forget, apart from McMillan's win a second half handicap event.

The next day, Monk was honoured with a place in the Great Britain World Team Cup quintet. He only scored one point as his team finished third behind Poland and Sweden and ahead of Russia.

At long last Nils Paulsen was back. He was in the team to face West Ham on 10 September as the Tigers entered their third home Knock Out Cup encounter on another wet evening in Glasgow. It was a close meeting with the Hammers drawing away over the last two heats. It is unusual for the home team to win only four of the 16 heats. The east London side had 12 race winners in their 50–43 victory. The Tigers had nine bonus points to the Hammers' four. Monk scored 12 with Scott on eight and – rising at reserve Templeton – who beat Ovenden in a pre-match race to secure his spot, added seven. Six had come from his two programmed rides.

He had a blown motor, then came out in heat 13 on McMillan's bike. In this heat Mattingley again had bike problems thanks to a malfunctioning magneto and his replacement, Templeton ended up third on a slowing bike. Paulsen, who had partnered Templeton, fell. Four points behind, the Tigers levelled again at the end of heat 14. Heat 15 saw four exclusions. Malcolm Simmons broke the tapes. In the rerun Paulsen fell and was excluded as was Tony Clarke who wasn't under power when the red lights came on. Coombes then faced Harrfeldt in another rerun. His bike had problems and gave up, but he gallantly tried to restart it, only to be excluded when he was lapped. There were cries for Harrfeldt to be excluded for using two hands to remove his goggles, presumably deemed not to be trying to race, but he finished and was awarded the win.

West Ham were led by former Glasgow Tiger and now veteran Scot Ken McKinlay on 14. He was still a class act and was supported by Sverre Harrfeldt and Norman Hunter. The visitors' top three were involved in the last two heats grabbing all the vital points, McKinlay and Hunter took a 5–1 in heat 16.

The weatherman made it no contest of the Tigers, Sheffield and Glasgow, on 17 September as he reported rain in Glasgow that night. For the record Trevor Redmond held off the decision to 6.30pm.

A week later, the meeting against Halifax got to heat eight before the weather saw contest over with the Tigers 31–17 ahead. The meeting came to an end in heat nine when Monk slid off and into the fence. It was abandoned before any rerun was staged.

October

The weather interfered again on 1 October. The meeting between the Tigers and an Edinburgh and Newcastle Select never started.

It was a drier night on 7 October as White City hosted the Glasgow Open Championship. The promotion pushed the boat out, maybe because of the previous three weeks, and Barry Briggs raced to a 15-point maximum. Sverre Harrfeldt eclipsed third man Olle Nygren, also on 13, in heat 20. Ivan Mauger, another potential winner scored 12 while Ken McKinlay was next on 11. Charlie Monk was missing, unhappy with the promoters because he was not on his way home to Australia. In his absence, the best Tigers were Bluey Scott and Coombes with eight points. The second and third places and top Tiger award were decided in the same heat with Harrfeldt beating Nygren and Scott beating Coombes for the top Tiger spot.

The Tigers' last trip to London for 1965 was on 8 October to Hackney. The Hawks widened the gap in almost all heats and won 54–24 win. Monk top scored with nine. Paulsen was next on 5 and Mattingley returned 4+1. The rest of the line-up did not score well. Monk had a chance to regain the Silver Sash but lost to Colin Pratt,

The Halifax Dukes returned to White City on the slightly drier night of 14 October. They almost immediately stamped their authority on the match on another wet, heavy, track. Without Paulsen, injured at Hackney, the Tigers gave Hicks another outing, but he and the normally reliable Coombes, along with McMillan all had stinkers on the wet track. To be fair to Coombes, he fell in his opening ride, had broken the frame of his bike and sat out the rest of the meeting. Three tactical substitute rides produced little and Monk again headed the Tigers' score chart with 13. Against old team mates at Middlesbrough, Scott rode well for 10+1 but the next best was Templeton on 6+3.

The final score this time was 44–33 to Halifax. In the original staging, the Tigers were winning 31–17 when the match was called off.

Glasgow's away swansong for 1965 was at Wolverhampton on 15 October and the Tigers gave an outing to Trevor Chamberlain who failed to score. Monk was the visitors' sole race winner with 10 points, but his fellow Tigers were very poor as they lost 56–21. None of the other six riders scored more than three points.

The British League Riders' Championship was staged at Belle Vue on 16 October. Glasgow had a winner! It was not Charlie Monk, rather it was Mae Marr became the 1965 Speedway Queen. Monk had a poor for him night and only gathered nine points and finished sixth.

The curtain on 1965 was brought down on 22 October and Sheffield blighted the end of season event by winning 41–37. Scott scored a paid maximum and Monk returned 11. Templeton signed off with seven. Mattingley, stranded at fog bound London airport, failed to arrive which meant the Tigers could only field one man in two heats.

The Tigers fans, had they delayed their departure, would have witnessed history as Jim McMillan took to White City for the first time in public and completed a few tentative laps.

The Tigers had started the season so well with riders really pulling their weight. As the season wore on, only Monk maintained his consistency and the others scored in fits and starts. Key rider Paulsen missed a big chunk of the season, others were missing for short spells and the team never had a settled septet. The Tigers used their second half riders, but they were often just making up numbers.

The icing on a pretty poor cake was Charlie Monk and the Scottish Cup win so it wasn't all doom and gloom. Harry Houston of the *Evening* Citizen, wrote in the *1966 British Speedway Handbook:* "...Bu the end of April, [the] Tigers ... were sitting at the top of the British League ... midway through the season ... injuries to top stars and a really dreadful away record in which they only succeeded in winning only two matches ... lost them their position at the top of the league." However, he did conclude that it was a "satisfying season for the Glasgow fans."

Glasgow finished 13th out of 18 teams in the British League. They had 31 league points from their 34 matches.

Two other stories for 1965 are: Charlie Monk was lucky to be alive. He had been scheduled to fly to London on a plane on 27 October but missed it because he did not have a confirmation of booking. The plane crash landed on the fog shrouded Heathrow runway and all occupants of it were killed.

Also, Monk was voted the 12th best rider in the World by a panel of experts from the six main speedway countries.

18. 1966: Scottish Cup triumph

Glasgow made few changes for 1966 from the stuttering 1965 outfit. The British League added King's Lynn to its ranks, making it a 19-team league. There was also the Knock Out Cup, and various regional competitions including the Scottish Cup. Hopes that gaps in teams would be filled by Swedish riders were generally stopped by the Speedway Riders' Association (SRA), but a few did ride. Guests were allowed to cover missing riders and they would become a regular feature.

Although it looked like Bengt Brannefors or Runo Wedin were earmarked for Glasgow, neither came north to the Tigers. However, Bengt Jansson joined Edinburgh.

Nils Paulsen retired and stayed in Norway. Another loss was Bruce Ovenden, who got married and stayed in New Zealand. Rider control, introduced in 1965, did nothing for the Tigers and the other powers that be both home and abroad did little to help either. Trevor Redmond just got on with it and it must have been stressful for him and his silent partners. In the end, Glasgow added two riders: tall Kiwi Alf Wells and Bill McMillan became a more permanent team member.

Wells had ridden for Edinburgh without ever hitting the heights. He developed well at White City. The Tigers retained their top star, Charlie Monk, who had wintered in Australia. They also kept Bluey Scott, Maury Mattingley, Willie Templeton and Graham Coombes, but the latter soon returned to parent track Newcastle.

The usual second halfers could be used to plug gaps and guests were used until the Tigers could sign a new rider. The Tigers sounded out Neil Street, but he declined their offer, preferring to seek a track closer to his base in the Midlands.

Tommy Bergqvist, a Swede, appeared for a second half try out, but never returned and then the SRA prevented the signing of another Swede, Bengt Brannefors. Eventually Redmond recruited another Norwegian, Jonny Faafeng, who arrived in May. Jonny had his moments, but never quite managed to replace Paulsen. Later in the season, the Tigers gave opportunities to Jim McMillan who took full advantage to learn his trade.

Monk had a lot of bike problems early on as he tried to convert from JAP to JAWA. After a few months he gave up, reverted to his JAP and started to look like the Monk of old.

The Tigers were involved in several last heat deciders that went the wrong way. Had they capitalised on them with a 5–1, they would have had 11 more league points and finished higher up the table.

April

Had any fan not been at the opening meeting on 1 April, they would have thought pals telling them that Monk had only scored three points were trying an April Fool stunt on them. Sadly, it was true as three bike failures on borrowed equipment cut his score. The first bike seized, the second flew then fizzled out. Thankfully, the rest of the Glasgow Tigers gathered enough to beat Sheffield 42–35, purging the 1965 last night defeat. Templeton and Wells were best on 9+2 and Scott added nine. Glasgow gradually pulled away during the meeting and a 5–1 to Sheffield in heat 13 made the score look more respectable.

After the match, Tommy Bergqvist beat fellow Swede Allan Dahlof in a race which featured Jack Monteith and Jim McMillan who fell. Bergqvist then came second in the second half final. In late April, the Tigers' move for Bergqvist was stopped by the Swedish speedway authorities because he had not ridden in their championships and was not allowed to ride outside Sweden. A local novice, Jimmy Jack, got good reviews about his second half performances, but he never made the grade.

On 8 April, the Tigers laid the West Ham spectre to bed with a narrow 39–38 win. Yet again, Monk had a bad night with five points from two completed rides. He then fell in his third ride. He was knocked out, ruling him out of his last outing. Scott was best on nine and Wells took seven. Once again, the Tigers had a collective steel in their riding. It was Graham Coombes's swansong; he rode as a guest ahead of the anticipated arrival of Bergqvist. Mattingley was the last heat hero, separating first visiting guest Eric Boocock from 1964 Tiger Terry Stone, who beat Coombes for third place

Glasgow were ahead from heat three, but a 4–2 to the visitors in heat 12 put them within three points of the Tigers. The Hammers were kitted out in high visibility gear meant to help them easily pick out team mates. The experimental attire was dropped fairly soon thereafter.

Again without Bergqvist, the Tigers pulled off a narrow hat-trick of wins as they saw off Coventry Bees on a bitterly cold 15 April. They used Doug Templeton as a guest. He rode because the Tigers' next hoped-for recruit, Bengt Brannefors, was not cleared to ride. He was there and watched the meeting, but did not come back. Monk improved; he scored 10 points after losing to Jim Lightfoot twice. Scott was on eight and Willie Templeton took seven. His brother Doug had a poor night and scored a paltry 3.

Snow at Swindon on 16 April and rain in Glasgow 22 April ruled out any action against Cradley Heath. Brannefors arrived, but had no riding permit, so Graham Coombes was ready to take his place.

It was drier in Edinburgh on 23 April, but the Tigers went down 46–31. Scott, who was turned down by Edinburgh twice, in 1950 and 1963, showed them what they missed with 12 points. Monk again had bike troubles and finished with five points from his last two rides. With four former Monarchs in the line-up, it wasn't a memorable return.

Odd refereeing decisions surfaced in heat three. Dudley McKean fell and was excluded. In the rerun, Jansson made a poor start and the race was stopped because it was deemed a false start. In the second rerun, Monk, on Mattingley's bike, had an engine failure leaving both riders without a bike. Sportingly, George Hunter gave Monk his bike and, mounted on it, he beat Jansson in heat 12.

The 'will he, won't he Brannefors saga' rumbled on to an unsatisfactory conclusion. It was later established he was riding in Sweden. In his absence, Red Monteith was drafted into the Tigers team. There were wrangles over the status of both Brannefors and Edinburgh's Swede Runo Wedin. While the UK promoters' association were happy to welcome the Swedes, the SRA were not. This was because a few Swedes planned to return home and the SRA would not allow them to be classed as non-resident. As a result, the temporary licences expired well before the end of April. Neither Brannefors nor Wedin came back.

On 26 April, the Tigers were at West Ham in the vast stadium at Custom House. It was demolished in 1972, and some of the local street names commemorate its past. Both teams used guests, Roy Trigg for Glasgow and Ron Mountford for the Hammers. Trigg was the top Tigers scorer with nine points from three wins. His last race zero in heat 11 let the Hammers get ahead. Monk struggled with seven points from three completed rides. Four Tigers all scored four. Monk and Trigg's engine failures both occurred when in scoring positions.

The Tigers had opened up a six-point lead by heat five; the Hammers levelled in heat seven, and after 10 heats it was 30–30. A last three heats flourish took the score to 43–35 to the east London team.

The 1966 fixtures planner seemed a bit kinder to Tigers and they only had to travel the relatively short distance to King's Lynn the next day for their first league match at the venue. The Stars' 'old-timers' gave their team a good middle order, whereas the Tigers were solid without any big scorers. Templeton was the best with seven, guest Ray Wilson, in for Brannefors, scored 6+1 and Wells 5+2. For Monk, his glowing performances of 1965 still eluded him as he took a couple of second places. The Tigers briefly had the lead early and were close up to heat 11. Then two 5–1s to the Starts resulted in a 45–33 defeat.

The end of April saw the Tigers avenge another 1965 home defeat as they sent Halifax Dukes packing on 29 April. Monk seemed to have turned the corner to head the Tigers' score chart on 10 points. Wells managed the same and became an instant Tigers' hero. Bill McMillan rose to the occasion with 7+1. Three Tigers, including guest Graham Coombes, took five points. Scott had a torrid night, falling in his second scheduled race. Different reports about his injuries indicate he had bruised leg muscles or an injured shoulder sustained in a crash with Dave Younghusband when the two riders locked together. He had to withdraw from the meeting and failed to score. The net result was a 42–36 win for Tigers, although Halifax were in contention throughout.

May

The Friday before had been a false dawn for Monk who turned out to race on the wet track wearing his overalls. Against Oxford on 6 May, bike problems returned robbing him of points when his ESO failed in heat five. He only scored 6+1. However, the Tigers were again solid throughout and it was Templeton who shone. He scored 10+1. Scott contributed nine points and Mattingley seven.

The Tigers had given up their bid for Brannefors and in this match had a new rider, Norwegian Jonny Faafeng. On his debut he scored a modest 4+1. His score was restricted by a couple of engine failures. The air filter was at fault and Jonny borrowed a lady's nylon stocking to cover the air intake to prevent it from drawing in dust. This wasn't unusual in the 1960s and these versatile items of clothing were also used as a temporary replacement car fan belt. A poor overall Oxford team performance is reflected in the 45–33 win for the Tigers

The Tigers extended their winning streak at White City on Friday 13 May when they downed Edinburgh Monarchs 43–35 in the league in front of cameras from STV. Stadium announcer Don Cummings, who worked for STV, became a commentator for the night. The Monarchs opened with a 5–1, then they hit problems. In heat two, Bengt Jansson fell and smashed his foot against a fence post. He broke his ankle and had a lengthy lay off. This was the only meeting the author saw at White City and I vividly recall watching Bengt's encounter with the fence from the terracing on the first / second bend.

Anyway, it was a close encounter until the last heat and the more solid Tigers eventually got the upper hand sufficient to take the win. Wells topped the charts with eight points and Scott and Monk were next best on 7+1. For the Monarchs, native Glaswegian and former Tigers fan Bert Harkins scored eight.

After a short break, the Tigers were on the road for the long trip to Wimbledon in South London on 14 May to face the Dons on a stock car damaged track. Their form to date suggested they would not give Dons much of a contest. However, they ran the Dons close until the end of heat seven, before the home team cut loose to win 48–30.

Alf Wells, relishing his move to Tigers, was top scorer with 11 points. However, riding at number two, he probably benefitted from facing the Wimbledon lesser lights. That said he did beat Bob Dugard and Reg Luckhurst. Monk was still struggling with six points. He blew his motor in his first ride on the way to the tapes. Bill McMillan was next best with 5+2. Faafeng travelled with the supporters in their bus, bike and all. Mattingley arrived late after working on his bike at Southampton and scored only 1+1 from three rides.

Sunday was a day off before the Tigers headed down to Devon to face the Exeter Falcons. After a poor run, Monk struck form and posted an 11-point return from four rides. Despite his revival, the Tigers gradually fell behind the Falcons to lose 46–32. Scott, who crashed with Colin Gooddy and Jimmy Squibb in heat 11, scored six. Mattingley, who was also in heat 11, missed the mayhem behind him and took the win. He gathered six points and was the next best Tiger. Gooddy followed fellow Falcon, heat 10 faller, Chris Blewett to hospital.

The World Championship Qualifying Round at White City was on 20 May. It was on a wet track and was a break from team meetings for the Glasgow faithful. Monk was in good form. However, his 14 points wasn't quite good enough to take the top money as Coventry's Ron Mountford raced to a 15-point maximum to take the top prize. Gritty Yorkshire star Eric Boocock again showed his liking for White City to finish third with 13 points. Mattingley had an all too seldom show of form and gathered 11 and Scott had eight. Templeton, with four, and McMillan at reserve had five, beating Mattingley in the process. Only Monk progressed to the next round from the qualifying round meetings.

The team's home league unbeaten run was extended again. Newport Wasps returned to South Wales on 27 May following a 46–32 Tigers' triumph. The Tigers top scorers were – back on his trusty JAP – Monk on 11 and Wells on 10. Faafeng was third highest with 6+2 in another solid showing by the Tigers septet. McMillan was rewarded with a move into the team and Mattingley's poor run of league form, largely due to motor problems yet again, saw him drop to a reserve berth for the first time in a long time in his lengthy career.

June

For the return meeting against Exeter at White City on 3 June, Mattingley moved back to the team. He was replaced at reserve by Faafeng, who retired from heat eight with bike problems. It was another solid home display by the Tigers that saw them win 45–32. The margin might have been larger, but McMillan was excluded for receiving outside help after falling in heat three. Monk took his first maximum of the season. The others maintained their solid showing and Mattingley, with nine, who dropped points due an engine stutter, and Scott on eight, were his best supporting acts.

A week on and the Long Eaton Archers came to White City. Long Eaton started the season with legend Ove Fundin in their team, but his heart didn't seem in it for whatever reason and he left. However, the gap was being filled by guests of the highest calibre and this time it was Ivan Mauger.

Monk' replicated his maximum of the previous week and Mattingley seemed rejuvenated with 10 points including two wins. He was beaten by Mauger and Archers star Ray Wilson in his other rides. Yet again, Wells rode well for nine points.

Ivan Mauger, normally a certainty for double figures, managed a poor, for him, seven. He was beaten by six of the Tigers and on the wrong end of two 5–1s which must have been very rare. The rest of the Archers were extremely poor and never managed a heat advantage as they lost 50–28.

The Knock Out Cup draw did not favour the Tigers as they had to go to Halifax on 11 June. It was like old times as Monk top scored with 13. However, the rest of his team, while scoring reasonably well, did not have enough in the tank to beat the Dukes. Mattingley, with seven points was again second-best Tiger while Scott and Wells both contributed six. With the Dukes 20–4 up after four heats, the Tigers were never really in the hunt and lost 57–39.

On 16 June, the Tigers were at non-league Middlesbrough for a Northern Cup match and another rain-soaked track. The cobbled together Bears looked a reasonable septet that night, but for the six-man Tigers, who were without Mattingley, their team work was an advantage and they won 45–32. Monk gathered another away maximum and former Bear Scott took 11, showing his mastery of the track. Faafeng (pronounced Farfeng) took a liking to the rough Cleveland Park surface to post eight points.

Four of the six Scotland team to face England at White City on 17 June, plus the two reserves were Scots. Seventh man Bluey Scott was one by name only and fellow Australian Monk made up the octet. It was the second test in a five-match series. The Scots had won the first at Edinburgh, and won this one 61–46. However, once the series switch to England, the English team won the last three to take the series. On this occasion, Monk top scored with 14 for his adoptive team and Scott added 13. Top native was West Ham's Ken McKinlay who also scored 13.

England's cause wasn't helped by Mike Broadbank retiring from heat one and not riding again. Without the talented Swindon rider, it was an uphill struggle for the visitors. Trevor Hedge was the best England rider on 13 with Dave Younghusband on 11 and Eric Boocock with 10+3 riding well. For a change, Mattingley raced for England with three points in two races. He wasn't given Broadbank's other three rides because his bike did not arrive until heat 13.

Few people would have predicted the 60–17 hammering the Tigers gave Poole on 24 June. The Tigers fans must have been pleased with the result but maybe disappointed by the racing. Mattingley led the rout with his 1966 maiden maximum, Monk, Templeton and Bill McMillan were all paid for maximum points. Only Wells and Scott missed out on four ride maximums and debutant Jim McMillan, Bill's younger brother, scored 3+1. Scott lost points when he was excluded after a coming together with Bill Andrew. The Tigers fans thought Andrew was at fault.

Around this time, the British League introduced the Rider Replacement rule to cover for a missing rider. The team had to have a seventh man at number eight. They had to have two races in the meeting, but they could be taken in the second half.

Energised by their big win against Poole, the Tigers went to Oxford on 30 June and nearly toppled the Cheetahs. It was a close encounter with the teams never more than two points apart and the lead changing hands twice. Monk took 11 and the rest of the team were solid with next best Templeton and Mattingley both on six points.

The Cheetahs won 40–38. If the Tigers had had a good second heat leader, they would have won. The match was blighted for both teams by problems at the starting gate with the referee being blamed for the problems. The Cheetahs' McDermott was left at the tapes in heat eight and Wells and Templeton had clutch disasters in heats two and 12 respectively.

July

A season highlight was at White City on 1 July. Scottish speedway fans had the chance to see the best from the Union of Soviet Socialist Republics (USSR) take on Scotland. In 1966 visits from Russian riders were very rare and tales of these throttle thrashers were glowing as red as their flag.

Having won relatively easily in 1965 on a rain-soaked Old Meadowbank, this had been eagerly anticipated encounter. After 18 heats the Scotland team had, perhaps somewhat surprisingly, beaten the visitors 57–51. Adopted Scots Monk, 15+1, and Scott 7+1, scored 22 points between them, and the balance of 35 was gathered by the native Scots. Doug Templeton 11+1, Willie Templeton 9+3, Ken McKinlay 9+2 and George Hunter 7+1 did their bit too.

Boris Samorodov, a growing star on the world stage was the USSR's best with 15. Established top star Igor Plechanov did not do as well as expected on eight points. The other double figure riders were Gennady Kurilenko on 13 and Yuri Chekeranov with 12+2. For whatever reason, famed reserve Gab Kadirov never took a ride, probably much to the disappointment of the crowd who must have anticipated seeing him in action.

In the days when sponsorship was a rarity, both Scottish tracks managed to land a two-leg event high profile event, the High Speed Gas Trophy. The prize for the winner over the two legs was a brand new, immaculately chromed Jackson Rotrax JAP bike. Unusually, the competition was restricted to members of the two Scottish teams.

On 8 July Glasgow staged it's round almost two weeks after the round at Edinburgh on 25 June. At White City, Monk gathered 14 points after an opening race defeat by Edinburgh's new Norwegian, Reidar Eide. After that set back, he was unbeaten and spoiled the maximum aspirations of big rival George Hunter who also amassed 14 points. Surprise with 13 points was Willie Templeton who only dropped points to Monk and Hunter. Eide was fourth with 11. The Tigers' other riders scored as follows: Bill McMillan 10, Scott and Wells nine each, Jim McMillan six, Maury Mattingley five, Joe Hicks two and reserve Red Monteith zero. The meeting highlight was the coming together of Doug Templeton and Bluey Scott.

The winner on aggregate was George Hunter who was unbeaten at Old Meadowbank to total 29. Monk was second with 26. Aggregate scores for the other Tigers were: Scott 21, Templeton 20, Wells and Mattingley 17 each, Bill McMillan 13, Jim McMillan seven, Joe Hicks and Red Monteith two. Hunter, now using ESO equipment, sold his prize.

Back to league business on 13 July, the Tigers comfortably beat the visiting Hackney Hawks. Both Monk and Wells scored maximums. This was Wells's first in Tigers colours, showing how his move west had benefitted him. Templeton was next best with nine points.

The solid Tigers won 52–26. The big downside was Scott breaking his ankle in heat six after a paid win in his first ride. The Hawks had opened with a 4–2, but from heat two onwards offered little resistance.

There was a momentous moment for the Tigers two days later, when they went to Newport's notorious Somerton Park and won 40–38. By the end of heat four, they looked to be heading for defeat, 15–9 down, but three heats later they were ahead and, despite the efforts of the Wasps' riders, Wells and Bill McMillan split the Gote Nordin / Geoff Penniket in heat 13 pair to achieve legendary speedway happiness.

Using the new rider replacement rule for Scott, the six-man Tigers were inspired by Monk's 14 points. Mattingley backed him with 10 and Wells with 9+1. Monk, disgruntled with some refereeing decisions, pulled out the meeting after the match and was reported to the Control Board. The row centred on the status of one of Charlie's rides which was claimed by Tigers to be a tactical substitute ride which would have allowed for his next unprogrammed outing as a rider replacement for Scott, but the referee ruled the first non-programmed outing was the rider replacement one and by then the closeness of the scores ruled out using Monk as a tactical substitute.

The following night, 16 July, Coventry Bees were not a pushover. They did not have it all their own way on a very wet track. Former Bee, Mattingley, flew round his old home Brandon to gather 14 points from six rides and Wells added 10+1. Monk had a torrid night, and, scored only four from his first two rides. He then wrecked his bike in a crash with Nigel Boocock. Nigel also bent his bike and that was both of them out of the meeting. Faafeng was involved in a crash which wrote off his bike and Jim McMillan had a couple of outings replacing the Norwegian. The Bees won 42–36.

The supporters had transport problems after this fixture. The supporters club bus broke down and had to be abandoned. A replacement wasn't secured until the afternoon and it pulled into Glasgow at 9pm on Sunday, six hours after it had set off.

Poole had a chance to pay back the Tigers on 20 July which they did with a 48–30 win. Poole were ahead from the first heat. It was like the repeat of a long running stage show with a plot that had Monk as the hero and the supporting cast failing to shine. Monk scored 13 points. The next best were Mattingley and Templeton on five each.

With both teams used rider replacement. As they cancelled each other out, both sides had to promote their reserves to replace the missing rider in the team and bring in the number eights at reserve.

Two days later, the Tigers, who had not had a home team fixture since June, visited Hackney. The trip coincided with the Glasgow Holidays period. The six-man team performed well, and entertained the crowd, but were not quite enough. They were beaten in a last heat decider 5–1 as Hawks Colin Pratt and Roy Trigg showed their class. It was another meeting that got away from the Tigers who entered heat 13 level at 36–36. Monk scored 11+1 from five rides while Mattingley and Wells rode five times to amass 9+1 each in this 41–37 reverse.

The next night, the Tigers were at Belle Vue. Again, they put up a good fight, but went down 42–36. It was another heat 13 5–1 by the Aces that widened the gap to six points.

Monk was the Tigers' top scorer again with 14, but next best was Templeton on seven then Wells with 6+1. Mattingley had a win and ongoing bike problems which kept him on a three-point return. Without Scott again, it was possibly another one that got away.

The homecoming on 29 July was lost to the weather when Cradley Heath made their second visit to Glasgow in 1966.

Around now, the Tigers' Supporters Club, which had bought souvenir tartan shawls for the Scots and Russian teams, decided to splash out to buy a track spare for their team. The club members had also redecorated the Tigers' changing room.

August

On 1 August, The Newcastle Diamonds outshone the Tigers 52–26. Both teams used rider-replacement, so Dave Gifford and Jim McMillan were promoted to the reserve berths. On a very wet track it was a lacklustre performance from Glasgow and no one managed a double figure score. Monk again was best on eight points and the next two were Wells with six and Mattingley on five. Monk did beat Ivan Mauger in heat three, but that was his only win. There really wasn't a weak link in the Diamonds team that had only four last places.

At long last the Glasgow fans saw a home meeting as the Tigers took on Wolverhampton Wolves on 5 August. Once again, both reserves were promoted as both teams were using rider-replacement. The home riders took until heat seven to lead by four points and the margin stretched to eight by heat 11. Wolves could have levelled in heat 13 because a 5–1 for them in heat 12 made it 38–34. Facing Wolves star of the night Peter Vandenberg and reserve Dave Hemus, who replaced Alan Cowland in heat 13, were Mattingley and inexperienced Jim McMillan. Mattingley managed to split the Wolves pair and ensured that their 4–2 wasn't enough to give a draw. Again, happiness for the Tigers' fans was 40–38.

Mattingley was the Tigers top scorer with 10 points. Templeton and Wells were on seven each. Monk started brightly, but pulled out of his last two races because he felt the starting process had become a fiasco. One race was started three times, twice due to rider transgressions and a third time due to the referee not turning off the red lights from the previous stoppage. As a result, he only scored five points and was booed by his normally loyal Tigers fans.

With Monk back on song with a maximum, King's Lynn were dispatched 53–25 on 12 August. The Tigers provided race winners in 11 of the 13 heats. He also won the Scottish Match Race Championship by beating George Hunter. Willie Templeton scored a paid maximum; Wells chipped in with 8+1 and Faafeng, using a new engine, did better until he fell in his last ride. It is well known he sold the old one to George Hunter, who had nothing but trouble with the engine as well.

Scottish Cup rivalry was renewed on 19 August. The Monarchs used Ray Wilson as a guest for Bengt Jansson. The Tigers were missing Bluey Scott, whose anticipated comeback did not happen. In his place, they elevated Faafeng into the team, used Ron Mountford as a guest and Jim McMillan at reserve. Whilst Faafeng did not replace Scott's scoring power, the Tigers' fortunes were boosted as Mattingley rose to the occasion with 11 points from five rides. Monk was at his best, this time with a fine 15 points maximum. Wells slotted in between Mattingley, who had another engine failure in one of his five rides, and Monk, with 12. They led the charge to a 57–39 victory. The Tigers loved to put one over on the Monarchs and the Glasgow fans must have been well pleased with their team.

Would the Monarchs pull back 18 points the next night, 20 August? The question was never answered on that day because rain intervened with the Monarchs 19–11 ahead. So, the second leg was delayed to another day. Both teams were unhappy to carry on and the captains made their views clear to the referee. The bikes did not like the wet and the riders were covered in mud. Probably the final straw was when Monk fell off.

The Tigers visited Swindon on 24 August, a rare Wednesday night fixture for the Robins. They won easily, 53–25, as the Tigers used rider-replacement for Scott. It was back to the Tigers of old. Monk topped the chart with 12 after an opening race duck, but lacked support. However, the efforts of Mattingley and Jim McMillan were applauded.

On the road home, the Tigers visited their namesakes in Sheffield on 25 August, but lost 49–29 at Owlerton. Again, Monk on 14 points was the top Tiger. His only support came from Mattingley, who looked like overcoming a string of magneto problems, on eight points.

Swindon followed the Tigers up the road a day later, and, without Scott, the home side were up against it. The match was unusual in that from heats four to 12, the teams were level-pegging. It all hinged on the last heat and the Tigers' top man Monk and a stuttering Mattingley with 11 and two points respectively before the race, faced an unbeaten Barry Briggs, reported to be carrying a shoulder injury, and Frank Shuter who was on five from three rides.

Left: Trevor Redmond, who came out of retirement as a rider in 1964 to strengthen the Tigers. He is wearing a 1960 Bristol race jacket.
Right: Norwegian Jonny Faafeng, who ride for the Tigers in 1966 and 1967.

Sadly for their fans, the Tigers could not prevent Shuter from taking third place as Briggs flew to another win. He did not win by a big margin, but it was enough. Monk ended with 13 on as the Tigers top scorer again, with Wells giving his all with 12 points. Templeton scored eight from five rides, but having won his first two, took 2+1 from his last three.

Danny Taylor hosted a meal for both teams and it reported he and Trevor Redmond were observed to be doing a lot of talking – a portent of Danny's takeover in 1967 perhaps?

The next day, with their 18 points lead, the Tigers returned to Edinburgh for the second leg of the Scottish Cup. Although they lost 54–42 on the night, the aggregate and cup winning score was 99–93 in their favour. This probably wiped out the disappointment from the defeat by Swindon.

Monk was the hero with 14+1 from six rides as the six-man Tigers took the Cup. Mattingley stuttering again early on but redeemed himself in his last three rides to gather 11+1. Former Monarchs Willie Templeton 8+1, Bill McMillan 5+2 and Alf Wells with five did the rest. A 5–1 by Monk and Mattingley over Hunter and Harkins clinched the two-leg aggregate score for the Tigers.

The Tigers held on to the silverware and its red and white ribbons from 1965. A small group of Edinburgh fans, very unsportingly, threw stones from the run-down Old Meadowbank terracing which, thankfully, was a rare unsavoury display from normally mild-mannered fans. It was also reported that Monk and Wells had their cars damaged. This did not take the gloss off their win. However, Monk gave up his Scottish match race Championship and did not ride in the Scottish Open later in the season because of the stone throwing and car damaging incidents.

On the road again, the Tigers travelled to Long Eaton on 30 August to find the track very wet and slippery from day long rain. Water was pumped from the track and the meeting went ahead. The Archers won 48–30. The Tigers' line up was weaker than usual, without Wells and Faafeng. They brought in a fairly inexperienced trio in Joe Hicks, and guests Ian Champion and Tom Leadbitter. Of the other four riders, only Monk, who had a rare fall in his six rides, recorded 13 and Templeton, who was quite accomplished on tricky venues, rode well on the usually fast Station Road track to score 11.

September

Tigers used a seven-rider line up, showing confidence in Jim McMillan to take the number seven berth against Belle Vue on 2 September. He didn't let them down, scoring 3+1 from two rides. Monk again completed his customary maximum and the rejuvenated Templeton added 11 points. Wells was paid the same with 10+1. Faafeng featured in a couple of 5–1 winning heats as he scored 7+1. The Tigers won 54–24.

For the Aces, Cyril Maidment ruined the maximum aspirations of both Templeton and Wells, had to be content with three seconds in his other rides to score 12, half his team's total. Sandor Levai, who had escaped Hungary in 1966 to come to the UK was next best with seven. Sandor had a battle with Templeton in the first heat. The author remembers seeing Sandor in his antiquated two-piece leathers riding for Stoke in 1963 and being unimpressed. However, he stuck at it and became a very fine rider. At reserve, the Aces had now veteran former Tiger Gordon McGregor. Sadly, he was a shadow of his former self.

Before the match, the hard-working supporters' club presented the team members with cheques for retaining the Scottish Cup.

Cradley Heath came to Glasgow for the third time, but due to the rain, not a wheel turned on 9 September.

The next day, the Midlands weather was a bit kinder and the Tigers were away to Cradley Heath. Jim McMillan moved to number eight as the six-rider Tigers used rider replacement for Scott, who was still out with an ankle injury. Monk again starred with 14, only losing to Tigers' old boy Chris Julian. Faafeng was second highest scorer with 7+1. The Tigers stayed close to the Heathens and were in striking distance of a win, 37–35, before heat 13 started. Faafeng and Mattingley conceded a 4–2 and so the Tigers lost 41–37 to Cradley guest Geoff Mudge and Australian Joe Weichlbauer. Mudge gated, but Mattingley had flew past on the outside to lead the race with Faafeng in third. With a draw on the cards, Mattingley's bike shed a chain and with it went an away draw. It was another last heat decider that went the way of the opposition in 1966.

On 12 September, champions elect Halifax tore the Tigers to bits at The Shay. The visitors were again without Scott and the Dukes won 60–18. Monk was, as always, top scorer, but with a poor – for him – nine from six rides. The Tigers had only one race win and had the last man in every heat.

Perhaps inspired by the return of Scott, or maybe having been given a talking to by the promoters, the Tigers faced Newcastle on 16 September at White City. Their task turned out to be easier than expected and the Tigers won 45–33. Another factor was that Ivan Mauger dropped out of two races with bike failures. Had his bikes worked, it would have been closer. Monk scored nine, and in his first ride laid down to avoid Mauger and was excluded. Templeton topped the chart again with 10+1. Returnee Scott contributed 7+1.

A week later, Wimbledon came to White City and were not impressive. The Tigers, on the other hand, were and, after losing the first heat 5–1, had three consecutive 5–1s and established a lead. They built on it over the match and won 48–29.

Monk, on a new bike, scored another full maximum and Wells scored a paid maximum. Settling back into the groove, Scott added 9+1. Mattingley had another poor night in what was a see-saw season for him.

The Dons' Olle Nygren had a good night with 10 points from five rides, but lost the Silver Sash to Monk after the match.

Monk had given up his Scottish Match Race Championship title. The prize was contested by Maury Mattingley who took on Monarch Bengt Jansson. However, it went east as Mattingley missed the gate in heat one and then his bike let him down when he was leading the second heat.

On 30 September, Glasgow staged the Glasgow Open Championship on another wet White City track. It was not a star-studded line up. Olle Nygren was back and powered his way to 14 points and the Trophy. Another recent visitor, Ivan Mauger, rode a bit closer to form and took silver with 12 points.

Surprise joint third place riders were often unsung Tigers Jonny Faafeng and Bill McMillan on 10 each. Perhaps the shock of the night was Monk falling twice and only gathering nine points.

The remaining Tigers' scores were: Alf Wells nine. Bluey Scott eight, Willie Templeton seven, Jim McMillan five, Maury Mattingley two, with Red Monteith at reserve zero. Big attractions Arne Pander and Trevor Hedge did not arrive. Arne was injured the night before and Trevor had declared that he was unavailable.

October

Cradley Heath arrived for the fourth time on 7 October. Both teams hoped to wrap up their fixtures for 1966 and enjoy the start of the close season. However, big rain clouds were back and with the Tigers 36–29 ahead the track was declared unfit to continue. The match was abandoned and the result stood. No re-staging was attempted.

The curtain came down with Monk on nine points after three races and Templeton and Wells on seven each. As the match wasn't completed, the Silver Sash stayed with Monk.

The Tigers' final fixture of 1966 was at Wolverhampton on 14 October. Wells was missing, so they drafted in Dai Evans, a Wolves junior, at reserve. He did not score. Former Wolf Mattingley, suffering from an injured hand and with his machinery still letting him down, also failed to score. The Tigers' best rider was Faafeng with 11+2 from five rides. He said that Monmore Green was much the same shape as his home track in Norway. Without his great efforts, the Tigers would have lost by more than 45–33. Monk scored eight from five rides while Scott and Templeton, both with 6+1, were joint third highest scorers.

Wolverhampton's Peter Vandenberg rounded off a good night by beating Monk in the Silver Sash in the second half.

That was it for the Tigers in a roller coaster of a season. They were often on the wrong side of the last heat deciders and match and league points within their grasp were snatched away. While Monk was undoubtedly the top rider, he had some below par meetings. Wells was a revelation and Bluey Scott was steady, but probably below his best in an injury wrecked season. The rest of the team rose to the heights, unfortunately at different times, but never managed to be consistent enough to keep big scores coming in. The one bright light on the horizon was Jim McMillan. He started the season in the second half and had enough team outings to demonstrate his potential to kick on in 1967.

In the grand scheme of things, the Tigers finished in eighth place, with 36 points from 36 matches. They were above Edinburgh in the league and held onto the Scottish Cup. It was the best post return season to date, but not one to light up the speedway sky. Harry Houston said in the *1967 British Speedway Handbook* "Tigers did live up to expectation although they were still disappointing away from home. As for glory, they won the Scottish Cup for the second year running and there was individual glory too for Charlie Monk who, for a period, held the Silver Sash..." He also noted the improvement in Alf Wells' form.

The match against Cradley turned out to be Trevor Redmond's swansong as a promoter at Glasgow and there were fireworks to mark his exit. The weather didn't just 'finish' the meeting, it also turned the fireworks into 'damp squibs'. Redmond was replaced as promoter by Danny Taylor by the start of the 1967 season.

19. 1967: Charlie Monk's last season

The 1967 Tigers saw a new promoter fronting the operations after buying out his predecessor. Danny Taylor stepped in to replace Trevor Redmond, for whom travelling to cover all his speedway and stock car interests was wearing him down. Taylor also managed the team until August when Neil McFarlane, the chairman of the Tigers' Supporters' Club, took over. Taylor was a farmer in the Borders area and stayed for one season at Glasgow before moving to set up a new team at Berwick in the newly formed Second Division.

He was prepared to release Maury Mattingley and when inviting Monk and Scott back he offered Scott the captaincy. However, Scott had retired in Australia after sustaining a back injury and decided he did not want to return to Glasgow. In the event, Taylor replaced him with Swede Nils Ringstrom, who was not of a similar status. Ringstrom had been with Long Eaton in 1966 and not stood out.

Taylor reversed his thinking on Mattingley; invited him back and retained him as captain. However, Mattingley did not see out the season and, after Monk turned Taylor down, Willie Templeton became the Tigers' captain.

So, Charlie Monk was back along with Mattingley, Ringstrom., Alf Wells, Willie Templeton, Jonny Faafeng, and Bill McMillan. Monk made his return conditional on basing himself in Yorkshire, so he could get more open meeting bookings.

Changes happened during the season, including the firing of Norwegian Faafeng who was replaced by another Scandinavian in Swede Bo Josefsson.

Mattingley had problems and this opened the door for drafting in Scots born Australian Brian Whaley. Jim McMillan rode regularly and increased his average. Jim was often in the away fixtures to start with and then became a permanent team member home and away.

Veteran onetime Tiger Gordon McGregor had a handful of meetings as stop gap. Former Newcastle rider Russ Dent arrived in August to replace the suspended Alf Wells and stayed on, replacing Brian Whaley when Wells returned.

All 19 teams from 1966 continued in the British League and the guest and rider replacement regulations continued.

March

The Tigers' season started at Hackney in London on 24 March. It was a promising start as the six riders from 1966 plus Ringstrom took a 39–39 draw from the fixture. As so often in 1966, a last heat stumble cost them a win. Monk split Bengt Jansson and Colin Pratt, but the Hawks 4–2 saved the home side from defeat.

It was Monk's only dropped point as he had been unbeaten before that and scored 11. Mattingley again made a good start to the season with 10 as did Wells on 9+1. Newcomer Ringstrom failed to score.

The match was dominated by eight 3–3 heat results. The Tigers took a first heat 5–1 and a 4–2, then the Hawks hit back with three 4–2 wins. Hackney finished fifth in the league and this was the only league point they dropped at Waterden Road.

A draw at Hackney must have set alarm bells ringing at King's Lynn as they prepared to face Tigers the next day. Despite using rider replacement for Peter Moore, who was injured at Oxford the night before, the Stars sextet stayed ahead from the off to win 42–35.

Monk repeated his best form to score a maximum, the first ever visiting rider to do so at King's Lynn, but Mattingley, with eight, apart, the Tigers were not as solid as the Stars. Ringstrom scored his first points as a Tiger with three from four rides, including an exclusion for breaking the tapes. King's Lynn finished bottom of the league, with seven home defeats, so this was a missed opportunity for the Tigers.

However, the shine came off a relatively good start when the Tigers opened at White City on 31 March. The Newcastle Diamonds horrified the Tigers fans as they sped to a 42–36 win. By heat seven they were 12 points up and coasting. The Tigers reduced the gap in the remaining six heats but it was too little, too late.

Monk was imperious with a five-ride maximum, but the next best Tiger was Wells on seven, then Templeton on five points. Mattingley's bike problems from 1966 continued and he had only one scoring ride before his bike packed in in his second and he pulled out of the meeting. This score indicated that the Tigers needed riders who could score regularly at White City. Unfortunately, Ringstrom was not doing this, probably due to unfamiliarity with the Scottish tracks.

April

Ringstrom improved a bit on 7 April scoring 5+2 against the Coventry Bees at White City. The score at heat 11 was 39–26 indicates that the Tigers had it won. A 4–2 and 5–1 to the Bees made the final score 42–35. Monk finished last in heat 13 and scored eight. Surprise top Tiger was Jonny Faafeng on 10.

Templeton added 7+1 as the Tigers produced a solid show to take their first home points. Mattingley had bike problems again, this time it turned up late and he missed his first ride as he had to warm it up before riding it; then it blew up in the second half. This was his third engine blow up only four meetings into the season.

Normally smooth riding Nigel Boocock was excluded for taking out Ringstrom who missed the rerun, but came back for a second in his last race.

The next day, the Tigers were at Belle Vue without Mattingley, who was replaced by Bill McMillan. Mattingley could have borrowed an engine from Doug Templeton, but decided not to tempt fate with it. Alas, it was the Tigers of old – Monk in great form with 14 from five rides while the rest gave him almost no support. The best were Faafeng, and guest Taffy Owen, both on six points. The 47–31 score reflected the difference between the two teams.

Back in Glasgow on 14 April, the Tigers faced the Exeter Falcons. The Tigers fans had a bit anxiety until the points were in the bag with a 42–34 win. The match was safe by the end of heat 12. Monk took his second maximum of the season. Templeton was next best with 9+1 and Mattingley, benefitting from being paired with Monk, scored 8+2. Problems with engines hit other riders. Wells's bike did not last a race and he was out of the meeting. Bill McMillan's gave up in two of his five rides and Ringstrom had one bike failure.

The Tigers travelled to Edinburgh the next day and caused a major upset – for the Monarchs' fans – by taking both league points. Happiness at a 40–38 win was tinged in red and white.

Glasgow dominated most of the meeting and any chance of a late draw for the Monarchs went when Ringstrom split the George Hunter and Bernt Persson pairing in heat 13. Up to that point Ringstrom had scored 3+2 from three rides. The Tigers' top two were Monk on 11 and Mattingley with 10+1. He showed he was up for it on a track he loved. The Tigers had shown a great deal of determination to produce the goods, something that wasn't always the case on the road.

The Monarchs had a chance to redeem themselves on 21 April at White City. They did not, but were ahead in the first half of the meeting. The Monarchs were still in with a chance before heat 13, but Monk and Willie Templeton took a 4–2 to win 41–37. The Tigers had taken the lead for the first time after heat nine.

Monk scored yet another home maximum, but none of his team mates did better than six points. The Tigers seemed to be developing a steeliness which had eluded them before.

Faafeng took part in the race of the night when he came from the back to pass Bill Landels before nailing Reidar Eide on the line. Later, in heat 10, Landels fell and Ringstrom hit his bike and fell. Landels remounted to finish which did not please the Tigers' fans because they were convinced that he had received outside assistance to get his bike going again. It appears the point wasn't awarded until the match was over. Around this time, Bill McMillan resolved his bike problems which saved him from buying new equipment.

For the supporters, completing the double against their biggest rivals made up for the opening night defeat by Newcastle.

The Tigers were due to race at Halifax on 22 April, but rain saw the meeting postponed.

Sadly for their fans, the Tigers did not build on the week before because on 28 April they had to win heat 13 4–2 to snatch a draw with Poole Pirates.

Monk did the business with another 12-point maximum. Wells, with opening race engine tappets problems, and Bill McMillan, both on seven points were the next best. The lead changed hands three times as the meeting progressed and the Tigers needed a 5–1 in heat 13 to win. However, Gote Nordin split Monk and Templeton to secure a draw as the Tigers fortunes continued to fluctuate. Mattingley's bike problem saga continued and thanks to a bike failure in his opener he ended his night without scoring. Ringstrom's four did a little to help. He was losing points after gating well and then being overtaken on his way to the flag.

The next day the Tigers travelled to Yorkshire to visit Halifax. The Dukes had a relatively easy passage over the 13 heats and won 45–33. However, it was a night of incidents which favoured neither side. Two thirds of the Tigers points were scored by Monk and Mattingley with 11 each. Without Ringstrom, the Tigers brought in Jim McMillan at reserve and with 3+1 he was Tigers forth highest scorer, behind Templeton on 4+3.

Both teams had their share of bad luck. Bert Kingston dropped points due to a fall and exclusion. He was ruled out after falling in front of Bill McMillan. McMillan could not avoid him and his bike in the ensuing crash and the damage was done. Kingston was off to hospital. Eric Boocock, like Wells, Dennis Gavros, and Greg Kentwell, had an engine failure. However, unlike Gavros and Kentwell, Wells did not appear after his bike failed.

May

Still without Ringstrom and Faafeng, the Tigers made their second trip of the season to London on 2 May. The match at West Ham was similar to many in this era. Monk was the Tigers' top rider with 13 and the rest were poor, scoring only 14 with three non-scorers. Wells's zero was due to a blown motor. To add insult to injury, his car broke down between Wet Ham and Sheffield. Jim McMillan made a contribution, scoring 4+2, finishing as third best Tiger behind Monk and Templeton. The Tigers had Gordon McGregor replacing Faafeng and the veteran scored 4+1. Mattingley's machine had another off night with another blown motor which left him pointless.

The Hammers won easily, 51–27. They did not lose a heat to the Tigers. To be fair to Glasgow, the Hammers were held to a draw in six of the heats.

Glasgow Tigers went down at a wet Owlerton track in Sheffield on 4 May. That said, the home Tigers didn't win it until heat 12. Glasgow operated rider replacement for Wells, who had wrecked an engine at West Ham. With Wells not having a spare serviceable engine, it was a Charlie Monk show meeting again. His team mates were, Templeton on eight apart, like movie extras – in the background with no starring roles. Monk scored a 15-point maximum, almost half the team's total. Due to his efforts, Glasgow made it close for most of the match. McGregor and Jim McMillan covered for Ringstrom and Faafeng. Sheffield won by 10 points, 44–34.

The teams met again in Glasgow the next day and this time the home men had the best of it. Glasgow pulled away almost from the start and built on their lead in all but one heat to win 49–29. Monk scored his usual maximum and he was matched by Bill McMillan who scored his first 12-point maximum. Templeton nearly matched him but was beaten in his last outing by Arnie Haley. This was the last outing as a Glasgow team member for Gordon McGregor. Alf Wells borrowed Brian Whaley's bike for his six-point return after his motor seized on the parade.

The next visitors to White City were Belle Vue on 12 May. The Aces had the match won after heat 12, despite having two non-scoring riders at numbers six and seven. Bill McMillan literally went from hero to zero somewhat unkindly – he was ruled out after an opening heat fall which resulted in a broken ankle. Again, without the two Scandinavians, Tigers used Jim McMillan in the team and newcomer Brian Whaley at reserve.

Monk was a bit subdued, returning only 9+1. The revelation was Jim McMillian, who had six rides and scored eight points, his best return thus far. Wells and Templeton each contributed 7+1. Glasgow had been six points up after heat six, but a tactical substitute rider for Tommy Roper reduced the deficit to two points, and they won 41–36.

Belle Vue were not happy following heat eight as Dave Hardy, who had finished third after Whaley had fallen ahead of him, causing him to take avoiding action, was excluded. Hardy had he rejoined the race unaware his sojourn onto the centre green was his undoing, no matter the reason. Despite the protest, the referee held firm on his decision to exclude Hardy for leaving the track.

A World Championship Qualifying Round meeting was raced on a very soft surface at White City on 19 May. Monk scooped the winners' prize with a 15-point maximum. He had won the qualifying meeting at Swindon the Saturday before, beating Martin Ashby from the back in a run-off. Bob Kilby, the rising Swindon rider with 12 points from two wins and three seconds, was next on the Glasgow podium. The third placed man was, on 11, perhaps, a surprise in the shape of Mattingley. He again showing how good he could be at White City when he was up for it and his bike was working. But for one bad last place, he might have been runner up. Belle Vue's Cyril Maidment was next on 10, level with another rising star, Sheffield's Arnie Haley. For the Tigers, Alf Wells scored nine and Jim McMillan, replacing Eric Boothroyd, six. Reserve Brian Whaley did not score in his only outing. Apart from points and start money for 14 points in two meetings to show for it, Jim McMillian's efforts had a downside as the Speedway Control Board ruled out any further participation in the Championship. The field was the subject of criticism for its poor quality, but did include the popular former Tiger, Graham Coombes.

1967 Glasgow Tigers: Jim McMillan, Brian Whaley, Alf Wells, Charlie Monk, Bo Josefsson, Nils Ringstrom; front: Danny Taylor (promoter on bike), Willie Templeton (on bike)

Willie Templeton, who scored nine points, was not helped when he reared at the start of his last race. He hit Dai Evans who ended up in the fence and was ruled out due to injury. Templeton took a third in the rerun.

With Mattingley stepping down as captain, the Tigers' new skipper was Willie Templeton. Maybe some of the gloss was taken off this a bit as he was second choice after Monk had turned it down. However, he certainly had the right credentials for the job and deserved it.

The Tigers introduced new signing, Swede Bo Josefsson, to the home fans and he took his place at number two paired with Alf Wells on 26 May against Long Eaton at White City. This signalled to the fans and the wider speedway community that Faafeng's time was over. Ringstrom was back too and Jim McMillan was retained at number seven. He had extra rides as Mattingley's bike troubles surfaced once more, as Mattingley rode twice.

A relatively strong looking Long Eaton Archers were swept aside after an early match flourish and the Tigers established their supremacy. They won 50–28. Maybe the Tigers riders were inspired by the new female cheer leaders. Needless to say, Monk topped the Tigers scorers with a maximum. Three Tigers, Wells, Templeton and surprise package Jim McMillan all scored 10+1. The four top Tigers did enough on their own to win the match with 42 points. Josefsson scored a reasonable 5+2.

For Archers Ray Wilson retained his Silver Sash, beating Monk after the match. The Archers' new Swede and future World Champion Anders Michanek scored eight on his Glasgow debut.

A visit to Coventry was the Tigers next meeting. They were 12–6 down after three heats on 27 May when a thunderstorm finished racing for the night. Coventry promoter Charles Ochiltree was often portrayed as hard-nosed, but he arranged for the visiting Tigers fans to be able to use their readmission tickets at White City.

At Newcastle on 29 May, the Tigers were without Charlie Monk and his place was covered by rider replacement. Mattingley's place was filled by Jim McMillan. Mattingley had travel problems once again. Alan 'Skippy' Paynter guested at number seven.

The Tigers' hopes might have been raised by the absence of Ivan Mauger, at Wimbledon alongside Monk for the Internationale meeting, but the Diamonds' new Dane, Ole Olsen, filled the gap without fully replacing Mauger's fire power. Monk had a poor night at Wimbledon, scoring only three points.

Wells was the top Tiger on eight, but he had no real support and his team lost 56–22 after a steady couple of heats followed by a string of heat defeats. He was a relieved man as a threatened two match ban for missing a meeting was converted to a severe reprimand and fine.

June

A solid Tigers team faced King's Lynn on 2 June at White City. It was a night that quite literally the Stars were out. Betts, Moore and Crane were missing so Eric Boocock and Bert Harkins guested for them. Another fine display by the Tigers saw them take a relatively easy 48–30 win. Templeton was best on 10 with Monk 'only' managing 9+1. Wells was next best on nine but Ringstrom deserves a mention he scored 7+4 riding with Monk.

The Tigers Knock-Out Cup progress ended at West Ham on 6 June. The score chart was a poor picture and the only Tigers race winner was Jim McMillan who top scored with eight points. Monk only scored 4+1 which was unlike him. This was one for Tigers to forget about. Ringstrom had an unhappy night as he broke the frame during a race, an unpleasant experience to say the least. West Ham won 67–29.

Monk used a JAP in an ESO frame which wasn't considered a wise option but, to be fair to the hybrid, it was good enough to carry Ove Fundin to a fifth World Championship later that season.

The result also shows the unfairness of the KO Cup ties being only one leg. The Tigers had no chance to reverse the result on their own track. However, West Ham were due at Glasgow on 9 June. Only Monk responded to the very strong opposition, led by Ken McKinlay. Monk did well to score 13 but, with Josefsson on seven their only other race winner, the Tigers lost 46–32. A last heat 5–1 for the Tigers made the score look better. It was another meeting to forget for the fans.

Thankfully 16 June wasn't a league encounter on a dry dusty track as a Tigers quartet faced another three teams, namely Europeans, Stockholm and the Monarchs. The teams pooled the Tigers and Monarchs assets and added Olle Nygren and Ivan Mauger, who rode for the Europeans. Two meeting reserves, Brian Whaley and Kenny Omand, were available and were used by Tigers and Edinburgh respectively

After 16 heats the Tigers team of Monk 12, Wells 10, Willie Templeton eight, Jim McMillan two and Brian Whaley one – both with two rides – came out on top with 33. The Europeans' best was Mauger with 10 and Tigers' Mattingley scored seven for the Europeans. Stockholm, with four bona fide Swedes, scored 22 thanks to 10 from Nygren. The Monarchs scored a miserable nine points with George Hunter best on four. It was a good win for the Tigers and a poor score for the Monarchs. This made the night for the Glasgow fans who were always happy to see their rivals founder.

The following week, the international flavour continued as White City hosted a round of the Great Britain versus Sweden test series. The home side, including Kiwis Barry Briggs and

Ivan Mauger, plus Australian Monk, won 66–41 on 23 June. The Top British riders were Eric Boocock with a paid maximum 15+3 and brother Nigel was next best on 14. Briggs let nobody down with 12+1. Monk had scored five points before his third ride fall when he was helped off by team mate Ron Mountford. Mountford tried passing Monk on the inside after passing the two Swedes. Few Tigers' fans believed his claim that his foot slipped off the footrest causing him to lose control. The move thankfully only wrecked Charlie's bike.

The Tigers' Swedes, Josefsson and Ringstrom, got caps but were out of their depth scoring one and zero respectively. They were replaced by reserves who also struggled. The bulk of Sweden's points were scored by Gote Nordin with 12, Olle Nygren 10+1 and Bernt Persson with 10.

This win for Great Britain was their largest of the series, and levelled it at 2–2. However, the Swedes won the final match at Belle Vue 63–44 to take the series 3–2.

The Tigers trip to struggling Cradley Heath on 24 June probably did not hold up much hope of a home win. The Tigers won 41–37 on a wet track. Monk again was the top Tiger, this time with 11 points. Next best were Templeton on nine and Josefsson with eight. It was another meeting that swung both ways until the home side levelled the score in heat 11 and kept it that way going into heat 13. The Tigers family duo of Templeton and Jim McMillan rose to the occasion and took a 5–1 to win the meeting. They had been steady up to heat 13 with Templeton on six and McMillan on 4+2.

The Heathens fans must have hoped that Ivor Brown could complete his maximum with a win to secure the draw – but he fell – and reserve Ken Wakefield could do no better than third place.

The Heathens came to Glasgow six days later and hoped to avenge the defeat. However, the solid Tigers turned them over 46–32. The visitors showed some resolve up to heat seven, but the Tigers levelled the scores and four 5–1 heat wins in the last six heats did the damage. Monk had another maximum; Wells and Templeton both gathered 10+1. The rest of the Tigers scored steadily. Cradley might lost more heavily, but Mattingley's plane was delayed and he only appeared in the second half.

For Cradley, former Tiger Graham Coombes scored seven points, overcoming tyre problems on the way.

The *Glasgow Citizen* columnist Harry Houston was still on crutches. He had tried an outing on a speedway bike with dire consequences. The only good thing was he had been in the same hospital ward as Bill McMillan.

July

The Tigers had a trip to Poole on 5 July. The Pirates had them walk the plank. That said, Josefsson showed his Viking heritage and put up a dogged fight for his best return thus far, 14 from five rides. Monk scored 11 from his four outings. The remainder did not contribute much. Josefsson earned a shot at the Silver Sash holder Gote Nordin, but he could not repeat his opening ride victory. Jim McMillan fell three times, trying to do his best, and his gutsy performance was appreciated by the Poole fans. Jim seemed to be caught out by the third bend. Josefsson and Monk scored 25 of the Tigers' 30 points in a 48–30 defeat.

A trip north saw the Tigers at Oxford the next day and they gave a reasonable account of themselves, only losing to a home 5–1 in heat 13. The margin going into the heat was 36–35 to Oxford, but McMillan and Templeton were beaten by Roy Trigg and Eddie Reeves.

Monk scored an away maximum, but the rest of the team could not muster the extra points to win the meeting. Templeton broke a frame which held him back to two points. Ringstrom and Josefsson had brought illegal Swedish tyres and had to use one legal tyre between them.

However, for the Tigers it was another meeting that got away at the last gasp. The Cheetahs put the closeness of the teams down to engine troubles, but at least they salvaged the situation. The Cheetahs' woes were temporary compared to the Tigers season long problems.

Back at home, Mattingley, now down to reserve, made another appearance in what was, for him, a bitty season so far. On 7 July at a rain-soaked White City, Newport with sensational Swede Torbjorn Harrysson in their ranks were the opposition. The Tigers seven were solid and won 43–34, never allowing Newport near enough to threaten. Monk was best with 11, Templeton, using an old frame, had another good night with 10 points and Josefsson contributed seven. Heat 12 saw the fans cheering Jon Erskine who suffered an engine failure and gamely pushed home for a point.

Harrysson raced to a full maximum, which was defined by his display in heat three when he beat Monk in his opening ride at White City.

On Wednesday 12 July, the Tigers faced fellow Friday night track Hackney. The Hawks never really caused any concern to Tigers. Templeton continued his good run of form with a 12-point maximum. A seized engine robbed Monk of a maximum, but Mattingley took the heat win to prevent a Hackney heat advantage. Wells was third highest Tiger on nine points.

The referee was not in the good books as he let Pratt lie on the track in heat one as the other three thundered by on the next lap. However, the rerun saw Tigers score a 5–1. The Tigers won comfortably, 48–30, and were never behind. Hackney had only scored 10 points by heat six.

Although their last trip to the Midlands had been fruitful, the visit to Wolverhampton on 14 July was not. Despite being often out-gated, Wolves just gobbled up the points, passing the Tigers almost at will. By heat 13 they had won 58–20. It was a very poor display by the visitors, with Wells the best on seven points and Monk next on six. The Wolves won every heat and were never in arrears.

The Glasgow Fair Holiday saw the Tigers in Wales at Newport on 21 July. This time the Wasps saw off the Tigers 44–34. Monk gained his revenge on Harrysson as he raced to a maximum. Templeton rose to the challenge on another acknowledged tricky track with seven, which was matched by Wells. This time it was a car breakdown that caused Mattingley to miss the meeting. Jim McMillan replaced him and junior Roger White became a Tiger for the night. Over the 13 heats the Wasps were a bit more solid.

With the number of tracks in the north it was necessary to stage qualifying meetings for the Northern Riders Championship. Glasgow staged theirs on 28 July. Monk demonstrated his mastery again and won his five races for 15 points. Bernt Persson, with 13, gave the Monarchs one of their two men on the podium. On the other side of Monk was Reidar Eide on 12 points. The round had a big attraction in the shape of four times World Champion Ove Fundin, but he probably wasn't pleased by his eight-point return.

The other Tigers in the meeting scored as follows: Nils Ringstrom 11 from seven rides at reserve, Willie Templeton 10, Bo Josefsson 10, Jim McMillan two, Alf Wells one and reserve Brian Whaley four from five rides. Alf fell in his third ride, damaged his ankle and pulled out of his last two rides. It has been suggested that Ringstrom's good score was down to his dander being up after a clash with the Monarchs' Bill Landels saw him sitting on the track.

Such was his annoyance that he went to have kick at Bill as he came round on the next lap, but the track rakers restrained him.

August

The first engagement in August was at Wimbledon on 3 August. It saw the Tigers slowly slip behind as the match progressed. The Dons had it won after heat 12. Alf Wells failed to turn up as he wasn't programmed to ride. Programmed Russ Dent also was a no show for the Tigers. Danny Taylor, possibly belatedly, knew Dent could not appear because of prior commitments. In order to try to prevent the Tigers being shorthanded, Taylor ordered Wells to ride at Wimbledon, but Wells ignored him.

Josefsson had another top scoring meeting with 11, losing only to fellow Swede Olle Nygren in his first ride. Monk was only one behind on 10, with a couple of seconds before winning twice, including beating Trevor Hedge who had beaten him earlier.

The Tigers had an illustrious guest in Garry Middleton, a soon to be speedway legend, although not always for good reasons. The guest and the rest of his adopted team mates failed to give the top two the backing needed. to win. The Tigers were not as well turned out as they should have been as Templeton, Monk and McMillan had no race jackets. The red jumpers they wore were smart, but not an adequate replacement for their race jacket featuring the Tigers' head. Those who did have race jackets, Josefsson apart, had the wrong number on the back. The Tigers also used the wrong helmet covers in heat 12, but at this time, the colour marshall was at fault, not the riders. He was confused by the wrong race jacket numbers. Managed by John S. Hoskins, the Tigers did not use Middleton for an extra ride. Amazingly, Hoskins thought it unsporting to use a Dons asset and win the match that way. The slightly more solid Dons won 43–35.

Back home the next day, the Tigers faced Swindon Robins with Mattingley, who was becoming even more an occasional Tiger, and Wells out. The latter was dropped by Danny Taylor for missing the meeting at Wimbledon. The Tigers introduced new signing Russ Dent who had been with Newcastle, and gave Brian Whaley an outing. Dent scored 1+1. Apart from Monk who scored a 15-point maximum, Josefsson, who nearly caught Briggs napping as he tried to slow a race, scored 9+1 and Templeton with eight points, there was no strong Tigers presence. This gave Robins a relatively easy run to the league points. The scores were level at the end of heat five, but after that Tigers slipped behind and a 5–1 in heat 13 only made the scores look more respectable. Despite his great show in the match, Monk failed to take the Silver Sash from Briggs. Monk pulled out of the meeting after the extra race because he was so tired. The Robins won 43–35.

The Scottish Cup first leg should have been on 11 August at White City, but rain prevented any action. Danny Taylor had flown in his two Swedes who could not have been there if they used ferries, but to no avail.

So, the contest was delayed for 24 hours and the first leg took place at Edinburgh the next day. The weather was kinder, but the Monarchs had a point to prove after their league defeat and won 56–39. There was no star showing for Monk. Out of kilter from a fall when he remounted to take third, he managed 7+2 from five rides on a track where he normally did well. Josefsson gathered 9+1 and Willie Templeton scored eight.

Despite the final score, the Tigers made a match of it, and, not for the first time lost a last heat 5–1. However, they did have a home second leg to redeem themselves.

The Tigers visited Long Eaton on 16 August, and were in another close encounter. The Tigers moved up a gear going into the last two heats. Drawing 33–33 after heat 11, they took a 5–1 in heat 12 to lead by four points; so even losing the final heat 4–2, the Tigers still managed to win 40–38. It was one of only three away league wins that season

Probably against all the odds it was reserve Brian Whaley who became the last heat hero when he split Ray Wilson, who was completing his maximum, and previously unbeaten guest Malcolm Simmons. It might be unfair to take the gloss of Brian's second place, but Simmons did have an engine failure when sitting behind Wilson. Whaley's partner, Alf Wells, had pulled out with bike problems, so Whaley was on his own. It is also notable that the Tigers' win was pulled off despite missing the on-form Josefsson.

Monk was the top Tiger with 10 points and Dent, 7+2 and Templeton on seven, were second and third best.

Not content with winning at Long Eaton, which made the Glasgow fans happy, the Tigers repeated the performance two nights later at White City against Wimbledon. Needless to say, it was another last heat decider and the Tigers won with a last heat 5–1 thanks to maximum man Monk and Templeton, who finished with 9+1. Jim McMillan scored seven points and Dent deserves a mention for his 6+3 return. The match seesawed most of the way. In heat 10 Wells penalised himself and his team by not moving from the gate as he thought Middleton had rolled at the start. The referee was happy with the start and Wells's bike had to be pulled from the track where he left it beside the start marshal.

The Dons had gone into the last heat two points to the good, but Monk and Templeton beat Garry Middleton, now in the Dons team at reserve, and Reg Luckhurst.

The next night, 19 August, the Tigers were in Coventry. The Bees were in good form downing Exeter 46–32, before facing Glasgow on a somewhat dusty surface. The Bees won 56–22 in a display of strength by six riders using rider-replacement for Rick France. The Tigers did not have a race winner and their best rider was Monk with four seconds for eight points. The rest contributed little.

The Halifax Dukes who had done well in Glasgow in the past, but could not quite raise the fire power to beat the Tigers on 25 August. For the Tigers, Mattingley was making another rare appearance. He replaced Ringstrom who had lost form in August, and took 3+2 as he eased himself into action again. Monk was top Tiger again with 11. Dent, mounted on Joe Hicks' bike, which was doubling up as the Tigers' spare machine, and Wells, pegged back by bike problems, both scored seven, Dent adding a bonus point.

To be fair, the Dukes never let the Tigers get too far ahead, but the Tigers, who won 43–35, were over the winning line before the last heat.

Neil McFarlane, who had been learning his trade as Glasgow team manager on away trips, was now given the role on a permanent basis.

September

On 1 September, the Tigers welcomed Oxford Cheetahs to White City. They were a bit faster than the live feline namesakes that had visited the stadium in 1940. The welcome didn't extend to allowing Oxford to win and the league points stayed in Glasgow. The visitors didn't roll over; it was only from heat eight onwards that the Tigers gradually took control. The match was secured by heat 12 and the last heat 3–3 did not affect the 44–34 ten-point gap.

Roy Trigg spoilt Monk's maximum hopes and Monk ended with 11. Wells scored a couple of thirds before taking two wins. Josefsson, who had been missing since early August, was back and was next best scorer on 7+3.

A Tigers 'B' team raced at a new venue, Nelson in Lancashire's Colne Valley on 2 September. The 'B' team included Josefsson, Dent, Whaley and Jim McMillan. The latter appeared to get the hang of the place after a second place in his opening ride. He raced to 14 points. Dent mastered it from the off to score 12+1 while Josefsson scored 9+1, maybe exercising more caution.

The Tigers used second half riders Ken Omand and Forbes MacKenzie with Harry Appleby at reserve. Ringstrom was programmed but had to pull out due a family bereavement – the death, back in Sweden, of his father.

The home team consisted mostly of league second strings and reserves, and they won 49–47. It was a closely contested match and the home team's two-point advantage came in heat 14 and was maintained over the last two heats.

The Scottish Cup contest concluded on 8 September. Mattingley displaced Whaley at reserve as the now confident Edinburgh Monarchs won at White City. This time it was the Monarchs who were up for the cup. The Tigers' top two were Monk on 14 and Josefsson with 11 while Wells added nine points. The Tigers had a slim lead on the night up to heat 12 when Monarchs levelled the scores. The last four heats favoured the Monarchs, but the Tigers could have won in heat 16, had not George Hunter raced to a win. Dent had a miserable night with magneto troubles in all his races.

Glaswegian Bert Harkins, with 9+1 played a big role in sinking the team he supported as a boy. The Monarchs 50–46 win meant the aggregate score was a convincing 106–85 for a soon to become homeless Edinburgh team.

Russ Dent was missing on 13 September for the visit of Wolverhampton. However, Ringstrom was there. His place in the side was not a given and according to Doug Nicholson he had to face Brian Whaley for the privilege in a "Vultures Match Race". Ringstrom led from the tapes and pulled away, but his bike packed in so Whaley took the reserve spot. The Tigers top two, Monk and Josefsson both managed full maximums. Sadly, it was Josefsson's last outing of the season at White City. Templeton again showed up well, scoring a paid maximum. The rest of the team did well and Wolves, were on the wrong end of a 57–21 defeat. Wolves missed Swede Hasse Holmqvist and used Bill McMillan, still trying to get back in the groove after a long layoff, as a guest

Tigers invited Monarchs back on 22 September in a challenge match for the Supporters' Trophy. It was on a bumpy track and turned out to be the season finale, although not planned as such. The 14 heat eight-a-side contest used the old match format from the early 1950s. The return of Ken McKinlay for the night as a guest for Glasgow was quite appropriate. The Tigers were without Josefsson. They were also missing Wells who was on the wrong end of two disciplinary actions, one by Taylor and the other by the Speedway Control Board (SCB). Taylor disciplined him for missing the meeting at Wimbledon in August, and the SCB action was for the same misdemeanour. However, even without Josefsson and Wells, the eight-man Tigers, boosted by McKinlay, took revenge on the Edinburgh Monarchs and won 53–31 to compensate for the Scottish Cup defeats. McKinlay showed he still had mastery of White City by scoring a 12-point maximum, which was emulated by Monk. This was a farewell to White City for Monk. Maury Mattingley also finished his White City career. He returned a great eight points. The silverware was a welcome addition for the Tigers' trophy cabinet which otherwise had been bare this season.

With two league matches left, the Tigers were in action the next day at Swindon. The Tigers did not expect to win at Blunsdon, where the Robins had won every league meeting in 1967, but they didn't quite want go down without a fight. Swindon had four very good home track riders and the Tigers were up against it from the start. The Tigers used Pete Smith as a guest for Josefsson and he did well with 8+1. Monk also returned eight points. Mattingley, with a short road trip for this meeting, did well with 7+1. Not unusually, the rest of the Tigers had a poor night away from home. Glasgow were also without Wells, who was serving the first of a two meeting suspension for non-payment of a recent fine. The Robins top three scored more than Tigers team in this 52–26 home win. Briggs also retained his Silver Sash when he beat Monk just after the match.

The Tigers trip to Exeter for the following Monday was postponed due to rain. The same fate befell the Glasgow Open on 29 September but no attempt was made to re-stage it.

October

The curtains came down for the 1967 Tigers at Exeter on 9 October, when the Falcons beat both Scottish teams in a double-header at the County Ground. The Tigers were marginally better than the Monarchs, but lost 50–28. Monk finished as he had done most of the season as top scorer, this time with 10. Mattingley bowed out with six and guest, Monarchs' Oyvind Berg, replacing the suspended Wells, scored 4+2. Mattingley finished with a heat 13 winning flourish. Wells was not suspended at the time for missing the match at Wimbledon. He was fined £25, but did not pay up and the suspension was for non-payment of the fine.

The season-ending British League Riders' Championship at Belle Vue was a big disappointment for the Tigers' fans because Monk only managed to score six points. He had finished the season with the second highest league average, only behind Barry Briggs, but this wasn't reflected in his low return.

An up-and-down season saw the Tigers finish 13th in the 19-team league. They were often within striking distance of a win only for it to be snatched away from them in the last few heats. The team won seven league points away from home, their best in the British League, but dropped nine at White City.

They started out without the heat leaders needed to give them more of a cutting edge. Monk ended the season on a massive average of 10.72 and did what he could. However, he probably would have appreciated better backup. Next best was Bo Josefsson with an average of 7.24, albeit from only 16 meetings. In the *British Speedway Handbook*, Harry Houston said that the Swede was "a winner who could get all the fans screaming".

Mattingley and Wells, who averaged 6.41 and 6.48 respectively, could have done better but had their more than their share of machine problems. Often the bike problems started before the meeting had progressed far beyond the opening heats. This put pressure on the relatively inexperienced reserves. However, this benefitted the promising Jim McMillan who gained a lot of experience. This helped the team in the coming years. Harry Houston said that he was a "star in the making". Houston also noted that Russ Dent had "made a big impression". Monk apart, the rest of the riders did not consistently perform as well as they might have done. Also, the team wasn't really a settled unit over the season.

And to add to the fans' concerns, Charlie Monk put in a transfer request in December. Also, Danny Taylor had stepped back from fronting the team during the season and was clear that he fancied running a team in 1968 in the new Second Division, closer to his home in the Borders. Les Whaley, the father of young reserve Brian Whaley, took over as promoter.

20. 1968: Final season at White City

During the winter big changes took place. In the British League a new Second Division was formed. It meant that Glasgow were in Division One. There were still 19 teams in the top tier and 10 in the lower one, which was aimed at giving young riders the chance to develop.

Edinburgh Monarchs had lost their stadium at Old Meadowbank, which was demolished to make way for a new arena for the 1970 Commonwealth Games. This stadium was recently demolished and replaced by a new arena. They became the Coatbridge Monarchs and were geographically nearer to Glasgow. The Long Eaton Archers moved the short way down the M1 to become the Leicester Lions.

The new 10 team Division Two included new tracks at Berwick and Canterbury. It also included Reading and Crayford, venues which had staged speedway before the Second World War. The remainder comprised Nelson which had opened in 1967, Belle Vue's second team, the Colts, and former venues in Middlesbrough, Plymouth, Rayleigh and Weymouth reopened.

Danny Taylor moved from Glasgow to open Berwick and the Tigers promoter was Les Whaley. On the riding side, Charlie Monk was gone. He moved to Sheffield while Alf Wells was moved by the powers that be to Newcastle under the rider control system. Maury Mattingley was allocated to Newcastle but decided to retire rather than move there.

The 1968 Glasgow Tigers were never properly compensated for the loss of their star man and the new promoters were never able to sort out a reasonable replacement, despite their season long efforts. The process started out with them being allocated another top Australian, Jim Airey, but he declined the move. The Tigers were also allocated Swede Gunnar Malmqvist who never came to Glasgow.

They took a bit of a gamble and snapped up promising Swede Lars Jansson, brother of Bengt. They also added Ovyind Berg, a Norwegian, who had ridden for Edinburgh in 1967, and shown a fair turn of speed at White City. These two joined returnees Willie Templeton, Bill and Jim McMillan, Bo Josefsson and Brian Whaley. The general consensus in the speedway press was that Glasgow were much weaker than the 1967 team. Sadly, this was confirmed as they collected the wooden spoon at the end of the season.

As the season advanced, Jansson dropped out and was replaced by another Swede Ake Andersson, who did not stay long. Another change during the campaign was the return of Russ Dent. He came back to replace Brian Whaley, who moved to Berwick and shone there.

The Tigers never really had a settled side. Only Templeton and Jim McMillan were ever present. Towards the end the season Alf Wells returned after being released by Newcastle.

It was not all doom and gloom. A big positive was Jim McMillan's rise to the top of the Tigers' team, a position he retained and flourished in until he moved south to Hull in 1974. Another positive development was the young talent of Bobby Beaton who took his early steps in the Tigers' ranks. He is another rider who grew in stature before he also moved south to further his career.

This was also last season of speedway at White City because the site of the stadium was on the planned route of the M8 motorway. The track was located at what was a 'pinch point' between Bellahouston Park and the railway. Taking a slice off the park was not an option compared to taking the land occupied by the stadium to facilitate the road. At that time, the long-term future at Hampden Park was viewed as a better option than staying at White City. The stadium could have been required for the redevelopment at relatively short notice and have left Tigers homeless. In the eventuality, it did not close until early 1972, approximately 44 years after it had opened. The Tigers could have stayed another three years.

March

The Tigers' season started on 29 March as in 1967 with a trip to fellow Friday night track Hackney. With Lars Jansson on the way to replace Gunnar Malmqvist, his place was taken by Olle Nygren as a guest. The Hackney meeting reporter, maybe not aware of the swap, reported that Nygren replaced Malmqvist. Nygren was top scorer for the Tigers with 10 points. New Tiger Berg was next best with 7+1 and Josefsson third on 5+1. The result was 47–31 – a relatively easy win for Hawks. Josefsson had taken a second in his first ride, suffered a blown motor, then took another three on borrowed equipment. Berg was fined for not having a nameplate on his bike. A breach of the regulations, but one that could have been addressed by a small amount of paint or a bit of Elastoplast and a biro.

The Tigers were never really in touching distance once the Hawks were ahead by six points after four heats, but Nygren and Templeton made sure there were no maximums for the Hawks.

The next night, the Tigers were at King's Lynn. Josefsson seemed to step up to the plate and take over Monk's starring role. He raced to a 12-point maximum on a rebuilt motor, suggesting he was going to kick on from his best showings in 1967. Nygren, guesting again, scored 11 and was only beaten by Malcolm Simmons. Berg gave a reasonable show with eight points, suggesting he could slot in as a heat leader.

The solid Tigers moved ahead in heat two and widened the gap to eight by heat six. There were small swings in the Tigers' winning margin in the ensuing heats, but King's Lynn were not allowed to get ahead and the Tigers ran out winners 42–36.

Jim McMillan scored only six points but, even at this early stage of the season, he got rave reviews from the *Speedway Star* correspondent, Martin Rogers.

April

With Lars Jansson in the team, the Tigers faced the Coatbridge Monarchs for the first time on 5 April in the Champagne Derby first leg. The Monarchs remained the Tigers' fiercest rivals so it was good for the fans in red and white for the team to win 51–45 at White City.

Perhaps, before the match, the blue and gold fans were peeved that Berg was now a Tiger. After the match, they would have been stunned as he produced a 15-point maximum. Jansson scored a promising 11+1 and Josefsson added 10+2. There were no other notable scorers, but the team's efforts took the Tigers over the winning line by heat 13.

Jim McMillan was lucky. He slipped on exiting the second bend and fell in the path of Doug Templeton. Doug managed to lift the front of the bike up in the air like a modern-day wheelie, but could not avoid running over his nephew's head in the process. Obviously shaken, but not seriously injured, McMillan returned to bag four points. The Monarchs had shown up well early on, but did not have just enough power to win.

The Tigers helped Monarchs settle in the new Cliftonhill Stadium track in the second leg of the Champagne Derby the next day. There were complaints about the new strip, but Ian Hoskins promised they would be sorted out. The track was unusual as it was banked, yet not bowl shaped all the way round. Bends three and four went up and down the old sloping terracing area. This opening meeting showed up inadequacies with the track lighting, which was not designed to illuminate what had been terracing.

Despite this, Jim McMillan – riding as partner to Jansson – excelled. He showed his team mates how to get round the new circuit. His 11 points from five rides was his best return so far. Josefsson had five second places to score 10. The third best Tiger was Berg with 9+1. Jansson had a very rare score of five third places with a bonus point foreach one to be paid for 10 points. Unfortunately for the Tigers, the Monarchs won 54–42 win to take the trophy and any Champagne on the go. Unlike the meeting the night before, the Tigers were in charge until heat eight, then the Monarchs nosed in front and stayed there to the end. The aggregate result was 99–93 to Coatbridge.

On 12 April, the Tigers met the Leicester Lions at White City, and the newcomers went back to the Midlands having lost 47–31. Jim McMillan scored another maximum and again Josefsson was his best backer with 11. Berg was the third highest scorer with nine points.

The Lions were unhappy with the track surface. Briefly ahead after heat two, they soon started to lose ground as the match progressed and never could catch up. Race of the night was heat nine when Berg and Templeton faced Boulger and Wilson. The Lions took the lead from the tapes only for Berg to pass both riders to secure a 3–3. He fell in heat 13 when chasing Michanek, but remounted to pass Vic White to take a point.

The next day, the Tigers visited Coventry and lost 48–30. The visitors' top scorers, Jim McMillan and Josefsson, both returned 7+1, not enough for a win. Jansson scored six with two falls suggesting he might not be ready to be a heat leader in the British League. Josefsson teamed up with Bill McMillan to nab a 5–1 in heat 11.

The Tigers called in to Brough Park, Newcastle on their way back to Scotland on 15 April, but were beaten 45–33. The match saw the Tigers chasing from the off and they only had a single 5–1 in their favour. Jansson top scored for the first time with 9+2, with support from Berg on 8+1 while Jim McMillan and Josefsson both managed 7+1. At a time when safety standards were not as high as today, Whaley crashed into the fence and a lamp standard, thankfully without incurring any undue injuries. Safety hazards like these were, in time, moved back from the edge of the fence. There was a bit of a dispute before heat one was settled. It started with a tape breaking, followed by the respective camps arguing over the rules before the rerun – won 4–2 by the Diamonds – sorted it all out.

Coventry made the trip north on 19 April and the Tigers almost matched the score at Brandon six days earlier, but fell a point short. They were strengthened by the return of Russ Dent who took a place in the team, relegating Templeton to reserve. Brian Whaley rode in the second half again.

Jim McMillan was again the Tigers' best rider with 11, beaten only by Nigel Boocock. Jansson had a fall when his bike reared at the start as he faced Boocock, but won his other three rides for nine points. Berg, using a bike borrowed from Whaley, after damaging his before the meeting started, scored 7+4. Josefsson added seven points, but still wasn't doing as well as expected.

Nigel Boocock was helped by former Tiger Charlie Monk in the pits. Monk sold his bike to another former Tiger, Alf Wells, after the meeting. Sadly, for Wells, the motor's crank pin broke in his first meeting on the bike at Newcastle.

The Tigers' trip to Swindon the next day turned out to be almost a whitewash. Dent was their top scorer with five points. Berg wasn't available because he had been working on his bike and arrived late, so Whaley came back into the team. Like Jansson, Whaley had bike problems and failed to score.

Glasgow Tigers 1968: Russ Dent, Oyvind Berg, Bill McMillan, Brian Whaley, Lars Jansson, Jim McMillan and Willie Templeton (on bike).

Lars Jansson and Jim McMillan riding for Glasgow at Coventry, April 1968.

Jim McMillan and Bill McMillan with their uncle, Willie Templeton in 1968.

Left: Oyvind Berg; right: Russ Dent.

The 61–17 score was painful reading for Tigers' fans. However, a positive point was that the Tigers did make it difficult for the second strings and reserves, although they could not live with the Robins heat-leaders, Barry Briggs, Bob Kilby and Mike Broadbank.

Berg was back for the trip to Exeter on the following Monday, 22 April. It was a better show from the Tigers. The 50–28 result was more respectable but still a heavy defeat. Jansson, who with Josefsson had been in Sweden at the weekend, led the line with eight and Jim McMillan scored six. However, the Tigers' trip south had not been a productive one.

A home match might have eliminated some of the bad vibes and on 26 April, the Tigers faced Cradley Heath at White City. The short run of defeats ended, but a win was not the outcome of this encounter as the Heathens best two on the night could not do enough to snatch a win. The Tigers' Berg and Jansson split the Roy Trigg and Chris Julian pairing in heat 13. Berg passed Julian early on and Jansson just pipped him on the line. The match ended 39–39, much to the Tigers' fans relief. However, there was frustration that Julian had 'got away' with a flier of a start in the last heat. The Tigers had been six points ahead after heat nine, but then immediately conceded a 5–1.

The new king of White City, Jim McMillan, gave his all with another maximum. He was ably backed by Templeton with 8+1. Josefsson and Jansson stuttered again when both should have done better. Jansson fell in his first ride and was excluded, but more was expected from Josefsson who had shown real promise towards the end of 1967.

Referee Ernie Chapman was criticised by the fans when he had to take four attempts at starting heat one. In the first, Berqvist made a flying start and, as Jansson drew level, Bergqvist moved over and Jansson ran into him. The injured Bergqvist was excluded. Chapman then decided there should be an all four back rerun. He then decided to reaffirm his exclusion of Bergqvist. Then, and finally, he excluded Jansson. Bergqvist was injured in the incident and reserve Chris Julian taking his place. The final result was a 3–3 draw.

The author recalls Mr Chapman, who was still refereeing into the late 1970s. He was a tall, slightly stooping elderly gentleman with thick glasses who was often accompanied by a big dog which joined him in the referee's box. In a pre-meeting encounter between Chapman and Jack Millen in the Powderhall pits in 1977, Millen, somewhat sarcastically, but reasonably politely for him, asked how Chapman had managed to get there without a guide dog.

The Tigers' woes continued the next day when they travelled the short distance to Coatbridge. Glasgow were drawn away in the first round of the KO Cup and it was the Monarchs who progressed after turning over the Tigers 66–42. Jim McMillan was now ensconced at number one and his 13+1 confirmed that status. Unusually, he had seven rides in the 18 heat eight-man teams match. Templeton was next with 8+1. Bill McMillan was next best with 7+1, matching his brother's two wins in the three rides he took as reserve. Jansson, Josefsson and Dent had a poor night, with six points between them.

For the Monarchs, Glaswegian Bert Harkins, soon to be a master of Cliftonhill, scored 12+1. Doug Templeton had a rare fit of pique, parked his bike on the track and lay down in protest after being excluded under the two-minute time rule. The Tigers were always up against it and were 10 points down after five heats. Alarm bells about the riders' performances must have been starting to ring.

May

The home fixture for 3 May against Wimbledon, which would have seen the McMillan brothers paired together, fell victim to the rain. The wet weather was also present at Halifax the next day, and washed out the meeting at The Shay as the teams got ready to race. Glasgow's two Swedes would have missed the Wimbledon match because they were racing back home. Josefsson, who qualified for the next round of the World Championship in Sweden, also failed to make Halifax due to injury, but Jansson was ready to ride at The Shay.

The weather was better in Leicester on 7 May, but the Lions were in no mood to be kind to rival big cats. Their defeat at White City was repaid as they won 43–35. Jim McMillan top scored for the Tigers again with 9+1 and Dent scored 8+2. Berg was third highest with 7+1. All the top riders took five rides as they used rider-replacement for the injured Josefsson.

The Lions had a longish, but more solid tail, and, apart from a couple of heat losses, moved ahead steadily over the match. They effectively had the match won by heat 11.

Without Berg, in Denmark seeking to progress in the World Championship, on 10 May the Tigers entertained Oxford Cheetahs. The track had received a lot of attention, including pumping water away, to recover from a rainy week. The preparation work included using sawdust to mop up water. The 49–29 home win saw four of the Tigers return double points. 'Mudlark' Dent, who tried a new gear ratio, showed some good form and gathered an 11+1 paid maximum. Jim McMillan scored 11, losing only to Ronnie Genz. Josefsson scored 10+2 for another paid maximum. Finally showing the form expected of him, Jansson added 10+1.

With rider-replacement available to both teams, Whaley and Peter Seaton were brought in at reserves.

The Tigers' promoters must have felt the team was turning the corner. Jim McMillan faced Bernt Persson in a Scottish Match Race Championship encounter, but could not beat the Swede and fell in trying to do so.

On 16 May, the Tigers ran into their favourite son when they visited Sheffield. However, Glasgow went down 51–27. A tapes exclusion pegged back Jim McMillan, who was Glasgow's only race winner, to eight points. However, he was still the best in his team. Next was Dent on six points. It was clear that the team had not really improved. Berg had a nightmare, with a fall after his frame broke. He pulled out of the meeting. The visiting Tigers fell behind in heat two and went further behind throughout the match. Needless to say, former Glasgow favourite Charlie Monk returned a 15-point maximum.

The next day, back at White City, the Tigers did not get any comfort from Monarchs. At least Berg snapped back into form to top score with 10 points. Jim McMillan was paid the same with 9+1 and Bill McMillan added 6+2. Jansson redeemed two bad rides with two wins for six points, but Josefsson, on the face of it, had a poor night. He was unlucky to be in the wrong place at the wrong time in heat 10. George Hunter lost control of his rearing bike as he neared the flag and Josefsson ended up collecting George, who then hit the starting gate post and snapped it in two. The race was stopped and rerun without Hunter who was excluded. Bill McMillan took the battered and bruised Josefsson's place in the rerun. This, and an engine failure for Dent, did not help Tigers.

The Monarchs went ahead from the start and were ahead by eight after heat six. The Tigers clawed things back to a deficit of two points going into heat 13. Reidar Eide was the Tigers heartbreaker as he won the decider, to complete a 15-point maximum. He won the match ahead of Berg and Jim McMillan. Bert Harkins scored nine points and the rest of the Monarchs did enough to win 40–38.

The Tigers fans were not pleased with improvised starting technique used to replace the gate. The elastic stretched across the track was released by former Tiger Larry Lazarus. Jim McMillan wasn't impressed by Eide's heat 13 'flier' of a start and the Tigers fans backed him to the hilt. Unfortunately for Jim, the referee did not agree and the result stood.

This performance, and the prospect of the all JAP mounted West Ham team coming the next week must have had the Tigers' fans worried, given the Hammers' record in Glasgow since 1965. Their fears proved justified on 24 May. West Ham moved ahead in heat two, then widened the gap over the next 11 to win 47–31.

Without Josefsson, the Tigers did not have enough fire power. Jim McMillan took their only race win in gathering 11+1. Berg was next best on six and the other riders' returns made dismal reading. Scottish speedway and former Glasgow legend Ken McKinlay scored 11+1 for the visitors.

The Glasgow management must have been distraught as their team seemed to be sinking down the league with defeat after defeat. The Tigers' bad luck was not restricted to the track. The West Ham match programme carried a prize quiz, and, thanks to a printer's error, the answers were given on the back page.

The fans had a week's break from league action as the Glasgow World Championship qualifying round meeting was up next on 31 May. Four programmed riders failed arrive – Tim Bungay, Norman Nevitt, Allan Butterfield and Ronnie Genz. The three reserves Brian Whaley, Lex Milloy and Brian Collins had 18 of the 20 spare rides on offer.

Swindon's Bob Kilby won the meeting with a 15-point maximum. Coatbridge's Bert Harkins scored a superb 14 for second place on the podium. One behind, Jim McMillan restored the Tigers' pride with 13. This gave him 31 from his three qualifying meetings and a passage to the British semi-finals. Other Tigers on show were Dent with 11, Willie Templeton with seven, and Bill McMillan with five.

June

The match on 7 June was against Wimbledon, a team with good consistent heat-leaders so Glasgow had to improve on their recent performances. A breakdown delayed the Wimbledon bus with six of their team and the Glasgow management ran the second half of the meeting first. Lone traveller Nygren was there early, but his leathers were on the bus and he could not change until they arrived. This meant another change – heat two was raced before heat one.

Berg's rides could be taken by any of the other six Glasgow riders, who included John Boulger as a guest for the injured Josefsson. Jim McMillan was the Tigers' top scorer with 11+1. Boulger chipped in a reasonable nine and Dent scoring 8+2, the Tigers responded as required. At the end of heat 13, the Tigers had won 40–38. Happiness for the Tigers.

Six points down after 11 heats, the Dons closed the gap to two with a heat 12 5–1. Reg Luckhurst and Bob Dugard faced Boulger and Dent in heat 13. Luckhurst won, but Dugard could not pass the Tigers and the resulting 3–3 was enough for the aforementioned home win.

There were reports that Les Whaley was looking to sign Gunnar Malmqvist, who was expected to be available from mid-June, to improve the team. However, that came to nothing. There was glimmer of hope on the horizon in the shape of Bobby Beaton, who was starting to be seen as a good prospect in the second halves at Coatbridge and White City.

The following night, the Tigers were at Halifax as the first half of a double-header. Again, they used rider replacement for Berg and Geoff Mudge was a guest for Josefsson. Jansson was also missing and his place went to Bill McMillan with Brian Whaley taking the reserve berth.

Mudge started well, but tailed off to contribute 10 points from six rides. Templeton added 6+1 and Jim McMillan scored six. With the other three scoring five points between them, the Tigers lost 50–27 and conceded six 5–1s. The second match featured Sheffield and Charlie Monk scored 10 points for the other Tigers.

Halifax came north for the return match on 14 June. They never let the Tigers settle and ended heat 13 ten points up and with a 44–34 win. Berg was back, but the gap left by the still injured Josefsson was filled by using rider-replacement. Yet again, the lower scoring riders did not perform well and Jansson, only scoring one, was disappointing.

Berg scored a good 12 from five rides and Templeton did well scoring with an impressive 11+2 from six rides. Jim McMillan was a bit subdued, but still was next best on eight points.

Les Whaley organised work on the track to deal with the aftereffects of a longish period of drought. It was spearheaded by the Monarchs' Doug Templeton. Unfortunately, the improved strip, as the result shows, suited the Dukes better than the Tigers.

Josefsson was still missing when the Tigers were at Belle Vue the next day. But for an engine failure, Jansson probably would have scored double figures rather than 9+1. He was unlucky to break a primary chain and suffer an ankle injury caused by the flailing chain before one of his races started. Bikes have, for many years since, a small bolt known as the Dutch Peg to stop flailing primary chains. Jim McMillan matched him, but the other four Tigers only gathered 10 points between them. The Aces won 50–28.

Dent had a rare off night when his bike packed up in heat one and he withdrew from the meeting after another pointless outing.

Charlie Monk was back at White City on 21 June and showed that he had not forgotten the quickest way round the track. As so often, his return was a maximum.

Still without Josefsson, the remaining six Tigers tried hard, but just fell short by two points. It was another case of losing in the last heat as Sheffield snatched the match with a 4–2. A better performing Jansson could not beat Bob Paulson, who had been unimpressive prior to the heat, as had his race mate Brian Maxted, who beat a toiling Dent.

It was a better all-round Glasgow effort, but a few more points before heat 13 were needed. On the night, the Tigers fans probably would have blamed Dent and reserve Whaley. Jansson showed what he could do with 12 from five rides and Jim McMillan, who had his handlebars break mid-race, scored nine points. Templeton contributed 7+3.

For the visitors, Bengt Larsson took a tactical ride after Sheffield had fallen six points behind after heat eight. The heat nine Monk & Larsson 5–1 pulled them back into the contest. Sheffield completed the match with two 4–2s to take the league points.

Les Whaley's efforts to improve the team now saw him look at Czechoslovakia, in particular Jan Holub and Lubous Tomicek. Again, nothing came of this bold initiative by Les to strengthen the team, looking to replace Lars Jansson. In the end Jansson's big score against Sheffield did not save him from being released by Whaley. However, the Swede was soon back in the British League riding for Cradley Heath.

The Tigers gave a debut to another Swede, the relatively unknown in the Britain, Ake Andersson on 28 June. Reports suggest that Whaley had also tried to sign Ove Fundin and Leif Enecrona, but in the event the arrival of the new rider did not please many fans. At least Whaley had taken some, possibly long overdue, action. Andersson was reportedly a victim of sea sickness caused by a rough North Sea crossing.

He opened with a race win against the visiting Swindon Robins on 28 June, but only scored one more point from four rides. It is open to conjecture if the move geed up Tigers, who won 43–35, or was it Barry Briggs and Bob Kilby missing from the Robins' line-up. In any event, it was a much welcomed home win and solid displays from Jim McMillan with 10 points and Berg, who rode a bike loaned by Monarchs' Bernt Persson and scored nine. Injury returnee Josefsson scored 8+1. It was their first win for almost a month.

July

July started with a challenging fixture against the Poole Pirates on 5 July. The improvement at the end of June continued and the new look Tigers won 46–32. Once again, Jim McMillan was the best Tiger with 10 points. He lost to Bill Andrew twice, Berg was excluded in heat seven for tape breaking, but won his other three rides for nine points. Josefsson was next on seven. The Tigers were a solid team. Whaley impressed with five points from four rides. He replaced Berg and two-minute exclusion victim Templeton as well as taking his two programmed outings.

The Tigers, who had effectively recalled Whaley from Berwick, allowed Bill McMillan to move to Berwick to take his place. McMillan made his debut on 5 July. It was a fair exchange in the circumstances.

The next day, the travel-sick Tigers arrived at Dudley Wood to face Cradley Heath. They did not, Dent apart, perform well. He won a couple of races as he gathered an impressive 9+1. Jim McMillan opened with a win, then added another four points from his next three rides to score seven. Berg had a poor night including two falls. In heat 10 he fell and brought down Josefsson and Cradley reserve Ken Wakefield in the process. In heat six he had been an unlucky victim of first bend bunching.

The Tigers' two Swedes were described as being unbelievably bad by the *Speedway Star* reporter. The Heathens won 53–25. For the home side, former Tigers Lars Jansson and Coombes rode together and scored two 5–1s.

It was three wins in row for the Tigers at home when they downed Wolverhampton at White City on 10 July. It was another solid showing against what turned out to be a virtually one-man team without star Swede Hasse Holmqvist and Peter Jarman. Ironically, their number one man was Jim Airey, the rider who had refused to move to Glasgow before the start of the season.

The top Tiger was Berg with 11 after losing to Airey in heat one. Jim McMillan scored 10+1 and Templeton returned 8+1. The Tigers started with losing the first heat 4–2, but then moved ahead in the next heat. The gap eventually became 20 and the Tigers won 49–29. Jim Airey with 14 swept all before him until heat 12 when he was beaten by McMillan There were no home meetings on the next two Fridays because of the Glasgow Fair Fortnight Holidays which usually started on the third Monday in July.

The Tigers' fans could visit Wolverhampton on Friday 19 July to see their team. The home team won 43–35, again without Hasse Holmqvist, but this time with home advantage.

Berg gave a sound five ride show to collect 12 and Jim McMillan scored 7+1. He fell while trying to go fast round the fence. Templeton added 7+1, but the two Swedes were toiling. Josefsson scored two points and Andersson failed to score. The Tigers started with a 4–2, but slipped behind like the Wolves had done at White City. Heat eight was the race of the night. Mick Handley just managed to pass Bill McMillan and prevent a Tigers' 5–1.

The fixture planners ignored the Glasgow holidays as a chance for the Tigers' fans to tour with their team. The next fixture was on 25 July at Wimbledon. The Dons pulled away and were 20 points ahead after heat nine. They won 49–29. Berg topped the Tigers' chart with 11+1 and Jim McMillan, growing in stature as the meeting progressed, scored 11 including a win over Olle Nygren. Both Berg and Jim McMillan took five rides. This time the two Swedes scored four, with Andersson again failing to score. The Glasgow management must have been wondering if they had blundered in replacing Jansson.

It should be noted that the next stage in the saga of their team improvement plan was torpedoed with Alan Jay's refusal to go to Glasgow and opting for Newcastle instead. Alan, the son of Wilf Jay who included Ashfield and Edinburgh in his CV, would have helped the tail end. However, the real problem was the failure to replace the dominant fire power of Charlie Monk from the beginning of the season.

Holidays over, the Glasgow fans were ready for the second half of the season. First up on 26 July were Belle Vue who this time managed to get a full team north in these days before the motorways. Traffic jams had prevented the full Aces team arriving at Coatbridge on 19 July when Monarchs raced a side dubbed the Northern Aces. In Glasgow, the Aces lost 44–34 with the reliable duo of Berg and Jim McMillan scoring 12 and 10 respectively from four rides. This was Berg's first maximum for the Tigers. His hardest ride was a struggle to beat Tommy Roper in heat seven. Andersson was next best, with 4+3. Two wins for Templeton saw him third best scorer with six.

It was a solid display from Tigers as they eased to the two league points, but Josefsson's form was becoming a source of concern.

August

At the start of the month, Brian Whaley decided to retire due to being dropped by his dad at Glasgow. However, the Berwick fans convinced him to change his mind and he went back to the Bandits with Bill McMillan going the other way.

The Tigers' latest run of home wins came to an end on 2 August when they faced Hackney at White City. Tigers led to heat four, the visitors levelled and it stayed that way until heat eight when the Hawks edged ahead. Thereafter, the Tigers played catch up, but a 5–1 for Bengt Jansson and Colin Pratt in heat 12 pushed Hackney over the winning line. A 3–3 in heat 13 was academic and Hackney won 42–36.

Without Josefsson, who was covered by rider replacement, and Andersson who was gone, the six-man Tigers had the usual two star riders, Berg on a full 15-point maximum and Jim McMillan on 12+1 from six rides. A rare last place in Jim McMillan's final ride in heat 12 did not help. The rest were pretty poor, no one scored more than four points. As it was, neither of the two Swedes did return, so the Tigers used guests and brought Whaley back yet again on occasions.

An upside of the night was that Oyvind Berg completed a great night by beating Bernt Persson to become Scottish Match Race Champion. Down sides, the defeat apart, were Bill McMillan blowing an engine, as did Dent, who also had a tapes exclusion.

A meeting of the Northern Riders Championship Qualifying Round was on offer the following week. Charlie Monk was back and scored 14 from his five rides to win the meeting and the winner's cheque. Jim McMillan was a point behind and took second place. Ole Olsen was a point behind him in third. The other Tigers scored: Bill McMillan 11, Oyvind Berg 10, Russ Dent five, Willie Templeton two, Brian Whaley two and Bobby Beaton, making his debut, one. Bill's display was worth fifth place and a notable effort for a man who had been consigned to the second half for much of the season until the trip to Wolverhampton in July.

An international challenge match provided the entertainment on 16 August. The visitors were Red Star Prague with the best riders from Czechoslovakia. The Tigers used Charlie

Monk as a guest and he scored another paid maximum at his old home. He was matched by both Berg and Jim McMillan on the same score. Red Star, who went down 51–27, were best served by Jaroslav Volf [Wolf] on 7+1. Frantisek Ledecky scored six and Jan Holub and Antonin Svab were next best on four. Miroslav and Vaclav Verner at numbers six and seven in the team became the best known of these seven riders. The final of the second half event was interesting as Jim McMillan won it from Berg and Monk showing he was now the top Tiger at White City.

Scottish Cup action was next, at Coatbridge the next day. The Tigers managed half the Monarchs' total and lost 64–32 on a slick track. The Tigers' demise was attributed their poor gating. Guest Martin Ashby was top scorer for the Tigers with 10 points. Unusually, Jim McMillan did not win a race and ended with 7+1 from five rides. Berg failed to shine with six, and fell in his first ride. It was a big defeat, but could the Tigers turn the tables the following Friday? The answer was no on aggregate, but yes to the match result.

Not for the want of effort on 23 August, the Tigers won at White City 57–39, a positive showing in front of a bumper crowd. Berg showed that his move to White City was worthwhile as he dropped one point in five rides for 14. Jim McMillan was next best with 11+1 and guest Charlie Monk added 11. Also back in the Tigers' team was Alf Wells after his enforced spell at Newcastle. The tall Kiwi had been replaced at Newcastle by Tigers target Alan Jay. Wells showed his gratitude by gathering 6+3. The Monarchs added to their aggregate lead early on, but the Tigers then started to erode that lead. However, they did not do quite enough despite a spirited effort.

For the Monarchs, Brian Collins was not pleased with the referee. He had featured in heat 13. At the first asking, Berg broke the tapes and was reinstated. In the rerun, Collins broke the tapes and expected to be reinstated as well. No such luck so Collins showed his displeasure by riding through a third set of tapes. This earned him a £10 fine. However, he had the last laugh as the Monarchs fans collected £15 for him, so he ended up £5 to the good! The Cup went to Coatbridge on aggregate 103–89.

The Tigers made their third visit of the season to London, this time to West Ham. Given the Hammers' home record, the result must have had fans thinking the result in the press was the wrong way round. The 42–36 score for the Tigers was correct.

The Hammers, who were missing the injured Sverre Harrfeldt, had an off night, but credit to the Tigers as they did not let the opportunity slip. Jim McMillan scored a maximum 12, by far the best on the night, and there were no other stand out stars in a very solid Tigers team showing. The match was level after heat 11 and the Tigers won the next two, 4–2 and a 5–1 to secure the win. Jim McMillan and Wells took heat 13 against George Barclay and Brian Leonard, who fell when in sight of a double figure return. Berg scored eight and Wells 6+3.

Normally a star man, Glasgow legend Ken McKinlay won his first ride then a shoulder blade bursting fall and exclusion ended his night. Stan Stevens was also involved in the heat five mayhem and went to hospital with a broken leg. A below par return from Norman Hunter did not help. The Tigers were in the right place to reap the rewards of their opponents' misfortunes for a change. It was Glasgow's second – and last – away win in the 1968 season.

The same 'lucky breaks' did not happen at Poole the following night and the Pirates were a much tougher proposition. Jim McMillan scored 13 points. Berg 'fell' in his first ride, laying his bike down to avoid the fallen Bill McMillan and was clearly shaken. Thereafter he only managed three points and a bonus. Best of the rest were Dent and Wells, both with 6+2. The home team won 42–36.

The Tigers next stop was Oxford on 29 August. It was another last heat decider. With the score 37–35 to Oxford, Jim McMillan was relegated to third place after Wells broke the tapes to be replaced by Whaley who was also excluded. To be fair to McMillan, he was up against home specialists Ronnie Genz and Colin Gooddy.

He had started with two wins and added two more to total eight, but was unlucky to lose points when his handlebars broke mid-race. Berg was top Tigers scorer on 10 and Dent was one behind on nine. The scores were never far enough apart to allow a tactical outing. They were often level and never more than apart until the final score of 42–36.

Back at White City, King's Lynn were close to the Tigers. The 44–34 score was enough to give the league points to Glasgow on 30 August. It was close until heat six. The Stars started with a 5–1 from Howard Cole and guest Bert Harkins over Jim McMillan and Templeton. The Tigers levelled by heat four and pulled away from heat seven. Berg was top Tiger again with 11 and Jim McMillan, in the number one race jacket, was next on 10. His brother Bill had a good 7+1. Alf Wells was lucky to be reinstated in heat nine after missing the start and throwing his bike on the centre green. The race was restarted with him and he finished last. King's Lynn were close to withdrawing in protest, but were appeased by the referee allowing Harkins back into the same race after he had broken the tapes in the first attempt to stage the re-rerun.

September

Newcastle came calling on 6 September, but without Ivan Mauger, who was away to Sweden for the World Championship Final. They used their own riders and lost narrowly 41–37. For the record, Mauger completed a faultless 15-point maximum to bag his first of his six World titles. For the Tigers, Berg scored a full maximum. It was a solid, rather than tops and tails, Tigers performance. Jim McMillan scored eight and brother Bill 7+1. The Tigers went ahead in heat four. The scores were always close with the Tigers in ascendancy throughout. The Diamonds' management made full use of tactical substitutes and used Dave Gifford and Ole Olsen to effect in heat 12 when they took a 5–1 ahead of Dent.

Up next at White City were Exeter, a team hitherto not very great on the road. However, this time they swooped to a 42–36 win thanks to a last heat 5–1 by Martin Ashby and Wayne Briggs over Berg and Dent. The Tigers were two points down before heat 13 and the result was not a foregone conclusion, although the Falcons were ahead from heat four.

Berg gave the crowd a scare as he mono-wheeled for some distance away from the tapes in heat one in the days when wheelies were not so controlled. However, he still scored 11+1 from five rides. Jim McMillan scored nine from four. The Falcons got a big break in heat 13 when Wells broke the tapes and was excluded. Brian Whaley was then excluded so, short of the two Exeter riders failing to finish, even a win from Jim McMillan could not see them lose. Wells was the Tigers third highest scorer with 7+3. The Falcons team included Chris Blewett, who had a short spell with the Tigers in 1964.

The last ever league encounter at White City was against Newport Wasps. The battle of the Celtic (Keltic) fringe saw the Scots repulse the Welsh 55–23 on 18 September. Jim McMillan was the Tigers top scorer with 11 after a first heat defeat by Jimmy Gooch. Berg was excluded from his opening ride for breaking the tapes, but went on to gather nine points from his other three rides. Dent scored 8+4, a paid maximum from four rides, having missed a scheduled outing. Wells scored nine from three wins but he, like Berg, broke the tapes in one outing. The Tigers gave Bobby Beaton three rides at number seven and he chipped in two points for a quiet and probably much belated debut. The Tigers were 10 points up after five heats and Exeter's only heat winner was Jimmy Gooch in heat one.

The league fixtures were completed on two days later at Newport. The Tigers were the first team to face the Wasps in a double header which also featured Newcastle. Newport turned the tables on the Tigers, winning 49–29. Torbjorn Harrison, who had missed the trip to Glasgow, scored a paid maximum.

Jim McMillan was the best Tiger on 11, rounding up a great season for him when he stepped up the plate on so many occasions. Berg was next best with nine, showing that he was a class act, and, on the basis of his scores at Coatbridge in 1968, showed that his move to Glasgow was really good for him. The Tigers' third top scorer was Dent with 6+4, an often-unsung Tiger, who showed he was a solid team man.

Alf Wells had a car breakdown, but did arrive at the stadium after the match had started. He did not ride. Some sources record him as a non-starter, others as being replaced in all his programmed outings to facilitate tactical substitute rides by Jim McMillan, Berg and Dent.

The curtain at White City came down at the end of the Glasgow Open Championship meeting on 27 September. Sadly, no the Tigers made it to the podium. The event was won by Nigel Boocock with 14 points. Ole Olsen scored 13 and third place went to former Glasgow icon Charlie Monk with 12. The Tigers scored: Oyvind Berg 11, Jim McMillan six, Russ Dent four, Alf Wells four, Willie Templeton three, Bill McMillan two and reserve Bobby Beaton one.

For the record, the last ever race was won by Ivan Mauger, the 1968 World Champion, ending the life of the track just over 40 years from when it opened in 1928.

Harry Houston, in the *1969 British Speedway Handbook*, said that Jim Airey had refused to come to Glasgow to replace Charlie Monk, and "... that started a series of disappointments as one after another, heat leaders arrived – and left – without making the grade." He also noted that Jim McMillan "shouldered his responsibilities magnificently and was undoubtedly the speedway discovery of the season." He also said that Oyvind Berg "was a model of consistency and his brilliant riding made him a tremendous favourite with the fans." He also noted the "tragic and sudden" death of former Glasgow promoter Danny Taylor.

Thus ended the White City era. As so often in the sport's history, the stadium was lost not because of poor attendances, but because of building work. In this case, a new motorway went through the site.

The 1968 campaign had been a roller coaster of a year with riders coming and leaving. The weak from the start the Tigers saw them finish as bottom of the league and without a new home for 1969. However, they moved to Hampden Park and survived. The story of the following years will be chronicled in the future.

The programmes from the last meetings at White City: the league match with Newport. And the Glasgow Open Championship.

21. Glasgow riders 1946 to 1954

The records for these pieces are for the seasons raced as a Glasgow Tiger only. The riders are arranged in alphabetical order. NL2 and NrL includes League and National Trophy statistics. NT = Northern Trophy, ACUC = ACU Cup, BSC = British Speedway Cup; AC = Anniversary Cup, NS = North Shield staged in both 1950, 1951 and 1954. 1954 records expunged and shown in italics. International appearances and individual tournaments are given for periods as a Tiger.
All Internationals are show irrespective of status. No caps or numbers will be shown for unofficial internationals. Bonus points will be shown as additional points e.g. +2 where appropriate.

Adler, Ted

Ted had a second half at Newcastle in 1946 then was called into service at Brough Park for his only Tigers outing in his second and last recorded meeting.

Year	Comp	M	R	P	BP	TP	CMA	FM	PM
1946	NT	1	2	2	0	2	4.00	0	0

Arlett, Joe

A Glasgow junior in the year immediately after the war. An irregular second halfer in 1946 to 1949, Joe had three outings for the Tigers in 1946.

Year	Comp	M	R	P	BP	TP	CMA	FM	PM
1946	NrL	3	5	0	0	0	0.00	0	0

Bainbridge, Ronald Arthur (Junior)
Born: 19 April 1924, Melbourne, Victoria, Australia.
Died: 5 November 2000.

Although he hailed from Melbourne, 'Junior' was spotted riding in Brisbane by former Australian international Charlie Spinks in 1946 joining Glasgow a year later as one of the influx of Australians and New Zealanders.

Despite being somewhat overshadowed in his time in Scotland by Tommy Miller and Jack Young, 'Junior' was a mainstay of the Tigers until the end of the 1953 season. when the club sold him to Ipswich to help clear debts. In 1947 and 1948 he was a bit inconsistent, but between 1949 and 1953 he consistently recorded averages of over eight points. A popular Tiger, his best season was 1951 when he achieved an 8.95 NL2 average and challenged for the Silver Helmet and Scottish Match Race Championship. When the track closed, he had scored 37 League maximums, despite a fractured knee cap sustained in 1952.

Never a fan of wet tracks, Junior, who co0promoted Glasgow's short 1956 season, retired from racing in the UK at the end of 1957. He continued to ride for a while in Australia.

Year	Comp	M	R	P	BP	TP	CMA	FM	PM
1947	NL2	26	99	117	15	132	5.33	0	0
1947	BSC	12	47	48	11	59	5.02	0	0
1948	NL2	33	136	166	14	180	5.29	1	1
1948	AC	16	66	99	18	117	7.09	0	0
1949	NL2	44	177	345	18	363	8.20	7	3
1950	NL2	22	84	173	11	184	8.76	6	3

1950	NS	14	54	104	3	107	7.92	0	0
1951	NL2	28	114	248	7	255	8.95	5	1
1951	NS	10	38	63	5	68	7.15	0	0
1952	NL2	34	145	293	18	311	8.58	2	1
1953	NL2	36	150	275	24	299	7.97	4	3

Individual Honours
British Riders Championship 1948 Did not progress beyond NLD3 round
World Championship 1949 Did not progress beyond Round three
1950 Did not progress beyond Championship round
1951 Did not progress beyond Round three
1952 Did not progress beyond Championship round
1953 Did not progress beyond Round one

Silver Helmet 1951 Lost 2–0 to Tommy Miller

Scottish Match Race

11 May 1949	White City	Ken Le Breton bt Junior Bainbridge	2–1
19 July 1949	Ashfield	Ken Le Breton bt Junior Bainbridge	2–0
7 July 1951	Edinburgh	Jack Young bt Junior Bainbridge	2–1
25 July 1951	White City	Junior Bainbridge bt Jack Young	2–1
31 July 1951	Ashfield	Jack Young bt Junior Bainbridge	2–0
30 July 1952	White City	Tommy Miller bt Junior Bainbridge	2–1

International Honours
Australia   1948   5+1 points v England (Division Two Teams)
                     1949   11 points v England (Division Two Teams)
                     1950   1 cap   1 point v England
                     1951   3 caps 6+2 points v England
                     1952   2 caps 0 points v England
Overseas   1947   1 cap   1 point v Britain
                     1950   4 caps 6+1 points v Britain
                     1951   3 caps 20+3 points v Britain
                     1952   2 caps 30 points v Britain
                     1953   3 caps 10 points v Britain
                     1951   1 cap   DNR v England
Scotland   1948   1 cap   8+1 points v England
                     1949   1 cap   6+2 points v England
                     1951   4 caps 21 points v England
                     1952   3 caps 15+2 points v England
                     1953   5 caps 16+1 points v England
Great Britain   1956   1 cap   5 points v Overseas

Scottish Championships
                     1949   4 points
                     1950   7 points
                     1951   9 points
                     1953   9 points

Baird, William Alexander (Bill)
Born: 16 March 1922, Forth, Scotland.

Initially a post-war junior at Glasgow, Bill spent his six-year racing career in his native Scotland, apart from a short spell at Bradford in 1947. He proved to be a popular performer despite rarely rising much above a reserve role riding at different times for all four Scottish venues in operation in the late 1940s and early 1950s. His best spell in the sport came while riding for Edinburgh in 1948.

Year	Comp	M	R	P	BP	TP	CMA	FM	PM
1946	NrL	18	50	37	8	45	3.60	0	0
1946	NT	3	3	4	0	4	5.33	0	0
1946	ACUC	10	26	18	1	19	2.92	0	0
1947	NL2	15	56	54	7	61	4.36	0	0
1947	BSC	1	4	4	1	5	5.00	0	0

Individual Honours
British Riders Championship 1946 Did not progress beyond NL Round

Bates, Billie
Born: Scotland.
Died: September 2001.

Billie spent three seasons in and out of the Glasgow team, mainly riding in second half races. In 1946, Middlesbrough made a bid for him but Glasgow refused to allow him to leave. He rode for the Tigers in 1947, making nine appearances. After a few team outings in 1948 Billie was given a chance again in 1949. Apparently, he was given a choice by his father of plumbing or speedway and chose plumbing.

Year	Comp	M	R	P	BP	TP	CMA	FM	PM
1947	NL2	4	10	12	3	15	6.00	0	0
1947	BSC	5	14	16	3	19	5.42	0	0
1948	NL2	3	6	4	2	6	4.00	0	0
1949	NL2	10	20	10	2	12	2.40	0	0

Beardsall, Stanley (Stan)
Born: 3 November 1919, England.

A pre-war junior at Sheffield, Stan rode briefly in the immediate post-war years for Glasgow, He went on to ride for Bradford, Wigan and Wombwell, retiring after a short spell at Fleetwood in 1949. He drove midget cars in the 1950s.

Year	Comp	M	R	P	BP	TP	CMA	FM	PM
1946	NrL	3	7	5	1	6	3.43	0	0

Blyth, Jim*
Born: c. 1928, Glasgow, Scotland. (* the spelling of his name confirmed by the late Glyn Shailes)

Jim come through the ranks in the late 1940s and early 1950s. He rode for the Tigers for much of 1951, but loss of form saw him dropped. He moved to Ashfield 'Giants' for 1952, then Ipswich for 1953 and part of 1954.

Year	Comp	M	R	P	BP	TP	CMA	FM	PM
1951	NL2	22	48	42	10	52	4.33	0	0
1951	NS	8	22	20	7	27	4.90	0	0

Individual Honours
1951 Winner White City Novice Championship

Byrnes, Bernard Francis (Bat)
Born: 15 July 1915, Sydney, New South Wales, Australia.
Died: 1976.

A former road racer who came to England in 1947. He joined Harringay then, after struggling there, moved to Glasgow where he became a crowd favourite.

He spent three seasons at White City. Road racing commitments delayed his return in 1948, but when he did arrive, he lost no time, scoring double figures in his first three matches. He was even better in 1949. In his last season in Britain, 'Bat' topped the Glasgow averages with an 8.35 CMA. A fractured skull sustained at Norwich in September ended his season early. He found himself suffering from deafness in one ear and serious headaches as a result of the crash and decided not to return for 1950.

Year	Comp	M	R	P	BP	TP	CMA	FM	PM
1947	NL2	17	69	96	10	106	6.14	0	0
1947	BSC	13	56	93	8	101	7.21	0	0
1948	NL2	19	81	149	13	162	8.00	1	1
1948	AC	12	52	78	5	83	6.38	0	0
1949	NL2	21	85	170.5	7	177.5	8.35	3	0

Individual Honours
British Riders Championship   1947 Did not progress beyond NLD2 Round

Australian Championship   1949 3rd

International Honours:
Overseas	1948		7+2 points v Britain
Scotland	1948	1 cap	9+1 points v England
	1949	1 cap	5 points v England

Craig, Douglas

Douglas Craig was a Scot who was given his chance in 1954 in that season's short-lived team. He rode in all six fixtures. He did not continue in speedway after the closure of the track

Year	Comp	M	R	P	BP	TP	CMA	FM	PM
1954	NS	6	12	6	1	7	2.33	0	0

Crowther, Joseph Cameron (Joe)
Born: 27 April 1913, Stanley, County Durham, England.
Died: 22 February 1991.

Apart from being a fine speedway rider, Joe listed professional footballer and comedian in an opera company as previous occupations He was a well-loved character and performer in the Scotland. He started riding at Middlesbrough in 1937, but his best years were at Glasgow.

He was a Glasgow Lion in 1939 and returning in 1946 as a Tiger. In the immediate post-war seasons, he was a mainstay of an often-struggling side, forming an admirable spearhead with fellow heat leader Will Lowther and excelling around the White City circuit. He scored over 1,400 points in his five seasons with the Tigers and maintained an average of around eight points per match until 1949. His best season was 1948 when he dominated the second half events, winning an exceptional number of trophies.

Hampered by a run of injuries, his scoring dropped and he moved to Motherwell in 1951. Joe raced on, but more injuries restricted his scoring in 1951 and 1952 and an attempted return in 1953 failed. He spent 1954 as the Eagles mechanic and later had a spell as team manager at Leicester.

Year	Comp	M	R	P	BP	TP	CMA	FM	PM
1946	NrL	24	100	191	9	200	8.00	1	0
1946	NT	4	19	37.5	2	39.5	8.31	0	0
1946	ACUC	10	47	98	4	102	8.68	1	0
1947	NL2	25	98	178	12	190	7.76	1	0
1947	BSC	8	30	39	5	44	5.86	0	0
1948	NL2	36	148	275	22	297	8.03	2	3
1948	AC	16	76	171	5	176	9.26	2	2
1949	NL2	29	108	198	20	218	8.07	2	1
1950	NL2	15	59	79	16	95	6.44	0	1
1950	NS	14	56	60	7	67	4.78	0	0

Individual Honours
British Riders Championship 1946 Did not progress beyond NrL Round
                                 1947 Did not compete
                                 1948 Did not progress beyond NLD2 Round
World Championship   1949 Did not compete
                                 1950 Did not progress beyond NLD2 Round

International Honours
Britain   1946   2+2 points v Overseas
                                 1947   8+4 points v Overseas
Scotland   1948 1 cap   13+1 points v England
                                 1949 1 cap   0 points v England

Others   1946 Won 50 Guineas Trophy at Sheffield
                                 1948 Won 50 Guineas Trophy at Edinburgh

Downham, Alfred (Nobby)
Born: 25 January 1922, Wisbech, Cambridgeshire, England.
Died: April 1991.

East Anglian Nobby learned to ride while stationed in Italy during the war. He impressed the Glasgow management and was offered a team place. Nobby spent three years with Glasgow, part of which was on loan with Edinburgh in 1948. He overcame a foot injury setback and became a useful reserve for the Tigers in early 1949. A loss of form saw him lose his place in July and he retired thereafter.

Year	Comp	M	R	P	BP	TP	CMA	FM	PM
1947	NL2	3	6	3	0	3	2.00	-	-
1947	BSC	1	3	1	0	1	1,33	0	0

Year	Comp	M	R	P	BP	TP	CMA	FM	PM
1948	NL2	8	24	25	5	30	5.00	0	0
1949	NL2	23	56	52	13	65	4.64	0	0

Individual Honours
World Championship   1949   Did not progress beyond first round

Dykes, Charles Peter Van Wren
Born: 23 October 1928, Christchurch, New Zealand.
Died: 14 December 1998.

A protégé of former Australian international Charlie Spinks, Peter Dykes started riding at Christchurch in 1947 before coming to the UK in 1950. He joined the colonial contingent at Glasgow. He missed only one meeting and scored a paid maximum at home to Stoke in June. He missed the 1951 campaign and returned in 1952 to resume as a Tiger.

In 1952, he was inconsistent, excellent at home matches but his away form, like so many of the Tigers, was often poor. He improved in 1953, but struggled to make the sport pay, and took a job in the insurance industry in South Africa at the end of the season, eventually returning home to New Zealand.

Year	Comp	M	R	P	BP	TP	CMA	FM	PM
1950	NL2	31	86	116	25	141	6.56	0	1
1950	NS	14	39	45	5	50	5.12	0	0
1952	NL2	50	194	213	43	256	5.28	0	0
1953	NL2	38	144	185.5	33	218.5	6.07	0	1

Individual Honours
World Championship   1950   Did not progress beyond Qualifying Round
                           1952   Did not progress beyond NLD2 Round
International Honours
New Zealand   1953   1 cap   10 points v Scotland
Overseas   1952   2 caps 1 point v Britain

Scottish Championship   1952   7 points

Fairhurst, Harold
Born: 12 March 1913, Wigan, Greater Manchester, England.

Wigan born; Harold Fairhurst emigrated to New Zealand aged seven. It was suggested that he was a true Kiwi with Wigan origins was invented to ease overseas rider restrictions which greatly affected Glasgow. Based in Auckland, he was one of the finest early post-war 'Kiwi' riders. He won the New Zealand Championship in 1949 and 1954.

After trials at Bradford in 1947, he joined the Tigers and his uncompromising riding style made him a popular Tiger. In 1949, he moved to local rivals Edinburgh and showed slow, but steady improvement, almost reaching heat leader status by the end of 1952.

He did not return in 1953 but raced in New Zealand. Harold was sadly killed in a mining accident a few years later.

Year	Comp	M	R	P	BP	TP	CMA	FM	PM
1947	NL2	21	64	60	14	74	4.63	0	0
1947	BSC	11	42	47	11	58	5.52	0	0
1948	NL2	36	145	189	24	213	5.88	0	1

Year	Comp	M	R	P	BP	TP	CMA	FM	PM
1948	AC	16	63	59	19	78	4.95	0	0
1949	NL2	14	49	59	13	72	5.88	0	0

Individual Honours
World Championship   1949   Did not progress beyond Round one

New Zealand Championship   1949   Winner (March 1949)

International Honours
Australia   1948   0 points v English Stars (Division Two Teams)
Overseas   1947   2 points v Britain

Garland, Cecil Alfred (Gruff)
Born: 29 January 1915, Sydney, New South Wales, Australia.
Died: 1989.

Gruff, a former rugby league player, first rode speedway at Sydney Royale in 1936. He came to the UK in 1939, joining Glasgow. He married a local girl later that year. He rejoined Glasgow after the War. In 1946, Gruff was the fourth best Tiger and it was his best season. Injury problems ruined his 1947 campaign. He was not able to recapture his form in later spells at Bradford and Ashfield, and returned home at the end of 1949. He rode in Australia, but a badly broken arm ended his career. Gruff used his nickname as he thought Cecil wasn't suitable for a speedway rider.

Year	Comp	M	R	P	BP	TP	CMA	FM	PM
1946	NrL	21	85	143	19	162	7.62	0	0
1946	NT	4	20	25	5	30	6.00	0	0
1946	ACUC	10	46	51	6	57	4.59	0	0
1947	NL2	9	33	46	2	48	5.82	0	0
1947	BSC	7	32	39	1	40	5.00	0	0
1948	NL2	6	13	9	0	9	2.77	0	0
1948	AC	7	22	7	2	9	1.63	0	0

Individual Honours
British Riders Championship   1946   Did not progress beyond NrL round
                                  1947   Did not progress beyond NLD2 round
International Honours
Overseas   1946   4+2 points v Britain

Gordon, William Cunningham (Will, Bill, and Jock)

Born: 16 June 1920, Elderslie, Scotland.

A Scottish junior who tried his luck at Stoke in 1947, but broke a leg late that season. He returned in 1948, but lost his team place by the end of May. Will returned north of the border and had unsuccessful spells at both Edinburgh and Glasgow. He spent most of the 1950 season racing in Ireland at Wally Lloyd's Dunmore track in Belfast and was a great success.

Year	Comp	M	R	P	BP	TP	CMA	FM	PM
1950	NL2	1	2	1	0	1	2.00	0	0
1950	NS	1	3	0	0	0	0.00	0	0

Green, John (Johnny)
Born: 25 May 1927, Burnley, Lancashire, England.

Johnny started his career at Hull in Division Three in 1949. He moved to Glasgow early in 1950, but a poor run of scores saw him go to Sheffield. In 1951, he started at Sheffield before moving to Edinburgh. Towards the end of 1952 he moved to Motherwell replacing Keith Gurtner who joined the Monarchs. After Motherwell closed, he spent the next two seasons at Leicester. A come back at Newcastle in 1961 was unsuccessful.

Year	Comp	M	R	P	BP	TP	CMA	FM	PM
1950	NS	10	25	11	2	13	2.08	0	0

Hodgson, Ernest Frank
Born: 25 May 1908, Middlesbrough, North Yorkshire, England.
Died: 9 May 1983.

A former sign writer, Frank Hodgson saw speedway at Hackney and tried it out at Dagenham in 1936. He rode for Nottingham before returning to Hackney and captained them until the War. Following service with the RAF, Frank joined Middlesbrough in 1946, but was out of action for a spell due to a back injury. Back in the saddle, he made up for lost time as part of their Northern League winning team. He captained the Bears to the 1947 title, and starred in 1948. Frank was a top-class performer and reached the British Riders Championship Finals in 1946 and 1948.

Following the closure of Cleveland Park, he moved to Newcastle for 1949 and part of 1950. As a Magpie then Diamond, his form dipped and he moved to Glasgow in August 1950 where he scored solidly. With the Tigers, back pain eventually took its toll and reduced his returns. He ended 1952 as a useful reserve. Earlier glory days may have been over, but he scored a pile of race and especially bonus points for the Tigers.

Year	Comp	M	R	P	BP	TP	CMA	FM	PM
1950	NL2	19	76	111	21	132	6.95	0	1
1951	NL2	32	124	170	30	200	6.45	1	3
1951	NS	10	37	50	11	61	6.59	0	0
1952	NL2	33	89	79	17	96	4.31	0	0

Individual Honours
World Championship   1951   Did not progress beyond Third Round
     1952   Did not progress beyond First Round

Scottish Championship   1950   2 points

Hodgson, John Thusson (Jack)
Born: 21 June 1915, Middlesbrough, North Yorkshire, England.
Died: September 1989.

While not achieving the individual success of his elder brother Frank, Jack Hodgson's career followed a similar path and he picked up Championship medals in 1946 and 1947. Jack rode on the grass tracks pre-War and served with the RAF before taking up speedway. He provided superb back up to the Bears' heat leader trio of Fred Curtis, Wilf Plant and his elder brother.

He moved to Newcastle in 1949, then swapped to Glasgow in an exchange deal for Will Lowther. He spent the rest of his career as a dependable middle order rider. He retired at the end of 1952, closely followed by Frank. This ended the Hodgson era in northern Second Comp speedway.

Year	Comp	M	R	P	BP	TP	CMA	FM	PM
1949	NL2	9	36	60	2	62	6.89	0	0
1950	NL2	31	123	177	29	206	6.70	1	1
1950	NS	14	51	68	10	78	5.77	0	0
1951	NL2	31	121	152	29	181	5.98	0	1
1951	NS	10	36	56	9	65	7.22	0	1
1952	NL2	28	86	75	20	95	4.42	0	0

Individual Honours
World Championship   1950   Did not progress beyond NLD2 round
                             1951   Did not progress beyond Third round
                             1952   Did not progress beyond NLD3 round

International Honours
England   1949–50 6 caps 34 points (v South Africa)

Scottish Championship   1950   2 points

Irvine, Stuart
Born: c. 1927, Glasgow, Scotland.

A former Merchant Navy seaman, Stuart had an outing in 1951 and was a second halfer in 1952 before being given a team place. Put in the body of the team in a National Trophy tie, he was replaced by more experienced reserves. Most of his time was in a reserve berth. He had a few second half outings 1953 and 1954. His brother Slim was a second halfer in 1951 and 1952.

Year	Comp	M	R	P	BP	TP	CMA	FM	PM
1952	NL2	13	24	11	1	12	2.00	0	0

Lack, Edward Ivan (Eddie)
Born: 13 October 1922, West Ham, London, England.
Died: November 2009.

A former RAF pilot, East Londoner Eddie spent almost his whole of his speedway career in Scotland. A Tigers regular in 1946, a broken arm in 1947 meant he missed the rest of the season. He joined Edinburgh in 1948 and rode there until mid-1954 when the Monarchs closed. He ended his racing days with a spell at the short-lived Weymouth club before becoming a leading track curator.

Year	Comp	M	R	P	BP	TP	CMA	FM	PM
1946	NrL	21	82	71	16	87	4.24	0	0
1946	NT	4	20	19	6	25	5.00	0	0
1946	ACUC	8	36	29	8	37	4.11	0	0
1947	NL2	1	1	0	0	0	0.00	0	0

Individual Honours
British Riders Championship   1946   Did not progress beyond NrL Round

International Honours
Britain   1946   DNR v Overseas

Lazarus, John (Larry)

Born: 15 December 1918, Glasgow, Scotland.
Died: June 2007.

A sand racer before the War, Larry had his early speedway experience on the Army tracks in Germany. He rode for Ashfield from 1949 to 1952 where he was a popular Giant.
1n 1953 Larry joined Glasgow Tigers, and scored steadily, then moved to Motherwell in 1954. He had a short spell at Ipswich in 1955 and 1956 before retiring. He was a part of the speedway scene in the 1960s.

Year	Comp	M	R	P	BP	TP	CMA	FM	PM
1953	NL2	37	141	179	31	210	5.96	0	4

Individual Honours
World Championship   1953   Did not progress beyond NLD3 round

International Honours
Scotland   1953   1 cap   2 points v New Zealand

Scottish Championships   1953   7 points

Lindsay, Norman John
Born: 9 April 1917, Melbourne, Victoria, Australia.
Died: 1998.

Norman was tutored by Charlie Spinks. In 1939, he rode for Bristol and Harringay. He saw wartime fire service action in the UK, then joined the Australian Air Force fighting in New Guinea. In 1947 he joined Harringay's Australian contingent, but was swapped for Wal Morton.

A popular Tiger, he was a fixture in the team for almost five seasons and made a massive number of appearances from 1947 to 1951. He was something of an unsung hero and rarely hit the headlines, but was the type of rider who, as his record shows, could be relied upon for a solid score at almost every meeting.

Year	Comp	M	R	P	BP	TP	CMA	FM	PM
1947	NL2	20	81	100.5	14	114.5	5.65	0	0
1947	BSC	8	32	57	4	61	7.62	0	0
1948	NL2	35	124	162	20	182	5.87	0	1
1948	AC	15	54	67	11	78	5.77	0	0
1949	NL2	46	176	230	30	260	5.91	0	1
1950	NL2	32	131	190	33	223	6.81	0	2
1950	NS	13	51	73	8	81	6.35	0	0
1951	NL2	32	123	156	25	181	5.89	0	2
1951	NS	10	40	72	3	75	7.50	0	0

Individual Honours		
British Riders Championship	1948	Did not progress beyond NLD2 round
World Championship	1949	Did not progress beyond Third round
	1951	Did not progress beyond Second round
International Honours		
Australia	1949	6+1 points v England (Division Two)
Overseas	1947	10 points v Britain
	1950	1 cap 1 point v Britain
Scotland	1948	1 cap 5+2 points v England
	1950	1 cap 1 point v England
Scottish Championship	1949	3 points

Lloyd, Peter
Born: 2 May 1929, Middlesbrough, North Yorkshire, England.
Died: 2021.

Peter was a Middlesbrough junior when he rode for the Tigers in a single meeting at his home track. He had his longest spell at Newcastle in 1947. In the two following years Peter appeared for a few teams including Edinburgh, Ashfield and Poole, but never rode full-time. He made a brief comeback in 1961.

Year	Comp	M	R	P	BP	TP	CMA	FM	PM
1946	NrL	1	2	0	0	0	0.00	0	0

Lockley, John (Johnny)
Born: 18 January 1913, Preston, Lancashire, England
Died: 1959.

After riding at Preston in the early days, he was a mechanic at Glasgow White City in 1946 and had four outings for Glasgow. Comebacks in the late 1940s quickly fizzled out.

Year	Comp	M	R	P	BP	TP	CMA	FM	PM
1946	NrL	1	2	0	0	0	0.00	0	0
1946	ACUC	3	5	0	0	0	0.00	0	0

Lowther, William Atkinson (Will)
Born: 11 February 1913, Low Fell, Tyne & Wear, England.
Died: 1982.

Will was a much-travelled rider before the War, riding for several teams including Glasgow in 1939. He was signed by Glasgow in 1946 to lead the Tigers. He and Joe Crowther formed the early spearhead. He was a top heat leader in all seasons from 1946 to 1949, among the top 10 riders in the league in 1946 and 1947.

His form dipped in 1948 and 1949. A dispute over non-selection for an international led to him moving to his favourite track, Newcastle, with Jack Hodgson going the other way. The transfer did not bring about an upturn in scoring and in 1951 he joined Motherwell. He retired at the end of 1952. He is a Tigers legend.

Year	Comp	M	R	P	BP	TP	CMA	FM	PM
1946	NrL	22	94	220	5	225	9.57	7	0
1946	NT	4	20	38.5	1	39.5	7.90	0	0
1946	ACUC	8	39	69	7	76	7.79	0	1
1947	NL2	30	121	288	0	288	9.52	9	0
1947	BSC	14	69	168	3	171	9.91	3	0
1948	NL2	36	149	254.5	19	273.5	7.34	2	1
1948	AC	16	73	149	8	157	8.60	3	0
1949	NL2	37	151	265	18	283	7.50	3	1

Individual Honours
British Riders Championship   1946   Did not progress beyond NrL round
                                   1947   Did not progress beyond NLD1 round
                                   1948   Did not progress beyond NDL2 round

World Championship   1949   Did not progress beyond Third round

International Honours:
Britain   1946   11+2 points v Overseas
                                   1947   16 points v Overseas
Scotland   1948   1 cap   7+1 points v England

Northern Riders Championship 1946   8 points

Northern Match Race Challenge Cup

17 Sept 1947	White City	Will Lowther bt Tommy Bateman 2–0
27 Sept 1947	Wigan	Will Lowther bt Dick Geary 2–0
1 Oct 1947	White City	Will Lowther bt Dick Geary 2–0

McGregor, James Ramsay (Gordon)
Born: 28 November 1921, Linlithgow, Scotland.
Died: 29 September 2001.

Started out with Glasgow in 1947 after racing in the Army in Germany. He steadily improved from 1947 second halves and had a few team outings by the end of the season. Between 1948 and 1950 Gordon was a regular rising to heat leader status. He could be good, but would sometimes have a poor meeting or two. Dubbed 'The Tash' Gordon was famous for his bushy moustache which he trimmed as his Tigers career progressed.

In 1951 Gordon moved to Motherwell to spearhead the new Eagles and remained there for four years. His form did decline a little and a possible move to Leicester in 1954 did not happen, with Ken McKinlay 'beating' him to a place.

Perhaps he could be described as an enigma as at his best he could beat anyone. He moved south in 1955 and rode for Leicester in 1955 and 56, Oxford 1958 to 1962, Belle Vue 1963 to 1966, Long Eaton 1967, King's Lynn II 1969, Doncaster 1970 and Birmingham in 1971. The last three saw high scores in the lower level league.

Year	Division	M	R	P	BP	TP	CMA	FM	PM
1947	NL2	6	16	10	5	15	3.75	0	0
1947	BSC	1	4	6	0	6	6.00	0	0
1948	NL2	32	71	54	15	69	3.89	0	0

1948	AC	12	36	38	7	45	5.00	0	1
1949	NL2	46	182	260	30	290	6.37	2	1
1950	NL2	32	133	229	23	252	7.58	0	1
1950	NS	14	55	108	7	115	8.36	1	1

Individual Honours
World Championship 1949 Did not progress beyond Third round
  1950 Did not progress beyond NLD2 round

International Honours
Britain   1950 1 cap 0 points v Overseas
Scotland 1949 1 cap 4+2 points v England
  1949 1 cap 9 points v Holland
  1950 1 cap 1 point v England

Scottish Championship 1949 11
  1950 10

McGuire, William (Angus)
Born: 5 March 1921, Hamilton, Scotland.

A wartime dispatch rider, Angus started at Glasgow in 1946 appearing in one meeting. He had a few more outings in 1947 and 1948, but made little of it. He rode for Liverpool in 1949 having the odd good meeting and started as a Chad in 1950 before moving to Fleetwood for the rest of 1950 and some of 1951.

Year	Comp	M	R	P	BP	TP	CMA	FM	PM
1946	ACUC	1	1	0	0	0	0.00	0	0
1947	NL2	5	16	7	1	8	2.00	0	0
1948	NL2	8	16	5	1	6	1.50	0	0

McIntosh, Alfred (Alf)
Born: 27 September 1926, Glasgow, Scotland.
Died: c.1999.

A grass track rider before racing on shale in 1948, he remained in Scotland for his whole speedway career. He took two years to establish himself as a Tiger and another two to progress to the full team on a regular basis. Progress in 1950 was restricted by a pre-season knee complaint. He hurt his ankle later that year. In 1952, Alf finally developed, averaging 5.60 and recording his debut paid maximum. When Glasgow closed in 1954, he had a short time as a Monarch before they closed as well. A joiner by trade, Alf became a teacher.

Year	Comp	M	R	P	BP	TP	CMA	FM	PM
1948	NL2	1	2	2	0	2	4.00	0	0
1949	NL2	21	56	42	11	53	3.79	0	0
1950	NL2	15	33	39	8	47	5.70	0	0
1951	NL2	32	90	82	21	103	4.58	0	0
1951	NS	10	30	44	4	48	6.40	1	0
1952	NL2	43	167	208	26	234	5.60	0	1
1953	NL2	21	89	122	12	134	6.02	0	1
1954	*NS*	*6*	*24*	*21*	*4*	*25*	*4.16*	*0*	*0*

Individual Honours
World Championship   1951   Did not progress beyond Second round
                               1953   Did not progress beyond NLD3 round
International Honours
Scotland   1949   1 cap   9+3 points v Holland
                               1953   1-point v New Zealand

McKinlay, John Robert Vicars (Ken)
Born: 7 June 1928, Blantyre, Scotland.
Died: February 2003.

Born John Robert Vicars, McKinlay was renamed by Johnnie Hoskins. He started as a second halfer in 1948, then, in 1949 progressed into a reserve berth by early June. He was in-and-out for much of the season.

From May 1950, he rode for the Tigers regularly and fluctuated between reserve and a team place after August. He was an established team man from 1951 to 1954. He rose to heat leader from 1952 onwards showing phenomenal form before the Tigers closed.

He rode for Leicester from 1954 to 1961, then transferred to Coventry where he rode from 1962 to 1964. He went on to lead West Ham for five seasons, including winning the triple in 1965 – league championship, KO Cup and London Cup. He then appeared for Oxford, Scunthorpe, Kings' Lynn, Coatbridge and Cradley before retiring after 1973.

He is acknowledged as Scotland's best ever rider on the basis of multi world final appearances. His greatest years were after he left Glasgow. He had steadily learned his trade as a Tiger, but sadly they never reaped much of benefit from him in terms of trophies.

Year	Comp	M	R	P	BP	TP	CMA	FM	PM
1949	NL2	20	47	27	3	30	2.55	0	0
1950	NL2	27	71	89	17	106	5.97	0	0
1950	NS	4	10	18	3	21	8.40	1	0
1951	NL2	31	122	171	13	184	6.03	2	0
1951	NS	10	40	50	13	63	6.30	0	0
1952	NL2	49	203	394	20	414	8.16	2	3
1953	NL2	40	173	360	24	384	8.88	7	2
1954	*NS*	*6*	*24*	*67*	*0*	*67*	*11.6*	*3*	*0*

Individual Honours

World Championship   1951   Did not progress beyond Round one
                               1952   Did not progress beyond Round one
                               1953   Did not progress beyond Round three

International Honours
Britain   1952   1 cap   0 points v Overseas
                               1953   3 caps 28+ 4 points v Overseas
Scotland   1949   7+2 points v Holland
                               1951   1 cap   1+1 points v England
                               1952   3 caps 28+3 points v England
                               1953   5 caps 53+7 points v England
                               1953   11+2 points v New Zealand

	Scottish Championship	1951	2 points
		1952	8 points
		1953	7 points

McWilliams, Vernon (Vern)
Born: 17 February 1931, Germiston, South Africa.

Vern was due to come to Motherwell but an injury ruled him out. He joined Glasgow in 1954, but was not a big scorer. He moved to Wolverhampton which closed soon after his arrival. He was third time lucky with Poole. He never returned to the UK.

Year	Comp	M	R	P	BP	TP	CMA	FM	PM
1954	NS	5	15	7	0	7	1.86	0	0

Malm, Arthur
Born: 11 September 1934, Manly, New South Wales, Australia.
Died: March 2011.

Billed as a new speedway sensation, Arthur came to Tigers in 1953 with high expectations placed on his shoulders. Sadly, he did not live up to those expectations and only had a few team outings in 1953. He rode in most of the Tigers curtailed 1954 season. He rode in Australia and had a try out at Edinburgh in 1961 before going home. His name is pronounced Marm.

Year	Comp	M	R	P	BP	TP	CMA	FM	PM
1953	NL2	5	12	1	0	1	0.33	0	0
1954	NS	5	13	5	0	5	1.53	0	0

Miller, Thomas Ogilvie (Tommy)
Born: 22 February 1924, High Blantyre, Scotland.
Died: 1975.

One of Scotland's best riders. Tommy Miller had a few second halves in late 1949 and practiced at Bothwell over the winter. Starting at reserve, he became a top six regular by mid-May and scored his first full maximum by mid-July. A truly meteoric rise, although he tended to be better at home than away. That said, he scored his first away maximum at the tricky Yarmouth track in mid-August. After a winter in Australia, he came back and was an amazingly prolific scorer for his next three seasons as a Tiger. He became the Silver Helmet holder beating Jack Young in 1951. His mastery in 1952 and 1953 is reflected in the number of maximums he collected in league meetings. He did not quite become the fourth Scottish rider to qualify for the World Final, missing out by a very narrow margin.

In 1954, he was transferred to Motherwell, a track where he was the master. This move helped fund the aborted season at White City. Disputes with Motherwell promoters led to a move to Coventry which signalled the start of a decline in the 1955 season. His scoring fell away and in 1956 he moved to Oxford without any resulting improvement. He retired after the pre-season practice at Oxford in 1957 to pursue his business interests.

He and Junior Bainbridge tried to revive White City in 1956 but it wasn't a success. Tommy's last direct involvement was as an umpire (referee) for the 1964 'black' Provincial

League. Tommy had a relatively short but spectacular career and his achievements speak for themselves.

Year	Comp	M	R	P	BP	TP	CMA	FM	PM
1950	NL2	31	130	281	15	296	9.11	6	4
1950	NS	14	45	48	11	59	5.24	0	0
1951	NL2	32	131	339	5	344	10.50	12	2
1951	NS	8	12	83	1	84	10.50	3	1
1952	NL2	49	208	564	4	568	10.92	21	1
1953	NL2	39	171	462	3	465	10.88	23	0

Individual Honours

World Championship
- 1950 Did not progress beyond NLD1 round
- 1951 Did not progress beyond Round thee
- 1952 Did not progress beyond Semis
- 1953 Did not progress beyond Round three

International Honours

England
- 1951 1 cap 10 points v Overseas
- 1952 2 caps 5 points v Australia
- 1953 1 cap 1 point v Australia

Britain
- 1950 1 cap 2 points v Overseas
- 1951 2 caps 12+4 points v Overseas
- 1952 4 caps 51+3 points v Overseas
- 1953 4 caps 62+3 points v Overseas
- 1956 1 cap 8 points v Overseas

Scotland
- 1950 1 cap 18 points v England
- 1951 5 caps 52+5 points v England
- 1952 5 caps 72+4 points v England
- 1953 5 caps 67+2 points v England
- 1953 1 cap 16 points v New Zealand

Silver Helmet 1951 Beat Jack Young, 0–2, 2–1, 2–0 to win and defended against Junior Bainbridge, 2–1, 2–0.

Scottish Match Race

19 July 1950	White City	Jack Young bt Tommy Miller	2–1
5 August 1950	Edinburgh	Tommy Miller bt Jack Young	2–0
29 August 1950	Ashfield	Tommy Miller bt Jack Young	2–0
19 Sept 1950	Ashfield	Ken Le Breton bt Tommy Miller	2–0
20 Sept 1950	White City	Ken Le Breton bt Tommy Miller	2–0
16 May 1951	White City	Tommy Miller bt Jack Young	2–0
2 June 1951	Edinburgh	Jack Young bt Tommy Miller	2–0
22 June 1951	Motherwell	Jack Young bt Tommy Miller	2–1
31 May 1952	Ashfield	Tommy Miller bt Derrick Close	2–0
13 June 1952	Motherwell	Tommy Miller bt Harold Fairhurst	2–0
30 July 1952	White City	Tommy Miller bt Junior Bainbridge	2–1
16 August 1952	Edinburgh	Tommy Miller bt Don Cuppleditch	2–0

Scottish Championship	1950	10	
	1951	14	
	1952	12	
	1953	15	Winner

Monteith, Jack (Red)
Born: 2 July 1931, Paisley, Scotland.
Died: 12 January 2010.

A never say die rider, Jack was a popular second half rider who entertained the fans with his neck or nothing efforts. It proves that a rider does not always have to be a star in speedway to be a favourite. He had a few outings in 1949 but featured more regularly in the period 1952 to 1956. He was only given two outings with the Tigers, one each in 1952 and 53, but had a few at Motherwell in 1958 and at Edinburgh in 1963 before turning out for Tigers from 1964 to 1966 (see next chapter). Tales about Jack are legion and his biggest claim to fame was leading a rescue of the Tigers in 1997 and 1998.

Year	Comp	M	R	P	BP	TP	CMA	FM	PM
1952	NL2	1	2	1	1	2	4.00	0	0
1953	NL2	1	1	1	1	2	8.00	0	0

Morton, Walter Neville (Wal)
Born: 17 January 1911, Birmingham, West Midlands, England.
Died: 21 April 1995.

Wal started in speedway before the War and rode for many tracks. After the War he was lined up for Norwich but, when Bert Spencer refused to move north, Wal became a Tiger instead. He was a popular rider, scoring well everywhere. In particular, he delighted in showing his home town team, Norwich, what they were missing out on. For some reason he only raced in the British Championship round at Glasgow in 1946. He did not stay for 1947 and transferred to Harringay as part of deal involving Norman Lindsay. Living up to his nickname of 'Wandering Wal', he changed clubs on a regular basis and retired in 1963 aged 52 after spells in the Provincial League with Liverpool, Middlesbrough, Bradford and Hackney.

Year	Comp	M	R	P	BP	TP	CMA	FM	PM
1946	NrL	20	85	178	7	185	8.71	2	0
1946	NT	4	20	34	4	38	7.60	0	0
1946	ACUC	8	39	66	2	68	6.97	0	0

Individual Honours
British Riders Championship   1946   Did not progress beyond NrL round

International Honours
Britain   1946   4 + 3 points v Overseas

Other   1946   Eastern Counties Champion Norwich 11
Northern Riders' Championship Bristol 8

Murray, William (Bill)

A junior rider at Glasgow, Bill made his debut for the Tigers at Sheffield on 24 April 1947 and rode two nights later in the league fixture at Birmingham. He was replaced in the side after those two matches by Junior Bainbridge and never appeared in a home fixture for his club.

Year	Comp	M	R	P	BP	TP	CMA	FM	PM
1947	NL2	2	3	1	0	1	1.33	0	0

Nicholson, Len
Born: England

Based in Northallerton, Len started at Newcastle in 1951 before moving to Glasgow in July where he was a reserve. He was initially a reserve in 1952 before rising into the team, but his scores did not improve until August. His promising career was suddenly ended when he suffered serious head injuries in Glasgow's final league match of 1952, an accident which left him on the danger list for a while. There is no telling how good Len might have been but he was certainly showing a lot of promise before his injury.

Year	Comp	M	R	P	BP	TP	CMA	FM	PM
1951	NL2	16	39	34	9	43	4.41	0	0
1952	NL2	39	122	127	18	145	4.75	0	0

Individual Honours
World Championship   1951   Did not progress beyond Round one

Oates, Charles Ronald (Charlie)
Born: 24 May 1912, Liverpool, Merseyside, England.
Died: 15 January 2005.

Charlie was a Liverpool rider before the War. In 1946 he became a Tiger, but did not score much in the first half of the campaign. He moved up to Bradford for the second half of the season. Dropping down he rode for Tamworth 1947 and Tamworth, then Wombwell in 1948. A return to Liverpool for in 1949 and part of 1950 didn't boost his career and he retired after a short spell at Long Eaton 1952. He famously helped Peter Craven into speedway.

Year	Comp	M	R	P	BP	TP	CMA	FM	PM
1946	NrL	9	26	18	6	24	3.69	0	0
1946	NT	2	2	1	1	2	4.00	0	0
1946	ACUC	3	8	7	2	9	4.50	0	0

Riddell, Malcolm
Born: Scotland.

A Scottish junior, Malcolm rode just twice for Glasgow in the 1949 season, being called upon when the Tigers' Australian contingent sailed for home before the completion of the league programme. He failed to score on his debut in a record 70–14 defeat at Bristol. Malcolm opened his account with a point at home to Coventry five days later.

He was a popular and successful performer in Belfast in the late 1940s and early 1950s and also had a spell at Motherwell early in 1951, but without ever making another league appearance.

Year	Comp	M	R	P	BP	TP	CMA	FM	PM
1949	NL2	2	4	1	0	1	1.00	0	0

Rogers, Fred
Born: 1 January 1929, Sheffield, South Yorkshire, England.
Died: November 2001.

Fred began his speedway career as a teenager after the War and was discarded by Glasgow after two meetings. He tried out at Bradford and Newcastle before trying his luck in East Anglia towards the end of 1948. He showed decent form at Yarmouth before finally joining Norwich where he stayed until 1954. He retired in 1956 after two seasons at Belle Vue.

Year	Comp	M	R	P	BP	TP	CMA	FM	PM
1947	NL2	2	5	2	0	2	1.60	0	0

Ryan, Keith Vincent (Buck)
Born: 30 December 1922, Mittagong, New South Wales, Australia.
Died: May 2018.

Buck Ryan was a steady scorer for Glasgow at White City, but was never able to reproduce the form that made him one of his country's leading riders on home soil. Something of an all-round motorcyclist, he overcame a broken neck while riding at Brisbane. He made a full recovery and was offered a team spot at Glasgow in 1947, making his debut at home to Wigan at the end of April. He put in some useful displays, including two unbeaten performances from the reserve berth, and returned to ride for the Tigers the following year.

The 1948 season was his best in Britain. He scored his debut maximum in the home derby against Edinburgh and was paid for double figures on four other occasions in an average of over seven points per match. A spell on the sidelines due to the limit on overseas riders imposed by the Speedway Riders' Association did not help him in 1949. His average slipped by over two points per match in what was a disappointing final season in Britain.

Electing not to return to Glasgow for domestic reasons, he continued to ride in Australia for many years after leaving these shores, winning the Australian Championship in 1952 and repeatedly defying strong rumours that he was to return to Glasgow. He actually departed from New South Wales in 1953, but got off the boat at Freemantle and returned home when promoter Ian Hoskins had pencilled him in to the White City team.

Year	Comp	M	R	P	BP	TP	CMA	FM	PM
1947	NL2	20	72	71	11	82	4.56	0	0
1947	BSC	12	42	48	6	54	5.14	0	0
1948	NL2	28	111	179	18	197	7.10	1	0
1948	SC	16	63	82	6	88	5.58	0	0
1949	NL2	33	123	130	26	156	5.07	0	1

International Honours
Australia   1948   4 points v England (Division Two Teams)
Overseas   1947   6 points v Britain

Saunders, Harold Walter (Harry)
Born: 1 August 1917, New Malden, Surrey, England.
Died: 1979.

The younger brother of George Saunders, Harry rode pre-War. He had a single outing for the Tigers in 1946. Man of many tracks, including Wimbledon, Eastbourne Tamworth, Wombwell, Oxford and Wolverhampton, he was a steady rider at all these venues.

Year	Comp	M	R	P	BP	TP	CMA	FM	PM
1946	NrL	1	5	1	0	1	0.80	0	0

Seers, Richard Rock (Dick)
Born: 14 August 1926, Sydney, New South Wales, Australia.
Died: 10 September 2022.

Dick had a few outings for Fleetwood in 1948 and for the Tigers in 1949 before moving to Halifax. Such was his progress that he moved to Bradford in 1950. However, an injury mid-season halted his progress. He stayed home in Australia in 1951 and 1952, but returned to Bradford for 1953 and 1954. He retired at home after injuries had spoiled his 1954 season. For the Tigers and Fleetwood. He was another who 'got away'.

Year	Comp	M	R	P	BP	TP	CMA	FM	PM
1949	NLD2	2	6	4	1	5	3.33	0	0

Sharp, Robert Henry (Bob)
Born: 17 February 1934, Arcadia, New South Wales, Australia.
Died: 12 September 2012.

Bob appeared at Sydney as a 16-year-old in the 1950–51 season. He created a storm when he arrived in Britain in 1952 billed as 'Cowboy' Bob Sharp at Ashfield, complete with 10-gallon hat and cowboy regalia. He struggled badly in his first season, and had outings with both Glasgow clubs, and spent most of the year in second halves. He improved with the Tigers in 1953 and was an ever present. Known affectionately as 'Last Bend Bob' because of his often belated moves to pass, he started with Tigers in 1954 and moved to Ipswich when they closed. He increased his average between then and 1958 when he returned home. He rode regularly in Australia before retiring in the late 1960s.

Year	Comp	M	R	P	BP	TP	CMA	FM	PM
1952	NL2	11	26	21	11	32	4.92	0	0
1953	NL2	40	110	118	26	144	5.24	0	0
1954	NS	6	24	42	1	43	7.16	0	0

Sharpe, Harold
Born: 25 January 1916, Kendal, Cumbria, England.

A rider who first rode in the Army in Germany, Wembley asset Harold rode at Glasgow for a short spell in 1947. He then moved to become a regular at Plymouth. He had an outing for New Cross in 1948, then signed and never rode for Oxford in 1949.

Year	Comp	M	R	P	BP	TP	CMA	FM	PM
1947	NL2	8	23	17	5	22	3.83	0	0
1947	BSC	5	15	10	2	12	3.20	0	0

Shearer, Thomas (Bert)
Born: 19 April 1916, Motherwell, Scotland.

Bert was a popular Scottish junior who had his best spell in the sport with Glasgow in 1947, averaging over five points a match. He fluctuated between reserve berth and second string. He started the 1948 season with Edinburgh, but struggled at Old Meadowbank, seeing his average fall by around one and a half points per match. He ended the season back at Glasgow before retiring at the end of the year.

Year	Comp	M	R	P	BP	TP	CMA	FM	PM
1946	NrL	4	9	1	1	2	0.89	0	0
1946	NT	2	2	0	0	0	0.00	0	0
1946	ACUC	1	1	0	0	0	0.00	0	0
1947	NL2	23	72	81.5	12	93.5	5.19	0	0
1948	NL2	1	4	1	1	2	2.00	0	0

International Honours
Britain   1947   4+2 points v Overseas

Smith, Ivor
Born: c. 1926, Hamilton, Scotland.

A Hamilton based builder, Ivor was a wartime dispatch rider in the Army in Burma. He learnt to ride speedway at the Bothwell Training School in Scotland. He showed good progress and rode for the Tigers at the end of 1949 when they were seriously shorthanded. Plans to include him in the 1950 were scuppered by a neck injury. Reports indicate that he was killed in a building site accident.

Year	Comp	M	R	P	BP	TP	CMA	FM	PM
1949	NL2	6	17	7	1	8	1.88	0	0

Steward, Jim

Jim had second half outings at Newcastle in 1951. He was given a single outing by the Tigers near the start of the 1952 season, standing in for the late returning Junior Bainbridge. Jim had a few more second halves and a pointless outing for Yarmouth, who turned up short handed, before disappearing from the speedway scene.

Year	Comp	M	R	P	BP	TP	CMA	FM	PM
1952	NL2	1	2	1	0	1	2.00	0	0

Stobbart, Maurice
Born: 22 December 1913, Aspatria, Cumbria, England.
Died: 27 February 2001.

The younger brother of Rol Stobbart, Maurice rode for Wembley, Newcastle and his local Workington track pre-War. He dabbled in promotion and staged meetings including two at Ayr in 1937. A Tiger in 1946, he was an ever-present, scoring in every official match that year. Usually better at home than away, he retired at the end of 1946. He had a couple of meetings for the Tigers in 1947 and had outings at Newcastle in 1948 and trials at other tracks before finally retiring after a short spell with Ashfield in 1949.

Year	Comp	M	R	P	BP	TP	CMA	FM	PM
1946	NrL	24	100	133	24	157	6.28	0	1
1946	NT	4	20	28	8	36	7.20	0	0
1946	ACUC	10	47	66	6	72	6.12	0	0
1947	NL2	2	6	5	1	6	4.00	0	0

Individual honours
British Championship   1946   Did not progress beyond NrL round

International honours
Britain   1946   DNR v Overseas

Templeton, Douglas (Doug)
Born: 18 June 1928, Maybole, Scotland.
Died: 21 December 2019.

One of the greatest figures in the history of Scottish speedway, Doug Templeton rode for 21 years. The Maybole born, Fifeshire farmer was a grass track rider who had one speedway second half in 1952. He made his debut for the Tigers in 1953 and was Scottish Junior Champion that year. After Glasgow closed in 1954, he moved to Motherwell. Doug had a few outings at Glasgow in 1956, for Ipswich the same year and Motherwell in 1958. He was a pillar of the Edinburgh Monarchs from 1960 to 1969. He then rejoined the Tigers from 1970 to 1972 and 1975 to 1976, with a spell at Berwick from 1972 to 1974.

Year	Comp	M	R	P	BP	TP	CMA	FM	PM
1953	NL2	11	30	16	4	20	2.67	0	0
1954	*NS*	*6*	*24*	*19*	*5*	*24*	*4.00*	*0*	*0*

International Honours
Scotland   1 cap   6+1 v New Zealand

Templeton, William Muir (Willie)
Born: 12 September 1930, Maybole, Scotland.
Died: 15 August 2008.

The younger brother of Doug Templeton, Willie was a Tiger for a brief period in 1954 before a slightly longer spell at Edinburgh. He rode at Glasgow in 1956 and was a Golden Eagle at Motherwell in 1958. He then rode for Edinburgh from 1960 to 1964, then moved to Glasgow in 1965 where he was a formidable opponent. Willie moved to Berwick in 1972 and was a Bandit until he retired at the end of 1978.

Year	Comp	M	R	P	BP	TP	CMA	FM	PM
1954	NS	2	8	2	0	2	1.00	0	0

Thomson, Walter (Wally)
Born: England.

County Durham based Wally was a Sergeant-Major in the Commandoes during the War. He had outings at both Newcastle and Glasgow in the 1946 Northern League. His longest run came with the Scottish side, making 10 appearances for the Tigers and recording a top score on his home debut.

Year	Comp	M	R	P	BP	TP	CMA	FM	PM
1946	NrL	10	22	13	4	17	3.09	0	0
1946	ACUC	6	8	2	1	3	1.50	0	0

Tidbury, Kenneth Frank (Ken)
Born: 23 August 1913, Hockley, Essex, England.
Died: October 1992.

Ken started riding grass and speedway for West Ham and Birmingham pre-War. He started out in the post-War era with Glasgow, riding seven times for the Tigers before losing his place in the side. He was with Eastbourne in 1947 and Hastings in 1948 and 1949 before a dip in form led to his retirement.

Year	Comp	M	R	P	BP	TP	CMA	FM	PM
1946	NrL	7	22	12	2	14	2.55	0	0

Tye, John (Jack)
Born: 7 April 1907, Liverpool, Merseyside, England.
Died: 1984.

Based in Preston, Jack rode pre-War. He made a brief comeback in 1946 at Bradford then had rides at Glasgow before having one outing as a Tiger.

Year	Comp	M	R	P	BP	TP	CMA	FM	PM
1946	ACUC	1	3	0	0	0	0.00	0	0

Urquhart, Raymond Clifford (Jack Martin)
Born: 3 February 1921, Newcastle, New South Wales, Australia.
Died: 14 August 2018.

Urquhart (Jack Martin) joined Glasgow on the advice of Bat Byrnes, having come over from Australia with Bill Maddern. He started 1948 with the Tigers, but his spectacular style was not translated into points. Jack only had five matches before moving to Newcastle. He was briefly at Ashfield in 1949 before returning home. He was born Raymond Clifford Urquhart, but rode as Jack Martin throughout his racing days.

Year	Comp	M	R	P	BP	TP	CMA	FM	PM
1948	NL2	5	10	4	3	7	2.80	0	0

Venier, Bruce
Born: c. 1913, United States of America.

Bruce was American born, but based in Toronto, Canada. A pre-war Newcastle rider, he joined Glasgow in 1947. After two meetings he had failed to finish a race and retired.

Year	Comp	M	R	P	BP	TP	CMA	FM	PM
1947	NL2	1	4	0	0	0	0.00	0	0

Welch, Harry
Born: 1 July 1912, Liverpool, Merseyside, England.
Died: 1967.

Harry started in speedway before the War, but did not make the grade until 1947 at Wigan. In 1948 he dropped down to Wombwell where he improved in a lower league. He rode for Liverpool from 1949 until it closed mid-season 1953. The Tigers grabbed him and he did not let them down as a second string. He did not return for 1954 due to a cost cutting exercise.

Year	Comp	M	R	P	BP	TP	CMA	FM	PM
1953	NL2	11	31	30	6	36	4.65	0	0

Individual Honours:
World Championship   1953   Did not progress beyond Round three

Wilkinson, William Derek Rutherford (Don)
Born: 13 November 1926, Morpeth, Northumbria, England.

Don rode second halves at Newcastle, then rode for Hull in Division Three in 1947. He then returned to Tyneside and eventually forced his way into the side at Brough Park. He was a handy second string by 1951, posting some big scores at home. He left Newcastle when they closed and was signed by Glasgow for 1952. He retired at end of 1953, but came back in 1961, initially at Middlesbrough, then Newcastle. He retired after injury in 1962. After a ride at Edinburgh in 1963, he decided not to return again.

Year	Comp	M	R	P	BP	TP	CMA	FM	PM
1952	NL2	49	180	191	35	226	5.02	0	0
1953	NL2	40	132	152	29	181	5.48	0	0

Individual Honours
Scottish Championship   1952   2 points

Williams, John (Butch)

A former mechanic and rider at West Ham speedway, Butch was a mechanic at Glasgow after the War. He had one meeting in 1946 to prevent Tigers being short-handed. He managed Rayleigh in the early 1950s.

Year	Comp	M	R	P	BP	TP	CMA	FM	PM
1946	NrL	1	2	0	0	0	0.00	0	0

Wilson, Brian
Born: 5 February 1929, Sheffield, South Yorkshire, England.

Brian was a man of many tracks and an inconsistent performer. He had one race for the Tigers at Birmingham in 1946.

Year	Comp	M	R	P	BP	TP	CMA	FM	PM
1946	ACUC	1	1	1	0	1	4.00	0	0

22. Glasgow riders 1964 to 1968

The records with these pieces only cover the riders' time with the Tigers. PL: Provincial League, BL: British League, BL1: British League First Division. Knock Out Cup matches are included in the league records.

Andersson, Åke
Born: 14 November 1936, Rödjenäs, Sweden.

Åke had an incredible 33 years in Swedish league speedway, stretching from 1954 to 1986. He came to Glasgow aged 31 in 1968 as the Tigers sought to improve their team by replacing Lars Jansson. Sadly, he did not produce the results, especially away and was discarded after seven meetings. He continued to ride in Sweden after leaving the Tigers.

Year	Comp	M	R	P	BP	TP	CMA	FM	PM
1968	BL1	7	23	19	5	24	4.17	0	0

Individual honours
World Championship   1968   Eliminated at Swedish Qualification stage

Beaton, John Robert Thompson (Bobby)
Born: 14 May 1952, Blantyre, Scotland.

Bobby made his debut for the Tigers aged 16 in 1968. He played a small role at White City. He progressed to become one of Scotland's best, riding for Tigers at Hampden Park and Coatbridge, then moving to Hull to remain in the top flight. He raced for Newcastle and Edinburgh before ending his 21-year career at Glasgow.

Year	Comp	M	R	P	BP	TP	CMA	FM	PM
1968	BL1	3	8	3	0	3	1.50	0	0

Berg, Oyvind Sandem
Born: 8 October 1943, Askim, Norway.
Died: January, 2008.

Good scores at White City in 1967 saw Oyvind, always programmed as Oyvind S. Berg, move from Edinburgh to White City, rather than Coatbridge with the Monarchs. He took the opportunity of a heat leader role that this move offered. He rode well in 1968 and stayed for two more years before moving to Oxford where he stayed a couple of years before retiring. He returned to Poole in 1974, and after that only raced in Europe.

Year	Comp	M	R	P	BP	TP	CMA	FM	PM
1968	BL1	33	140	265	12	277	7.91	3	0

Individual Honours
World Championship   1968   Eliminated at British – Nordic stage.

Scottish Match Race   1968   August beat Berndt Persson
                                        September lost to Reidar Eide

Scottish Championship	1968	8		
International Honours				
Scotland	1968	1 cap	10 points v England	

Blewett, Christopher Henry (Chris)
Born: 18 June 1929, Toronto, Ontario, Canada.
Died: 5 June 2002.

Although born in Canada, Chris was raised in Cornwall. Most of his team experience from 1961 to 1969 was with relatively local tracks, Plymouth, St Austell and Exeter. His links with Trevor Redmond saw him ride for Glasgow for a couple of meetings.

Year	Comp	M	R	P	BP	TP	CMA	FM	PM
1964	PL	2	2	0	0	0	0.00	0	0

Coombes, Graham
Born: 25 October 1939, Auckland, New Zealand.

Graham was a novice in Auckland in 1956 and 1957. He came to England in 1959 for two seasons at Belle Vue. He returned in 1964 and moved to Glasgow when Sunderland folded. He had a second season at Glasgow before being moved to Newcastle in 1966. He rode for Cradley Heath for three seasons before retiring.

Year	Comp	M	R	P	BP	TP	CMA	FM	PM
1964	PL	12	37	23	9	32	3.46	0	0
1965	BL	37	131	130	40	170	5.19	0	1

Individual Honours
World Championship	1965	Eliminated at Round Two stage
Scottish Championship	1966	DNR (Reserve)

Dent, Allan Russell (Russ)
Born: 22 July 1940, Consett, County Durham, England.

Russ started at Newcastle in 1961 and rode until 1975. He was signed by Glasgow as a replacement for Maury Mattingley, and stayed until the end of 1969. He did well at White City and was a solid team man as shown by his 36 bonus points in 1968.

He also had his starring moments. Russ did well for the Diamonds and was probably a surprise signing at the time. He had spells at Newcastle and Sunderland after leaving the Tigers. He was a great servant to northern speedway in his 14 years in the saddle.

Year	Comp	M	R	P	BP	TP	CMA	FM	PM
1967	BL	8	31	32	8	40	5.16	0	0
1968	BL1	32	128	149	36	185	5.78	0	2

Individual Honours
World Championship   1968   Eliminated at Qualifying Round stage

International Honours
England   1968   1 cap   0 points v Scotland

Faafeng, Jonny
Born: c. 1943 Norway.
Died: December 1967.

Jonny joined the Tigers in May 1966, but did not prove to be the prolific scorer they had hoped. He did have his moments, especially at White City. He returned for 1967, but after a trip home on World Championship business, he failed to return and was sacked. He was fatally injured in a road accident in Norway a short time later.

Year	Comp	M	R	P	BP	TP	CMA	FM	PM
1966	BL	28	89	97	21	118	5.30	0	0
1967	BL	10	40	48	6	54	5.40	0	0

Individual Honours
World Championship   1966   Eliminated at Nordic / British Final stage
                                  1967   Eliminated at Nordic Final stage

Scottish Championship   1966   7 points (Held in 1967)

Hanlon, Eric
Born: Scotland.

Eric rode second halves at Edinburgh, in the early 1960s and moved to Glasgow in 1964. He had a few reserve outings for the Tigers, but was never considered for any more permanent opportunities and retired.

Year	Comp	M	R	P	BP	TP	CMA	FM	PM
1964	PL	3	7	6	1	7	4.00	0	0
1964	NrL	1	2	0	0	0	0.00	0	0

Hicks, Joe
Born: 16 May 1943, New Plymouth, New Zealand.

Joe arrived with Bruce Ovenden, but struggled to secure a team place in 1964. He had a few appearances in 1965 and 1966, but failed to gain a permanent spot. Nonetheless he rode in many second halves and was highly valued as part of the Tigers set up, acting as a mechanic for the benefit of the team.

Year	Comp	M	R	P	BP	TP	CMA	FM	PM
1965	BL	4	12	4	2	6	2.00	0	0
1966	BL	2	4	0	0	0	0.00	0	0

Jansson, Lars
Born: 27 November 1944, Danderyd, Sweden.
Died: 27 October 2011.

Lars, brother of Bengt, joined the Tigers in 1968 when a proposed move for Gunnar Malmqvist fell through. He lacked the experience and scoring power that the Tigers needed at the time. After 17 matches he was replaced by (Lars) Ake Andersson, an expected quick fix which did not work.

Year	Comp	M	R	P	BP	TP	CMA	FM	PM
1968	BL1	17	76	97	11	108	5.68	0	0

Individual Honours
World Championship   1968   Eliminated at Swedish Qualification stage

Josefsson, Bo
Born: 11 July 1940, Forserum, Sweden.

Nicknamed 'Bo the Bomb' by his fans at Glasgow, he was added to the Tigers' squad in 1967, replacing Jonny Faafeng. A top end Swedish league performer, he had some notable meetings and was usually a reliable performer. He started 1968 very well, but his form tailed off as the season progressed. Added to his non availability for the Tigers due to other commitments at home, he was axed as a part of a cost savings exercise. He rode until 1975 in Sweden.

Year	Comp	M	R	P	BP	TP	CMA	FM	PM
1967	BL	17	73	111	15	126	6.90	1	0
1968	BL1	20	73	114	10	124	6.79	1	1

Individual Honours
World Championship   1967 Eliminated at Nordic Qualifier stage
                             1968 Eliminated at Swedish Final stage

International Honours
Sweden   1967   3 caps 1 point v Great Britain

Other
Swedish Championship   1967 Runner up
Silver Sash Match Race Championship   1967 Challenger – Lost to Gote Nordin

Julian, Christopher Denis (Chris)
Born: 4 March 1937, Fraddon, Cornwall, England.
Died: 17 May 1997.

Cornishman Chris started out at Exeter in 1958. He rode at Bristol, Plymouth, Neath and St Austell before taking on the 1,000 miles round trip to Glasgow, mostly by road. He had an injury disrupted spell as a Tiger. After the Tigers, Chris then rode for Cradley Heath, Newport, Exeter and Mildenhall before bowing out at Weymouth in 1977.

Sadly, his gyrocopter flying hobby resulted in his premature death, aged 60, in 1997 when his machine crashed in Gloucestershire.

Year	Comp	M	R	P	BP	TP	CMA	FM	PM
1964	PL	15	59	97	5	102	6.92	0	0
1964	NL	9	37	57	1	58	6.27	0	0
1965	BL	1	4	7	2	9	9.00	0	0

International Honours
Scotland   1964   3 caps 4+1 points v England

Lagrosse, Bernie Lewis (Roy Williams)
Born: 2 August 1939, Christchurch, New Zealand.
Died: 30 June 2007.

Bernie Lagrosse rode at many northern tracks and had a few outings for the Tigers in 1965. He had started speedway in 1958 in New Zealand and spent time in Australia. He stayed at home in 1966 and 1967, then turned out for Berwick from 1968 to 1970 as Roy Williams with some success

Year	Comp	M	R	P	BP	TP	CMA	FM	PM
1965	BL	4	8	1	0	1	0.50	0	0

McMillan, James Dunn Templeton (Jim)
Born: 3 December 1945, Glasgow, Scotland.

The younger brother of Bill McMillan and nephew of the famous Templeton brothers, Jim started at Cowdenbeath in 1966. After a spell in the second half was given a reasonable number of outings by Glasgow Tigers at reserve without securing a team place on a permanent basis. 1967 was Jim's breakthrough season. He became a permanent fixture and his scores improved as the season progressed. The experience gained in those two campaigns was put to good use in 1968 when Jim became the top Tiger. After White City closed, Jim continued to improve and, when the Tigers dropped down, he moved to Hull for two seasons, Wolverhampton for five seasons and then rode at Belle Vue for two seasons. After another stay with Glasgow in 1983, Jim saw out his career at Berwick. His career records show he rarely missed a meeting. Since retiring, Jim has become a highly valued technical expert with the Speedway Control authorities and FIM.

Year	Comp	M	R	P	BP	TP	CMA	FM	PM
1966	BL	13	26	17	6	23	3.54	0	0
1967	BL	29	111	113	17	130	4.68	0	0
1968	BL1	37	168	333	16	349	8.31	3	0

Individual Honours
World Championship   1968   Eliminated at British – Nordic stage

Scottish Match Race   1968   May   Lost to Berndt Persson

International Honours
Scotland	1968	1 cap 10+2 points v England
Great Britain	1968	1 cap 7+1 points v Sweden

Scottish Championship
	1967	0
	1968	8

McMillan, William Alexander (Bill)
Born: 16 July 1940, Glasgow, Scotland.

Bill started speedway in 1962 at Edinburgh beside his uncles Doug and Willie Templeton. When White City opened, Bill moved west to Glasgow. He was very underrated and could slam in the occasional big score. Perhaps if the Glasgow promoters had shown a bit more faith in him, and he had avoided an injury after a maiden home maximum in 1967, he might have scored a lot more. Too often, he was used in a stopgap role which is a testament to his loyalty to the Tigers – and Monarchs for that matter. He had a short spell at Berwick and some time in Australia before a shortish spell with the Tigers before retiring in 1971.

Year	Comp	M	R	P	BP	TP	CMA	FM	PM
1964	PL	22	75	53	16	69	3.68	0	0
1964	NrL	10	38	37	7	44	4.63	0	0
1965	BL	20	65	53	17	70	4.31	0	0
1966	BL	37	135	130	37	167	4.95	0	1
1967	BL	14	45	40	5	45	4.00	1	0
1968	BL1	30	106	107	20	127	4.79	0	0

Individual Honours
World Championship
	1965	Eliminated at Qualifying Round stage
	1966	Eliminated at Qualifying Round stage
	1968	Eliminated at Qualifying Round stage

International Honours
Scotland	1964	1 cap 0 points v England
	1966	2 caps 0 points v England
	1968	1 cap DNR v England

Scottish Championship   1968   1

Others
Scottish Junior Championship   1965   12   Winner

Mattingley, Maurice William (Maury)
Born: 22 October 1923, Totton, Hampshire, England.
Died: November 2007.

Maury Mattingley started at his local Southampton track in 1952, aged 28. He stayed in speedway until he retired aged 44. He rode for Southampton, Coventry and Plymouth. He joined Wolverhampton in 1963, then Glasgow in 1964 as 1963 Scottish Open Champion.

Given the commuting distance between Glasgow and his Southampton base, the Tigers promoters sweetened the move by flying him north for meetings. Maury's form fluctuated week by week over the four years he raced for Tigers, often due to bike problems. At his best he could beat anyone. Maury retired in 1968.

Year	Comp	M	R	P	BP	TP	CMA	FM	PM
1964	PL	23	96	176	10	186	7.75	1	0
1964	NrL	10	41	78	4	82	8.00	1	2
1965	BL	30	116	154	22	176	6.07	0	2
1966	BL	37	143	206	21	227	6.35	1	0
1967	BL	22	78	105	20	125	6.41	0	0

Individual Honours
World Championship   1965   Eliminated at Qualifying Round stage
                            1966   Eliminated at Qualifying Round stage
                            1967   Eliminated at Qualifying Round stage

Scottish Match Race   1966   September Lost to Bengt Jansson 2–0

International Honours
Scotland   1964   3 caps 11+4 points v England
                            1967   1 cap   0 points v England

England   1965   1 cap   8 points v Scotland
                            1966   2 caps 6 points v Scotland

Scottish Championship   1964   10
                            1965   5
                            1967   2

Other
Silver Sash Match Race Championship   1964 Challenger Lost to Ivan Mauger

Mitchell, Gordon William
Born: 3 December 1931, Hamilton, Scotland.
Died: September 2021.

Gordon started in the same race at White City as Tommy Miller after learning speedway at Bothwell. However, for various reasons he did not ride in many meetings. He rode at White City in 1956 and Motherwell in 1958. He only made a league breakthrough in 1960 at Edinburgh. He moved to Newcastle for 1961, retired for a time, then returned to second halves at Glasgow in 1964. He had a few outings for the Tigers, but could not secure a long-term place. He was a regular visitor to Scottish venues after he retired

Year	Comp	M	R	P	BP	TP	CMA	FM	PM
1964	PL	2	5	4	1	5	4.00	0	0

Monk, Warren Edric (Charlie)
Born: 5 February 1940, Adelaide, South Australia, Australia.

Charlie started riding in his home city of Adelaide before coming to the UK in 1962. He signed for new Welsh venue Neath. He moved to Long Eaton before joining Glasgow in 1964. Something of a shy and introverted character, he was the top Tiger from 1964 to 1967. His exploits in 1965 shocked the speedway world. It was his best ever season in a long and illustrious career. He won the Internationale, contested the British Match Race Championship with nye invincible Barry Briggs. In the World Championship, he was pretty hard done by at the last hurdle which prevented his appearance in the World Final.

Despite early season mechanical problems in 1966, he scored well thereafter and was back in double figures in 1967. At his own request he moved to Sheffield, but he did return to Glasgow for the Hampden Park era, then rode for Halifax, before joining Edinburgh in 1977 then retired after spending 1978 at Barrow.

Year	Comp	M	R	P	BP	TP	CMA	FM	PM
1964	PL	24	106	284	5	289	10.91	11	0
1964	NrL	9	36	99	0	99	11.00	5	0
1965	BL	37	163	415	4	419	10.28	9	1
1966	BL	37	158	362	4	366	9.27	6	1
1967	BL	36	152	396	3	399	10.50	14	0

Individual Honours

World Championship
- 1965 Eliminated at British Final stage
- 1966 Eliminated at British Semi Final stage
- 1967 Eliminated at British Final stage

Gold Helmet
- 1965 Leg 1 Beat Barry Briggs 2–0
- 1965 Leg 2 Lost to Barry Briggs 0–2
- 1965 Decider Lost to Barry Briggs 0–2

Scottish Match Race
- 1964 July Beat Doug Templeton 2–0
- August Beat George Hunter 2–1
- 1965 May Beat George Hunter 2–1
- June Lost to George Hunter 2–1
- 1966 August Beat George Hunter 2–0 then resigned

Internationals

Australia 1967–68 1 cap 12+1 points v England

Great Britain
- 1965 5 caps 50+5 points v Russia
- 1966 1 cap 1 point World Team Cup
- 1967 2 caps 17 points v Sweden

Overseas 1964 4 caps 43 points v Great Britain

Scotland
- 1964 3 caps 43+1 points v New Zealand
- 1964 5 caps 82+3 points v England
- 1965 1 cap 13 points v Russia
- 1965 1 cap 5 points v Poland
- 1965 2 caps 35 points v England

1966	1 cap	15+1 points v Russia
1966	5 caps	71 points v England
1967	1 cap	11+2 points v Poland

Scottish Championship
1964	14	Runner Up
1965	11	
1966	13	Held in 1967

Others
1964	Provincial League Riders Championship 13 runner up
1965	Internationale Winner
1965	British League Riders Championship 9 points
1966	British League Riders Championship 5 points
1967	British League Riders Championship 6 points

Silver Sash Match Race Championship
1964	Holder – Lost to George Hunter,
	Challenger – Lost to Ivan Mauger twice
1965	Challenger – Lost to Colin Pratt
1966	Challenger – Beat Olle Nygren
	Holder – Lost to Peter Vandenberg
1967	Challenger – Lost to Ray Wilson
	Challenger – Lost by default to Barry Briggs
	Challenger – Lost to Barry Briggs

Monteith, Jack (Red)

The rider profiles for 1945 to 1956 include details of Jack's brief Tigers career in that era. He also rode for the team in 1964, and made a handful of appearances in the British League in 1965 and 1966.

Year	Comp	M	R	P	BP	TP	CMA	FM	PM
1964	PL	4	10	9	1	10	4.00	0	0
1964	NrL	9	23	15	3	18	3.13	0	0
1965	BL	2	7	6	0	6	3.43	0	0
1966	BL	1	2	0	0	0	0.00	0	0

Ovenden, Bruce Walter
Born: 15 June 1940, New Plymouth, New Zealand.

Bruce started riding on grass then moved to shale. He come to the UK and became a Tiger for 1964. He stayed for the first British League season before returning to New Zealand for good. He was never a star, but his improvement in 1965 suggests he might have kicked on in 1966.

Year	Comp	M	R	P	BP	TP	CMA	FM	PM
1964	PL	22	85	57	16	73	3.44	0	0
1964	NrL	9	36	33	11	44	4.88	0	0
1965	BL	30	99	95	24	119	4.81	0	1

Individual Honours
World Championship   1965   Eliminated at Qualifying Round Two

Paulsen, Nils Kristian
Born: c. 1936, Norway.

Nils was a top rider in Norway and came to Glasgow to strengthen the Tigers for 1965. He suffered his share of injuries which reduced his overall contribution, He soon settled in the UK and had a purple patch mid0season. He did not return to Glasgow for 1966 and retired after a short spell at Exeter.

Year	Comp	M	R	P	BP	TP	CMA	FM	PM
1965	BL	24	92	135	13	148	6.43	0	1

Individual Honours
World Championship   1965   Eliminated at Nordic Qualifier stage

International Honours
Norway   1965   1 cap 4 points in World Team Cup QR

Other
Silver Sash Match Race Championship   1965   Challenger – lost to Bob Andrews

Redmond, Trevor John
Born: 16 June 1927, Christchurch, New Zealand.
Died: 17 September 1997.

Trevor started riding in the UK at Aldershot in1950 before being signed by the Wembley Lions, where he rode from 1952 to 1956. Between 1957 and 1963 he was at Bradford, Swindon, Bristol, Wolverhampton, Neath and St Austell for varying spells of time. Trevor was a World finalist and New Zealand international.

He retired to promote at Glasgow in 1964, but he was needed by the Tigers and scored very well. He did retire at the end of that season. As well as a rider Trevor promoted speedway at several venues, including in South Africa in the 1950s, and masterminded the return of the Wembley Lions in 1970. He also promoted stock car racing.

Year	Comp	M	R	P	BP	TP	CMA	FM	PM
1964	PL	20	89	163	7	170	7.64	0	0
1964	NrL	2	7	7	2	9	5.14	0	0

International Honours
Overseas   1964   3 caps 29+7 points v Great Britain
Scotland   1964   3 caps 21+7 points v England

Individual Honours
Scottish Championship   1964   8

Ridgeon, Victor William (Vic)
Born: 6 December 1928, Hackney, London, England.
Died: 12 May 2009.

Vic was at Yarmouth from 1950 to 1953, then was the uncrowned Southern Area king at Rye House until 1957. He then rode at Wolverhampton from 1961 to 1962, Rayleigh 1963, Sunderland 1964 and then became a short-term Tiger. He retired after a short spell at Exeter in 1966. Later had a few outings with The Men in Black using his JAP at Peterborough and High Beech celebrations.

Year	Comp	M	R	P	BP	TP	CMA	FM	PM
1964	PL	5	17	8	1	9	2.12	0	0

Ringstrom, Nils
Born: 2 October 1943, Huddinge, Sweden.

Nils rode for Long Eaton in 1966 and was signed by the Tigers for 1967. He never really set the heather on fire like so many of his countrymen and did not return to race in the UK. To be fair to Nils, he had a few good meetings but was not the heat-leader the Glasgow promoters were hoping he would be. Nils later became a top FIM grade referee.

Year	Comp	M	R	P	BP	TP	CMA	FM	PM
1967	BL	27	98	75	18	93	3.80	0	0

Individual Honours
World Championship   1967   Eliminated at Swedish Qualifier stage

International Honours
Sweden   1967   2 caps 0 points v Great Britain

Scottish Championship   1966   6   (Held in 1967)

Scott, Eric William (Bluey)
Born: 10 July 1929, Auburn, New South Wales, Australia.

Bluey was the darling of the Motherwell fans from 1951 to 1954. The red-haired Bluey then had spells at Southampton and Ipswich in 1955 before returning home, where he continued to ride. He returned in 1963 and rode well for Long Eaton, after a Scottish berth was not offered to him, then was at Middlesbrough in 1964, He spent 1965 and 1966 with the Tigers, based in familiar family Scottish surroundings before retiring to Australia after an injury interrupted last season.

Bluey had intended to return for 1967, but a crash and resulting back injury ruled out a return as a rider. His experience gained in the 1950s served him well and he was perhaps a slightly stronger performer on his home tracks. Bluey spent some time in Scotland serving the Tigers in off track roles, but eventually returned to Australia, settling on the Gold Coast

Year	Comp	M	R	P	BP	TP	CMA	FM	PM
1965	BL	37	155	271	24	295	7.61	2	2
1966	BL	22	85	134	16	150	7.06	0	0

Individual Honours
World Championship	1965	Eliminated at British Semi Final stage
	1966	Eliminated at Qualifying Round stage

International Honours
Scotland	1965	1 cap 6 points v England
	1966	5 caps 25 points v England
	1966	1 cap 7+1 points v Russia

Scottish Championship	1965	4

Stone, Terrence Harry (Terry)
Born: 2 May 1938, Rainham, Essex, England.

A real speedway enthusiast and a tremendously popular larger than life figure, Terry started at Rayleigh in 1960. He then had spells at Exeter, Rayleigh, Wolverhampton and New Cross. Recruited by the Tigers in 1964 to help shore up the team, he was discarded after a short spell. He went on to ride for Exeter, Poole, West Ham and Rayleigh before retiring in 1973. Terry suffered knocks and injuries at inopportune moments in his career and always bounced back. He only stopped riding in Men in Black events and vintage grass track events, where he mastered the art of leg trailing on a Douglas, because the powers that be said so. 'The original Stoney' is an unsung hero and a great ambassador for speedway.

Year	Comp	M	R	P	BP	TP	CMA	FM	PM
1964	PL	14	46	28	5	33	2.87	0	0
1964	NrL	6	28	30	6	31	4.80	0	0

Templeton, William Muir (Willie)
Born: 12 September 1930, Maybole, Scotland.
Died: 15 August 2008.

Willie was often under the shadow of brother Doug in his early days in the mid-1950s and in the Provincial era at Edinburgh. However, his loan move to Glasgow in 1965 saw him blossom. He did not quite maintain that level from 1966 to 1968, but was a well0respected opponent at White City. He moved with the Tigers to Hampden Park, which probably did not require the same level of throttle control as White City, and stayed until 1972. The Tigers' move to Coatbridge saw Willie move to Berwick where he stayed until he retired in 1978. He rode alongside Doug from 1960 to 1964 and at Hampden and Berwick. He was a reliable team member throughout his career, rarely missing meetings through injury or illness.

His brief time at the Tigers in 1954 is covered in the profiles for that period.

Year	Comp	M	R	P	BP	TP	CMA	FM	PM
1965	BL	31	123	200	22	222	7.22	1	1
1966	BL	37	150	217	36	253	6.75	0	2
1967	BL	37	151	218	22	240	6.36	1	1
1968	BL1	37	148	159	23	182	4.92	0	0

Individual Honours
World Championship	1965	Eliminated at Round Two stage
	1966	Eliminated at Qualifying Round stage

| | 1967 | Eliminated at Qualifying Round stage |
| | 1968 | Eliminated at Qualifying Round stage |

International Honours
Scotland

	1965	3 caps 9 points v England
	1965	1 cap 0 points v Russia
	1966	5 caps 20 points v England
	1966	1 cap 2 points v Poland
	1967	1 cap 0 points v England
	1967	1 cap DNR (res) v Poland
	1968	1 cap 1 point v England

Scottish Championship

	1965	1	
	1966	7	(Held in 1967)
	1967	3	
	1968	6	

Other
Silver Sash Match Race Championship   1968   Challenger – lost to Reidar Eide

Vale, Arthur Nelson Victor Kenneth (Ken)
Born: 24 June 1924, Milland, West Sussex, England.
Died: 3 December 2012.

Ken rode for several teams from 1959 to 1971, but only had regular spots at Long Eaton, Oxford, Newport, Canterbury and Workington. One of the most enthusiastic riders of his era, Ken never really made the big time in speedway, but gave 100 per cent effort and was always a popular rider. He had one outing for the Tigers in 1964 and another in 1969.

Year	Comp	M	R	P	BP	TP	CMA	FM	PM
1964	PL	1	2	2	0	2	4.00	0	0

Wells, Alfred Richard James (Alf)
Born: 28 January 1942, Christchurch, New Zealand.

Spotted by Dick Campbell, Alf arrived at with him at Edinburgh in 1961 and spent five years as a Monarch. After an illness ruined his 1965 season, Alf moved to White City where he had his best performances of his career, despite various problems. After two seasons he was allocated to Newcastle where his form declined. He ended 1968 back at Glasgow. He rode for a season at Hampden Park, then rode for Nelson and moved with the team to Bradford. He did not ride in 1973 then, after a short period at Berwick 1974, he retired.

Year	Comp	M	R	P	BP	TP	CMA	FM	PM
1966	BL	35	144	242	27	269	7.47	1	1
1967	BL	31	115	173	13	186	6.47	0	0
1968	BL1	8	28	42	10	52	7.43	0	0

Individual Honours
World Championship

| | 1966 | Eliminated at Qualifying Round stage |
| | 1967 | Eliminated at British Semi Final stage |

Scottish Championship   1966   1

Whaley, Brian
Born: 26 August 1944, Edinburgh, Scotland.

A native Scot who moved to Australia with his family, he joined the Tigers in 1967. He rode mainly at reserve, usually covering absences of more regular Tigers.
He was used in a similar role in 1968. He showed flashes of potential which were not nurtured and was never really given a long secure run to improve and establish himself. He had spells in Division Two in 1968. He returned to Australia in 1972.

Year	Comp	M	R	P	BP	TP	CMA	FM	PM
1967	BL	17	42	26	7	33	3.14	0	0
1968	BL1	23	54	26	6	32	2.37	0	0

Wickett, Raymond (Ray)
Born: 19 January 1938, Stratton, Cornwall, England.

Started speedway at Rye House in 1959 and 1960, then rode for Plymouth in 1961 and 1962 and St Austell in 1963. He was then taken to Glasgow by Trevor Redmond. He appeared briefly as a Tiger, but left because of the travelling involved. He had short spells with Exeter in 1964 and 1965, and West Ham in 1965 and 1966, without establishing himself as a regular. He retired in 1966, but did ride in some second halves in the early 1970s.

Year	Comp	M	R	P	BP	TP	CMA	FM	PM
1964	NL	3	12	12	2	14	4.66	0	0

Appendix: Statistics and Records

The team

National league results

Season	League	Played	Won	Draw	Lost	For	Against	Points	Place
1930	NrL	17	4	0	13	259	339	4	10/13*
1931	NrL	12	2	0	10	249	387	4	6/6*
1946	NrL	20	6	0	14	810	862	12	6/6
1947	NL2	28	10	0	18	1044	1299	20	8/8
1948	NL2	32	14	3	15	1289	1390	31	6/9
1949	NL2	44	20	0	24	1757.5	1924.5	40	8/12
1950	NL2	28	18	0	10	1272	1074	36	2/15
1951	NL2	30	14	1	15	1303	1215	29	10/16
1952	NL2	44	23	1	20	1837	1853	47	5/12
1953	NL2	32	16	2	14	1423.5	1262.5	34	4/9
1964	PL	22	6	2	14	805	906	14	12/12
1965	BL	34	15	1	18	1315	1329	31	13/18
1966	BL	36	18	0	18	1395	1394	36	8/19
1967	BL	36	16	2	18	1343	1557	34	13/19
1968	BL1	36	13	1	22	1312	1495	27	19/19

* Competitions not competed. Glasgow closed before the end of the 1931 season.

Other league competitions

Season	Comp	Played	Won	Draw	Lost	For	Against	Points	Place
1946	ACU C	10	3	0	7	184	282	6	5/6
1947	BSC	14	5	0	9	625	717	10	7/8
1948	Ann C	16	8	0	8	750	780	16	4/9
1950	Nor S	14	4	0	10	536	639	8	7/7
1951	Nor S	10	7	0	3	441	393	14	2/6
1954	Nor S	5	0	0	5	179	238	0	W*
1964	NrL	10	5	0	5	368	408	10	4/6

*Glasgow did not complete their 1954 North Shield fixtures

National cup competitions

Season	Comp	Opponents	Round	Venue	F	A	Notes
1946	NT	Sheffield	2-1L	H	61	47	
1946	NT	Sheffield	2-2L	A	47	61	Agg 108–108
1946	NT	Sheffield	2R-1L	H	62	45	
1946	NT	Sheffield	2-2L	A	44	63	Agg 106–109
1947	NT	Newcastle	2-!L	A	45	63	
1947	NT	Newcastle	2-2L	H	60	46	Agg 105–109
1948	NT	Edinburgh	1-1L	H	70	38	
1948	NT	Edinburgh	1-2L	A	46	62	Agg 116–100
1948	NT	Birmingham	2-1L	H	45.5	61.5	

1948	NT	Birmingham	2-2L	A	28	80	Agg 73.5–141.5
1949	NT	Norwich	1-1L	H	67	41	
1949	NT	Norwich	1-2L	A	36	71	Agg 103–112
1950	NT	Stoke	1-1L	A	43	65	
1950	NT	Stoke	1-1L	H	70	38	Agg 113–103
1950	NT	Norwich	2-!L	H	70	38	
1950	NT	Norwich	2-2L	A	30	78	Agg 100–116
1951	NT	Sheffield	2 Walk over				
1951	NT	Norwich	3-1L	H	64	44	Agg 91–125
1951	NT	Norwich	3-2L	A	27	81	
1952	NT	Glasgow Ashfield	2-1L	H	65	43	
1952	NT	Glasgow Ashfield	2-2L	A	56	52	Agg 121–95
1952	NT	Leicester	D2-SF-1L	H	53	55	
1952	NT	Leicester	D2-SF-2L	A	62	46	Agg 115–101
1952	NT	Poole	D2 F-1L	A	47	61	
1952	NT	Poole	D2-F-2L	H	58	50	Agg 105–111
1953	NT	Edinburgh	2-1L	H	75	33	
1953	NT	Edinburgh	2-2L	A	61	47	Agg 136–80
1953	NT	Wolverhampton	3-1L	A	59	49	
1953	NT	Wolverhampton	3-2L	H	76	32	Agg 135–81
1953	NT	Rayleigh	4-1L	H	69	39	
1953	NT	Rayleigh	4-2L	A	44	64	Agg 113–103
1953	NT	Birmingham	QF-1L	A	38	70	
1953	NT	Birmingham	QF-2L	H	56	52	Agg 94–122
1953	QC	Wolverhampton	2	H	71	37	
1953	QC	Ipswich	QF	A	55	53	
1953	QC	Exeter	SF	H	72	36	
1953	QC	Edinburgh	F-1L	A	43	65	
1953	QC	Edinburgh	F-2L	H	56	52	Agg 99–117
1964	PL KOC	Sheffield	1	H	59	37	
1964	PL KOC	Newport	QF	H	46	49	
1965	KOC	Sheffield	2	H	64	32	
1965	KOC	Swindon	3	H	49	46	
1965	KOC	West Ham	SF	H	43	50	
1966	KOC	Halifax	2	A	39	57	
1967	KOC	West Ham	2	A	29	67	
1968	KOC	Coatbridge	1	A	42	66	

Scottish Cup

Season	Opponents	Round	Venue	F	A	Notes
1951	Lanarkshire	1-1L	H	57	51	
1951	Lanarkshire	1-2L	A	61	47	Agg 118–98
1951	Edinburgh	F-1L	A	42	66	
1951	Edinburgh	F-2L	H	64	42	Agg 106–108
1952	Edinburgh	SF-1L	A	52	56	
1952	Edinburgh	SF-2L	H	67	41	Agg 119–97
1952	Ashfield	F-1L	A	53	50	
1952	Ashfield	F-2L	H	75	33	Agg 128–83
1964	Edinburgh		H	52	43	

1964	Edinburgh		A	43	53	Agg 95–96
1966	Edinburgh		H	57	39	
1966	Edinburgh		A	42	54	Agg 99–93
1967	Edinburgh		A	39	56	
1967	Edinburgh		H	46	50	Agg 85–106
1968	Coatbridge		A	32	64	
1968	Coatbridge		H	57	39	Agg 89–103

Season results

Glasgow Team meetings only. Venue only shown for neutral stadiums. Full heat details and riders' scores are available on the *Speedway Researcher* website.
1929 to 1956 Abbreviations: NS = North Shield Ch = Challenge NTr = National Trophy BC = Border Cup NL2 = National League Division Two BT Border Trophy PG = Press Gala SC= Scottish Cup LC = Lanarkshire Cup SCC = Scottish Coronation Cup QD = Queen's Cup
DH = Double Header meeting IC = International Challenge ICC = Inter-Continental Challenge
1964 to 1968 abbreviations: NrL = Northern League PL = Provincial KOC = Knock Out Cup I = International NC = Northern Cup CD = Champagne Derby ST = Supporters' Trophy

1929
1/5 Manchester White City 23 Glasgow 4 Ch
28/8 Newcastle Gosforth 19 Glasgow WC 9 £100 Ch
10/9 Glasgow WC 14 Newcastle Gosforth 14 Ch
17/9 Glasgow WC 14 The Rest 28 Ch
24/9 Glasgow WC 19 Newcastle Gosforth 9 £100 Ch
8/10 Glasgow WC 10 Edinburgh 17 White Horse Tr
12/10 Edinburgh 16 Glasgow WC 12 White Horse Tr

1930
22/4 Glasgow WC 23 Leicester Super 13 NrL
26/4 Leicester Super 10 Glasgow WC 8 NrL Abn
6/5 Glasgow WC 16 Belle Vue 20 NrL
10/5 Edinburgh 12 Glasgow WC 10 White Horse Tr
13/5 Glasgow WC 16 Manchester White City 19 NrL
17/5 Rochdale 20 Glasgow WC 13 NrL
24/5 Belle Vue 21 Glasgow WC 13 NrL
27/5 Glasgow WC 17 Warrington 18 NrL
4/6 Sheffield 26 Glasgow WC 10 NrL
10/6 Glasgow WC 18 Sheffield 17 NrL
17/6 Glasgow WC 17 Rochdale 19 NrL
1/7 Glasgow WC 19 Edinburgh 17 White Horse Tr
8/7 Glasgow WC 16 Newcastle Gosforth 20 NrL
12/7 Leicester Super 24 Glasgow WC 11 NrL
15/7 Glasgow WC 10 Liverpool 26 NrL
23/7 Liverpool 26 Glasgow WC 10 NrL
5/8 Blues 26 Reds 9 Ch
15/8 Warrington 23 Glasgow WC 12 NrL
16/8 Liverpool 23 Glasgow 13 Ch
Glasgow WC 20 Preston 12 NrL
21/8 Preston 26 Glasgow WC 9 NrL
26/8 Glasgow WC 13 Wembley 21 Ch
23/9 Glasgow WC 8 Blantyre 10 ST

1931
14/4 Glasgow WC 21 Belle Vue 31 NrL
23/4 Preston 35 Glasgow WC 18 NrL
28/4 Glasgow WC 28 Preston 25 NrL
12/5 Glasgow WC 31 Leicester Super 23 NrL
23/5 Belle Vue 40 Glasgow WC 14 NrL
26/5 Glasgow WC 43 Preston 52 NT
4/6 Preston 70 Glasgow WC 26 NT
13/6 Leicester Super 39 Glasgow WC 15 NrL
16/6 Glasgow WC 23 Leeds 31 NrL
18/6 Sheffield 35 Glasgow WC 19 NrL
27/6 Leeds 39 Glasgow WC 14 NrL
30/6 Glasgow WC 24 Belle Vue 30 NrL
7/7 Glasgow WC 25 Sheffield 28 NrL
11/7 Leeds 35 Glasgow WC 18 NrC DH
11/7 Leeds 31 Glasgow WC 17 NrL DH

1939
6/5 Glasgow Lions 23 Newcastle 31 Ch
13/5 Glasgow Lions 25 Middlesbrough 27 Ch
20/5 Glasgow Lions 30 Sheffield 24 Ch
27/5 Glasgow Lions 22 Colonies 31 Ch
3/6 Glasgow Lions 34 Southampton 20 Ch
10/6 Glasgow Lions 32 Newcastle 21 Ch
17/6 Glasgow Lions 24 Australians 30 Ch
20/6 Edinburgh Thistles 32 Glasgow Lions 22 Ch
24/6 Glasgow Lions 33 New Cross 21 Ch
1/7 Glasgow Lions 28 Wembley Lions 25 Ch
8/7 Glasgow Lions 34 Edinburgh Thistles 18 Ch
22/7 Glasgow Lions 41 Sheffield 43 ACUNC
25/7 Edinburgh Thistles 56 Glasgow Lions 27 ACUNC
29/7 Glasgow Lions 45 Edinburgh Thistles 36 ACUNC
5/8 Glasgow Lions 41 West Ham 42 Ch
7/8 Newcastle 58 Glasgow Lions 22 ACUNC
19/8 Glasgow Lions 29 Newcastle 53 ACUNC

1940
8/5 Glasgow 40 Belle Vue 43 Ch
15/5 Glasgow 59 West Ham 48 Ch
22/5 Glasgow 29 Harringay 43 Ch
25/5 Belle Vue 46 Glasgow 37 Ch
29/5 Glasgow 34 The South 37 Ch
12/6 Glasgow 51 Harringay 39 Ch

1945
11/8 Bradford 46 Glasgow 37 Ch
15/8 Glasgow 61 London 47 Ch
29/8 Glasgow 56 Newcastle 51 Ch
5/9 Glasgow 42 North London 39 Ch
10/9 Newcastle 49 Glasgow 35 Ch
19/9 Glasgow 46 The Rest 37 Ch
26/9 Ron Johnson's Sel 34 Bill Kitchen's Sel 50 Ch
3/10 Glasgow 37 The Midlands 46 Ch
10/10 Ron Johnson's Sel 42 Bill Kitchen's Sel 42

1946
22/4 Newcastle Diamonds 40 Glasgow Tigers 43 Ch
24/4 Glasgow Tigers 61 Sheffield Tigers 47 NTr
25/4 Sheffield Tigers 61 Glasgow Tigers 47 NTr
1/5 Glasgow Tigers 40 Newcastle Diamonds 44 NrL
6/5 Newcastle Diamonds 44 Glasgow Tigers 40 NrL
8/5 Glasgow Tigers 62 Sheffield Tigers 45 NTr RM
9/5 Sheffield Tigers 63 Glasgow Tigers 44 NTr RM
15/5 Glasgow Tigers 40 Birmingham B 42 NrL
22/5 Glasgow Tigers 44 Norwich Stars 38 NrL
25/5 Norwich Stars 41 Glasgow Tigers 43 NrL
29/5 Glasgow Tigers 58 Sheffield Tigers 26 NrL
1/6 Birmingham Brummies 46 Glasgow Tigers 37 NrL
3/6 Newcastle Diamonds 48 Glasgow Tigers 48 NrT
8/6 Newcastle & Middlesbrough 33 Sheffield & Glasgow 50 Ch
12/6 Glasgow Tigers 50 Newcastle Diamonds 46 NrT
13/6 Sheffield Tigers 45 Glasgow Tigers 39 NrL
19/6 Glasgow Tigers 47 Birmingham B 36 ACUC
20/6 Norwich Stars 51 Newcastle & Glasgow 33 Fr
24/6 Newcastle D 47 Glasgow Tigers 36 ACUC
26/6 Glasgow Tigers 37 Norwich Stars 46 ACUC
3/7 Glasgow Tigers 34 Middlesbrough Bears 50 NrL
24/7 Glasgow Tigers 37 Sheffield Tigers 47 NrL
29/7 Newcastle Diamonds 46 Glasgow Tigers 38 NrL
31/7 Glasgow Tigers 52 Newcastle Diamonds 32 NrL
3/8 Birmingham Brummies 39 Glasgow Tigers 45 NrL
7/8 Glasgow Tigers 54 Norwich Stars 42 NrT
8/8 Sheffield Tigers 48 Glasgow Tigers 36 NrL
10/8 Norwich Stars 59 Glasgow Tigers 36 NrT
14/8 Glasgow Tigers 51 Sheffield Tigers 42 ACUC
15/8 Sheffield Tigers 55 Glasgow Tigers 41 ACUC
21/8 Glasgow Tigers 37 Middlesbrough Bears 47 NrL
22/8 Middlesbrough Bears 54 Glasgow Tigers 30 NrL
28/8 Glasgow Tigers 42 Middlesbrough B 54 ACUC
11/9 Glasgow Tigers 58 Birmingham B 26 NrL
12/9 Middlesbrough B 54 Glasgow Tigers 41 ACUC
19/9 Middlesbrough Bears 52 Glasgow Tigers 30 NrL
25/9 Glasgow Tigers 51 Newcastle D 45 ACUC
28/9 Norwich Stars 64 Glasgow Tigers 32 ACUC
30/9 Newcastle Diamonds 50 Glasgow Tigers 34 Fr
2/10 Glasgow Tigers 40 Norwich Stars 44 NrL
5/10 Norwich Stars 51 Glasgow Tigers 32 NrL
9/10 Glasgow Tigers 51 Bradford Boomerangs 33 Fr
12/10 Birmingham B 62 Glasgow Tigers 34 ACUC
16/10 Glasgow Tigers 38 Wembley Lions 43 Fr

1947
9/4 Glasgow Tigers 43 Oliver Hart's Select 39 Ch
23/4 Glasgow Tigers 31 Sheffield Tigers 52 NL2
24/4 Sheffield Tigers 58 Glasgow Tigers 26 NL2
26/4 Birmingham B 60 Glasgow Tigers 24 NL2
30/4 Glasgow Tigers 43 Wigan Warriors 41 NL2
7/5 Glasgow Tigers 48 Bristol Bulldogs 36 NL2
14/5 Glasgow Tigers 40 Birmingham B 44 NL2
16/5 Bristol Bulldogs 57.5 Glasgow Tigers 26.5 NL2
17/5 Norwich Stars 58 Glasgow Tigers 25 NL2
21/5 Glasgow Tigers 38 Middlesbrough Bears 58 BSC
22/5 Middlesbrough Bears 62 Glasgow Tigers 33 BSC
28/5 Glasgow Tigers 42 Sheffield Tigers 54 BSC
29/5 Sheffield Tigers 56 Glasgow Tigers 40 BSC
30/5 Bristol Bulldogs 59 Glasgow Tigers 37 BSC
31/5 Birmingham B 59 Glasgow Tigers 37 BSC
2/6 Newcastle Diamonds 63 Glasgow Tigers 45 NT
4/6 Glasgow Tigers 60 Newcastle Diamonds 46 NT
16/6 Newcastle Diamonds 43 Glasgow Tigers 41 NL2
18/6 Glasgow Tigers 45 Newcastle Diamonds 38 NL2
25/6 Glasgow Tigers 52 Wigan Warriors 44 BSC
2/7 Glasgow Tigers 48.5 Bradford B 35.5 Ch
9/7 Glasgow Tigers 48 Bristol Bulldogs 36 NL2
10/7 Middlesbrough Bears 46 Glasgow Tigers 38 NL2
12/7 Wigan Warriors 56 Glasgow Tigers 27 NL2
16/7 Glasgow Tigers 56 Wigan Warriors 27 NL2
23/7 Glasgow Tigers 51 Newcastle Diamonds 44 BSC
30/7 Glasgow Tigers 55 Norwich Stars 41 BSC
13/8 Glasgow Tigers 47 Sheffield Tigers 37 NL2
15/8 Bristol Bulldogs 57 Glasgow Tigers 27 NL2
16/8 Birmingham B 59 Glasgow Tigers 24 NL2
20/8 Glasgow Tigers 54 Bristol Bulldogs 42 BSC
27/8 Glasgow Tigers 62 Birmingham B BSC
30/8 Wigan Warriors 45 Glasgow Tigers 39 NL2
3/9 Glasgow Tigers 48 Middlesbrough Bears 36 NL2
6/9 Norwich Stars 63 Glasgow Tigers 33 BSC
10/9 Glasgow Tigers 50 Norwich Stars 34 NL2
17/9 Glasgow Tigers 54 Birmingham B 29 NL2
20/9 Wigan Warriors 51 Glasgow Tigers 45 BSC
24/9 Glasgow Tigers 36 Middlesbrough Bears 48 NL2
29/9 Newcastle D 39.5 Glasgow Tigers 44.5 NL2
1/10 Glasgow Tigers 40 Newcastle Diamonds 44 NL2
8/10 Glasgow Tigers 46 North of England 38 Ch
9/10 Sheffield Tigers 57 Glasgow Tigers 27 NL2
11/10 Norwich Stars 61 Glasgow Tigers 23 NL2
13/10 Newcastle D 50 Glasgow Tigers 46 BSC
15/10 Glasgow Tigers 45 Jack Parker's Select 38 Ch

1948
31/3 Glasgow Tigers 47 Newcastle Diamonds 35 NL2
1/4 Middlesbrough Bears 61 Glasgow Tigers 22 NL2

7/4 Glasgow Tigers 49 Fleetwood Flyers 34 NL2
8/4 Sheffield Tigers 55 Glasgow Tigers 28 NL2
14/4 Glasgow Tigers 48 Birmingham B 36 NL2
17/4 Edinburgh Monarchs 39 Glasgow Tigers 44 NL2
21/4 Glasgow Tigers 41 Norwich Stars 42 NL2
24/4 Norwich Stars 53 Glasgow Tigers 31 NL2
28/4 Glasgow Tigers 37 Middlesbrough Bears 47 NL2
30/4 Bristol Bulldogs 53 Glasgow Tigers 31 NL2
1/5 Birmingham B 53 Glasgow Tigers 31 NL2
5/5 Glasgow Tigers 36 Bristol Bulldogs 48 NL2
12/5 Glasgow Tigers 49 Edinburgh Monarchs 35 NL2
15/5 Hamilton 41 Rest of Glasgow 39 Ch
(at Hamilton Palace Grounds)
19/5 Glasgow Tigers 51 Birmingham B 45 AC
25/5 Newcastle Diamonds 37 Glasgow Tigers 46 NL2
26/5 Glasgow Tigers 55 Sheffield Tigers 29 NL2
27/5 Middlesbrough Bears 54 Glasgow Tigers 42 AC
1/6 Fleetwood Flyers 48 Glasgow Tigers 36 NL2
2/6 Glasgow Tigers 40 Middlesbrough Bears 55 AC
16/6 Glasgow Tigers 70 Edinburgh Monarchs 38 NTr
19/6 Edinburgh Monarchs 62 Glasgow Tigers 46 NTr
23/6 Glasgow Tigers 45.5 Birmingham B 61.5 NTr
29/6 Fleetwood Flyers 62 Glasgow Tigers 34 AC
3/7 Birmingham Brummies 80 Glasgow Tigers 28 NTr
7/7 Glasgow Tigers 54 Newcastle Diamonds 42 AC
14/7 Glasgow Select 46 Vic Duggan's Select 37 Ch
17/7 Norwich Stars 64 Glasgow Tigers 32 AC
21/7 Glasgow Tigers 71 Edinburgh Monarchs 24 AC
22/7 Sheffield Tigers 69 Glasgow Tigers 27 AC
26/7 Newcastle Diamonds 50 Glasgow Tigers 46 AC
28/7 Glasgow Tigers 68 Fleetwood Flyers 28 AC
1/8 Santry Saints 30 Glasgow Tigers 42 Ch
3/8 Fleetwood Flyers 40 Glasgow Tigers 44 NL2
4/8 Glasgow Tigers 56 Bristol Bulldogs 40 AC
6/8 Bristol Bulldogs 55 Glasgow Tigers 39 AC
7/8 Birmingham Brummies 69 Glasgow Tigers 27 AC
11/8 Glasgow Tigers 63 Edinburgh Monarchs 21 NL2
23/8 Newcastle Diamonds 50 Glasgow Tigers 34 NL2
25/8 Glasgow Tigers 55 Middlesbrough Bears 29 NL2
26/8 Middlesbrough Bears 42 Glasgow Tigers 42 NL2
1/9 Glasgow Tigers 51 Sheffield Tigers 45 AC
2/9 Sheffield Tigers 34 Glasgow Tigers 50 NL2
8/9 Glasgow Tigers 46 Bristol Bulldogs 38 NL2
11/9 Edinburgh Monarchs 47 Glasgow Tigers 49 AC
15/9 Glasgow Tigers 54 Newcastle Diamonds 30 NL2
18/9 Sheffield Tigers 41 Glasgow Tigers 43 Ch
at Old Meadowbank, Edinburgh
22/9 Glasgow Tigers 60 Norwich Stars 24 NL2
24/9 Bristol Bulldogs 65 Glasgow Tigers 18 NL2
25/9 Birmingham B 65 Glasgow Tigers 19 NL2
29/9 Glasgow Tigers 39 Birmingham B 45 NL2
6/10 Glasgow Tigers 42 Fleetwood Flyers 42 NL2
9/10 Norwich Stars 66 Glasgow Tigers 18 NL2
13/10 Glasgow Tigers 42 Sheffield Tigers 42 NL2
16/10 Edinburgh M 52 Glasgow Tigers 32 NL2

1949
6/4 Glasgow Tigers 50 Edinburgh Monarchs 24 NL2
9/4 Edinburgh Monarchs 43 Glasgow Tigers 41 NL2
13/4 Glasgow Tigers 59 Coventry Bees 25 NL2
15/4 Southampton Saints 43 Glasgow Tigers 41 NL2
20/4 Glasgow Tigers 52 Walthamstow W 32 NL2
26/4 Ashfield Giants 35 Glasgow Tigers 46 NL2
27/4 Glasgow Tigers 53 Newcastle Magpies 31 NL2
30/4 Norwich Stars 57 Glasgow Tigers 27 NL2
2/5 Newcastle Magpies 43 Glasgow Tigers 40 NL2
4/5 Glasgow Tigers 47 Belle Vue Aces 36 Ch
6/5 Cradley Heath Cubs 56 Glasgow Tigers 27 NL2
11/5 Glasgow Tigers 64 Southampton Saints 20 NL2
12/5 Sheffield Tigers 59 Glasgow Tigers 25 NL2
25/5 Glasgow Tigers 48 Norwich Stars 36 NL2
1/6 Glasgow Tigers 27 Bristol Bulldogs 57 NL2
8/6 Glasgow Tigers 54 Cradley Heath Cubs 30 NL2
15/6 Glasgow Tigers 67 Norwich Stars 41 NTr
18/6 Norwich Stars 71 Glasgow Tigers 36 NTr
22/6 Glasgow Tigers 52 Ashfield Giants 32 NL2
29/6 Glasgow Tigers 51 Newcastle Magpies 32 NL2
9/7 Coventry Bees 45 Glasgow Tigers 39 NL2
13/7 Glasgow Tigers 48 Edinburgh Monarchs 34 NL2
19/7 Ashfield Giants 51 Glasgow Tigers 33 NL2
20/7 Glasgow Tigers 45 Sheffield Tigers 39 NL2
23/7 Edinburgh Monarchs 61 Glasgow Tigers 23 NL2
27/7 Glasgow Tigers 49 Ashfield Giants 35 NL2
30/7 Edinburgh Monarchs 30 Glasgow Tigers 24
Newcastle Magpies 22 Sheffield Tigers 19
at Old Meadowbank, Edinburgh
1/8 Fleetwood Flyers 38 Glasgow Tigers 46 NL2
3/8 Glasgow Tigers 39 Walthamstow Wolves 45 NL2
9/8 Glasgow Tigers 28 Edinburgh Monarchs 56 Ch
10/8 Glasgow Tigers 68 Fleetwood Flyers 16 NL2
12/8 Bristol Bulldogs 62 Glasgow Tigers 22 NL2
13/8 Coventry Bees 52.5 Glasgow Tigers 30.5 NL2
17/8 Glasgow Tigers 58 Southampton Saints 26 NL2
22/8 Walthamstow W 48 Glasgow Tigers 34 NL2
27/8 Amsterdam 34 Scotland 38 Ch
28/8 Feyenoord Tigers 45 Glasgow Tigers 39 Ch
31/8 Glasgow Tigers 51 Cradley Heath H 33 NL2
1/9 Sheffield Tigers 68 Glasgow Tigers 16 NL2
7/9 Glasgow Tigers 35 Bristol Bulldogs 49 NL2
9/9 Cradley Heath H 59 Glasgow Tigers 25 NL2
10/9 Norwich Stars 58 Glasgow Tigers 26 NL2
14/9 Glasgow Tigers 45 Sheffield Tigers 39 NL2
19/9 Newcastle Magpies 49 Glasgow Tigers 34 NL2
21/9 Glasgow Tigers 47 Norwich Stars 36 NL2
26/9 Walthamstow W 56 Glasgow Tigers 27 NL2
27/9 Southampton Saints 52 Glasgow Tigers 32 NL2
28/9 Fleetwood Flyers 56 Glasgow Tigers 28 NL2
5/10 Glasgow Tigers 51 Fleetwood Flyers 33 NL2
7/10 Bristol Bulldogs 70 Glasgow Tigers 14 NL2
12/10 Glasgow Tigers 35 Coventry Bees 49 NL2

1950
5/4 Glasgow Tigers 41 Newcastle Diamonds 43 NS
12/4 Glasgow Tigers 55 Fleetwood Flyers 28 NS
17/4 Newcastle D 12 Glasgow Tigers 12 NS abn
19/4 Glasgow Tigers 34 Stoke Potters 50 NS
26/4 Glasgow Tigers 47 Edinburgh Monarchs 37 NS

29/4 Edinburgh Monarchs 63 Glasgow Tigers 21 NS
3/5 Glasgow Tigers4 7 Sheffield Tars 37 NS
5/5 Sheffield Tars 53 Glasgow Tigers31 NS
6/5 Stoke Potters 55 Glasgow Tigers 29 NS
9/5 Ashfield Giants 44 Glasgow Tigers40 NS
10/5 Glasgow Tigers 41 Ashfield Giants 43 NS
13/5 Giants & Tigers 35 Bothwell Bulls 48 Ch at Hamilton
17/5 Glasgow Tigers 51 Halifax Dukes 33 NS
19/5 Halifax Dukes 50 Glasgow Tigers34 NS
20/5 Fleetwood Flyers 47 Glasgow Tigers 37 NS
22/5 Newcastle Diamonds 56 Glasgow Tigers 28 NS
27/5 Stoke Potters 65 Glasgow Tigers 43 NTr
31/5 Glasgow Tigers70 Stoke Potters 38 NTr
7/6 Glasgow Tigers 70 Norwich Stars 38 NTr
10/6 Norwich Stars 78 Glasgow Tigers 30 NTr
14/6 Scottish Select 51 Vic Duggan's 33 Ch
17/6 Ashfield Giants 52 Glasgow Tigers 56 BC
21/6 Glasgow Tigers 60 Stoke Potters 23 NL2
24/6 Edinburgh Monarchs 44 Glasgow Select 40 Ch
28/6 Glasgow Tigers 60 Ashfield Giants 48 BC
30/6 Santry 33 Glasgow Select 27 Ch
1/7 Coventry Bees 47 Glasgow Tigers 37 NL2
2/7 Shelbourne Tigers 55 Glasgow Tigers 28 Ch
4/7 Southampton Saints 56 Glasgow Tigers 28 NL2
12/7 Glasgow Tigers 50 Cradley Heath H 34 NL2
19/7 Glasgow Tigers 68 Yarmouth Bloaters 16 NL2
20/7 Edinburgh Monarchs 15 Glasgow Tigers 9 PG
22/7 Fleetwood Flyers 40 Glasgow Tigers 44 NL2
26/7 Glasgow Tigers 56 Halifax Dukes 28 NL2
27/7 Plymouth Devils 24 Glasgow Tigers 30 NL2
2/8 Glasgow Tigers 49 Ashfield Giants 35 NL2
9/8 Glasgow Tigers 43 Walthamstow Wolves 41 NL2
14/8 Walthamstow W 53 Glasgow Tigers 31 NL2
15/8 Yarmouth Bloaters 43 Glasgow Tigers 41 NL2
16/8 Glasgow Tigers 47 Coventry Bees 36 NL2
18/8 Belfast Bees 39 Glasgow Tigers 32 Ch
23/8 Glasgow Tigers 45 Sheffield Tars 39 NL2
26/8 Edinburgh Monarchs 49 Glasgow Tigers 35 NL2
30/8 Glasgow Tigers 61 Plymouth Devils 23 NL2
1/9 Lanarkshire Eagles 37 Glasgow Tigers 47 Ch
2/9 Stoke Potters 38 Glasgow Tigers 43 NL2
4/9 Cradley Heath H 52 Glasgow Tigers 32 NL2
7/9 Glasgow Tigers 51 Southampton Saints 33 NL2
13/9 Glasgow Tigers 60 Edinburgh Monarchs 24 NL2
20/9 Glasgow Tigers 61 Norwich Stars 23 NL2
23/9 Norwich Stars 54 Glasgow Tigers 29 NL2
25/9 Newcastle Diamonds 41 Glasgow Tigers 43 NL2
27/9 Glasgow Tigers 56 Fleetwood Flyers 28 NL2
4/10 Glasgow Tigers 56 Newcastle D 28 NL2
10/10 Ashfield Giants 37 Glasgow Tigers 47 NL2
11/10 Glasgow Tigers 46 Edinburgh Monarchs 62 BC
12/10 Sheffield Tigers 48 Glasgow Tigers 36 NL2
14/10 Edinburgh Monarchs 71 Glasgow Tigers 37 BC
18/10 Halifax Dukes 51 Glasgow Tigers 33 NL2

1951
28/3 Glasgow Tigers 56 Fleetwood Flyers 28 NS
4/12 Glasgow Tigers 47 Newcastle Diamonds 37 NS
11/4 Glasgow Tigers 42 Edinburgh Monarchs 41 NS
13/4 Lanarkshire Eagles 46 Glasgow Tigers 35 NS
16/4 Newcastle Diamonds 47 Glasgow Tigers 37 NS
18/4 Glasgow Tigers 51 Lanarkshire Eagles 32
21/4 Edinburgh Monarchs 61 Glasgow Tigers 23 NS
25/4 Glasgow Tigers 57 Ashfield Giants 27 NS
30/4 Fleetwood Flyers 35 Glasgow Tigers 49 NS
2/5 Glasgow Tigers 51 Newcastle Diamonds 33 NL2
9/5 Glasgow Tigers 39 Belle Vue Aces 45 Ch
14/5 Liverpool Chads 47 Glasgow Tigers 37 NL2
15/5 Ashfield Giants 40 Glasgow Tigers 44 NS
16/5 Glasgow Tigers 49 Walthamstow W 35 NL2
19/5 Stoke Potters 53 Glasgow Tigers 31 NL2
23/5 Glasgow Tigers 57 Lanarkshire Eagles 51 SC
25/5 Lanarkshire Eagles 47 Glasgow Tigers 61 SC
26/5 Norwich Stars 14 Glasgow Tigers 4 NTr Abn
28/5 Newcastle Diamonds 45 Glasgow Tigers 39 NL2
30/5 Glasgow Tigers 64 Norwich Stars 44 NTr
6/6 Glasgow Tigers 53 Leicester Hunters 31 NL2
9/6 Norwich Stars 81 Glasgow Tigers 27 NTr
15/6 Halifax Dukes 55 Glasgow Tigers 29 NL2
18/6 Cradley Heath H 55 Glasgow Tigers 29 NL2
20/6 Glasgow Tigers 60 Stoke Potters 24 NL2
27/6 Glasgow Tigers 57 Yarmouth Bloaters 27 NL2
29/6 Fleetwood Flyers 45 Glasgow Tigers 39 NL2
14/7 Coventry Bees 42 Glasgow Tigers 42 NL2
18/7 Glasgow Tigers 54 Liverpool Chads 30 NL2
19/7 Edinburgh Monarchs 11 Glasgow Select 19 PG
25/7 Glasgow Tigers 46 Coventry Bees 38 NL2
28/7 Edinburgh Monarchs 66 Glasgow Tigers 42 SC
1/8 Glasgow Tigers 53 Norwich Stars 30 NL2
8/8 Glasgow Tigers 64 Edinburgh Monarchs 42 SC
11/8 Ashfield Giants 55 Glasgow Tigers 29 NL2
15/8 Glasgow Tigers 56 Ashfield Giants 28 NL2
17/8 Leicester Hunters 51 Glasgow Tigers 33 NL2
18/8 Norwich Stars 59 Glasgow Tigers 25 NL2
24/8 Lanarkshire Eagles 46 Glasgow Tigers 38 LC
29/8 Glasgow Tigers 52 Halifax Dukes 32 NL2
30/8 Oxford Cheetahs 47 Glasgow Tigers 37 NL2
5/9 Glasgow Tigers 40 Lanarkshire Eagles 44 NL2
14/9 Lanarkshire Eagles 50 Glasgow Tigers 34 NL2
19/9 Glasgow Tigers 57 Oxford Cheetahs 27 NL2
24/9 Walthamstow W 49 Glasgow Tigers 35 NL2
25/9 Yarmouth Bloaters 46 Glasgow Tigers 38 NL2
26/9 Glasgow Tigers 44 Edinburgh Monarchs 40 NL2
29/9 Edinburgh Monarchs 55 Glasgow Tigers 29 NL2
3/10 Glasgow Tigers 65 Fleetwood Flyers 19 NL2
10/10 Glasgow Tigers 60 Cradley Heath H 23 NL2
12/10 Lanarkshire E 42 Glasgow Tigers Sel 48 Ch

1952
25/3 Reds 18 Blues 28 Tigers 31 Eagles 19 4TT at Ashfield
26/3 Tigers 44 The Ex-Tigers 40 Ch Reunion
2/4 Glasgow Tigers 56 Liverpool Chads 28 NL2
9/4 Glasgow Tigers 47 Coventry Bees 37 NL2
16/4 Glasgow Tigers 58 Yarmouth Bloaters 26 NL2
19/4 Edinburgh Monarchs 53 Glasgow Tigers 31 NL2

23/4 Glasgow Tigers 49 Poole Pirates 35 NL2
26/4 Coventry Bees 48 Glasgow Tigers 36 NL2
30/4 Glasgow Tigers 53 Stoke Potters 31 NL2
1/5 Oxford Cheetahs 53 Glasgow Tigers 29 NL2
2/5 Cradley Heath H 56 Glasgow Tigers 28 NL2
3/5 Stoke Potters 53 Glasgow Tigers 31 NL2
7/5 Glasgow Tigers 42 Ashfield Giants 42 NL2
9/5 Lanarkshire Eagles 40 Glasgow Tigers 44 NL2
Glasgow Tigers 43 Motherwell Eagles 41 NL2
Leicester Hunters 48 Glasgow Tigers 36 NL2
Yarmouth Bloaters 56 Glasgow Tigers 28 NL2
19/5 Poole Pirates 61 Glasgow Tigers 23 NL2
21/5 Glasgow Tigers 65 Ashfield Giants 43 NTr
24/5 Ashfield Giants 52 Glasgow Tigers 56 NTr
30/5 Wigan Panthers 41 Glasgow Tigers 43 Ch
31/5 Glasgow Tigers 50 Lanarkshire Eagles 34 LC at Ashfield
4/6 Glasgow Tigers 49 Cradley Heath H 35 NL2
7/6 Ashfield Giants 36 Glasgow Tigers 48 NL2
11/6 Glasgow Tigers 49 Leicester Hunters 35 NL2
3/6 Lanarkshire Eagles 44 Glasgow Tigers 40 LC
18/6 Glasgow Tigers 53 Leicester Hunters 55 NTr
20/6 Leicester Hunters 46 Glasgow Tigers 62 NTr
23/6 Liverpool Chads 41 Glasgow Tigers 43 NL2
25/6 Glasgow Tigers 56 Oxford Cheetahs 28 NL2
28/6 Edinburgh Monarchs 56 Glasgow Tigers 52 SC
30/6 Poole Pirates 61 Glasgow Tigers 47 NTr
2/7 Glasgow Tigers 58 Poole Pirates 50 NTr
6/7 Shelbourne Tigers 35 Glasgow Tigers 37 Ch
12/7 Coventry Bees 54 Glasgow Tigers 30 NL2
14/7 Poole Pirates 56 Glasgow Tigers 28 NL2
16/7 Glasgow Tigers 38 Leicester Hunters 45 NL2
18/7 Lanarkshire Eagles 41 Glasgow Tigers 43 NL2
23/7 Glasgow Tigers 67 Edinburgh Monarchs 41 SC
26/7 Stoke Potters 54 Glasgow Tigers 30 NL2
29/7 Yarmouth Bloaters 57 Glasgow Tigers 27 NL2
30/7 Glasgow Tigers 40 Cradley Heath H 44 NL2
4/8 Liverpool Chads 47 Glasgow Tigers 37 NL2
12/8 Ashfield Giants 50 Glasgow Tigers 58 SC
13/8 Glasgow Tigers 56 Yarmouth Bloaters 28 NL2
18/8 Glasgow Tigers 75 Ashfield Giants 33 SC
20/8 Glasgow Tigers 45 Lanarkshire Eagles 39 NL2
27/8 Glasgow Tigers 52 Stoke Potters 32 NL2
3/9 Glasgow Tigers 56 Edinburgh Monarchs 28 NL2
10/9 Glasgow Tigers 61 Liverpool Chads 23 NL2
12/9 Cradley Heath H 55 Glasgow Tigers 29 NL2
17/9 Glasgow Tigers 47 Ashfield Giants 37 NL2
20/9 Ashfield Giants 45 Glasgow Tigers 38 NL2
24/9 Glasgow Tigers 45 Poole Pirates 38 NL2
25/9 Oxford Cheetahs 35 Glasgow Tigers 49 NL2
26/9 Leicester Hunters 58 Glasgow Tigers 26 NL2
1/10 Glasgow Tigers 38 Coventry Bees 46 NL2
4/10 Edinburgh Monarchs 46 Glasgow Tigers 38 NL2
8/10 Glasgow Tigers 59 Oxford Cheetahs 24 NL2
15/10 Glasgow Tigers 46 Edinburgh M 38 NL2

1953
1/4 Glasgow Tigers 41 Coventry Bees 43 NL2
3/4 Liverpool Chads 49 Glasgow Tigers 35 NL2

4/4 Coventry Bees 51 Glasgow Tigers 33 NL2
8/4 Glasgow Tigers 51 Wolverhampton W 33 NL2
15/4 Glasgow Tigers 57 Stoke Potters 27 NL2
17/4 Leicester Hunters 44 Glasgow Tigers 40 NL2
18/4 Stoke Potters 50 Glasgow Tigers 34 NL2
20/4 Poole Pirates 58 Glasgow Tigers 28 NL2
22/4 Glasgow Tigers 42 Leicester Hunters 42 NL2
29/4 Glasgow Tigers 49 Poole Pirates 35 NL2
6/5 Glasgow Tigers 75 Edinburgh Monarchs 33 NTr
8/5 Lanarkshire Eagles 44 Glasgow Tigers 40 LC
9/5 Edinburgh Monarchs 47 Glasgow Tigers 61 NTr
9/5 Motherwell & Dist. Select 40 Glasgow Sel 42 Ch at Hamilton
13/5 Glasgow Tigers 59 Lanarkshire Eagles 25 NL2
20/5 Glasgow Tigers 57 Liverpool Chads 27 NL2
29/5 Wolverhampton W 49 Glasgow Tigers 59 NTr
6/6 Edinburgh Monarchs 43 Glasgow Tigers 41 NL2
8/6 Liverpool Chads 37 Glasgow Tigers 47 NL2
9/6 Yarmouth Bloaters 57 Glasgow Tigers 27 NL2
10/6 Glasgow Tigers 45 Yarmouth Bloaters 39 NL2
19/6 Wolverhampton W 40 Glasgow Tigers 44 NL2
24/6 Glasgow Tigers 76 Wolverhampton W 26 NTr
1/7 Glasgow Tigers 69 Rayleigh Rockets 39 NTr
4/7 Rayleigh Rockets 64 Glasgow Tigers 44 NTr
11/7 Birmingham B 70 Glasgow Tigers 38 NTr
15/7 Glasgow Tigers 56 Birmingham B 52 NTr
18/7 Stoke Potters 42 Glasgow Tigers 42 NL2
21/7 Ashfield 11 Tigers 24 Eagles 29 Monarchs 20
23/7 Edinburgh Monarchs 20 Glasgow Tigers 10 SG
24/7 Lanarkshire Eagles 43 Glasgow Tigers 41 NL2
28/7 Eagles 38 Tigers 22 Ch at Ashfield
29/7 Glasgow Tigers 46 Poole Pirates 38 NL2
5/8 Glasgow Tigers 71 Wolverhampton Wasps 37 QC
8/8 Edinburgh Monarchs 44 Glasgow Tigers 40 NL2
12/8 Glasgow Tigers 52.5 Lanarkshire E 31.5 NL2
19/8 Glasgow Tigers 58 Edinburgh Monarchs 26 NL2
20/8 Ipswich Witches 53 Glasgow Tigers 55 QC
24/8 Poole Pirates 47 Glasgow Tigers 37 NL2
25/8 Yarmouth Bloaters 58 Glasgow Tigers 26 NL2
26/8 Glasgow Tigers 49 Wolverhampton W 35 NL2
28/8 Glasgow Tigers 61 Edinburgh Monarchs 47 SCC
31/8 Exeter Falcons 69 Glasgow Tigers 39 QC
2/9 Glasgow Tigers 57 Coventry Bees 26 NL2
9/9 Glasgow Tigers 54 Leicester Hunters 30 NL2 DH
9/9 Glasgow Tigers 64 Stoke Potters 20 NL2 DH
11/9 Wolverhampton W 45 Glasgow Tigers 39 NL2
12/9 Coventry Bees 51 Glasgow Tigers 33 NL2
16/9 Glasgow Tigers 62 Yarmouth Bloaters 21 NL2
16/9 Glasgow Tigers 55 Edinburgh Monarchs 29 NL2
18/9 Leicester Hunters 48 Glasgow Tigers 36 NL2
23/9 Glasgow Tigers 72 Exeter Falcons 36 QC
26/9 Edinburgh Monarchs 65 Glasgow Tigers 43 QC
2/10 Lanarkshire Eagles 50 Glasgow Tigers 58 SC
5/10 Glasgow Tigers 56 Edinburgh Monarchs 52 QC
7/10 Glasgow Tigers 65 Lanarkshire Eagles 43 SC

1954
10/4 Edinburgh Monarchs 47 Glasgow Tigers 36 NS
14/4 Glasgow Tigers 32 Coventry Bees 51 NS

16/4 Leicester Hunters 47 Glasgow Tigers 37 NS
17/4 Ipswich Witches 48 Glasgow Tigers 36 NS
21/4 Glasgow Tigers 38 Edinburgh Monarchs 45 NS
23/4 Lanarkshire Eagles 58 Glasgow Tigers 25 NS

1955
14/5 Lanarkshire Eagles Sell 54 Glasgow Tigers Select 29 Ch @ Hamilton

1956
16/5 Scotland 49 England Select 57 IC
30/5 Glasgow Tigers 48 Birmingham B 48 ASC
13/6 Britain 56 Overseas 52 ICC
27/6 Glasgow Tigers 58 Bradford Tudors 38 ASC
11/7 Glasgow Tigers 54 Norwich Stars 41 ASC

1964
1/4 Glasgow Tigers 44 Middlesbrough Bears 34 NrL
2/4 Sheffield Tigers 59 Glasgow Tigers 19 NrL
8/4 Glasgow Tigers 49 Sheffield Tigers 29 NrL
10/4 Middlesbrough Bears 46 Glasgow Tigers 32 NrL
15/4 Glasgow Tigers 41 Edinburgh Monarchs 37 NrL
18/4 Edinburgh Monarchs 56 Glasgow Tigers21 NrL
29/4 Glasgow Tigers 50 Sunderland Saints 28 NrL
4/5 Newcastle Diamonds 46 Glasgow Tigers 29 NrL
6/5 Glasgow Tigers 53 Newcastle Diamonds 25 NrL
12/5 Sunderland Saints 48 Glasgow Tigers 30 NrL
13/5 Glasgow Tigers 40 Newport Wasps 38 PL
20/5 Glasgow Tigers 41 Exeter Falcons 36 PL
25/5 Exeter Falcons 43 Glasgow Tigers 35 PL
26/5 Long Eaton Archers 45 Glasgow Tigers 33 PL
29/5 Glasgow Tigers 39 Poole Pirates 39 PL
10/6 Glasgow Tigers 35 Wolverhampton W 42 PL
17/6 Glasgow Tigers 59 Sheffield Tigers 37 KOC
18/6 Sheffield Tigers 42 Glasgow Tigers 36 PL
22/6 Newcastle Diamonds 51 Glasgow Tigers26 PL
24/6 Glasgow Tigers 37 Edinburgh Monarchs 41 PL
3/7 Glasgow Tigers 44 Long Eaton Archers 34 PL
10/7 Glasgow Tigers 31 Newcastle Diamonds 46 PL
15/7 Glasgow Tigers 46 Newport Wasps 49 KOC
17/7 Wolverhampton W 39 Glasgow Tigers 38 PL
22/7 Poole Pirates 43 Glasgow Tigers 35 PL
24/7 Hackney Hawks 49 Glasgow Tigers 29 PL
31/7 Glasgow Tigers 42 Hackney Hawks 36 PL
14/8 Glasgow Tigers 52 Edinburgh Monarchs 43 SC
15/8 Edinburgh Monarchs 53 Glasgow Tigers 43   SC
28/8 Glasgow Tigers 41 Cradley Heath H 37 PL
4/9 Glasgow Tigers 44 Sheffield Tigers 34 PL
11/9 Newport Wasps 48 Glasgow Tigers 30 PL
18/9 Glasgow Tigers 37 Middlesbrough Bears 41 PL
19/9 Edinburgh M 39 Glasgow Tigers 39 PL
17/10 Cradley Heath H 42 Glasgow Tigers 36 PL

1965
2/4 Glasgow Tigers 59 Hackney Hawks 19 BL
16/4 Glasgow Tigers 56 Coventry Bees 22 BL
17/4 Edinburgh Monarchs 36 Glasgow Tigers 42 BL
22/4 Sheffield Tigers42 Glasgow Tigers 36 BL
23/4 Glasgow Tigers 48 Edinburgh Monarchs 30 BL
30/4 Glasgow Tigers 37 Wimbledon Dons 41 BL
1/5 Belle Vue Aces 36 Glasgow Tigers 42 BL
7/5 Glasgow Tigers 54 Exeter Falcons 24 BL
8/5 Coventry Bees 51 Glasgow Tigers 26 BL
14/5 Glasgow Tigers 40 Swindon Robins 38 BL
21/5 Glasgow Tigers 45 West Ham Hammers 32 BL
22/5Halifax Dukes 39 Glasgow Tigers 39 BL
28/5 Glasgow Tigers 60 Long Eaton Archers 18 BL
1/6 Long Eaton Archers 41 Glasgow Tigers 37 BL
3/6 Oxford Cheetahs 48 Glasgow Tigers 30 BL
5/6 Cradley Heath H 43 Glasgow Tigers 35 BL
7/6 Exeter Falcons 46 Glasgow Tigers 32 BL
11/6 Glasgow Tigers 38 Oxford Cheetahs 40 BL
25/6 Glasgow Tigers 49 Poole Pirates 29 BL
2/7 Glasgow Tigers 64 Sheffield Glasgow Tigers KOC
9/7 Glasgow Tigers 53 Cradley Heath Heathens 25 BL
15/7 Glasgow Tigers 43 Wolverhampton Wolves 34 BL
19/7 Newcastle Diamonds 48 Glasgow Tigers 30 BL
24/7 King's Lynn Stars 40 Glasgow Tigers 38 Ch
6/8 Glasgow Tigers 42 Newcastle Diamonds 36 BL
13/8 Glasgow Tigers 49 Swindon Robins 46 KOC
17/8 West Ham Hammers 47 Glasgow Tigers 30 BL
18/8 Poole Pirates 49 Glasgow Tigers 26 BL
20/8 Glasgow Tigers 55 Edinburgh Monarchs SC
21/8 Edinburgh Monarchs 54 Glasgow Tigers 41 SC
27/8 Glasgow Tigers 43 Newport Wasps 35 BL
28/8 Swindon Robins 54 Glasgow Tigers 24 BL
30/8 Newport Wasps 50 Glasgow Tigers 28 BL
3/ Glasgow Tigers 42 Belle Vue Aces 32 BL
4/9 Wimbledon Dons 49 Glasgow Tigers 29 BL
10/9 Glasgow Tigers 43 West Ham Hammers 50 KOC
24/9 Glasgow Tigers 31 Halifax Dukes 17 BL abn
8/10 Hackney Hawks 54 Glasgow Tigers 24 BL
14/10 Glasgow Tigers 33 Halifax Dukes 44 BL
15/10 Wolverhampton W 56 Glasgow Tigers 21 BL
22/10 Glasgow Tigers 37 Sheffield Tigers 41 BL

1966
1/4 Glasgow Tigers 42 Sheffield Tigers 35 BL
8/4 Glasgow Tigers 39 West Ham Hammers 39   BL
15/4 Glasgow Tigers 41 Coventry Bees 37 BL
23/4 Edinburgh Monarchs 46 Glasgow Tigers 31 BL
27/4 King's Lynn Stars 45 Glasgow Tigers 33 BL
29/4 Glasgow Tigers 42 Halifax Dukes 36 BL
6/5 Glasgow Tigers 45 Oxford Cheetahs 33 BL
13/5 Glasgow Tigers 43 Edinburgh Monarchs 35 BL
14/5 Wimbledon Dons 48 Glasgow Tigers 30 BL
16/5 Exeter Falcons 46 Glasgow Tigers 32 BL
27/5Glasgow Tigers 46 Newport Wasps 32 BL
3/6 Glasgow Tigers 45 Exeter Falcons 32 BL
10/6 Glasgow Tigers 50 Long Eaton Archers 28 BL
11/6 Halifax Dukes 57 Glasgow Tigers KOC
16/6 Middlesbrough Bears 32 Glasgow Tigers 45 NC
24/6 Glasgow Tigers 60 Poole Pirates 17 BL
30/6 Oxford Cheetahs 40 Glasgow Tigers 38   BL
13/7 Glasgow Tigers 52 Hackney Hawks 26 BL
15/7 Newport Wasps 38 Glasgow Tigers 40 BL
16/7 Coventry Bees 42 Glasgow Tigers 36 BL

20/7 Poole Pirates 48 Glasgow Tigers 30 BL
22/7 Hackney Hawks 41 Glasgow Tigers 37 BL
23/7 Belle Vue Aces 42 Glasgow Tigers 35 BL
1/8 Newcastle Diamonds 52 Glasgow Tigers 26 BL
5/8 Glasgow Tigers40 Wolverhampton Wolves 38 BL
12/8 Glasgow Tigers 53 King's Lynn Stars 25 BL
19/8 Glasgow Tigers 57 Edinburgh Monarchs 39 SC
20/8 Edinburgh M 19 Glasgow Tigers 10 SC Abn
24/8 Swindon Robins 53 Glasgow Tigers 25 BL
25/8 Sheffield Tigers 49 Glasgow Tigers 29 BL
26/8 Glasgow Tigers 38 Swindon Robins 40 BL
27/8 Edinburgh Monarchs 54 Glasgow Tigers 42 SC
30/8 Long Eaton Archers 48 Glasgow Tigers 30 BL
2/9 Glasgow Tigers 54 Belle Vue Aces 24 BL
10/9 Cradley Heath H 41 Glasgow Tigers 37 BL
12/9 Halifax Dukes 60 Glasgow Tigers 18 BL
16/9 Glasgow Tigers 45 Newcastle Diamonds 33 BL
23/9 Glasgow Tigers 48 Wimbledon Dons 29 BL
7/10 Glasgow Tigers 36 Cradley Heath H 29 BL
Abn 11 heats, result stands
14/10 Wolverhampton W 45 Glasgow Tigers 33 BL

1967
24/3 Hackney Hawks 39 Glasgow Tigers 39 BL
25/3 King's Lynn Stars 42 Glasgow Tigers 35 BL
31/3 Glasgow Tigers 36 Newcastle Diamonds 42 BL
7/4 Glasgow Tigers 42 Coventry Bees 35 BL
8/4 Belle Vue Aces 47 Glasgow Tigers 31 BL
14/8 Glasgow Tigers 42 Exeter Falcons 34 BL
15/8 Edinburgh Monarchs 38 Glasgow Tigers 40 BL
21/4 Glasgow Tigers 41 Edinburgh Monarchs 37 BL
28/4 Glasgow Tigers 39 Poole Pirates 39 BL
2/5 West Ham Hammers 51 Glasgow Tigers 27 BL
4/5 Sheffield Tigers 44 Glasgow 34 BL
5/5 Glasgow Tigers 49 Sheffield Tigers 29 BL
12/5 Glasgow Tigers 36 Belle Vue Aces 41 BL
26/5 Glasgow Tigers 50 Long Eaton Archers 28 BL
27/5 Coventry Bees 12 Glasgow Tigers 8 BL Abn
29/5 Newcastle Diamonds 56 Glasgow Tigers 22 BL
2/6 Glasgow Tigers 48 King's Lynn Stars 39 BL
6/6 West Ham Hammers 67 Glasgow Tigers 29 KOC
9/6 Glasgow Tigers 32 West Ham Hammers 46 BL
16/6 Glasgow Tigers 33 Europeans 31
    Stockholm 22 Monarchs 9 4TT
24/6 Cradley Heath H 37 Glasgow Tigers 41 BL
30/6 Glasgow Tigers 46 Cradley Heath Heathens 32 BL
5/7 Poole Pirates 48 Glasgow Tigers 30 BL
6/7 Oxford Cheetahs 41 Glasgow Tigers 36 BL
7/7 Glasgow Tigers 43 Newport Wasps 34 BL
12/7 Glasgow Tigers 48 Hackney Hawks 30 BL
14/7 Wolverhampton W 58 Glasgow Tigers 20 BL
21/7 Newport Wasps 44 Glasgow Tigers 34 BL
3/8 Wimbledon Dons 43 Glasgow Tigers 34 BL
4/8 Glasgow Tigers 35 Swindon Robins 43 BL
12/8 Edinburgh Monarchs 56 Glasgow Tigers 39 SC

16/8 Long Eaton Archers 38 Glasgow Tigers 40 BL
18/8 Glasgow Tigers 40 Wimbledon Dons 38 BL
19/8 Coventry Bees 56 Glasgow Tigers 22 BL
25/8 Glasgow Tigers 43 Halifax Dukes 35 BL
1/9 Glasgow Tigers 44 Oxford Cheetahs 34 BL
2/9 Nelson Admirals 49 Glasgow B 47 Ch
8/9 Glasgow Tigers 46 Edinburgh Monarchs 50 SC
13/9 Glasgow Tigers 57 Wolverhampton W 21 BL
22/9 Glasgow Tigers 53 Edinburgh Monarchs 31 ST
23/9 Swindon Robins 52 Glasgow Tigers 26 BL
9/10 Exeter Falcons 50 Glasgow Tigers 28 BL

1968
29/3 Hackney Hawks 47 Glasgow Tigers 31 BL1
30/3 King's Lynn Stars 36 Glasgow Tigers 42 BL1
5/4 Glasgow Tigers 51 Coatbridge Monarchs 45 CD
6/4 Coatbridge Monarchs 54 Glasgow Tigers42 CD
12/4 Glasgow Tigers 47 Leicester Lions 31 BL1
13/4 Coventry Bees 48 Glasgow Tigers 30 BL1
15/4 Newcastle Diamonds 45 Glasgow Tigers 33 BL1
19/4 Glasgow Tigers 47 Coventry Bees 31 BL1
20/4 Swindon Robins 61 Glasgow Tigers 17 BL1
22/4 Exeter Falcons 50 Glasgow Tigers 28 BL1
26/4 Glasgow Tigers 39 Cradley Heath H 39 BL1
7/5 Leicester Lions 43 Glasgow Tigers 35 BL1
10/5 Glasgow Tigers 49 Oxford Cheetahs 29 BL1
16/5 Sheffield Tigers 51 Glasgow Tigers 27 BL1
17/5 Glasgow Tigers 38 Coatbridge Monarchs 40 BL1
24/5 Glasgow Tigers 31 West Ham Hammers 47 BL1
7/6 Glasgow Tigers 40 WimBL1edon Dons BL1
8/6 Halifax Dukes 50 Glasgow Tigers 27 BL1
14/6 Glasgow Tigers 34 Halifax Dukes 44 BL1
15/6 Belle Vue Aces 50 Glasgow Tigers 28 BL1
21/6 Glasgow Tigers 38 Sheffield Tigers 40 BL1
28/6 Glasgow Tigers 43 Swindon Robins 35 BL1
5/7 Glasgow Tigers 46 Poole Pirates 32 BL1
10/7 Glasgow Tigers 49 Wolverhampton W 29 BL1
19/7 Wolverhampton W 45 Glasgow Tigers 33 BL1
25/ WimBL1edon Dons 49 Glasgow Tigers 29 BL1
26/7 Glasgow Tigers 44 Belle Vue Aces 34 BL1
2/8 Glasgow Tigers 36 Hackney Hawks 42 BL1
16/8 Glasgow Tigers 51 Prague 27 Ch
17/8 Coatbridge Monarchs 64 Glasgow Tigers 32 SC
23/8 Glasgow Tigers 57 Coatbridge Monarchs 39 SC
27/8 West Ham Hammers 36 Glasgow Tigers 42 BL1
28/8 Poole Pirates 45 Glasgow Tigers 33 BL1
29/8 Oxford Cheetahs 42 Glasgow Tigers 36 BL1
30/8 Glasgow Tigers 44 King's Lynn Stars 34 BL1
6/9 Glasgow Tigers 41 Newcastle Diamonds 37 BL1
13/9 Glasgow Tigers 36 Exeter Falcons 42 BL1
18/9 Glasgow Tigers 55 Newport Wasps 23 BL1
20/9 Newport Wasps 49 Glasgow Tigers 29 BL1
28/9 Coatbridge Monarchs 48 Glasgow Tigers 30 BL1

The riders

Averages in national competitions – in alphabetical order. Minimum of six meetings for inclusion

1946

Riders	Comp	M	R	P	BP	TP	CMA	FM	PM
B Baird	NrL	18	50	37	8	45	3.60	0	0
	NT	3	3	4	0	4	5.33	0	0
	ACUC	10	26	18	1	19	2.92	0	0
J Crowther	NrL	24	100	191	9	200	8.00	1	0
	NT	4	19	37.5	2	39.5	8.31	0	0
	ACUC	10	47	98	4	102	8.68	1	0
G Garland	NrL	21	85	143	19	162	7.62	0	0
	NT	4	20	25	5	30	6.00	0	0
	ACUC	10	46	51	6	57	4.59	0	0
E Lack	NrL	21	82	71	16	87	4.24	0	0
	NT	4	20	19	6	25	5.00	0	0
	ACUC	8	36	29	8	37	4.11	0	0
W Lowther	NrL	22	94	220	5	225	9.57	7	0
	NT	4	20	38.5	1	39.5	7.90	0	0
	ACUC	8	39	69	7	76	7.79	0	1
W Morton	NrL	20	85	178	7	185	8.71	2	0
	NT	4	20	34	4	38	7.60	0	0
	ACUC	8	39	66	2	68	6.97	0	0
C Oates	NrL	9	26	18	6	24	3.69	0	0
	NT	2	2	1	1	2	4.00	0	0
	ACUC	3	8	7	2	9	4.50	0	0
B Shearer	NrL	4	9	1	1	2	0.89	0	0
	NT	2	2	0	0	0	0.00	0	0
	ACUC	1	1	0	0	0	0.00	0	0
M Stobart	NrL	24	100	133	24	157	6.28	0	1
	NT	4	20	28	8	36	7.20	0	0
	ACUC	10	47	66	6	72	6.12	0	0
W Thomson	NrL	10	22	13	4	17	3.09	0	0
	ACUC	6	8	2	1	3	1.50	0	0
K Tidbury	NrL	7	22	12	2	14	2.55	0	0

1947

Riders	Comp	M	R	P	BP	TP	CMA	FM	PM
J Bainbridge	NL2	26	99	117	15	132	5.33	0	0
	BSC	12	47	48	11	59	5.02	0	0
B Baird	NL2	15	56	54	7	61	4.36	0	0
	BSC	1	4	4	1	5	5.00	0	0
B Bates	NL2	4	10	12	3	15	6.00	0	0
	BSC	5	14	16	3	19	5.42	0	0
B Byrnes	NL2	17	69	96	10	106	6.14	0	0
	BSC	13	56	93	8	101	7.21	0	0
J Crowther	NL2	25	98	178	12	190	7.76	1	0
	BSC	8	30	39	5	44	5.86	0	0
H Fairhurst	NL2	21	64	60	14	74	4.63	0	0

	BSC	11	42	47	11	58	5.52	0	0
G Garland	NL2	9	33	46	2	48	5.82	0	0
	BSC	7	32	39	1	40	5.00	0	0
N Lindsay	NL2	20	81	100.5	14	114.5	5.65	0	0
	BSC	8	32	57	4	61	7.62	0	0
W Lowther	NL2	30	121	288	0	288	9.52	9	0
	BSC	14	69	168	3	171	9.91	3	0
G McGregor	NL2	6	16	10	5	15	3.75	0	0
	BSC	1	4	6	0	6	6.00	0	0
B Ryan	NL2	20	72	71	11	82	4.56	0	0
	BSC	12	42	48	6	54	5.14	0	0
H Sharpe	NL2	8	23	17	5	22	3.83	0	0
	BSC	5	15	10	2	12	3.20	0	0
B Shearer	NL2	23	72	81.5	12	93.5	5.19	0	0

1948

Riders	Comp	M	R	P	BP	TP	CMA	FM	PM
J Bainbridge	NL2	33	136	166	14	180	5.29	1	1
	AC	16	66	99	18	117	7.09	0	0
B Byrnes	NL2	19	81	149	13	162	8.00	1	1
	AC	12	52	78	5	83	6.38	0	0
J Crowther	NL2	36	148	275	22	297	8.03	2	3
	AC	16	76	171	5	176	9.26	2	2
N Downham	NL2	8	24	25	5	30	5.00	0	0
H Fairhurst	NL2	36	145	189	24	213	5.88	0	1
	AC	16	63	59	19	78	4.95	0	0
G Garland	NL2	6	13	9	0	9	2.77	0	0
	AC	7	22	7	2	9	1.63	0	0
N Lindsay	NL2	35	124	162	20	182	5.87	0	1
	AC	15	54	67	11	78	5.77	0	0
W Lowther	NL2	36	149	254.5	19	273.5	7.34	2	1
	AC	16	73	149	8	157	8.60	3	0
G McGregor	NL2	32	71	54	15	69	3.89	0	0
	AC	12	36	38	7	45	5.00	0	1
A McGuire	NL2	8	16	5	1	6	1.50	0	0
B Ryan	NL2	28	111	179	18	197	7.10	1	0
	SC	16	63	82	6	88	5.58	0	0

1949

Riders	Comp	M	R	P	BP	TP	CMA	FM	PM
J Bainbridge	NL2	44	177	345	18	363	8.20	7	3
B Bates	NL2	10	20	10	2	12	2.40	0	0
B Byrnes	NL2	21	85	170.5	7	177.5	8.35	3	0
J Crowther	NL2	29	108	198	20	218	8.07	2	1
N Downham	NL2	23	56	52	13	65	4.64	0	0
H Fairhurst	NL2	14	49	59	13	72	5.88	0	0
J Hodgson	NL2	9	36	60	2	62	6.89	0	0
N Lindsay	NL2	46	176	230	30	260	5.91	0	1
W Lowther	NL2	37	151	265	18	283	7.50	3	1
G McGregor	NL2	46	182	260	30	290	6.37	2	1
A McIntosh	NL2	21	56	42	11	53	3.79	0	0

Riders	Comp	M	R	P	BP	TP	CMA	FM	PM
K McKinlay	NL2	20	47	27	3	30	2.55	0	0
B Ryan	NL2	33	123	130	26	156	5.07	0	1

1950

Riders	Comp	M	R	P	BP	TP	CMA	FM	PM
J Bainbridge	NL2	22	84	173	11	184	8.76	6	3
	NS	14	54	104	3	107	7.92	0	0
J Crowther	NL2	15	59	79	16	95	6.44	0	1
	NS	14	56	60	7	67	4.78	0	0
P Dykes	NL2	31	86	116	25	141	6.56	0	1
	NS	14	39	45	5	50	5.12	0	0
J Green	NS	10	25	11	2	13	2.08	0	0
F Hodgson	NL2	19	76	111	21	132	6.95	0	1
J Hodgson	NL2	31	123	177	29	206	6.70	1	1
	NS	14	51	68	10	78	5.77	0	0
N Lindsay	NL2	32	131	190	33	223	6.81	0	2
	NS	13	51	73	8	81	6.35	0	0
G McGregor	NL2	32	133	229	23	252	7.58	0	1
	NS	14	55	108	7	115	8.36	1	1
A McIntosh	NL2	15	33	39	8	47	5.70	0	0
K McKinlay	NL2	27	71	89	17	106	5.97	0	0
	NS	4	10	18	3	21	8.40	1	0
T Miller	NL2	31	130	281	15	296	9.11	6	4
	NS	14	45	48	11	59	5.24	0	0

1951

Riders	Comp	M	R	P	BP	TP	CMA	FM	PM
J Bainbridge	NL2	28	114	248	7	255	8.95	5	1
	NS	10	38	63	5	68	7.15	0	0
J Blythe	NL2	22	48	42	10	52	4.33	0	0
	NS	8	22	20	7	27	4.90	0	0
F Hodgson	NL2	32	124	170	30	200	6.45	1	3
	NS	10	37	50	11	61	6.59	0	0
J Hodgson	NL2	31	121	152	29	181	5.98	0	1
	NS	10	36	56	9	65	7.22	0	1
N Lindsay	NL2	32	123	156	25	181	5.89	0	2
	NS	10	40	72	3	75	7.50	0	0
A McIntosh	NL2	32	90	82	21	103	4.58	0	0
	NS	10	30	44	4	48	6.40	1	0
K McKinlay	NL2	31	122	171	13	184	6.03	2	0
	NS	10	40	50	13	63	6.30	0	0
T Miller	NL2	32	131	339	5	344	10.50	12	2
	NS	8	12	83	1	84	10.50	3	1
L Nicholson	NL2	16	39	34	9	43	4.41	0	0

1952

Riders	Comp	M	R	P	BP	TP	CMA	FM	PM
J Bainbridge	NL2	34	145	293	18	311	8.58	2	1
P Dykes	NL2	50	194	213	43	256	5.28	0	0
F Hodgson	NL2	33	89	79	17	96	4.31	0	0
J Hodgson	NL2	28	86	75	20	95	4.42	0	0

Rider	Comp	M	R	P	BP	TP	CMA	FM	PM
A McIntosh	NL2	43	167	208	26	234	5.60	0	1
K McKinlay	NL2	49	203	394	20	414	8.16	2	3
T Miller	NL2	49	208	564	4	568	10.92	21	1
L Nicholson	NL2	39	122	127	18	145	4.75	0	0
B Sharp	NL2	11	26	21	11	32	4.92	0	0
D Wilkinson	NL2	49	180	191	35	226	5.02	0	0

1953

Riders	Comp	M	R	P	BP	TP	CMA	FM	PM
J Bainbridge	NL2	36	150	275	24	299	7.97	4	3
P Dykes	NL2	38	144	185.5	33	218.5	6.07	0	1
L Lazarus	NL2	37	141	179	31	210	5.96	0	4
A McIntosh	NL2	21	89	122	12	134	6.02	0	1
K McKinlay	NL2	40	173	360	24	384	8.88	7	2
T Miller	NL2	39	171	462	3	465	10.88	23	0
B Sharp	NL2	40	110	118	26	144	5.24	0	0
D Templeton	NL2	11	30	16	4	20	2.67	0	0
H Welch	NL2	11	31	30	6	36	4.65	0	0
D Wilkinson	NL2	40	132	152	29	181	5.48	0	0

1954

Riders	Comp	M	R	P	BP	TP	CMA	FM	PM
D. Craig	NS	6	12	6	1	7	2.33	0	0
A McIntosh	NS	6	24	21	4	25	4.16	0	0
K McKinlay	NS	6	24	67	0	67	11.6	3	0
B Sharp	NS	6	24	42	1	43	7.16	0	0
D Templeton	NS	6	24	19	5	24	4.00	0	0

A Malm and V McWilliams rode in five meetings each and W Templeton rode in two. Glasgow did not complete their North Shield fixtures and the results were expunged.

1964

Riders	Comp	M	R	P	BP	TP	CMA	FM	PM
G Coombes	PL	12	37	23	9	32	3.46	0	0
C Julian	PL	15	59	97	5	102	6.92	0	0
M Mattingley	PL	23	96	176	10	186	7.75	1	0
	NrL	10	41	78	4	82	8.00	1	2
B McMillan	PL	22	75	53	16	69	3.68	0	0
	NrL	10	38	37	7	44	4.63	0	0
C Monk	PL	24	106	284	5	289	10.91	11	0
	NrL	9	36	99	0	99	11.00	5	0
R Monteith	PL	4	10	9	1	10	4.00	0	0
	NrL	9	23	15	3	18	3.13	0	0
B Ovenden	PL	22	85	57	16	73	3.44	0	0
	NrL	9	36	33	11	44	4.88	0	0
T Redmond	PL	20	89	163	7	170	7.64	0	0
	NrL	2	7	7	2	9	5.14	0	0
T Stone	PL	14	46	28	5	33	2.87	0	0
	NrL	6	28	30	6	31	4.80	0	0

1965

Riders	Comp	M	R	P	BP	TP	CMA	FM	PM
G Coombes	BL	37	131	130	40	170	5.19	0	1
M Mattingley	BL	30	116	154	22	176	6.07	0	2
B McMillan	BL	20	65	53	17	70	4.31	0	0
C Monk	BL	37	163	415	4	419	10.28	9	1
B Ovenden	BL	30	99	95	24	119	4.81	0	1
N Paulsen	BL	24	92	135	13	148	6.43	0	1
B Scott	BL	37	155	271	24	295	7.61	2	2
W Templeton	BL	31	123	200	22	222	7.22	1	1

1966

Riders	Comp	M	R	P	BP	TP	CMA	FM	PM
J Faafeng	BL	28	89	97	21	118	5.30	0	0
M Mattingley	BL	37	143	206	21	227	6.35	1	0
B McMillan	BL	37	135	130	37	167	4.95	0	1
J McMillan	BL	13	26	17	6	23	3.54	0	0
C Monk	BL	37	158	362	4	366	9.27	6	1
B Scott	BL	22	85	134	16	150	7.06	0	0
W Templeton	BL	37	150	217	36	253	6.75	0	2
A Wells	BL	35	144	242	27	269	7.47	1	1

1967

Riders	Comp	M	R	P	BP	TP	CMA	FM	PM
R Dent	BL	8	31	32	8	40	5.16	0	0
J Faafeng	BL	10	40	48	6	54	5.40	0	0
B Josefsson	BL	17	73	111	15	126	6.90	1	0
M Mattingley	BL	22	78	105	20	125	6.41	0	0
B McMillan	BL	14	45	40	5	45	4.00	1	0
J McMillan	BL	29	111	113	17	130	4.68	0	0
C Monk	BL	36	152	396	3	399	10.50	14	0
N Ringstrom	BL	27	98	75	18	93	3.80	0	0
W Templeton	BL	37	151	218	22	240	6.36	1	1
A Wells	BL	31	115	173	13	186	6.47	0	0
B Whaley	BL	17	42	26	7	33	3.14	0	0

1968

Riders	Comp	M	R	P	BP	TP	CMA	FM	PM
A Andersson	BL1	7	23	19	5	24	4.17	0	0
O Berg	BL1	33	140	265	12	277	7.91	3	0
R Dent	BL1	32	128	149	36	185	5.78	0	2
L Jansson	BL1	17	76	97	11	108	5.68	0	0
B Josefsson	BL1	20	73	114	10	124	6.79	1	1
B McMillan	BL1	30	106	107	20	127	4.79	0	0
J McMillan	BL1	37	168	333	16	349	8.31	3	0
W Templeton	BL1	37	148	159	23	182	4.92	0	0
A Wells	BL1	8	28	42	10	52	7.43	0	0
B Whaley	BL1	23	54	26	6	32	2.37	0	0

Where Eagles Dared – Speedway in Motherwell by Jim Henry
Speedway came to Motherwell in 1950. The first season saw a makeshift team provide a variety of meetings to introduce the sport to the town. The positive response saw the Lanarkshire Eagles enter the National League Division Two in 1951. As speedway declined nationally in the early 1950s, the Eagles' fellow Scottish teams closed down – Glasgow Ashfield for league racing after 1952 and both the Glasgow Tigers and Edinburgh Monarchs in 1954. The Eagles were willing to race in 1955, but the English teams refused to travel north for only one meeting in Scotland, effectively forcing the team out of business.
A short resurgence in 1958 did not last and 1972 saw a flicker of bike action on the site of the demolished stadium. This book gives a fascinating insight into speedway in Motherwell, when the Eagles dared in Scotland's black county. **Published in 2021 @ £13.95**

My Crazy Speedway World by Bert Harkins
"Here we are folks, after many months of being stuck to my computer keyboard, I finally finished my autobiography having bashed out every word, dot and comma along the way. It covers my early days growing up in Glasgow, to cycle speedway, road racing, speedway and life after I had hung up my white boots and tartan leathers. This is the story of a wandering Speedway Scotsman and I hope that you enjoy it." **Bert Harkins**
Published in February 2018. Now available @ £16.95

For both books: order direct from the publishers: London League Publications Ltd post free in the UK. Visit www.llpshop.co.uk for credit card orders or write to (cheques payable to London League Publications Ltd): PO Box 65784, London NW2 9NS. Also available on Amazon, AbeBooks, EBay and as an E-Book on Amazon for Kindle. Or order from any bookshop.

Other speedway books from London League Publications Ltd

Life on the Edge – Split Waterman by Trevor Davies
Authorised biography of one of speedway's most famous riders. Covers his full speedway career and much more. Published in April 2021 @ £14.95

Freddie Williams – Double World Speedway Champion
By Peter Lush
The full story of the first British double World Champion. Also includes his brothers Eric and Ian, both international speedway stars, and the other sporting members of the Williams family. Published in March 2019 @ £13.95

Dave Jessup – A Speedway Journey by Peter Lush
Authorised biography of one of the top British speedway riders from the 1970s and 1980s. Also covers his time as England team manager and playing golf for the England Amateur Senior team. Published in October 2020 @ £14.95.

When the Lions Roared – the story of the famous Wembley Speedway team by Peter Lush & John Chaplin
The story of the Wembley Lions from 1929 to 1971. Includes full statistics and rider profiles. Published in October 2016 @ £14.95.

Warzone Speedway by Trevor Davies.
Last few copies of a speedway classic. Covers the riders who rode in speedway meetings in Europe while in the Army during and after the Second World War. £13.95

For all books: order direct from the publishers: London League Publications Ltd post free in the UK. Visit www.llpshop.co.uk for credit card orders or write to (cheques payable to London League Publications Ltd): PO Box 65784, London NW2 9NS. Also available on Amazon, AbeBooks, EBay and as an E-Book on Amazon for Kindle. Or order from any bookshop.